The Memoirs of Lady Hyegyŏng

The Memoirs of
Lady Hyegyŏng

The Autobiographical Writings of
a Crown Princess of Eighteenth-
Century Korea

Translated with an
Introduction and Annotations
by JaHyun Kim Haboush

UNIVERSITY OF CALIFORNIA PRESS

Berkeley / Los Angeles / London

University of California Press
Berkeley and Los Angeles, California

University of California Press, Ltd.
London, England

Library of Congress Cataloging-in-Publication Data

Hyegyŏnggung Hong Ssi, 1735–1815.
  [Hanjungnok. English]
  The memoirs of Lady Hyegyŏng : the autobiographical
writings of a Crown Princess of eighteenth-century Korea /
translated, with an introduction and annotations by JaHyun
Kim Haboush.
    p. cm.
  Includes bibliographical references and index.
  ISBN 978-0-520-20055-5 (pbk. : alk. paper)
    1. Hyegyŏnggung Hong Ssi, 1735–1815.   2. Princesses—
Korea—Biography. 3. Korea—Kings and rulers.   4. Korea—
History—1637–1864.   I. Haboush, JaHyun Kim. II. Title.
DS913.392.H94A3   1996
951.9'02'092—dc20
  [B]
                                                              94-40457

Printed in the United States of America

12   11   10

13   12   11   10   9

The paper used in this publication meets the minimum requirements
of ANSI/NISO Z39.48-1992 (R 1997) (*Permanence of Paper*). ∞

To the memory of my mother and grandmother

Contents

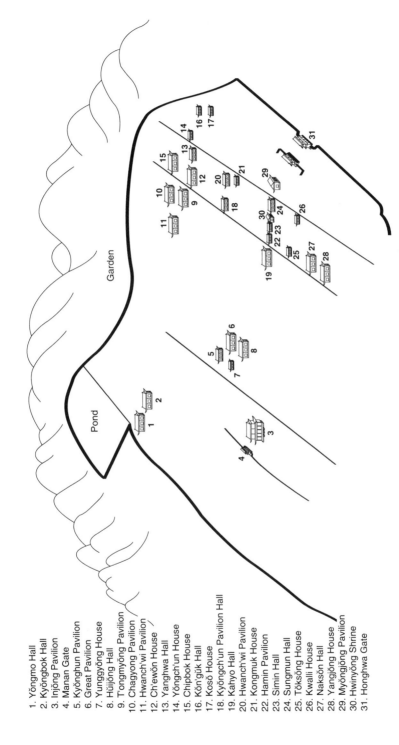

1. Yŏngmo Hall
2. Kyŏngbok Hall
3. Injŏng Pavilion
4. Manan Gate
5. Kyŏnghun Pavilion
6. Great Pavilion
7. Yunggyŏng House
8. Hŭijŏng Hall
9. T'ongmyŏng Pavilion
10. Chagyong Pavilion
11. Hwanch'wi Pavilion
12. Ch'ewŏn House
13. Yanghwa Hall
14. Yŏngch'un House
15. Chipbok House
16. Kŏn'gŭk Hall
17. Kosŏ House
18. Kyŏngch'un Pavilion Hall
19. Kahyo Hall
20. Hwanch'wi Pavilion
21. Kongmuk House
22. Hamin Pavilion
23. Simin Hall
24. Sungmun Hall
25. Tŏksŏng House
26. Kwalli House
27. Naksŏn Hall
28. Yangjŏng House
29. Myŏngjŏng Pavilion
30. Hwinyŏng Shrine
31. Honghwa Gate

Ch'angdŏk and Ch'anggyŏng Palace compound

Acknowledgments

This project was very long in the making, and I have benefited immensely from the comments, criticisms, and suggestions of my friends and colleagues. They are too numerous to mention here, but I would like to thank first the late Professors Chong Pyonguk and Kim Tonguk of Seoul National University and Yonsei University respectively, and Professor Kim Yongsuk of Sukmyong University for their encouragement and help. Gari Ledyard and Catherine Swatek read the entire manuscript and made many valuable suggestions. Patricia Ebrey, Laurel Kendall, Susan Mann, and James Palais read parts of the manuscript and they, too, made insightful comments. I would like to thank them all. I would also like to express my appreciation to Wolfgang Bauer, Edward Seidensticker, and Pei-yi Wu for answering my queries and sharing interesting ideas.

During the course of working on this manuscript, I used various libraries and archives and received invaluable assistance from scholars and librarians. I would like to thank Professors Yi T'aejin and Han Young-woo, the former and present directors of the Kyujanggak Library at Seoul National University, Mr. Yi Sangun also of the Kyujanggak, the entire staff of the Library at the Academy of Korean Studies, Ms. Amy Lee and Mr. Kenneth Harlan of the C.V. Starr East Asian Library at Columbia University, and Mr. Young-key Chu of the East Asian Library at the University of California, Berkeley. I would also like to thank Mr. Joseph Newland of the Asia Society, Ms. Chee-yon Kwon of the Sackler Gallery, and Mr. Kim Sontae of the Bureau for the Preservation of Cultural Properties in Seoul for helping me acquire illustrations. I would like to express my gratitute to Homer Williams for assisting me with several computer problems. Sheila Levine and Laura Driussi of the University of California Press offered me encouragement, expert professional counsel, and enthusiasm. I am grateful to them. I feel particularly indebted to Carolyn Hill, who edited my manuscript with meticulous care and admirable skill. Finally, I would like to thank the National Endowment for the Humanities, which provided me with a grant, and the Korea Research Foundation, which supported the publication of this book.

Introduction

The Author and Autobiographical Discourse

The Memoirs of Lady Hyegyŏng consists of four auto-biographical narratives written by Lady Hyegyŏng, an eighteenth-century Korean noblewoman. She was born in 1735, a daughter of Hong Ponghan (1713–1778) of the illustrious P'ungsan Hong family. As a consequence of Korean custom of the period, her personal name remains unknown.[1] In 1744, she married Crown Prince Sado (1735–1762). They were both nine years old at the time, and consummation did not take place until five years later. On the day of consummation, Prince Sado was appointed prince-regent and assumed an official role in governing. However, his father, King Yŏngjo (r. 1724–1776), still made the most important decisions. Lady Hyegyŏng bore Sado two sons and two daughters, the Princesses Ch'ŏngyŏn and Ch'ŏngsŏn. One of her sons died in infancy; the other later became King Chŏngjo (r. 1776–1800).

On one hot summer day in 1762, King Yŏngjo ordered Prince Sado, then twenty-seven, to get into a rice chest. The chest was sealed, and Sado died eight days later. This tragic episode hung over the Chosŏn court for many years, inexorably shaping the lives of those who had been close to Prince Sado. Despite deep chagrin

I

and a professed desire to end her life, Lady Hyegyŏng lived on and lent support to her son who had been left vulnerable by his father's tragic death.

This decision, however, haunted her all her life. Although widows were not expected to follow their husbands to death in Chosŏn Korea (1392–1910),[2] this was a special case. Prince Sado's bizarre execution by his father was an attempt to avoid the appearance of a criminal execution, which would, under Chosŏn custom, have required punishment of his entire family.[3] Sado's son, the only remaining heir to the throne,[4] would have likewise borne the stigma of criminality, something the Chosŏn court could not afford. Had Lady Hyegyŏng chosen to die, her death could have been seen as a protest against the royal decision or, alternatively, it might have deepened the suggestion that Sado had been guilty. Neither possibility would have furthered Chŏngjo's legitimacy. Lady Hyegyŏng's maternal allegiance as well as her sense of public duty to dynastic security precluded her suicide. In the context of the Chosŏn mentality, which would have seen suicide as an honorable alternative, to be indebted for her life to the king who had killed her husband definitely left her in a compromising position.

The circumstances of Prince Sado's death became a focal point for severe political turmoil. The immensity of its political implications cannot be exaggerated. That the conflict was between a reigning king and an heir apparent was troubling enough; more troubling was that the heir's son became the heir apparent and was subsequently enthroned. In 1764, to lessen the impact of the incident of Prince Sado on Chŏngjo's legitimacy, King Yŏngjo made Chŏngjo a posthumously adopted son of Prince Hyojang (1719–1728), the deceased older brother of Prince Sado. This measure legally severed Chŏngjo from Prince Sado; it meant that Chŏngjo was not in any legal sense the son of one who might be called a criminal. Despite these benefits, the adoption made an already delicate issue far more complex.

Because of the sensitive nature of this situation, any discussion of Chŏngjo's legitimacy became taboo, but the issue lurked just beneath the surface, always ready to ignite another round of political furor. Royal and affinal relatives, powerful families, and officials were divided on the issue of Chŏngjo's acceptability and became involved in debilitating feuds. Hong Ponghan, who served as a high-ranking minister on the State Council at the time of Sado's death, emerged as his grandson's principal protector, leading the faction known as *sip'a*, whereas the Kyŏngju Kim, the family of Queen Chŏngsun (1745–1805), King Yŏngjo's second queen, emerged as a major force in the opposing camp known as *pyŏkp'a*. In the post-Sado court of recriminating politics, Lady Hyegyŏng not only had to navigate with extreme caution for her own preservation but also had to witness attacks against her father and the decline of her family's political fortunes.

When Yŏngjo died in 1776, Chŏngjo succeeded his grandfather to the throne. He displayed a certain ambivalence toward his maternal family, and the Hong family did not fare well under him. In the first year of his reign, Hong Inhan (1722–1776), Hong Ponghan's younger brother, was suspected of disloyalty to Chŏngjo and was executed. This cast a terrible pall over the Hong family. Nevertheless, Chŏngjo was devoted to his mother, and after this initial shock, the Hong family was allowed to live for a time in peaceful retirement. If they entertained hope of returning to their former glory, it ended with the sudden death of Chŏngjo in 1800. The accession to the throne of Chŏngjo's son, Sunjo (r. 1800–1834), not yet eleven, necessitated the regency of Queen Dowager Chŏngsun, the archenemy of the Hong family. Soon the Hong family suffered another tragedy. In 1801, Hong Nagim (1741–1801), Lady Hyegyŏng's younger brother, was accused of having converted to Catholicism and was executed. With Sunjo's assumption of personal rule in 1804, Lady Hyegyŏng's trials finally seem to have ended. King Sunjo was attentive to his grandmother and did what he could to comfort her.

The four narratives that comprise *The Memoirs of Lady Hyegyŏng* were written from 1795 to 1805, a ten-year period spanning the end of Chŏngjo's reign and Sunjo's accession. Lady Hyegyŏng began writing when Chŏngjo was still on the throne and did not complete the last memoir until after Sunjo had personally assumed power. She lived for ten years after finishing her last memoir and died in 1815, at the age of eighty.

The Memoirs of Lady Hyegyŏng, known as *Hanjungnok* (Records written in silence) or *Hanjung mallok* (Memoirs written in silence), is viewed in contemporary Korea as a great literary masterpiece and an invaluable historical document. Rather than being composed in literary Chinese as were most writings by men before the modern era, these memoirs were written in Korean, in *han'gŭl* script, making them accessible to the modern reader. To a certain extent, the reader's fascination is with the incident itself—a frightening story of a filicide. The fourth memoir depicts, in all its terror, the father-son conflict that culminates in Sado's death. It explores the sources of Sado's madness—and the aberrant behavior, uncontrolled rages, and violence that threatened the safety of the dynasty. The fact that a woman narrates this most public of incidents, an event that can be described as the ultimate in male power rivalry, makes *The Memoirs* unique in autobiographical literature. In the West until the modern period, autobiographies by women were a mere fraction of the total number of autobiographies. Moreover, the overwhelming majority focus exclusively on the private and domestic sphere of life.[5] There seems to have been even fewer women autobiographers in East Asia. Japan produced a few self-narratives by women, but they tend to be diaries, and thus introspective and fragmentary.[6]

The Memoirs of Lady Hyegyŏng is much more than a description of filicide, however. Of the four memoirs, only the last is devoted to that event; the first three focus on the author and the lives of people other than the central players in that incident. Although the four memoirs were conceived of and written as separate works on separate occasions for specific audiences in defense of specific individuals, they constitute an integral whole that moves from the personal to the public. The first, written in 1795, is a narration of Lady Hyegyŏng's life and, to a lesser extent, the lives of her natal family. Addressed to her nephew, the heir of the Hong family, it is an apologia for herself and her father, defending their choices to live on after Prince Sado's death. Each of the last three memoirs, which are addressed to King Sunjo, is increasingly public in subject matter and genre. The second memoir, written in 1801, is a defense of Lady Hyegyŏng's younger brother, Hong Nagim, and her paternal uncle, Hong Inhan, both of whom had been executed. The third memoir, written in 1802, describes the unrelenting obsession of her son, King Chŏngjo, with restoring honor to his father. The fourth and last memoir, written in 1805, finally recounts the history of the Sado incident—the tension in the Yŏngjo-Sado relationship, the son's mental illness and violent outbursts, and his death ordered by his father. Although the first three memoirs describe at length the emotional turmoil and political repercussions of the Sado incident, the incident itself is referred to only cryptically. Hence, the last memoir functions almost as the resolution in a detective novel in that it answers many unanswered questions raised by the first three memoirs.

Written over a tumultuous ten-year period, these memoirs were in part prompted by external events such as Lady Hyegyŏng's sixtieth birthday or the execution of her brother. Writing a memoir was a very unusual activity for a woman at that time, and Lady Hyegyŏng had to surmount formidable cultural obstacles to do so. First, she had to overcome an inhibition against self-narration, and then she had to transcend, as she does in the final memoir, the reluctance to discuss the deficiencies and aberrant behavior of her husband and her father-in-law.

What motivated her? In the earlier memoirs, she was intent on justifying herself and her family. As her family lay in ruins, she felt it imperative to plead the causes of those members who had died in disgrace and to restore their honor, albeit posthumously. At some point, she decided that, for her and other members of her family to be judged fairly, their actions had to be seen in the proper perspective, which in turn required an accurate understanding of the Sado incident.

Lady Hyegyŏng also came to believe that the motives and actions of Prince Sado and King Yŏngjo, the central players in the incident, should be accurately portrayed and recorded. Discussion of the incident had been forbidden because it was against custom to mention royal misconduct. Moreover, it was hoped that silence would put those painful memories to rest. Instead, the silence only encouraged misrepresentation and misinterpretation. Exaggerated and distorted versions of royal motives and princely actions were whispered about and disseminated. Lady Hyegyŏng finally concluded that brushing the incident aside was not the answer. What had happened was horrible, but it would become even more monstrous in people's imaginations if left unexplained. She felt that the versions in circulation blamed or attributed willful misdeeds to one party or the other rather than seeing the event in the totality of complex human interaction, and she concluded that although she might not have been able to save them from their tragedy, she should at least rescue them from the more ignoble fate of being viewed as perverse villains by future generations. This required presenting them in their human complexity, caught between better intentions and inexplicable impulses. This conviction led her to surmount a powerful reluctance to expose the failings in her husband or her father-in-law.

It was clearly difficult for her to present this relentlessly gloomy and terrifying tale—that was why she resisted writing it for so long —but she tells it with compassion as each player moves toward the tragic denouement. A special sympathy is reserved for her husband, Prince Sado, as she portrays his suffering and pain. She felt that by not following her husband in death, she left her conjugal duty unfulfilled. Writing this memoir was her way of seeking forgiveness.

The "imperatives of imaginative discourse"[7] that an author follows when transforming a life lived into a life recounted are not confined to what the author professes them to be. In the process of recounting, the author desires to "recompose" as much as to "discover" self.[8] Through the very act of writing, Lady Hyegyŏng was engaged in a quest to recompose and discover historical or human truth. She took great pains to reconstruct how it all happened, what each individual did, and in what order. But on a deeper, almost subconscious level, she searched for something more fundamental, some understanding that would explain the vagaries of human fate and the waywardness of the moral order.

Narrating Lives and the Sense of Self

Writing *The Memoirs* was a political act for Lady Hyegyŏng; the very act of writing them meant that she wished to testify for herself and the actors in her narration and to persuade others of her testimony. To be persuasive, she had to present causes and represent lives in accordance with the cultural grammar of her time.[9] What resources in the repository of tradition did Lady Hyegyŏng possess? What paradigms of autobiographical and testimonial writing were available to her? Can her memoirs be described as identifiably in the feminine mode? How is her writing related to her sense of self?

Traditional Korean literature includes various kinds of first person, nonfiction narratives that are, if not necessarily autobiographical, revelatory of the writer's interior life. These include travel literature and *chapki* or *chapnok* (miscellaneous writings).[10] There are also straightforward memoirs, often with the title *mallok* (leisurely writing). Many powerful officials wrote reminiscences of their active service under this title. Most official memoirs, however, tend not to reveal anything remotely private in the lives of the royal family or the authors' own lives.[11] An interesting example is the memoir by Lady Hyegyŏng's father, Hong Ponghan, *Igikchae mallok*, which begins in 1733 when he was a young student and ends in 1748. He comments on his daughter's royal marriage in 1744, his passing the civil examination shortly thereafter, and the period when his career began to flourish. The memoir records several of his memorials[12] and various long conversations with Yŏngjo that were presumably indicative of his and the king's intellectual makeup and social stance. On the private or emotional life of either the king or himself, however, it is completely silent.[13]

Pei-yi Wu's study of autobiography in China underscores the enormous impact that biography had on autobiographical writing, which developed under its powerful and ubiquitous shadow. Wu argues that biography was conceived of as mainly fulfilling the historical function of transmitting moral principles; therefore it revealed only those facts deemed historically relevant, remaining silent about emotional and interior lives. Autobiographers had to overcome the inhibitions on self-expression imposed by the conventions of biography.[14]

In Korea, the biographies written in literary Chinese were in the same subgenres as those written in China, such as *chŏn/chuan* (biography), necrology, and *yŏnbo/nien-p'u* (life chronology).[15] Biographies of Hong Ponghan by his sons, for instance, give some indication of what topics were considered worthy of inclusion in works in that genre. One, a life chronology of Hong Ponghan by his oldest son, Hong Nagin (1730–1777), records his public career but makes no mention of his marriage or the birth of his children except for that of Lady Hyegyŏng.[16] The other, titled *Sŏnbugun yusa* (Memorable anecdotes from father's life), consists of reminiscences by his three younger sons.[17] This piece pays homage to his familial virtues, but the focus is on Hong Ponghan as a son and brother—the loss of his mother when he was six, his remembrances of her, his devotion to his stepmother, his generosity to his sisters and brothers especially when they were in need, and so on.

Very little is said of his immediate home life. Nothing is said of his marriage or his children, except for occasional admonitions by him.[18]

After the Korean script, *han'gŭl*, was devised in the mid-fifteenth century, the written culture, which had previously been composed exclusively in literary Chinese by men, greatly expanded its scope to include many more subjects, genres, and participants. The writing of a certain class of women, including court ladies, aristocratic *yangban* women, and some courtesans, came to constitute a special portion of the written culture in the latter half of the Chosŏn period.

Men continued to write in literary Chinese, except for letters to women, certain genres of poetry, and other incidental pieces that concerned mostly private aspects of their lives. Women wrote almost exclusively in Korean. They used the vernacular as a means of self-expression and communication as well as a mode of social and political empowerment. They wrote poetry, essays, and manuals of manners and housekeeping for other women. Letters were the most usual form of writing and generally fulfilled social obligations to kin such as greetings and condolence.[19] This custom changed the texture of social life by allowing women to play a distinct role in the written discourse, though within the limited sphere of domestic concerns.

Conscious attempts by women to seize control of the narratives of their own or others' lives also emerged, though tentatively. Epistolary form was occasionally resorted to for self-presentation.[20] In the royal court, palace ladies began to write about the lives of their mistresses in the form of romans à clef, which have been classified as "court novels" (*kungjŏng sosŏl*) but are increasingly viewed of late as documentary court literature (*kungjŏng silgi munhak*).[21] Recently, necrologies of men written by women in Korean have also come to light.[22]

It is commonly believed that writing in Chinese and writing in Korean were dichotomous traditions, separated, respectively, by the gender of author and audience (male versus female), subject matter (public versus private), and genre (classical versus vernacular). While this perception may be valid to some extent, there was a closer relationship between the two traditions than has been acknowledged, as well as a large area in which the two converged,[23] at least when it came to the practice of writing about lives. The common thread binding these writings is adherence to a paradigm of virtue. Necrologies, court novels, and narratives of self present their subjects as paragons of familial or social virtue and arrange chronological details to construct the closest approximation to the ideal.

Lady Hyegyŏng's memoirs depart from this model. It is not that she renounces the paradigm. Though she confesses to a deviation from the ideal, she never eschews her wholehearted commitment to it. Nonetheless, her narration is informed by a realization that life does not allow one to live up to the ideal. In the first three memoirs, this inability is attributed to the multiple roles with which one must contend, each carrying its own demands that can and often do clash with the demands of other roles. In the fourth memoir, the conflict is no longer presented as stemming from external factors alone but from internal forces as well. True, the conflict is between father and son, but each is driven by his innermost dark forces. As Lady Hyegyŏng probes the human psyche, she accepts the imperfections and weaknesses of her subjects and allows space for autonomous interior life. In this, her memoirs clearly depart from standard paradigmatic representations of lives.

Her narration is imbued with poignancy and complexity. She accepts human imperfection and acknowledges the inability to live up to the ideal but maintains the Confucian belief in the perfectibility of humanity and the notion that social privilege should be based on moral renewal. She is acutely aware of the exacting demands that exalted position makes on her and the other highly placed persons in her memoirs. The tension of her narration derives from the fact that she is influenced by two seemingly opposing forces, to each of which she appears strongly committed. In other words, she unfolds her extraordinary tale as "an elaborate drama of honour,"[24] a drama of her class and milieu.

In studies of Western autobiography, it has been posited that a sense of the discrete self, a consciousness of self as an isolated being, is a precondition for writing autobiography.[25] Women autobiographers, however, are seen in a somewhat different light. The female sense of self, as opposed to the male sense of the discrete self, is defined by its relationships to the persons surrounding the self.[26] This is given as a reason why women sometimes appended a short autobiography to long biographies of their husbands, as did Margaret Cavendish, Duchess of Newcastle, in the seventeenth century.[27] The English noblewoman, however, clearly wishes to assert her own identity.[28] She expresses a conscious desire to be different from the norm, declaring that she prefers writing to needlework and that this sets her apart from other women.[29] In contrast, Lady Hyegyŏng does not display the faintest desire to depart from the norm. Because of her exalted position, she seldom had a chance to speak of her own accomplishments in such skills as needlework, but she does boast of her mother's talent. In fact, her idea of being extraordinary was not to depart from but to adhere to and excel by the norm.

It is clear that Lady Hyegyŏng and Margaret Cavendish had different senses of self. One of the more obvious differences lay in the way they perceived the relationship between their private and public selves. Margaret Cavendish may sometimes express her sense of self through her relationship to other people around her, but there is no question that she regards her private self as distinct from and prior to her public self. In both, the private self is given a certain autonomy and space apart from the public self. In Lady Hyegyŏng's work, however, the space between private self and public self becomes quite small as the relationship between the two becomes ever more closely intertwined. She acknowledges the distinction between the private and public selves but feels that the redemption of her public self is indispensable to the integrity of her private self. Time and time again, Lady Hyegyŏng stresses the depth and acuteness of shame she felt for failing to live up to what she accepts as the legitimate demands of her multiple roles. She is convinced that only by feeling and confessing the acuteness of her shame, the degree of which should be proportional to the distance she has fallen from the ideal, can she be redeemed. She tries to atone for the failings of her public self by the intensity of the remorse of her private self, and in this way the interdependence between the two selves becomes complete. Even in the fourth memoir, though she allows space to the autonomous interior lives of Yŏngjo and Sado, she does not deviate from her belief in the close relationship between their private and public selves. For Sado, she merely replaces remorse with suffering. That is, she pleads for understanding of his public misconduct on the basis of the depth of his private suffering.

The Genres

The Memoirs of Lady Hyegyŏng has given rise to a certain ambiguity concerning genre, caused largely by a desire to define *The Memoirs* as a single integrated work. When these four memoirs were compiled into a composite work during the nineteenth and early twentieth centuries, compilers and editors did not respect the individual pieces; they split individual memoirs and rearranged them into a chronological account.[30] The titles given by different compilers to the integrated memoirs, *Hanjungnok* or *Hanjung mallok*, indicate that the work was regarded either as a testimony or reminiscence. In the modern era, until quite recently, *The Memoirs of Lady Hyegyŏng* has been classified as a court novel.[31] At present, there are a number of views concerning the genre of *The Memoirs*,[32] but the tradition of describing the four memoirs as a single work in a single genre persists. However, once we acknowledge that the four memoirs were separate pieces written in different genres, the task of defining these genres becomes much clearer.

From the beginning, Lady Hyegyŏng was keenly aware that narration was a mode of empowerment.[33] She drew not only from the resources of the tradition of women's writing in the *han'gŭl* script, including letters, testimonials, and court novels, but also from men's writing in literary Chinese. Not having a ready-made form available to her, she appropriated for each memoir a genre that had hitherto been used almost exclusively by men. As the subjects of the memoirs move from the personal to the public, so do the genres in which the memoirs are written.

The first memoir, addressed to the heir of her natal family, takes the form of a family injunction. The remaining three memoirs, adjusted to a royal reader, are in properly and progressively more public genres. The second memoir is in the form of a memorial, the third a biography, and the fourth a historiography. Lady Hyegyŏng transforms these formal and impersonal genres into narratives full of passionate testimony in a personal voice.

In 1795 when Lady Hyegyŏng wrote her first memoir, she had just reached her sixtieth birthday, and her son, King Chŏngjo, was on the throne. Although it was almost exclusively men who left injunctions to the younger members of their families, it is perhaps not strange that her nephew asked Lady Hyegyŏng, the Hong family's most prominent member, to write something for the family, or that she complied. To provide such a memoir for one's children has been a common practice in many cultures. In the West, auto-biography has frequently been addressed to the author's children. The format easily accommodates both the urge to impart to young-sters life's hard-learned lessons and the desire to be remembered by them for one's distinct self.[34]

In Korea, family injunctions tended to be purely instructional, brief, and written in an impersonal voice.[35] Lady Hyegyŏng's first memoir, *The Memoir of 1795*, departs from this usual form. Al-though it contains advice and exhortations to the younger gen-eration, its main body is a self-narration followed by a postscript devoted to short family remembrances. This is the only piece among the four that is in accord with the principle that Lejeune calls the "autobiographical pact," in which the writer, the narrator, and the protagonist are the same person.[36] Lady Hyegyŏng selects and orders her experiences into an integrated pattern, a process for the writing of autobiographies described by Northrop Frye.[37] In the postscript, as she briefly sketches the lives of her parents, her siblings, their spouses, her uncles and aunts, and even her servants, she attempts to bring order and meaning to their lives.

One is struck by a pointedly defensive tone in her presentation of self and other members of her family. It is the defensiveness of someone who feels that she has been deeply compromised by some terrible event and believes that she must assert her innocence. Though Lady Hyegyŏng does not discuss the death of Prince Sado in much detail here, she obviously felt that she and her family had been irrevocably marked by their association with the incident. Indeed, in the eyes of the world, this was the case. Although the political fortunes of the Hong family did not wane until a decade after the tragic incident, the decline was tied to issues associated with Sado's death. Inevitably, stinging attacks ensued on the moral character of its members, especially Hong Ponghan. Her writing should be understood in this context. She felt acutely responsible for her family's downfall, believing that her marriage into the royal house had led to their suffering and decline. That her marriage was not in the least at her own initiative did not diminish the deep sense of guilt that pervades her first memoir.

More to the point, she wrote the memoir as a rebuttal to decades of implicit and explicit accusations made against her family. Thus she persistently stresses the moral integrity of each of her subjects—how virtuous each was, and how, placed repeatedly at moral crossroads, each chose unfailingly the alternative that fulfilled the most public of his or her duties.

However unusual in form, *The Memoir of 1795* is in spirit a genuine family injunction. By refuting criticisms and charges made against herself and her family, she wishes more than anything else to reestablish their moral legitimacy so that younger generations will reclaim the honorable family tradition. She is fully aware that moral integrity is an elusive thing, subject to different views and interpretations. In this sense, she is clearly seizing narratives of self and family in order to control destiny, turning what is usually an impersonal form into a self-narration and family chronicle with which to restore family honor and integrity.

The Memoir of 1801, her second memoir, was written to protest the then-recent execution of her brother, Hong Nagim, during the 1801 persecution of Catholics that reflected the changing ideological climate in the Chosŏn government following the death of King Chŏngjo in 1800. These persecutions would continue for the rest of the nineteenth century.[38] The charges against Hong Nagim, however, were unsubstantiated and unfounded.[39] Lady Hyegyŏng attributes the accusations entirely to an acrimonious interfamilial feud. Still reeling from the grief of losing her son and the shock of seeing her brother executed, she reveals herself at her bitterest and most emotional as she defends not only her brother but also Hong Inhan, her paternal uncle, whose execution in 1776 had signaled the decline of the Hong family.

The Memoir of 1801 had been written for the king and was prompted by a profound sense of outrage. Hence, it is not strange that its form resembles a memorial. Although most memorials to the throne discussed matters of a public nature, there was a category reserved for those who felt aggrieved about something concerning themselves or persons close to them such as family members or mentors. These memorials tended to be narratives in which the authors refuted unfavorable accounts by presenting contrary evidence and displaying appropriate emotions. Hong Nagyun, Lady Hyegyŏng's younger brother, wrote such a memorial in 1809 and sent it to King Sunjo. He was provoked by a memorial criticizing Hong Ponghan, who was long since dead.[40] The younger Hong's memorial passionately defends his father and his older brother, emphasizing their loyalty, public spiritedness, and the terrible injustice of the accusations against them.[41] Although memorial literature has always been viewed as a forum for public policy, it would be more fitting to view memorials such as Hong Nagyun's as testimonial literature. There are many memorials of this type, and they perhaps should be studied as such.

The privilege of sending a memorial to the throne was open to educated men who were deemed qualified to participate in public discourse conducted in literary Chinese. Lady Hyegyŏng's *Memoir of 1801* is remarkable in that she privatizes a mode of writing that had been reserved exclusively for public discourse among men. Availing herself of her position as the grandmother of the king, she appropriates this genre and uses it for testimony in Korean. She contends that the charges used to send the two Hong men to the gallows were purely political and that both men's fates were extremely unjust. She makes these assertions by presenting as much evidence as possible with commensurate moral outrage.

The Memoir of 1802, written a year later, is much more sober. It discusses some of the same issues as the second memoir, but instead of flaring with outrage, it relies on the force of Chŏngjo's filial devotion. It presents a moving portrayal of Chŏngjo as a son obsessed with restoring honor to his ill-fated father, whose tragic death he witnessed as a ten-year-old boy. As discussed earlier, soon after Sado's death, probably fearing that Sado's criminality would undermine his grandson's legitimacy, Yŏngjo made Chŏngjo an adopted son of Sado's deceased older brother. Legally and ritually this limited the honor which Chŏngjo could render to Sado. Lady Hyegyŏng recounts that, in his unrequited obsession, Chŏngjo drew up a plan in which he would fulfill his dream of restoring honor to his father as well as to the dishonored members of the Hong family. Yet he died before he could enact his plan. In appealing to Sunjo by recounting to him Chŏngjo's unfulfilled aspirations, Lady Hyegyŏng privatizes the genre of biography as well as its subject. This memoir is the biography of a filial son rather than the biography of a king who was, in fact, one of the most brilliant rulers of the Chosŏn dynasty. Moreover, it is written by the mother of this filial son and addressed to his son, upon whom filiality presumably weighed just as heavily.

The Memoir of 1805 presents the incident of Prince Sado. With Lady Hyegyŏng's claim that it recounts the truthful history of the royal filicide of the crown prince, it enters the realm of historiography. However, historiography as practiced in Korea was written according to well-defined conventions. These included third person narration based on sources other than the writer's personal observations so as to impart objectivity and credibility to the narrative.[42] Since Lady Hyegyŏng's narrative of the incident of Prince Sado was a first person eyewitness account, it flagrantly defies historiographical conventions in several crucial aspects despite its claim to historiographical status.

The first violation of historiographical convention is its emphasis on the personal. Though Lady Hyegyŏng is aware that the incident was a complex mixture of the political and the personal and intimates the political dimensions of the affair, she presents the incident primarily as a personality conflict between father and son.

The second violation of convention is the mode of narration. Not only does she narrate in the first person, but she eschews the customary indirection in describing the failings of the king and the royal family. One senses her belief that the only redemption for them and the other players involved lies in her portrayal of them in their full human complexity and imperfection, causing and enduring pain. This offers the psychological insight so rarely found in historical documents.

The third violation concerns the source. In discussing Sado's life before she married him and entered the palace, she relies upon accounts she heard from other people. But as soon as the narration enters the period when she was present, she relies almost exclusively on her own memory and observation.[43]

The genre of Lady Hyegyŏng's *Memoir of 1805* constitutes a curious exchange of the public and the private. On the one hand, the history of a ruler and his heir is recounted as the story of father and son by the son's wife. Here, the privatization of an "impersonal" and "public" genre finds an extreme manifestation. On the other hand, it exteriorizes and historicizes her private memory as public history.

The Individual Memoirs: Themes and Issues

THE MEMOIR OF 1795

In *The Memoir of 1795*, Lady Hyegyŏng organizes her life into a simple pattern: her Edenic childhood, which ends abruptly with her wedding at the age of nine; her life in the palace, which soon turns into an unremitting ordeal, first because of her husband's strange illness and then, after his death, because of labyrinthine court politics; and her death wish, which repeatedly punctuates her interior life and finally dissolves in a moment of epiphany as she embraces life when her grandson, Sunjo, a long-awaited heir to the throne, is born on her fifty-fifth birthday in 1790. Despite the extraordinary life she recounts, this pattern is a variation on one of the most common archetypes. What gives her story its particular flavor and force is the exploration of what constitutes peace and ordeal and how the final resolution is reached.

The existence of peace or ordeal in her life is determined by the absence or presence of conflicting demands placed upon her. Childhood is characterized by their absence; adult life, by the presence of a multitude of sharply conflicting ones. Unable to meet all of them satisfactorily, she feels deep shame and guilt. The final resolution is achieved when Sunjo is born on her birthday, because she takes this as a sign that Heaven has affirmed her worthiness and approved of her life as one lived for the public cause.

Childhood functions as a special signifier in her narration. It represents a golden age of perfect harmony in which emotion and duty naturally and spontaneously cohere. She had only one role, that of a daughter. She was loved by her parents, and she loved and obeyed them in return; this mutual affection brought only pleasure to everyone concerned. Her move from her natal home to the palace, obviously a passage from childhood to adulthood, signifies passing from private life to public life and from a life of harmonious simplicity to a life of multiple roles. When she married and acquired other roles—wife, daughter-in-law, then mother, and Crown Princess Consort (*sejabin*)—she was no longer able to satisfactorily discharge the duties of all of these roles. The most conspicuous conflicts were between her role as a daughter to her natal family and her newly acquired roles in marriage. By the norms of eighteenth-century Korean Confucian society, she was to transfer her primary allegiance to her husband's family, yet this social prescription did not acknowledge the legitimacy of the emotions of newly married young women. It was unreasonable to expect that a young woman, on joining a husband whom in most cases she had not seen before, should naturally transfer her loyalty to him and his family of strangers.[44] Thus a discrepancy was created between her continuing affection for her natal family and the limits placed on what she was permitted to do for them. This was brought home to Lady Hyegyŏng when she was not permitted to wear proper mourning after her mother died.[45] In fact, this sense of unrequited affection for their natal families appears to have been a recurring theme in the daily lives of women.

In her study of autobiographies of Victorian women, Valerie Sanders proposes that in Britain, it was in women's autobiography that childhood was discovered. She attributes this to the fact that "many Victorian women are relatively unselfconscious," a tendency that enables them to describe this rather comical period of their life.[46] This is not the way Lady Hyegyŏng perceives herself as a child. She presents herself as having been a perfect little girl with no trace of childishness. Nonetheless, her idealization of childhood and her strong nostalgia for it are noteworthy. One seldom encounters such sentiment in writings by men during Chosŏn Korea. Lady Hyegyŏng, having left her childhood home, remembers childhood with special affection and "invents" it in her narration.

Lady Hyegyŏng also experienced conflict between the demands imposed by the roles that came with her marriage, each of which included both public and private aspects. The most extreme example of this concerned what was proper for her to do when her husband died. Wifely and maternal duty claimed her with almost equal force, but each required an opposite course of action. One demanded taking her own life, the other living on in shame. Lady Hyegyŏng justifies her decision to live as choosing the most public of her duties, the course that benefited dynastic security. This coincided with her maternal duty. However, the fact that this duty had a primary claim does not obliterate the fact that she failed to discharge her wifely duty. Thus she says, "Wishing to repay the throne and to protect the Grand Heir, I gave up the idea of killing myself. Nevertheless, how can I ever forget, even to the last moment of my consciousness, the shame of not having known the proper end and my regret over my long and slow life."

In defending her family, Lady Hyegyŏng applies the same logic, stating that they were placed in situations in which they had to choose the more public of their duties. Her father chose to remain in office in support of his grandson after Prince Sado's death. Her younger brother, Hong Nagim, chose to compromise his honor to save his father's life. The list goes on; the choice between personal honor and public cause is a familiar theme in her narration. The choices she and her father made required deep compromises of personal honor, which were the cause of her shame. But at the same time, she implies that it was also their ultimate sacrifice born of their devotion to the public cause.

Yet in one crucial instance she fails to reason in this manner. She greets with shock and bitterness Yŏngjo's decree of 1764 that made Chŏngjo an adopted son of the deceased Prince Hyojang. Though the reasons for this measure were not specified in the decree, it is difficult to see it as anything but an attempt to protect Chŏngjo's legitimacy, since the adoption passed the line of succession from Yŏngjo to Chŏngjo through Prince Hyojang, bypassing Prince Sado completely and avoiding the ominous shadow that Sado's death cast upon his son's legitimacy. Under this ruling, Lady Hyegyŏng lost her claim to status as the legal parent of the heir apparent and her future status as Queen Dowager. That she greeted the news with shock and bitterness is understandable. However, writing this narration thirty-one years after the ruling's enforcement, Lady Hyegyŏng still does not acknowledge that the decree might have been issued to protect her son's legitimacy or even that it served any public purpose. To the end, she maintains that the decree was unjust and needless. We can only speculate on Lady Hyegyŏng's refusal to view this more objectively. Perhaps it was too painful to acknowledge that she and her husband had become encumbrances to her son's legitimacy. If she had to sacrifice her personal honor for the public cause, then she could accept the sacrifice. But it was entirely different to believe that she and her husband had become the very sources of dishonor.

Although she does not confront certain issues, the act of writing the narrative probed her most profound doubt and disillusion over the discrepancy between her expectations and her experiences. She grew up believing in a correspondence between the moral order and human affairs. This belief, however, was constantly challenged. In her own life, she was repeatedly confronted by events beyond her wildest imaginings. More than that, life generally seemed chaotic and random. Thus it seemed to her that a vision of harmony and order was only briefly glimpsed during her childhood; with childhood's passing, that vision was irretrievably lost.

She had much to ponder. How could she explain her experiences? Why was there so much suffering and disorder? Could it be that calamities occurred because people were at fault? Were they personally responsible for their misery? By the cultural grammar of her society, a moral person was someone with good intentions and sound judgment. This made it difficult to accept the possibility that a good person could make fundamental errors or harbor a tragic flaw.

If people did not cause their own fate, then was it possible that Heaven had no concern for human society? This was tantamount to denying the existence of the moral order, an impossible thought for her. She had to believe that Heaven manifested its will in some logical pattern, but this pattern was certainly invisible and incomprehensible to her. Thus, it is almost in protest against Heaven that she records its inconsistencies as they were manifested in individual lives. It is as though, by bearing testimony to the suffering and misery in individual lives, she could counterbalance the incomprehensible designs of Heaven. Thus she laments all the imperfections of life. Her childhood, a time of perfect happiness that ended abruptly, becomes an emblem of everything that ends before it runs its natural course and of all the unfulfilled promises. In fact, this sense of unrequitedness defines sadness for her.

Despite her denials of personal responsibility, there lurked deep in her psyche a suspicion that perhaps she was the cause of her own fate. Why should she bear so much misery and tragedy otherwise? If she did not herself invite these terrible events, then at least she was placed in such situations. Did Heaven hate her? Was she somehow intrinsically despicable? This doubt explains her tremendous relief at her grandson's birth on her birthday. She took his birth as a sign that Heaven recognized her life-long devotion to the public cause and affirmed its worth. A tentative conciliation was struck between her belief and her life. It was a fragile peace. The divine sign did not take away her shame nor did it right the wrong, but it did affirm that her life had not been in vain.

THE MEMOIR OF 1801

This fragile peace was to be completely shattered a decade later. When Chŏngjo died in 1800 after a brief illness, Lady Hyegyŏng seems to have become prostrate with grief. He was in his prime, his forty-ninth year, and the death was very sudden. With the assumption of regency by Queen Dowager Chŏngsun, power began to reverse. Insults were heaped upon the Hong family. Lady Hye-gyŏng felt herself humiliated and unwelcome; she was pointedly reminded that she was not Chŏngjo's legal parent, a painful fact that had been glossed over as much as possible during her devoted son's reign. Her will to live was almost destroyed by the loss of her son, for whom she had sacrificed her other duties, and the insults that reawakened all of her terrible memories. But when her brother Hong Nagim was executed in 1801 on charges she thought completely ludicrous, she grew so enraged that she wished to live in order to vindicate him. She expresses a similar sentiment about restoring the honor of her uncle, Hong Inhan, who was executed in 1776.

Writing this memoir was the first step in this endeavor. Unlike *The Memoir of 1795*, this one is written to the king to protest and correct criminal verdicts and is public in content and purpose. It conveys a greater sense of urgency. If the writing of the first memoir can be seen as an attempt to reconcile belief and experience, this one can be seen as born of a sense of betrayal by fate, a sense that Heaven has dealt her more blows than she deserves and that she should take matters into her own hands in the limited time left to her. Thus, much more explicitly than the earlier memoir, this one is written to take control of history.

Written in the heat of aggrieved passion, *The Memoir of 1801* presents rancorous and gloomy views of life. In this description of the labyrinthine politics of the post-Sado court, even the mother-son relationship between Lady Hyegyŏng and Chŏngjo, which is presented in rosy tints in the other memoirs, is not without conflict. In the years between Prince Sado's death and Chŏngjo's accession, they labored under extreme tension. Chŏngjo was made Crown Prince two months after his father's death[47] and was never free of Sado's spectre and the terror and insecurity that were associated with his death. Under no circumstances could he alienate his grandfather, which was why Lady Hyegyŏng sent her son to live in the same palace precinct as Yŏngjo. Nor could Chŏngjo afford to displease anyone else who might adversely affect his relationship with his grandfather. Princess Hwawan, Yŏngjo's favorite daughter, was said to have exerted much influence over her father and posed special problems. Lady Hyegyŏng draws a damning portrait of Hwawan as a capricious, power-hungry, domineering, ignorant woman, but Chŏngjo had to stay in his aunt's good graces.

In addition, there were Chŏngjo's own complex feelings toward his maternal family. Although he appreciated his maternal grandfather's devotion, he was resentful of what he considered the older man's overbearing interference. One could also imagine that Chŏngjo resented that the Hong family, who initially and for the most part owed their prosperity to Prince Sado, behaved after his death as if nothing had happened. Lady Hyegyŏng argues that this behavior was to assuage Yŏngjo's uncertainty concerning Chŏngjo; if Yŏngjo were to retain as heir the grandson born of the son he had just put to death, he needed assurances of loyalty from everyone associated with the child. But as a child, Chŏngjo may not have understood that fact.

The events leading to Hong Inhan's execution came at the end of Yŏngjo's reign, and Lady Hyegyŏng presents them as the culmination of the tensions born of a highly charged political atmosphere. Yŏngjo was over eighty and in ill health. In an audience with ministers of the State Council in 1775, Yŏngjo proposed that Chŏngjo be appointed to the prince-regency. Hong Inhan, then the Minister of the Left, took a position in that audience that was judged to be seditious and disloyal to Chŏngjo.

The main charges of disloyalty were that Hong Inhan opposed the establishment of Chŏngjo's regency and used language in opposing it that undermined Chŏngjo's qualifications and thus his legitimacy. Both issues, the question of regency and the particular language Hong Inhan used, are so embedded in the intricacies of the history and politics of the eighteenth-century Chosŏn court that they warrant some explanation. There were two kinds of regency in the Chosŏn dynasty. The first type was established when the king was in minority and the most senior queen dowager acted as his regent. The second type, the prince-regency, was established when the king wished to delegate a portion of his administrative duties to the heir apparent either because of age or ill health. The latter variety, because of the tension intrinsic to the situation, was viewed with apprehension. During the political strife of the eighteenth century, when the prince-regency was riddled with factional implications, the question of the regency inevitably took on added complexity.

The prince-regency of Kyŏngjong, Yŏngjo's predecessor and older brother, seems to have set off a long sequence of chain reactions associated with this institution. That regency was installed in 1717 because of King Sukchong's failing health and poor eye-sight. Sukchong was not happy with his heir, Kyŏngjong, who appears to have been mentally and physically quite feeble and de-ficient.[48] Only with the pledge of the senior Noron Ministers' loy-alty was Kyŏngjong kept and his regency instituted.[49] Kyŏngjong had no children,[50] and soon after his accession, his only surviving brother, Yŏngjo, was appointed heir apparent. As Kyŏngjong's health weakened, a censor proposed that Yŏngjo be made regent. Since a prince-regency implied that the king was in some sense deficient, officials were expected to resist the proposal for a time and then agree to it only reluctantly even though the king himself broached the topic. However, the Noron were a little too eager for Yŏngjo's prince-regency, and the Soron used this to fuel Kyŏng-jong's resentment of them. No regency was instituted, but the discussion functioned as a catalyst for the famous purge of the Noron of 1721–1722.

The next prince-regency was the ill-fated one of Prince Sado. It was installed in 1749 when he reached his fifteenth year, and it ended with his death thirteen years later.[51]

In view of the menacing and complex associations the prince-regency had acquired, it was natural that when Yŏngjo brought up the issue of Chŏngjo's regency in an audience in 1775, those pres-ent responded with extreme nervousness and caution. No one as-sented, and Hong Inhan objected to it quite strongly. This much is clear, but exactly what he said, and when, and why, are not so clear. In fact, conspicuous discrepancies as well as different inter-pretations exist between the accounts by Lady Hyegyŏng and that presented in the *Sillok*, the official annals. Consistent with official views at the time of its compilation, the *Sillok* states that Hong Inhan was a traitor and presents his objection as an insolent and willful act based on ulterior motives.[52] Lady Hyegyŏng, on the other hand, attributes it to his flustered state of mind and his desire to get through the situation by saying something as noncommittal and innocuous as possible. Another point of disagreement between the two versions involves Lady Hyegyŏng's alleged note to Hong. The *Sillok* says that Lady Hyegyŏng, hearing of her uncle's stance, sent him a note pleading with him to accept the royal proposal, but that even after having been apprised of royal intentions, Hong still opposed the regency.[53] Lady Hyegyŏng says nothing about send-ing a letter.

Several factors lead one to suspect that though she probably sent a message to Hong Inhan, it was one urging him to oppose the regency. One may accept at face value the *Sillok* statement that she sent a message; *Sillok* historians are not known to fabricate events. They did, however, interpret them freely to suit their views, and so one may certainly question *Sillok* claims concerning the content of the message, which would have been sealed and treated with great discretion. In her *Memoir of 1801*, Lady Hyegyŏng professes a belief that the regency had been the origin of her husband's downfall and that she wished to avoid one for her son at all costs. Such a message to Hong Inhan would explain her acute sense of guilt for his death: "there is not one which is not my responsibility and my fault."

It should be noted that her uncle was judged to have been disloyal to her son, who put him to death, and that *The Memoir of 1801* was written after Chŏngjo had died. What did she say while her son was alive? In *The Memoir of 1795*, she refers to this incident only briefly: "My uncle mysteriously committed a slip of the tongue in the winter of *ŭlmi* (1775). This led to the ruin of the family." This brevity may have been a concession to her son's feelings, but she maintains that her uncle erred, not that he committed a crime. If Lady Hyegyŏng believed that Hong Inhan had engaged in hostile and seditious actions against her son as the *Sillok* alleges,[54] it is doubtful that she would have forgiven him, even given her concern to restore her family's honor. More to the point, it is even more unlikely that, during her son's reign, she would have presented her uncle's objections to his regency as a mere slip of the tongue. As it is, she seems to have regarded her uncle with a mixture of family loyalty and certain reservations about his intelligence and integrity.

She displays none of these reservations toward her brother Nagim, who she confesses was her favorite. As she presents it, Hong Nagim's life, more than that of any other member of her family, exhibits the greatest discrepancy between nobility of character and the cruelty of fate. She sees him as an innocent victim whose early promise for greatness was nipped prematurely because of his scruples and filial devotion, and whose life in the remote countryside and conscientious avoidance of worldly fame led to execution as a heretic. She is convinced that her brother was killed in her place. In seeing him as her surrogate, she identifies with him completely.

She does not see his or her plight as merely a personal misfortune; she sees it as a sign of the disruption of the social order. The tentative resolution she had achieved in 1795 is completely shaken, but she could not accept what she saw as prevailing disorder, a state in which personal honor and social justice had no place. This memoir was written in part as an attempt to restore this order. When Sunjo reinstated Hong Nagim's honor in 1807, a few years after he assumed personal rule,[55] she must have felt at least partially vindicated. Hong Inhan's reinstatement took longer. In 1855, one sexagesimal cycle after Lady Hyegyŏng's sixtieth birthday, King Ch'ŏlchong (r. 1849–1863) posthumously restored Hong Inhan's honor.[56] It appears that this was partly motivated by Lady Hyegyŏng's memoir. Though she did not live to see her uncle reinstated, her narrative ultimately prevailed.

THE MEMOIR OF 1802

This memoir covers more or less the same ground as the one written the previous year. But whereas *The Memoir of 1801* is a cry of despair, this is a much more reasoned and calm plea. Over time Lady Hyegyŏng composed herself and developed a more effective way to present her case. No longer are there suggestions of tension between her and her son; the mother-son relationship is once again restored to the pedestal of perfect understanding and devotion. In contrast to *The Memoir of 1801*, this memoir addresses her grandson directly and invokes the primacy of filial piety, a most prized virtue in Confucian society. In this way, she appeals to a personal and ethical imperative.

She rhetorically assumes that Sunjo, out of filial devotion, will wish to carry out those things his father had wanted to do but had left incomplete because of his premature death. Thus she claims that what she asks Sunjo to do is nothing more than what his father had hoped to accomplish. By equating her requests with Chŏngjo's unfulfilled hopes, she is implying that compliance with her wishes would not only please her but his father as well.

What exactly did Chŏngjo want to do for his parents? It was well known that he was extremely pained that his adoption kept him from rendering Prince Sado and Lady Hyegyŏng the full honor due to the parents of a reigning king. On the first day of his reign, Chŏngjo lamented, "Alas, I am really Prince Sado's son. The Late

Majesty made me an adopted son of Prince Hyojang since he thought the main line of the family should be given precedence. Isn't it sad!... Though propriety must be strict, human emotion cannot but be expressed."[57] Lady Hyegyŏng reveals that Chŏngjo had elaborate plans to mend this imperfect state of affairs and that the executor of these plans was to be Sunjo. Chŏngjo planned that in 1804, when Sunjo reached his fifteenth year, he would abdicate the throne to Sunjo, directing that he render full honors to his grandfather and, by extension, his grandmother. In this way, Prince Sado was to be posthumously made king without Yŏngjo's decree having been countermanded. This was obviously an extremely circuitous, even fanciful, plan. After the third monarch, T'aejong (r. 1400–1418), no Chosŏn king had abdicated voluntarily. Because Chŏngjo died in 1800, the question of the feasibility of this plan was moot.[58] Even as fantasy, it underscores the lengths to which Chŏngjo contemplated going to honor his father without violating the dynastic authority of the Yi royal house. If Chŏngjo had been willing to reverse Yŏngjo's decree, he could have offered honors to his father to his heart's content.[59] However, Chŏngjo seems to have felt that to reverse the decree would undermine the moral authority of the Yi royal house and, by extension, his own moral authority.[60]

Chŏngjo's unrequited filial devotion is the central force of this memoir. His affection for his father is characterized by intensity and pathos. Chŏngjo was one of the most able and accomplished monarchs of Chosŏn Korea, but what his reign immediately conjures up are the artifacts he left to commemorate his father. These include Suwŏn (Hwasŏng), the city in which he reinterred his father and that he rebuilt as a shrine to his father's memory, and magnificent processional paintings that depict Chŏngjo's entourage in full regalia on the way to Prince Sado's tomb.[61] We can speculate on the reasons for his obsession. One is the traumatic circumstance under which he lost his father. On the day that Sado was ordered to enter the rice chest, Chŏngjo, a child not yet ten, lay prostrate behind his father, begging Yŏngjo for his father's life until he was physically removed from the scene.[62] Could he ever have forgotten such a moment? Then, when he was made Crown Prince and assumed his father's role, he had to deal with Yŏngjo, a brilliant but tempestuous and erratic man, who probably was quite exacting of his new heir. One might imagine that Chŏngjo felt as no one else could the difficulty and pain that drove his father to insanity and that he developed a deep sympathy for him.

Beyond the purely psychological factors was the issue of legitimacy—his father's imperfect status signified his own imperfect authority. In the Chosŏn monarchy, the legitimacy of the royal house rested at least conceptually and rhetorically upon its moral authority,[63] and paternal criminality was unacceptable for the monarch. Despite the cautionary measures taken by Yŏngjo, the *pyŏkp'a* group apparently did not deem Chŏngjo acceptable. Though Chŏngjo ascended the throne and those who questioned his legitimacy were punished, the fact that he could not render full honor to his father was a constant signifier of his own compromised ancestry. He must have reasoned that the connotations of Sado's criminality, a moral failing that cast a shadow on the royal house, could only be countered through a display of extraordinary moral prowess on his part. Abdication carried out in the name of filial devotion was to be such a display. By relinquishing the throne, he would obliterate Prince Sado's imperfection and thus retroactively legitimate his ancestry.

The central issue, however, was whether the question of Sado's criminality could be resolved without an adequate disclosure of the 1762 incident. Discontent concerning the official court policy of silence on the event was widespread, as evident in the mounting protests to open the discussion.[64] Nor did the policy of silence prevent speculation and conjecture. Lady Hyegyŏng was troubled by this. She mentions that there were two prevailing opinions, which, depending on whether one assumed Sado's criminality or his innocence, defended either Yŏngjo or his son, and that both were false and distorted. In other words, whether Sado is made a criminal or Yŏngjo a cruel father, the moral authority of the royal house is compromised, and Chŏngjo's status is adversely affected. If she believes that a complete picture should be presented to establish truth, then to what extent is she willing to reveal that complete picture? Not much, at least not in this memoir. She mentions Prince Sado's illness, which she asserts made Yŏngjo's decision unavoidable. There she rests. She is not ready to go into detail.

Lady Hyegyŏng's defense of her father suffers from the same problem as her discussion of Sado's criminality. That is, she has to defend him without getting to the crux of the matter. She reassesses the cause of her family's persistent misfortune and concludes that the root of the problem lies in her father's involvement in the Sado incident. The most grave charge against him was that he suggested to Yŏngjo that Prince Sado be ordered into a rice chest and that he supplied the chest. She vehemently denies the truth of this charge, but her defense is limited because she cannot discuss the details of the incident, and thus is unable to place his role in context. This disturbed her deeply. She was as committed to reestablishing her own father's honor as Chŏngjo was to reestablishing Sado's, and she pursued this objective as persistently as her son pursued his. She was aware, however, that the filial devotion of a married woman to her natal parents belonged to the private sphere and that it could not be presented as a consuming passion, as that of a man could be. This is why she does not argue, as she does for Chŏngjo, from the primacy of her filial devotion to her father. Rather she evokes the authority of her son to confirm her claim by making a place for her father and her family in his unfulfilled wishes. She says that her son promised that at the time of Sado's posthumous elevation to king, her father's and her family's honor would be fully restored as well. These promises had already been mentioned in *The Memoir of 1801*, but here they are presented as Chŏngjo's wishes for his maternal family, paralleling his wishes for his father. In this way, she attempts to make public her private devotion to her father.

Still, Lady Hyegyŏng understood very well that Hong Ponghan's honor could not rest purely on her protestations of his innocence or, for that matter, on Chŏngjo's tributes. Rather, she had to establish her father's integrity as an implicit quality of his actions, and this required that she present him as a public man engaged in the complex moral and political issues of the court. This would have required a discussion of the incident of 1762. The constraints resulting from the policy of silence about the incident were obvious. They affected the honor of her family as well as the moral authority of the royal house. And finally they made *The Memoir of 1805* a necessity for Lady Hyegyŏng.

THE MEMOIR OF 1805

The Memoir of 1805 is testimony concerning the 1762 royal filicide. She again addresses Sunjo directly, but, unlike *The Memoir of 1802* in which she appeals to him as his grandmother, she befits this memoir's more public subject matter by speaking to him as a senior royal family member to a royal descendant. The decision to present the entire history of the 1762 incident was one to which she had come only reluctantly. She was aware that a discussion of the father-son conflict would require her to reveal the two principals' strange behavior, a revelation that not only violated Chosŏn sensibility and custom but also contradicted Chŏngjo's policy.

Two issues were involved. One was whether and how to present the strange and insane behavior of the crown prince. Sado's behavior during the last years of his life when he became mad was truly bizarre. In the West, the understanding of madness has undergone continuous change and has only recently come to be seen as mental illness.[65] We have only the most scant indications of how madness was understood in eighteenth-century Korea. We know that Chŏngjo had the description of his father's conduct deleted from the *Records of Royal Secretariat*, an official record of the court,[66] because he felt ashamed of the symptoms of his father's madness. In fact, any mention of the topic became taboo. The second issue was whether and how to portray Yŏngjo's role in his son's tormented life, to which he had to put an end. Because of the incident's sensitive implications for the moral authority of the royal house, the official historiography made only the most cryptic references to it, minimizing Yŏngjo's role. Although Lady Hyegyŏng was sympathetic toward her son's position and understood the rationale behind the official historiographical stance, she became convinced that the policy of silence to which she had hitherto adhered was destructive and that the entire history of the filicide including Sado's illness and Yŏngjo's role had to be disclosed. She cites several reasons for this.

The most immediate is the necessity of correcting speculation and theories about the incident that, festering in repression, circulated widely. Whether the theory was that Sado was a criminal, or that Yŏngjo needlessly killed his son, or that officials instigated Yŏngjo to carry out the cruel act, they all reduced a complex tragedy to ill-considered finger-pointing. Silence had been adopted as a way of burying the unfortunate past; instead, an untruthful past was being invented and circulated. Silence was maintained to protect the dead from being subjected to incessant gossip and ridicule; instead, the dead were transformed into monsters and criminals. It

was imperative that these versions be replaced by truthful eyewitness testimony.

Almost as crucial is the right of the living descendant to be
truthfully informed about his ancestors. In Sunjo's case, he was
entitled to this knowledge not only as a descendant but also as a
ruler. His office required him to evaluate and make judgments
upon history. Another reason cited, which is closely related to both
of these issues, is Lady Hyegyŏng's belief that her experience and
knowledge are unique and valuable and thus should be transmitted. Of those who suffered through the grim incident and
played a significant role, she was the only one still living. She felt a
personal obligation to correct distortions and misrepresentations
concerning the dead. This engendered in her a compelling desire
to break away from complicity in silence and to reclaim history by
recording her memories.

She appears to have been acutely aware that this was to be a
momentous endeavor and that its success would depend on her
credibility as a reporter. She is clearly mindful of the fact that her
claim as a participant in the 1762 incident is a double-edged sword.
Her very qualification as an eyewitness—living through the event
as the wife of Prince Sado—could also make her biased. She attempts to allay the reader's suspicions by stressing the autonomy of
her viewpoint. She maintains that she owes allegiance to both parties, and thus the only course open to her is to be truthful and
impartial. She promises "a clear and coherent picture of the incident" to show "how it unfolded from its beginning to its end."

The memoir traces the father-son relationship from its euphoric
beginning when Yŏngjo welcomes the long-awaited heir in 1735 to
its tragic end when Sado dies in a rice chest in 1762. In the course
of narrating the story, various aspects of their conflict are analyzed.
First, there were differences in their personalities; Yŏngjo was "articulate, bright," whereas Sado was "reticent and slow, deliberate
of movement." Then, more important, their relationship was col-
ored and shaped by their respective public positions as the present
and future occupants of the throne. The effects of these combined
factors seem to have been deadly. Lady Hyegyŏng presents a tale
of a father and a son inextricably locked in a long, tortuous journey
into tragedy—the distant abodes that separated them early in
Sado's infancy, the growing estrangement between them, Yŏngjo's

high expectations and exacting demands, Sado's fear of his father, Yŏngjo's impatience with his son and his subsequent harshness, Sado's rage over his father's disapproval and rejection, the deterioration of Sado's personality, his madness, his violent explosions, intimations of Sado's attempts at patricide, and the final act. It is a dramatic and shocking tale, complex and sorrowful.

Her presentation of Sado is at once sympathetic and terrifying. So much is at stake in her efforts to dissuade the reader of Sado's criminality that she does not attempt to hide his transgressions. Rather, she places the responsibility for Sado's insanity squarely with Yŏngjo, saying that Sado's illness was caused by rejection and lack of love. The underlying theme is that he lost his battle to meet his father's demands not because he did not want to comply, but because he desired so intensely to live up to his father's expectations that the constant paternal disapproval was too great to bear. She presents his suffering and pain as larger than life. Though she does not condone his transgressions, she implies that even his trangressions were testimony to the depth of his suffering.

However, her apparent sympathy for her husband does not prevent her from admitting that at some point, consumed by rage and madness, Sado turned violent and posed such a threat to his son and his father that there was no alternative but to safeguard the dynasty by eliminating him. Just as her description of the earlier stages of his illness is sorrowful, her description of his explosive rage in the final stage is frightening. She conjures up a vivid image of a court in which all, in shock, horror, and dismay, watch helplessly as Sado descends into destructive violence. This state of terror continues until Lady Sŏnhŭi, Sado's mother, urges Yŏngjo to protect the safety of the dynasty by carrying out the final act, and Sado is placed in the chest. Lady Sŏnhŭi's choice of duty over maternal affection is presented by Lady Hyegyŏng as a choice of tragic dimensions. Thus Lady Hyegyŏng absolves Yŏngjo of any hastiness or overreaction in killing his son.

The picture of the 1762 incident she presents is compelling enough to convince the reader that simple finger-pointing is woefully inadequate. She achieves this narrative authority despite the fact that this memoir is not fully cognizant of the complexities of the political milieu in which Yŏngjo and Sado lived. While she is aware that the relationship of Yŏngjo and Sado was one in which the political and the personal were inextricably linked, she does not fully grasp the extent of the impact of the political on the personal. For instance, she explains the establishment of Sado's regency by saying that Yŏngjo wished "to let the Prince-Regent take care of those cases which he [Yŏngjo] detested but which were too serious for eunuchs." This might have been a partial reason. The fact remains, however, that she is unable to imagine Yŏngjo at work, constantly battling intractable factionalism and the perpetual threat of rebellion.[67] Nor is she able to fathom the nature of his hopes for and disappointments in his son as public heir, which leaves much of Yŏngjo's fury and frustration unconsidered.

If Lady Hyegyŏng, with her essentially private perspective, fails to perceive Yŏngjo the public man, it is her understanding of him as a private individual with his own agonies that absolves him in the end. Despite her assessment that Yŏngjo's harshness caused his son's psychological problem, Lady Hyegyŏng does not morally condemn Yŏngjo. She achieves this by allowing for the mystery of the human psyche. She maintains a division between the human realm, which is knowable, and the cosmic realm, which is unknowable. Yŏngjo's behavior toward his son belonged to the human realm. Step by step she traces Yŏngjo's harshness, which caused Sado's illness and ended in human tragedy. But the reasons for this behavior belong to the cosmic realm. She implies that, though one can record exterior chronology and speculate on etiology, what compelled Yŏngjo or Sado to do and feel as they did at each point must remain a mystery. Thus, though she describes Yŏngjo as unloving and expresses resentment toward him, she concedes that he, too, battled his own private demons. In the final analysis, the human psyche is unknowable.

In this final memoir, she can claim no greater understanding of the mystery of the workings of Heaven than she did when she wrote the first memoir ten years previously. Unlike the first or second memoir, in which puzzlement is accompanied by a sense of outrage or betrayal, here she seems to acquiesce to the notion that Heaven must have its own way of operating even if it cannot be discerned. Lady Hyegyŏng acknowledges that if the workings of each sphere—the personal, the social, the human, and the cosmic—are quite complicated separately, the relationship between them is even more complex. She does not deny that there is a correlation between them, but she concedes that ultimately these forces are mysterious and not immediately apparent. Thus, while she validates the moral order, she does not demand its transparency in individual lives.

In the same vein, she upholds the primacy of the social order. Individual consideration, no matter how compelling, must be subservient to this public cause. This view, however, is accompanied by full sympathy for the human condition and respect for individual endeavors regardless of the results. For whatever reason, be it the conflicting demands of multiple roles or inexplicable psychic needs, it is impossible to be all that one is supposed to be. Disappointment, guilt, and sorrow are inevitable. Though people must struggle with conflicting impulses and desires, and though they often lose their battles, the effort to be moral has intrinsic worth. And even when people fail, they deserve sympathy for their suffering. Thus she renders sympathy to all of those who, in 1762, voluntarily or involuntarily had to do what was necessary to uphold the social order.

This cost each a great deal. For Sado, it meant dying in a sealed rice chest; for Yŏngjo, it meant putting his only surviving son to death by a gruesome method; for Lady Sŏnhŭi, it meant urging Yŏngjo to kill her son; for Hong Ponghan, it meant burying Sado, consoling Yŏngjo, and protecting Chŏngjo; for Chŏngjo, it meant inheriting his father's mantle by becoming someone else's son; for Lady Hyegyŏng herself, it meant relinquishing her son to Yŏngjo and living on in shame. While it meant different things for different people, it cost all of them deep pain. By describing their pain and their struggle, Lady Hyegyŏng in these extraordinary memoirs offers a historian's compassion and consolation.[68]

Texts

Despite the popularity of *The Memoirs of Lady Hyegyŏng* in contemporary Korea, only recently has it been widely disseminated. The first time any portion of the memoirs was introduced to the public was in 1939, when portions of the first and fourth memoirs were serialized in the short-lived literary monthly, *Munjang* (Literary style). *The Memoirs* was published from the first issue, in February 1939, until the issue of January 1940.[69] Until then, the memoirs had circulated within the narrow confines of the Yi royal family. However, this exclusive readership does not mean that the original remained intact or that the textual history is known or easily traced. With the possible exception of *The Memoir of 1795*, the original manuscript is lost.

Reflecting its exclusivity, there is no woodblock edition. Fourteen known handwritten manuscript copies of different varieties exist, and they fall into three categories.[70] The first contains the manuscripts of all four memoirs collected into a complete series. There are eight sets, six in Korean, two in a mixture of Korean and Chinese. The second category comprises manuscripts of the first memoir. Three are in Korean, and one in a mixture of Korean and Chinese. There is also a manuscript of the first half of the first memoir in Korean. The manuscripts of the first memoir came to scholars' notice after 1979. The third category consists of Chinese translations of the second and third memoirs.

For a long time, the manuscripts that were thought to be important were complete series of memoirs. Of these series, there are three important manuscripts. The first, known as the Karam manuscript, is named after the nom de plume of the late Professor Yi Pyŏnggi, who discovered it. This manuscript is believed to date from 1919. It consists of six volumes and has acquired the title *Hanjungnok*. The memoirs serialized in *Munjang* were based on the Karam manuscript. The second is the Ilsa manuscript, named after the late Professor Pang Chonghyŏn. It consists of three volumes entitled *Hanjung mallok*. The Minjung sŏgwan edition of 1961, edited by Kim Tonguk, which is still regarded as the standard modern edition, is based on the Ilsa manuscript, which is believed to date from approximately the turn of this century. Both are at the Kyujanggak Library at the Seoul National University. The third is in the Asami collection at the University of California, Berkeley. This has six volumes and is titled *Hanjung mallok*. When I acquired a copy of the Asami manuscript in 1978, it was not known to Korean scholars.

I had to make several decisions in the course of translating and studying the memoirs. The first involved which manuscripts I should use as a basis for my translation. After comparing the three manuscripts, I concluded that the Asami manuscript was the earliest and least corrupt version and thus decided to use it. Later I discovered that in 1979 Professor Kim Yongsuk had independently acquired a copy of the Asami manuscript and come to the same conclusion, dating it at about 1880.[71]

The second decision involved the order in which to present the four memoirs. This question arose because none of the complete series of memoirs follows the sequence in which Lady Hyegyŏng wrote them. With little variation, all three manuscripts rearrange the memoirs in temporal sequence. First came the first half of the first memoir, then the fourth memoir, followed by the second half of the first memoir. Then came the second memoir, followed by the third memoir. Was I to follow the order in the Asami manuscript or restore the memoirs to the sequence in which Lady Hyegyŏng wrote them? I chose to do the latter. It seemed that the narrative authority of the memoirs demanded this restoration of original order.

The third decision was considerably more difficult. After I finished translating all four memoirs based on the Asami manuscript, I found a manuscript of the first memoir, also in the Asami collection, which is a considerably earlier version than the one included in the Asami complete manuscript (Asami comp A). I had overlooked this manuscript, which I will call the Asami M (Memoir) 1-A. The catalogue described it as an "abridged" manuscript,[72] and when I briefly examined it on one of my visits to Berkeley in the 1970s, it seemed that the manuscript fit the description in the catalogue. Later I found that it had this appearance because it included, after Lady Hyegyŏng's *Memoir of 1795*, a Korean translation of Hong Nagyun's memorial. This memorial, the Chinese version of which was sent to King Sunjo in 1809, is a passionate defense of his father and older brother and thus discusses some of the same events that Lady Hyegyŏng does in her first, second, and third memoirs. Because Hong Nagyun's memorial was appended to the manuscript, it appeared to be "abridged." In any case, it came to my notice that Professor Kim Yongsuk, who has been working on Lady Hyegyŏng's memoirs for a long time, discovered this manuscript in 1979, and she concluded that this was most likely the original.[73] Upon close examination, I agreed that there was no question that the Asami M 1-A was far more authentic and less tampered with than the version of *The Memoir of 1795* included in the Asami complete manuscript. I then had to decide whether to keep translations of all four memoirs from the Asami complete manuscript, or to replace my translation of the first memoir with a new translation based on this earlier version.

Despite the superior claim to authenticity of the Asami M 1-A manuscript, it could be argued that, for stylistic consistency and flow, all four should come from the same manuscript. However, arguments in favor of the earlier version far outweighed this. First, it is infinitely preferable to go with the more authentic version even if it is only for the first memoir, which amounts to about one-third of the length of the four combined. Lady Hyegyŏng's voice is much more vivid and her conception of her world is much more clearly delineated in this version. Since the four memoirs were written as separate works, using a separate text for the first memoir did not seem to mar the coherence of the work as a whole. Moreover, this earlier version gives some indication of the process of change that the texts of the other three memoirs have probably gone through in the course of being copied and compiled. Thus I decided to translate the Asami M 1-A for *The Memoir of 1795*.

As they stand in this book, *The Memoir of 1795* is based on this earlier version, Asami M 1-A, while the remaining three memoirs, *The Memoir of 1801*, *The Memoir of 1802*, and *The Memoir of 1805*, are based on the Asami manuscript of the complete series, Asami comp A. In the *han'gŭl* texts, the style of the first memoir, the Asami M 1-A manuscript, differs rather considerably from the style of the three later memoirs, which are from the Asami comp A manuscript. The first memoir is written in a more informal and spontaneous style than the rest, which are more polished and contain numerous words of Chinese origin. I have tried to suggest this difference in the translation. The four memoirs are presented in the order in which Lady Hyegyŏng wrote them.

Translator's Note

Naming conventions in eighteenth-century Korea were extremely complicated. It was impracticable to follow Lady Hyegyŏng's usage faithfully in my English translation, and so I have made various modifications. Sometimes it has meant anachronistic usage, sometimes substituting for Lady Hyegyŏng's usage a more commonly known name. For instance, she refers to her husband by the name of his shrine, Kyŏngmogung. Since he is popularly known as Prince Sado, I used this name instead.

There is one rule to which I try to remain faithful. That is, during the eighteenth century, one's given name unaccompanied by one's family name was used almost exclusively as an expression of contempt or in referring to someone who is at least one generation junior or much lower in social class. Thus when Lady Hyegyŏng says Kwiju or Hugyŏm rather than Kim Kwiju or Chŏng Hugyŏm in referring to those persons who were archrivals of her family, she is explicitly displaying her contempt. She also refers to her nephews by given names, but in this case, this is because she is their elder. She does not refer to her younger siblings by their given names because they are of the same generation as she. She refers to them as my older brother, my second brother, my younger sister, and so on.

Members of the royal family are referred to by the titles they were given, Queen Chŏngsŏng, Princess Hwap'yŏng, and so on.

These were not regarded as given names but as titles. These titles changed with station, but I have adhered to one form whenever possible. An exception is Chŏngjo, Lady Hyegyŏng's son. He is referred to as the Grand Heir, the King, the present King, and the late King, depending upon the situation. Another exception is Princess Hwawan, often referred to by Lady Hyegyŏng as Madame Chŏng. I have followed her usage.

When a person is identified by a full name, I have placed the surname first, followed by the given name. I have also followed Korean custom in referring to married women outside the royal family by their maiden surnames. When this was not practicable, I have used their husbands' surnames.

In referring to age, I translate *se* as being in a certain year or I used true age in English usage. Fifteen *se*, for instance, becomes "he was in his fifteenth year" or "he was fourteen years of age." In traditional Korea, time was also measured in sixty-year cycles.

Principal Persons

THE HONG FAMILY

HONG HYŎNBO (1688–1740). Lady Hyegyŏng's paternal grandfather. He was a descendant of Princess Chŏngmyŏng, King Sŏnjo's daughter, and had a respectable official career that included an appointment as Minister of Rites.

HONG INHAN (1722–1776). Hong Ponghan's younger brother. After passing the civil service examination in 1753, he served in important posts. He was Minister of the Right in 1774 and Minister of the Left in 1775. He opposed Chŏngjo's regency in 1775. Upon Chŏngjo's accession in 1776, he was executed under charges of disloyalty to Chŏngjo.

HONG NAGIM (1741–1801). Hong Ponghan's third son. Referred to as the third brother by Lady Hyegyŏng. He passed the civil service examination in 1769 and shortly thereafter retired to private life. In 1801, he was accused of having converted to Catholicism, and executed.

HONG NAGIN (1730–1777). Hong Ponghan's oldest son. Lady Hyegyŏng's older brother. He had a successful official career.

HONG NAGYUN (1750–1813). Hong Ponghan's fourth and youngest son. Referred to as the fourth brother. He never served in office.

HONG NAKSIN (1739–?). Hong Ponghan's second son. Referred to as the second brother. He passed the civil service examination in 1766 but retired from office in 1770 to live in the countryside.

HONG PONGHAN (1713–1778). Lady Hyegyŏng's father. With his daughter's marriage to Crown Prince Sado and his subsequent passing of the civil service examination in 1744, he served in office for almost three decades. After Prince Sado's death, Hong emerged as Chŏngjo's protector. In his later years, he repeatedly came under attack for his supposed role in the Sado incident.

HONG SUYŎNG (1755–?). Hong Nagin's eldest son, thus the heir to the Hong family. *The Memoir of 1795* is addressed to him.

MADAME HONG (1746–?). Lady Hyegyŏng's younger sister. She married Yi Pogil in 1759, but because her husband's father was implicated in a seditious plot, she led a difficult life.

MADAME MIN (dates unknown). Hong Nagin's wife. Born to the illustrious Min of Yŏhung family, she married Hong Nagin in 1745.

MADAME YI (1713–1755). Hong Ponghan's wife and Lady Hyegyŏng's mother. She was the daughter of Yi Chip, who, at the time of his daughter's marriage, was serving as Governor of Hwanghae Province.

THE YI ROYAL FAMILY

MADAME CHŎNG. See Princess Hwawan.

KING CHŎNGJO (r. 1776–1800). Prince Sado's son born of Lady Hyegyŏng in 1752. Referred to as the Grand Heir, the King, and the late King. Appointed Crown Prince in 1762 after his father's death, he was appointed Regent in 1775 and succeeded to the throne in 1776 upon the death of Yŏngjo, his grandfather. He died in 1800.

PRINCESS CH'ŎNGSŎN (1756–1802).   Prince Sado and Lady Hyegyŏng's second daughter. Married Chŏng Chaehwa, known as Lord Hŭngŭn, in 1766.

QUEEN CHŎNGSŎNG (1692–1757).   Yongjo's first wife. Sŏ Chongje's daughter. Estranged from her husband, she was childless.

QUEEN CHŎNGSUN (1745–1805).   Kim Han'gu's daughter and Yŏngjo's second queen. The royal wedding took place in 1759. For four years from 1800 to 1804, she was the dowager regent to the minor king, Sunjo, during which time Lady Hyegyŏng's family suffered. Her family were archrivals of the Hong family.

PRINCESS CH'ŎNGYŎN (1754–?).   Prince Sado and Lady Hyegyŏng's first daughter. She married Kim Kisŏng in 1764.

LORD HŬNGŬN (dates unknown).   Chŏng Chaehwa. The husband of Princess Ch'ŏngsŏn and the brother-in-law of Chŏngjo. He is known as a fun-loving person who led Chŏngjo a bit astray in his adolescence and before he ascended to the throne. This event led to difficulties between Hong Ponghan and his grandson, Chŏngjo.

PRINCESS HWAHYŎP (1733–1752).   Yŏngjo's seventh daughter, born of Lady Sŏnhŭi. She died of measles.

PRINCESS HWAP'YŎNG (d. 1748).   Yongjo's third daughter, born of Lady Sŏnhŭi. Beloved by her father, she died in childbirth.

PRINCESS HWASUN (d. 1758).   Yŏngjo's second daughter, born of Lady Yi Chŏngbin. She starved herself to death upon her husband's death.

PRINCESS HWAWAN (1738–?). Yŏngjo's favorite daughter. She married Chŏng Ch'idal but was widowed young. While her father was alive, she wielded great power. She left the palace when Chŏngjo ascended the throne. In 1778, under official pressure, Chŏngjo stripped her of her royal title and the privileges associated with it and banished her to Kanghwa Island. In 1782 Chŏngjo allowed her to move to a location near the capital.

LADY HYEGYŎNG (1735–1815). The author of the memoirs. Hong Ponghan's daughter. She married Prince Sado in 1744 and bore him Chŏngjo and the Princesses Ch'ŏngyŏn and Ch'ŏngsŏn.

PRINCE HYOJANG (1719–1728). Yŏngjo's first heir apparent, but he died in his tenth year.

QUEEN HYOSUN (d. 1751). Prince Hyojang's widow and the daughter of Cho Munmyŏng. She was posthumously given the title of queen in 1776 when her adopted son, Chŏngjo, ascended the throne.

QUEEN HYOŬI (1753–1821). She married Chŏngjo in 1762. She was the daughter of Kim Simuk.

LORD ILSŎNG (d. 1757). Chŏng Ch'idal. Princess Hwawan's husband.

QUEEN DOWAGER INWŎN (1687–1757). Sukchong's third queen. Kim Chusin's daughter. Yŏngjo was said to have been devoted to this stepmother.

LADY KASUN (dates unknown). King Chŏngjo's secondary consort and King Sunjo's mother. Unlike most secondary consorts, she was the daughter of a high-ranking official. Her father, Pak Chunwŏn, served as Minister of Justice. She was selected and brought into palace in 1787 through a formal procedure.

LADY MUN (d. 1776).   Yŏngjo's secondary consort. She gave birth to the Princesses Hwanyŏng and Hwagil in 1753 and 1754. She was thought to have engaged in schemes to eliminate the heir apparent, Chŏngjo, and thus, upon Chŏngjo's accession in 1776, she was executed.

PINGAE (d. 1761).   Sado's secondary consort. Née Pak, she was given the title Kyŏngbin. She had been a lady-in-waiting to Queen Dowager Inwŏn, and so there was a taboo on Sado's taking her in. Sado was fond of her and took her in despite the taboo and stern paternal disapproval. She bore him two children, Prince Ŭnjŏn and Princess Ch'ŏnggŭn. In 1761 Sado, in madness, beat her to death.

PRINCE SADO (1735–1762).   Yŏngjo's son born of Lady Sŏnhŭi. Lady Hyegyŏng married him 1744. He was appointed heir apparent in 1736 and Prince-Regent in 1749. He became mad and violent. In 1762, Sado was ordered by Yŏngjo to enter a rice chest in which he died eight days later.

LADY SŎNHŬI (d. 1764).   Yŏngjo's secondary consort. She bore Prince Sado and several princesses. She is reported to have urged Yŏngjo to kill Sado when Sado became very violent.

KING SUNJO (r. 1800–1834).   Lady Hyegyŏng's grandson and King Chŏngjo's son born of Lady Kasun in 1790. Three of Lady Hyegyŏng's memoirs, *The Memoir of 1801*, *The Memoir of 1802*, and *The Memoir of 1805* were written for him. Referred to as the young King or the present King.

PRINCE ŬNŎN (1754–1801).   Prince Sado's son by Lady Yim Sukpin. He was named In. He was accused of involvement in Catholicism and executed in one of the persecutions of Catholics.

PRINCE ŬNSIN (1755–1771).   Prince Sado's son by Lady Yim Sukpin, and so, Ŭnŏn's younger brother. He was named Chin. Accused of having been involved in a seditious scheme, he was banished to an island in 1771 and soon died there.

KING YŎNGJO (r. 1724–1776). Sukchong's son born of Lady Ch'oe Sukpin in 1694. Referred to as His Majesty. Appointed heir apparent in 1721, he succeeded his brother to the throne in 1724. A brilliant but tempestuous ruler. Sado's father.

OTHERS

CHŎNG HWIRYANG (1706–1762). Chŏng Ch'idal's uncle. He had a successful official career that included an appointment as the Minister of the Left. When Prince Sado went to P'yŏngyang, Chŏng was the Governor of P'yŏngan Province.

CHŎNG HUGYŎM (1750–1776). Princess Hwawan's adopted son. He passed examinations in 1766 and wielded power while King Yŏngjo was on the throne. When Chŏngjo came to the throne in 1776, he was executed under a charge of disloyalty to Chŏngjo.

LORD CH'ŎNGWŎN. See Kim Simuk.

HAN YU (d. 1770). A country scholar. He sent memorials viciously attacking Hong Ponghan, which led to Hong's dismissal. He was executed.

HONG KUGYŎNG (1748–1781). Chŏngjo's confidant in the early years of Chŏngjo's reign. A member of another branch of the Hong family, but also a nemesis of Hong Inhan. Though he helped Chŏngjo to consolidate his power, he became too powerful. His schemes to become an affinal relative of the royal house did not succeed, and he died in banishment.

KIM CHONGSU (1728–1799). Related to the Hong family on his maternal side, but on bad terms with them. He worked closely with Hong Kugyŏng. When Hong Kugyŏng fell from power, he turned against him, and thus he was able to remain in office. He eventually rose to high positions, serving as Minister of the Right and Minister of the Left.

KIM HAN'GI (dates unknown). Kim Han'gu's brother and ally.

KIM HAN'GU (d. 1769). Queen Chŏngsun's father, thus Yŏngjo's father-in-law. He was given the title Lord Ohŭng. The Kim family were archrivals of the Hong family.

KIM KWANJU (1743–1806). Kim Kwiju's cousin and a political ally. He was banished after Chŏngjo's accession. During Queen Chŏngsun's regency (1800–1804), he reached the position of Minister of the Right. But subsequently, he was banished.

KIM KWIJU (d. 1786). Queen Chŏngsun's brother. The most politically active member of the Kyŏngju Kim family, who were in contention with the Hong family. Upon Chŏngjo's accession in 1776, he was banished to Hŭksan Island. In 1784 he was allowed to settle in Naju, where he died of illness.

KIM SIMUK (1722–1772). Father of Queen Hyoŭi and Chŏngjo's father-in-law. He was given the title of Lord Ch'ŏngwŏn and served in various posts.

The Memoirs of Lady
Hyegyŏng

The Memoir of 1795

From the time I came to the palace as a child,* each morning and evening I exchanged letters of greeting with my parents, and many of those letters should have remained with my family. However, upon my departure, my father† cautioned me, "It is not right that letters from the outside should be scattered about the palace. Nor would it be proper for you to write of anything at length aside from simple words of greeting. It would be best if, after reading the news from home, you wrote us on the same sheet of paper." As he instructed, I wrote to them on the top margin of the letters that Mother faithfully sent twice each day. Father's letters, as well as those of my brothers and sister, were answered in the same way. Father also cautioned my family not to strew the letters from the palace about the house. Thus my family gathered all my letters and, at regular intervals, washed away all that was written.‡ Hence, none of those writings remained in my family's possession.

My oldest nephew, Suyŏng,[1] regretted this and repeatedly urged me, "We have none of Your Ladyship's writings in our house. If Your Ladyship could write something for us, then we would treasure and transmit it to the family." He was correct, of course, and I

---

* When she married Prince Sado in 1744, both of them were in their tenth year.
† Hong Ponghan.
‡ Washing away the ink with water was the standard way of obliterating what was written. Paper was then reused.

49

meant to write something for him, but I did not manage to do it. This year I have completed my first sixty years and my remaining days are few. Completing this cycle, I have experienced a sharp longing for my deceased husband. Moreover, I fear that if I wait any longer my memory will grow even worse. So, complying with my nephew's request, I have recorded what I experienced and how I felt in the past, to let others know. My memory has declined, however, and I could not recall many things. Thus I have recorded only what I was able to remember.

I was born in my maternal grandparents' home at Kop'yŏng-dong in Pansong-bang,* at one o'clock in the morning on the eighteenth day of the sixth month of the *ŭlmyo* year (1735). Father is said to have come and prepared for Mother's delivery. He was not able to come to his in-law's on the eighteenth, but on the night of the seventeenth he is reported to have dreamt that a black dragon appeared on the wall of the room in which Mother was staying. This led him to expect that he would have a boy. Thus when I was born, he thought it strange that I was a girl, contrary to the portent of the dream.† Shortly after my birth, Grandfather‡ came to see me in person. He is said to have taken a liking to me, saying, "This child is no ordinary child."

I was told that my great-grandmother Yi also expressed high hopes for me. When Mother returned home with her newborn child twenty-one days after the birth, my great-grandmother came to see me. She told my mother, "She is different from other children. Bring her up well." She personally selected a wet nurse and sent her to us. That is how my wet nurse was chosen.

When I was growing up, Grandfather was unusually fond of me and scarcely allowed me out of his presence. He would always joke, saying, "This child is a little woman. She will grow up very quickly."

After I entered the palace, the memory of all this praise that I received as a child left me with a certain unease and fear that I

---

* The home was located in the western district of Seoul. While Chosŏn Korea accepted patriarchy, traces of native custom, which had included uxorilocal marriages, remained. Giving birth at a woman's parents' house was one such trace.
† A dragon dream connoted that the child would achieve distinction in public life. Her father was puzzled because women could not be active in public life.
‡ Hong Hyŏnbo.

might not live up to those expectations. Still, I used to wonder whether the high opinions of me expressed by two elder generations were not based on some foreknowledge, and I thought it quite strange.

When I was very young, I had an older sister, and my parents loved us both. When my sister died, I became the sole object of an affection that exceeded the bounds of normal parental love. Father in particular loved me. Although my parents had not reached such an age that they would dote on their children, they were still exceptionally partial to me. Can it be that it was because this unfilial daughter was fated to enter the palace? Whenever this thought occurs to me, it brings a pang to my heart and tears to my eyes.

My parents were, as a rule, strict in educating their young. For instance, discipline for my older brother* was very strict and formal. Strangely, they showed me only love and affection. Father favored me so much that, as a young child, I found it difficult to stay away from him even for a short while. In fact, I seldom left my parents' side. Even at night, I could fall asleep only if I slept in the same room with them.

In the third month of *kimi* (1739), my second brother† was born. In the same year Father's younger sister gave birth to my cousin, Chin'gwan. Father was unusually close to his siblings and, thus, arranged that his sister come and deliver her child at our house. Mother was sent somewhere else for my brother's delivery.

I was four at the time and was weaned from my wet nurse. I accompanied Mother to the place of delivery, where Grandfather visited often. He dropped by without fail on his way back from the palace. I remember well that I would wait for him. Because I had received much love from him, when he was ill in the *kyŏngsin* year (1740) I often accompanied Mother to visit him at his quarters.‡ After his death I was sent to Great-grandmother Yi because of my extreme youth. I remember that I hated being sent there, that I missed my parents, and that I felt deeply sorry for my youngest uncle.§ I had a special affection for him because of our closeness in

* Hong Nagin.
† Hong Naksin.
‡ They lived in the same house, but in different quarters.
§ Hong Yonghan.

age. I also recall that when I returned home, I saw Grandfather's tablet being brought back* and that I thought of him and missed him.

Father was exceptionally filial. He grieved profoundly over the death of his father and continued to serve his stepmother with utmost sincerity. He loved his brothers and instructed and educated them in a manner no different from the way in which he loved and educated his children. Mother was also outstanding in her virtuous conduct, her filial devotion, and her sisterly love. In caring for an ailing father-in-law, in serving her mother-in-law, in managing household affairs, and in loving her husband's three sisters, Mother left nothing to be desired. She was also on very friendly terms with the wife of her husband's second brother[2] who, since *kyŏngsin* (1740), had shared the mourning duties with her. My mother made sure that she consulted her sister-in-law on the particulars of each mourning ritual so as to deepen their friendship and harmony.

This aunt was also quite exceptional in her virtue. She respected her older-sister-in-law nearly as much as she respected her mother-in-law, and she loved her husband's brother's children as her own. I remember how affectionate she was toward me and how attentively she taught me to read Korean. I became quite attached to her. My mother used to say to my aunt, "She really adores you."[3]

As the great-grandson of a princess, Grandfather was born to an illustrious and wealthy family. He was incorruptible and simple in his habits, and thus he left no money. After his death, our household showed no sign that it had been that of a minister.[4] Rather, it was in every way the household of a poor scholar out of office.

In carrying out mourning and sacrificial rituals, my parents never deviated from perfect decorum. Our house had no household shrine.[†] Nonetheless, they were determined to construct Grandfather's shrine in time, and they put all their effort to it. When the three-year mourning period ended, the shrine was completed and the memorial tablet was in place. Given the financial state of our household at the time, this was an impossible feat carried out only because of Father's filial devotion and able management. It was truly an admirable accomplishment.

---

* This signaled that the funeral had just been completed.
† Hong Hyŏnbo was a second son, and as such, he moved out on his own. The ancestral shrine belonged to the main branch of the family.

My mother lost her mother in the *muo* year (1738). Before she recovered from this loss, she was confronted with the death of her father-in-law in the *kyŏngsin* year (1740). She had given birth to my third brother only three or four months before that.* Under heavy mourning duties, Mother grew exceedingly emaciated and weak. Concerned with her weakened state, Father asked her to take Grandfather's leftover restorative medicine. Mother, however, was very anxious to spend some time at her natal home. In her haste, she left without taking the medicine as he had asked. Feeling that his wife had behaved most inconsiderately, Father was deeply cha-grined. I had accompanied Mother to her home, but Father came and took me back and reprimanded Mother sharply. Unable to stay on at her natal home, Mother returned. Father would not see her and sent her many harsh messages. Mother was distressed. She thought that he was being excessively severe, and so she refused to eat. It was midwinter. Miserable that my parents were refusing food and upset that they were on bad terms, I went about forlornly and restlessly. I, too, could not bring myself to eat. Feeling sorry for my discomfort, Father began to eat. Lest she wound her child, Mother also resumed her usual pleasant air. This was really a happy turn. My parents complimented me, saying, "Such a young child knew enough to be unhappy over a parental disagreement." They gave me a toy pot and pan in reward. I was delighted and played happily with the toys.

I vividly remember my parents' filial conduct. Each day at dawn, Father visited the shrine. Afterwards, he would visit his stepmother to pay his respects, first bowing and then conversing with her in tender words and with a gentle expression. Grandmother responded in the same way, placing in him an affection and trust greater than that which she gave to her own children. Even to a child it was obvious that she treasured this stepson more than her own, and I understood that this was really exceptional. This was the result of Father's sincere devotion.

Father was also unusually affectionate to his sisters.[5] In the *sinyu*

---

* This is in error. Lady Hyegyŏng's third brother, Nagim, was not born until 1741. It would make more sense if she were pregnant with him. Lady Hyegyŏng may be attempting to avoid the suggestion that her brother was conceived during the mourning period for her grandfather, who died in the sixth month of 1740. Strict Confucian norms prescribed sexual abstinence during the mourning period for one's parents.

year (1741) his oldest sister was stricken by the epidemic. During her illness and after her death, no one else went to see her. But my father said, "How can one be so selfish as to neglect one's own sister when she is ill and fail to attend to her funeral after her death?" He went to her house and nursed her in her illness. When she died, he remained at the wake continuously, and he cried for a long time. One could see how he loved his sister. Soon afterwards, his brother-in-law died. Bereaved of their parents, my cousins were forlorn. My father took pity upon them and looked after them gladly as if he could not do enough for them. He brought one niece home and held her wedding at our house. My father was always kindhearted and generous like that and always affectionate. His home was always open to his two sisters, and they came very often to stay. He was particularly close to his second sister, and he frequently went to her home and brought her back with him.

Father had been raised by his grandmother for a time, and so he never missed a sacrifice for her. He also treated his cousins from the main house—an older male cousin and two female cousins— just as if they were his own siblings. Though I do not recall too many things from this period, I do remember seeing him being always filial and affectionate.

Father applied himself diligently to studying. He met every day with other scholars to discuss and exchange ideas. When this happened at our house, Mother would prepare the food with care and send it to the men's quarters.

Speaking of Mother, she was not only punctilious in her sacrificial duties to ancestors and her service to her parents-in-law but also extremely industrious. She wove and sewed day and night. It was not unusual for her to work until the early hours of the morning. She did not like old servants speaking of the light burning in her room till daybreak. To avoid this praise for diligence, she hung quilts over her windows when she worked at night. Working through those cold nights wore her hands rough, but she did not seem to mind at all. By early morning she was up, and after her morning toilet, she visited her mother-in-law punctually each day. Never once did she go until her hair had been piled neatly into a bun and she had put on a formal robe. The manner in which she served and assisted her husband was anything but ordinary, and it won his complete trust. I cannot forget how Father relied on her and how much he respected her opinion.

Father and Mother maintained an exceptionally frugal household. They insisted on simplicity in their own clothing and in the way they clothed their children, but never once were we siblings unseasonably or slovenly dressed. Our clothes may have been of coarse fabric, but they were always clean. In this alone, one could see that my mother was as neat as she was frugal. She did not lightly express joy or anger; at family gatherings she was always cheerful yet serious. There were none in the family who did not admire and respect her.

Mother and Father were married in the *chŏngmi* year (1727).* Her father died suddenly right after the wedding, and so Mother could not join her husband until the following year. Her mother died in *muo* (1738), but Mother could not remain there with her family very long. Thus, whenever she left for her husband's home, she and her brother always parted in tears. She looked up to her brother and her sister-in-law, Madame Hong, as though they were parents and treated them with deep affection. Though I was not yet of an age to observe these things, whenever I accompanied Mother to her family's home I was very impressed by the loving attitude she had toward her family. Both my uncle Lord Chirye,[6] and my cousin Sanjung were fond of me. My mother's family was known for incorruptibility, and hence they were poor. But they were devoted to each other. This was also true of the women in the family. Aunt Hong welcomed her sisters-in-law warmly whenever they visited and was careful to make them feel at home.

Mother was one of three sisters. The oldest married into the Andong Kim family[7] but was widowed young. Mother always thought of her. A son of this aunt, Kim Igi, was married in the late spring of *sinyu* (1741) at the home of his maternal uncle. Mother brought me to her brother's home on this occasion. Cousin Song was also there. She was the eldest daughter of Mother's second sister. Her father[8] was the deputy minister of some board at the time. She subsequently married my father's youngest brother and so became my aunt. When we were children, we often met at our maternal uncle's house and played together. In any case, when this cousin attended the wedding, she was dressed splendidly. Though I was not yet old enough to wear mourning, I still wore white.

---

* They were married in Haeju city at the governor's residence, since Lady Hyegyŏng's maternal grandfather was serving as Governor of Hwanghae Province.

Mother said, "She is wearing such beautiful clothes, but yours are so plain. Perhaps you should dress as she does?" I answered, "I am in mourning for Grandfather. I cannot do as she does. It is only proper that I wear a white blouse and a cotton skirt. I also want to stay inside with you and do not wish to go outside the gate."* Mother praised me for this. I was still too young to know proper decorum, and so my answer must have seemed quite strange. It must have been the influence of my education. It is odd how parental behavior influences even very young children.

In the third month of *kyehae* year (1743), Father, as a senior student in the Royal Academy, had an audience with the King. Later I was told that His Majesty had noticed Father's dignified manner and his courteous answers and had immediately taken to him. After the sacrifice at the Confucian Temple, the King announced that a special civil service examination would be held shortly, and he invited the students to take it. After I entered the palace, I heard that His Majesty on that evening had said to his confidant: "Today I met a very promising young scholar who will render me great assistance." Then he is said to have expressed a hope for Father's success in the examination. Previous generations in our family had placed upon my father the highest of expectations. Father held noble views and beliefs. His companions were like-minded people; they were all prominent scholars from illustrious families. Naturally, Father eventually attained the highest posts. But after reaching prominence, he always had to be cautious and discreet because of this unfilial daughter, and thus was unable to express his ability to the fullest. As responsibility for this lay entirely with me, how can I not feel pain? At any rate, on this occasion it was believed that Father would surely pass. My uncle from the main house,[9] the head of the senior branch of the Hong family, came to our house and the whole family awaited the results in an atmosphere of great expectancy. Father was unsuccessful however. I, too, was expectant, and my disappointment was so sharp that I cried.

In the winter of that year Father was appointed a ritual attendant at Ŭinŭng.† It was the first official post in the family since the

* Since Lady Hyegyŏng's mother was in mourning for her father-in-law, she had to stay inside the gate.
† Ŭinŭng was the tomb of King Kyŏngjong and Queen Sŏnŭi.

death of Grandfather. All were delighted. When the rice came in payment of his salary, Mother divided it evenly among the relatives, not keeping even one peck for us.

In the spring of *kyehae* year (1743) my older brother performed the capping ceremony, and his wedding was planned for *kapcha* (1744). I counted the days to the arrival of my new sister-in-law. But, to my complete astonishment, it was I who was selected as the bride of the Crown Prince. At first, Mother did not wish to send in my name for the royal selection.* She thought that there would be no harm done if a scholar's daughter were withheld from the list. But Father said, "As a subject, one does not dare to deceive the throne." And he sent in my name. But my family was extremely poor at the time and there was simply no money for a wardrobe. Mother made a skirt with a piece of fabric that she had originally saved for my deceased older sister's dowry; she made the lining and the undergarments of cloth taken from old clothes. How poor we were, indeed! I can still vividly picture Mother laboring to assemble the wardrobe.

The twenty-eighth day of the ninth month was the day of the preliminary selection.† I was the youngest among the candidates. I thought that since I was just too young [to be the favorite], I might as well take the opportunity to observe splendid scenes until I was allowed to return home. However, His Majesty noticeably favored me and Queen Chŏngsŏng observed me with particular interest.

Lady Sŏnhŭi, the Crown Prince's mother, was not among those seated in the selection chamber. Instead, I was summoned to her quarters beforehand. When she saw me, she seemed quite pleased and was very loving. I thought that she was kind to me because I was a young child. Ladies-in-waiting competed with each other to sit closer to me. All this made me quite uncomfortable. Then we were given gifts. Lady Sŏnhŭi and Princess Hwap'yŏng watched

---

* During the Chosŏn dynasty, selections of spouses for royal children, known as *samgant'aek* (three-step screening), were conducted as follows. A royal edict was sent out asking that families with eligible boys or girls send in their names. After prescreening, the remaining candidates were asked to come to the court. There a final choice was made after three screenings. The royal edict concerning the selection of a wife for Crown Prince Sado was sent out in 1743. *Yŏngjo sillok* (hereafter *YS*), in *Chosŏn wangjo sillok*, 58:15a.

† Eight girls were chosen in the preliminary selection. *YS*, 58:26a–b.

how I carried myself and taught me to improve my manners. I did as they taught.

That night I slept in my mother's room. Early the next morning, Father came in and said to Mother, "This child is the top candidate. How can that be?" He was obviously perturbed. Mother said, "After all, she is only the daughter of a poor and nameless scholar. Maybe we should not have sent in her name." Half asleep, hearing my parents express their concerns, I became very sad and started to cry. Then, remembering how kind everyone at the palace had been, I flew into a panic and became utterly inconsolable. My parents tried to comfort me, saying, "This is not something a child should worry about." For some reason, I became acutely despondent after the first presentation. Was it perhaps because I had a premonition of the myriad trials and tribulations that I would go through in the palace?

After the initial selection, word spread, and many relatives came to visit us; even the former servants who had stopped paying us visits after *kyŏngsin* (1740) came. One can see how people are, and what governs their affections.

On the twenty-eighth day of the tenth month, the second presentation was held.* Naturally, I was terrified. My parents, too, were deeply worried. When they sent me off, they seemed to be anxiously hoping that, by some stroke of luck, I would not be chosen. When I arrived at the palace, however, it appeared as though the decision had already been made. First of all, the way my tent was prepared and the way I was welcomed were quite different from the treatment the other girls received. My nervousness grew steadily. At the royal audience, it became obvious. Unlike the way he received other girls, His Majesty came behind the bamboo curtain. He put his arm affectionately on my shoulder and said, "I have found a beautiful daughter-in-law. You make me think of your grandfather." He also said, "When I met your father, I was glad to find a man of ability. You are every bit his daughter." He seemed very pleased. Queen Chŏngsŏng and Lady Sŏnhŭi also seemed happy and were loving and kind. The princesses were also affectionate. They held my hands and were reluctant to let me go.

Rather than being allowed to leave immediately, I was led to Kyŏngch'un Pavilion. Because of a delay, I had to stay quite a long

---

* Three girls were chosen in the second presentation. *YS*, 58:29a.

while. Lady Sŏnhŭi sent some food for the midday meal. A lady-in-waiting came in and tried to remove my ceremonial robe to measure me. I resisted removing my robe at first, but she coaxed me, and I gave in and let her measure me. I felt increasingly agitated. I wanted to cry, but lest the palace ladies see me, I withheld my tears with all my strength. As soon as I entered the palanquin, I burst into tears. Then I realized, to my utter amazement, that my palanquin was being carried by palace servants. Before I recovered from this shock, I noticed a lady messenger from the Queen, dressed completely in black, standing in the street, waiting to accompany me. My astonishment was simply indescribable.

When it arrived at our house, the palanquin was led through the gate to the men's quarters. My father raised the curtain of the palanquin and helped me down. He was dressed in ceremonial robes. He seemed awestruck and uncomfortable. How clearly I remember my father's manner on this occasion, reverent but disturbed. I was overwhelmed by a sharp sadness as I held my parents. Even now, when I recall this scene, I cannot keep tears from streaming down.

Mother also had changed into ceremonial robes. She covered the table with a red cloth. Bowing four times, she received the Queen's message and bowing twice, Lady Sŏnhŭi's. She, too, was reverent and uneasy. I was amazed to find that complete preparations had been made to invite the whole entourage to a repast with many different kinds of delicacies. I feel that, compared to the way in which the royal affinal families do things these days, we adhered to a much more elaborate and grand style.

From that day, my parents changed their form of address to me; now they spoke to me exclusively in respectful language.* The other elders in the family also treated me with deference. This change made me indescribably uncomfortable and sad. Realizing that his daughter was going to be the Crown Princess Consort and that it was irrevocable, Father seemed to experience an acute sense of apprehension. He perspired heavily, his clothes often became soaked, and he seemed to dread the parting. In his uneasiness, he counseled me, offering a thousand, ten thousand words of advice. I cannot record them all. The prospect of leaving my parents was, of

---

* The Korean language has different levels of speech. The language Lady Hyegyŏng's parents now used with her was of a level appropriate to one's elders and honored guests.

course, simply unbearable for me. This was so horrifying that whenever I thought of it, my insides seemed to just melt away. I fell into a state of such intense anguish that I lost interest in everything.

Meanwhile, every one of our relatives—not merely close ones, but even the most distant members of the lineage—came to see me before my departure. It got so that really distant ones had to be received by others in the outer quarters. My great grandfather's cousin from Yangju came. Several cousins of my grandfather also came. I remember in particular one elderly gentleman. He said, "Since life in the palace is so strict, this will be our farewell in this life. Please be respectful in your conduct and take good care of yourself." He then added, "My name is Kambo, Kam for 'mirror,' and Po, 'to help.' I hope you will remember me." Though I had never met this gentleman before, his words somehow saddened me.

The final presentation was scheduled for the thirteenth day of the eleventh month.* As the days dwindled, I became sadder, and every night I slept in my mother's arms. My aunts—Father's two sisters and Father's brother's wife, Aunt Sin—also grieved over my departure and stayed with me and were poignantly affectionate. I wanted to sleep between my parents, so I asked Father to come and sleep in the inner quarters. But, because there were so many guests to entertain, there were only two nights on which he could come to sleep in the inner quarters. On those nights, lying between Father and Mother, how sorrowfully did I cry! They caressed and consoled me. Pitying their child, they lay sleepless. Even now, so many years later, as I think of these things I am again overwhelmed with those same feelings.

I felt that it would be proper to pay a visit to the ancestral shrine of the Hong family and to the shrine of my maternal grandparents to bid farewell. However, I felt rather uneasy doing this of my own accord. My wish to pay a visit was related to Lady Sŏnhŭi through a family connection (the wife of the older brother of Lord Kŭm- sŏng, His Majesty's third son-in-law, was my second paternal aunt's husband's younger sister). Lady Sŏnhŭi reported my wish to His Majesty and royal permission was soon granted. Sharing a pa- lanquin, Mother and I went to the home of the main branch of the

---

* This was when Lady Hyegyŏng was officially chosen. *YS*, 58:31a.

Hong family. This uncle and his wife had no daughter. They had often invited me to their house, sometimes overnight, and they had showered me with affection. The King had heard of this relationship and had instructed this uncle: "Help with the royal wedding." He had been staying at our house since the selection, but Aunt Ŏ was very happy to see me and brought me to the ancestral shrine. Ordinarily, descendants would bow to the shrine in the courtyard, but contrary to custom, I was made to enter the main hall and to bow there. Coming down the steps, I experienced deep stirrings in my heart. My second cousins came forward, and I sadly bid them farewell. My mother then told me that since her marriage, she had never been able to bow in the main hall of the Hong ancestral shrine. On that day, because of me, she finally got to see it at close range.

Later that day we visited Mother's family. My mother's brother had died a few years previously, but his widow welcomed me warmly nonetheless. She seemed pensive and downcast during the farewell. My cousins, with whom I had been quite intimate—playing, riding piggy back on them, or receiving affectionate embraces—now kept a distance. They said few words and were respectful. This saddened me. It was particularly hard to say good-bye to my cousin's young wife, Sin. We had been so fond of each other.

After visiting Mother's sisters, I returned home. Soon the day of the final presentation came. Two nights before, on the night of the eleventh, my aunts suggested to me, "How about taking one last good look at the house?"* They led me around. The night air was cold and crisp and the moon shone brightly upon the snow-covered ground. As they led me by the hand through the garden, I wept silently. I returned to my room but could not fall asleep, and lay awake the night through.

Very early the next morning, royal messengers arrived to summon me to the palace. I put on the ceremonial costume that had been sent by the court. The house was full of women relatives that day, distant relations who came to bid me farewell and closer ones who gathered to leave for the bride's pavilion.† Soon the time came

* Yi royal family custom did not allow women who had married into the royal house to visit their natal homes.

† During the Chosŏn dynasty, women marrying into the royal family were housed in a pavilion near the palace between the final presentation and the wedding ceremony. This seems to have been a compromise between the demands of

for the ceremony in which I would announce my departure at my grandfather's shrine. I bowed deeply and read my farewell announcement. I could not help crying as I did this. My heart felt as though it would break. Father also struggled to hold back tears. How everyone lingered, unable to bring themselves to say goodbye!

The day after the second presentation, the Prince's governess, Palace Matron* Ch'oe, and Kim Hyodŏk, a lady-in-waiting in charge of ritual matters, came to our house. Unlike ordinary ladies-in-waiting, Palace Matron Ch'oe was a large woman with an air of authority about her. When she arrived at our house, a narrow straw carpet was rolled out on which she was to walk to a guest room decked with silk embroideries and patterned cushions. She had served at the palace through several reigns and was particularly well versed in the customs and manners of the court. Mother, leading several formally attired sisters-in-law, greeted the palace ladies graciously. Trays of delicacies and wine were sent in continually until quite late in the night. I wondered how food could be prepared so quickly! After measuring me for ceremonial costumes, they returned to the palace.

Just before the day of the final presentation, Palace Matron Ch'oe and another lady-in-waiting, Mun Taebok, came with clothing sent by Queen Chŏngsŏng. The box they brought contained an outfit consisting of a long T'ang robe in heavy green silk, a blouse in pale yellow silk with a grape pattern woven into it, and an underblouse of heavy purple silk. In addition, it contained a thin chemise and a soft silk skirt in patterned crimson.

Father's younger sister was extremely playful. When I was a young child, a newly available type of silk of patterned crimson was in great vogue. When the box of clothes arrived from the court, this aunt said, "Your Ladyship once said to me, 'Wouldn't it be nice to wear a moon-white silk blouse with a patterned crimson

---

Chosŏn custom, which prescribed that the wedding ceremony take place at the bride's residence, and Chu Hsi's *Family Rituals*, which requires that the groom personally go to the bride's home to bring her to his family home where the wedding is to take place.

   * *Sanggung*. Refers to a lady-in-waiting of the fifth rank, the highest rank that could be achieved by ladies-in-waiting. *Kyŏngguk taejŏn*, 2 vols. (Seoul: Pŏpchech'ŏ, 1962), 1:17–18.

silk skirt? My hair should have high points on top in the shape of crane wings and be rounded in the back.' Now you have a crimson silk skirt! Why do you not come and look at it?" Everyone in the room laughed at my aunt's remark. But I was in such a sad mood that I could not bring myself to lift my gaze.

I had not had any pretty clothes as a child, but I do not recall being envious of anyone who had. There was, for instance, my aunt's daughter, who was my age. Her parents were quite wealthy and just doted on her. There was nothing that she did not own, lovely clothes, jewels, and cosmetics. But I was never envious of her. One day she came to our house dressed in a skirt made of fine, almost transparent, red silk with a lining done in the same fabric. It was just striking and when my mother saw it, she asked me, "Would you not like to wear a skirt like that?" I answered, "If I already had one, I guess there is no reason why I would not wear it. But since it must be made for me, I do not want one." My mother praised me, "You are saying this because you know we are poor. But I will make a promise. Because of that answer, when you get married, I will make a skirt for you just like that one. Even an adult could not have been more thoughtful."

Once, just after the second selection, my mother burst into tears and said, "I never got to dress you in pretty clothes. I wanted to make you that skirt, but in the palace you won't be able to wear ordinary clothes. I had better make something pretty for you now, just as I always wanted to." Grieving all the while, my mother made me this skirt of double red silk and made me wear it before the final presentation. I wept, and I wore it.

Lately I have noticed that families whose daughters marry into the royal house do not hesitate to have clothes made for their daughters after the wedding and sent to them at the palace. I must say that, by comparison, my family was a trifle too cautious.

When I arrived at the palace, I was brought to Kyŏngch'un Pavilion for a rest and then to T'ŏngmyŏng Pavilion for an audience with the Three Majesties.* Her Highness Queen Dowager Inwŏn, who had not seen me before, spoke first. "You seem beautiful and virtuous. This is a great blessing for the nation." His Majesty, patting me affectionately, exclaimed, "What an intelligent daughter-in-law I have. I did indeed choose well." Her Highness Queen

* *Samjŏn.* Refers to the king, his legal mother, and his wife.

Chŏngsŏng also expressed profound delight, and Lady Sŏnhŭi, acting with maternal love for her son, was immensely kind and affectionate. My childish heart leapt with gratitude and admiration, and I was overwhelmed by a desire to please them. I corrected my makeup, put on a long ceremonial robe, and sat down to receive a formal repast. At dusk, I bowed four times to the Three Majesties and set out for the bride's pavilion.* His Majesty accompanied me to my palanquin. Taking my hand, he said, "Keep well until you return." He added thoughtfully, "I will send you a copy of the *Elementary Learning* (*Sohak/Hsiao-hsüeh*); study it with your father. Take care of yourself and come back in good health." By the time I left the palace after so much kindness and love had been bestowed upon me, it was completely dark and the lights were lit in the street.

From that day on, ladies-in-waiting attended me and I faced the terrible prospect of sleeping apart from my mother. Upset by this separation, I could not sleep. Mother, too, must have been quite distressed. But Palace Matron Ch'oe, always stern, made no allowance for personal feelings. "The rule of the palace does not permit it. Please go to your room," she commanded, and she just would not let me sleep in the same room with Mother. It was utterly heartless of her.

The next day, a copy of the *Elementary Learning* arrived from His Majesty. I studied it daily with Father. The uncle from the main house came in daily, as did my second uncle and my older brother. My third uncle,† who was still a child, also came often.

His Majesty soon sent me another book with a message suggesting that I read it in my spare time while studying the *Elementary Learning*. It was a book of instructions that His Majesty himself had written for Queen Hyosun‡ after her marriage to his older son. His Majesty had it copied for me.

The bride's pavilion was decorated with exquisite furniture, screens, and objets d'art. There was a gift from Lady Sŏnhŭi, an

---

* The bride's pavilion for Lady Hyegyŏng was a detached palace located at Ŏŭi-dong. It had been the residence of King Hyojong (r. 1649–1659) before he was appointed heir apparent.
† Hong Chunhan.
‡ The wife of Prince Hyojang, Yŏngjo's first Crown Prince, who died in 1728. Hyosun married Prince Hyojang in 1727 and died in 1751. She never was a queen while she lived. The honorary title Queen Hyosun was awarded posthumously.

ornamental object shaped like an eggplant and made of Japanese pearls. I was told that it had originally belonged to Princess Chŏng-myŏng, who had given it to one of her granddaughters on the occasion of her marriage into the Cho family. The Cho family must have sold it afterwards, since Lady Sŏnhŭi bought it for me through one of her ladies-in-waiting. It struck me as quite unusual. It could not have been just a coincidence that I, who was descended from Princess Chŏngmyŏng, now came to own this object that had belonged to her. But this was not all.

My grandfather had a weakness for paintings. He had once owned an embroidered screen, but one of his servants had sold it after his death. Strangely enough, Lady Sŏnhŭi bought it through a relation of another lady-in-waiting, turned it into a four-panel boudoir screen, and put it in my bedchamber. Father's younger sister recognized it immediately, remarking, "Odd how Grandfather's screen should find its way into his granddaughter's bedchamber here in the pavilion."

Lady Sŏnhŭi also placed one of her own screens in the pavilion. It was huge, with a dragon embroidered across its eight panels. When Father saw it, he stared at the screen. Then he said to his wife and sisters, "That dragon is exactly the color of the one I saw in my dream the night before my daughter's birth, on the seventeenth day of the sixth month, *ŭlmyo* year (1735). I really could not figure it out. Now seeing this, suddenly I can see that it is exactly like the one in my dream." My aunt exclaimed how extraordinary it was that Grandfather's screen turned up in my bedchamber and that the dragon in Father's dream should be so like the one in this other screen. The dragon was embroidered in black thread, but gold thread was used for the scales. Thus what was otherwise a jet black dragon seemed to shimmer with gold. Father still marveled at the dragon. "That one in my dream was not really black, but I could not describe it. This is so similar," he said.

At the bride's pavilion, my parents instructed me on the smallest aspects of daily conduct, teaching me even such things as how to sit and how to lie down. They also exhorted me, "Please serve the Three Majesties with care but, most of all, with filial devotion. In serving the Crown Prince, always assist him to find the right way. Be prudent in your choice of words." Thus they repeatedly instructed me. Although they counseled, it was always with sympathy and affection. Once, speaking on the subject of speech, Father said,

"There will be times when you will feel besieged on all four sides. It is on just those occasions that your words must be impeccable and rational." At the time, I was puzzled by what he meant. Later I came to realize that this had been a deeply thought-through and wise piece of advice. I stayed at the bride's pavilion for over fifty days. Not one day passed in which my parents did not instruct me on points of conduct.

During this stay, ladies-in-waiting came frequently, bearing messages of greeting from the Three Majesties. They came first to me to bear greetings. Then they would ask for my mother and would convey messages from the Three Majesties to her. My mother always received them with gratitude and humility. Invariably, ladies-in-waiting were offered food and delicacies. Officials from the Board of Rites often came, too. Each was offered a tray of food and wine. My mother made certain that the food was ample and of high quality and that the wine was warm. This hospitality was remembered at court for a long time. People often recalled my family's generosity during my wedding.

In addition to Mother, who stayed at the bride's pavilion most of the time, Father's two sisters came. Aunt Sin also came periodically. While I was at the bride's pavilion, Grandmother fell ill. Caught between the royal wedding and my grandmother's illness, my parents must have been extremely anxious.* Even if they had no other worry, the prospect of marrying me off would have made it a stressful period for them. However, as distressing as the illness must have been, my parents maintained their composure and concealed their anxiety, behaving cheerfully whenever they came to the bride's pavilion. But Grandmother took a turn for worse and so had to be moved elsewhere. Concerned for his mother's comfort, Father carried her on his own back to and from the palanquin. Word of this spread and, upon hearing of this, the ladies-in-waiting at the pavilion were full of admiration. Everyone at the court praised Father's extraordinary filial devotion to his stepmother. With Heaven's help, Grandmother recovered. This was truly a blessing for the country. I must say that I had never been so nervous over anything before that.

* If her grandmother had died, then her parents would have been obliged to go into mourning. Then they would have been unable to attend to the tasks required of them by the royal wedding.

My formal designation as the Crown Princess Consort was set for the ninth of the first month, and the wedding for the eleventh, two days later. As the day of parting from my parents approached, I could no longer contain my sadness. I spent those last days crying all day. My parents must have been feeling sad as well, but they were better able to restrain their emotion. Father advised me calmly, "Please make sure that you do not forget our instructions." Then he sternly admonished me for crying continually. Thinking back to that time, though I understand the sadness of the child, I realize that I should have been more considerate of my parents and that I should not have made things so difficult for them.

After the first part of the wedding ceremony at the bride's pavilion,[10] I again received instructions from Father and Mother. On this occasion my parents did not show the slightest sign of sadness. They behaved with perfect decorum. Father wore an official's red cloak and a scholar's cap and Mother wore a green ceremonial robe and a formal coiffure.* This ceremony was attended by my family and the relatives who had come to bid me farewell. Many from the palace also attended. I remember that Mother did not change her expression at all when she gave me counsel. My parents were barely over thirty years old at the time. Despite their youth, they comported themselves impeccably, with perfect decorum. They did not make even one error or false step. They always looked dignified and composed. Everyone who saw them remarked that the royal house had done well in its choice of in-laws.

The grand ceremony took place later that day at the palace. The next day, the twelfth, was the day of a bowing ceremony in which I bowed to His Majesty as his daughter-in-law. During a change of robes, His Majesty came over and said, "Now that I have formally received your gift as your father-in-law, allow me a word of advice. In serving the Crown Prince, please be gentle with him and do not be frivolous of voice or expression. If his eyes wander, pretend that you do not notice. It is not at all an unusual thing in the palace, and so it is best to behave normally, not letting him know that you noticed." He continued, "It is improper for a woman to show her undergarments to her husband. So do not carelessly loosen your clothes in his presence. There is another thing—the rouge stains on women's towels are not pretty, even though it is rouge. So do

---

* A lady's formal coiffure consisted of braided hairpieces piled on top.

not leave rouge marks on towels." Heeding his advice, I have always been careful with my clothes and taken special care not to smear towels with rouge.

On that day His Majesty, attended by the newly wed couple, received my father in an audience at T'ongmyŏng Pavilion. He was extremely cordial, offering Father a goblet of wine. Father took it gratefully, poured the contents on his sleeve, and clasped the orange seeds to his bosom.* His Majesty turned to me, saying, "Your father understands proper ritual." My father was moved by this royal grace and his eyes shone with tears of gratitude. Later I was told that at home Father summoned the family and recounted this story. Then, in tears, he burst forth, "Now that we are bestowed with such royal grace, we must pledge that, from today, we will repay his kindness with a devotion that transcends death."

On the following day there was a ceremony at Injŏng Hall in which the officials congratulated His Majesty. Not only did His Majesty permit me to view this grand spectacle; he also invited my family. He said, "Let the ladies also view it."

After the ceremony, with Mother accompanying me, I went to the Queen's residence to pay respect. Queen Chŏngsŏng greeted Mother personally with the utmost graciousness. Her Royal Highness approached her just as the mother of any groom might have approached the mother of her son's bride. Pointing at me, she thanked my mother. "You have raised your daughter beautifully and this has brought great joy to the nation. You have made a great contribution." I can still vividly recall how profoundly this affected Mother. Queen Dowager Inwŏn sent greetings to my mother through her chief lady-in-waiting. While Her Royal Highness did not receive my mother in an audience, the message she sent was warm and kind. The palace ladies observed that Madame Yi was received more warmly than Madame Cho† had been in the *chŏngmi* year (1727). In fact, Mother was popular and greatly admired at court. She was treated with respect and consideration. Palace ladies followed her about as though she were an old acquaintance. It

---

* According to a passage from the *Li chi* (Book of rites), "When one receives fruit from a ruler, if the fruit has seeds, then one should clasp them to his bosom." *Li chi*, in *Ch'ing shih-san-ching chu-shu*, ed. Yüan Yüan (Shanghai: Chung-hua shu-chu, 1930), vol. 43, 1:15a.
† The mother of Queen Hyosun, who married Yŏngjo's first son.

must have been that her manner, which was always pleasant, and her speech, which was concise yet thoughtful and generous, won the admiration of the ladies-in-waiting, who praised her to the skies until the whole court burst into a chorus of admiration.

The wife of my uncle from the main house of the Hong family was a first cousin to Queen Sŏnŭi, and several ladies-in-waiting from the Queen Dowager's residence knew her. So during our stay at the bride's pavilion, Mother was treated, at best, as well as this aunt. Once Mother made her appearance at court, however, the ladies-in-waiting from both the King's and Queen's residences gazed intently at her and noticeably praised her. Later, when Mother died in *ŭrhae* (1755), the old ladies-in-waiting at court who had known her shed tears and mourned her with true grief. This shows how well she was liked.

When we went to see Lady Sŏnhŭi, she led Mother in at once. They struck a fast and cordial relationship, one that would have been rare even among ordinary families.

After spending three nights at T'ongmyŏng Pavilion, I moved into what was to be my residence. It was a house called Kwanhŭi House, one of the buildings within the Crown Prince's residence. It was situated near Chŏsŭng Pavilion. Seeing that I had settled into my quarters, Mother prepared to leave. This was simply unbearable for me, but she showed no inappropriate emotion. Perfectly composed, she bid me farewell, offering a few parting words of advice. "The Three Majesties are very fond of Your Ladyship. His Majesty the King loves Your Ladyship as though you were his own daughter. Your Ladyship is in his sagacious grace. Your Ladyship's duty requires that you ever more exert yourself in filial devotion to the Three Majesties. That is the best way to serve your natal family. If Your Ladyship were to think of your parents, please apply yourself in filial devotion rather than crying." Mother then left calmly. Though she behaved this way in order not to excite me, just before she entered her palanquin, she burst into tears. Pleading with the ladies-in-waiting, she asked them to look after me. They were clearly touched. They promised, "Please do not worry, my lady. How could we turn our backs on such an earnest maternal request as yours?"

On the fifteenth I was ceremonially admitted to Sŏnwŏn-jŏn, the ancestral shrine. On the seventeenth, I was presented to the

Royal Ancestral Temple.* His Majesty commended me, saying that, despite my youth, I had comported myself well through the seven-day ceremony; even with my head weighed down with ornaments, I had made no misstep. Lady Sŏnhŭi was obviously pleased with my performance and expressed her happiness with it. On receiving such love and praise, my feelings of gratitude deepened.

The twenty-first was the birthday of His Highness the Crown Prince. Mother came to the palace to offer him her congratulations. Our delight at seeing each other was beyond description. Urged by Their Royal Highnesses, Mother stayed at court for a while before she left. I could hardly bear the sharp sense of dejection each time she left.

Father came to the palace twice monthly, on the first and the fifteenth, but I could see him only when His Majesty specifically permitted it. Even when he came to my quarters, he seldom stayed for long. "The palace rules are strict. Outsiders are not supposed to stay very long," he would say, promptly taking leave. Still, he was always ready with advice. When he did come, he always visited the Crown Prince, counseling him to study. With great care and patience, Father sought to explain famous writings and well-known historical events in such a way as to be easily understood by a young child. In fact, he spent more time with the Prince than with me. The Prince responded remarkably well and his affection and respect for his father-in-law grew noticeably. One need not go into detail about my father's devotion to the Prince and the extent to which he treasured him.

In the tenth month of *kapcha* (1744) Father passed a palace examination. "My father-in-law passed the examination," the Prince exclaimed in delight. I was staying at a different house, but he came, all smiles, to share the happy news with me. He was so excited. Perhaps to his young mind, passing the examination seemed quite extraordinary, for no one in Queen Dowager Inwŏn's family had passed one, and Queen Chŏngsŏng's family had not produced even one noteworthy person. His mother's family did not even merit such discussion. At any rate, after the ceremony in which the

---

* The ancestral shrine was where portraits were kept of King T'aejo, the founder of the dynasty, and King Sukchong, Yŏngjo's father. The ancestral temple, Chongmyo, was where Yi royal ancestors' tablets were kept. Matters considered to be of dynastic import were announced at this temple. Thus the Crown Prince's marriage was announced there, and his new wife was presented there.

King presented red plaques and flowers to the successful candidates, Father, with the flowers still on his lapel, came to see the Crown Prince. Overjoyed, the Prince stroked the flowers happily. His Majesty, too, was quite pleased. He had been a bit disappointed that my father had been unsuccessful in the previous year.

Their Royal Highnesses, Queen Dowager Inwŏn and Queen Chŏngsŏng, also summoned me to congratulate me on Father's success. "It is good fortune for the nation that a royal in-law should pass the examination," they pronounced. Queen Chŏngsŏng was especially happy. Her family was of the Noron faction* and had fallen victim to political upheaval. Thus, though she was not particularly partisan, she just naturally felt closer to Noron members, as if they were some sort of relations. For this reason, Her Highness had been overjoyed to have my family as royal in-laws. Now her genuine happiness over Father's success even brought tears to her eyes. At the time, I thought she was pleased because Father's success in the examination was the first for a royal affine since Lord Kwangsŏng and Lord Yŏyang.[11] There had been Lord P'ungnŭng,[12] but my family was Noron. In my youth and naivete, I casually accepted her generosity and consideration. Only in retrospect have I come to realize how exceptional her kindness was! It must have been because my parents were able to please the sagacious hearts of His Majesty and Her Highness that the Queen treated us with such special regard.

After Father passed the examination, he declined a post in the Censorate. Later, high posts either at the Office of Special Councilors or the Office of Royal Decrees eluded him.† When he came under consideration, he was indicted for some terrible crime that disqualified him. Thus he did not receive the opportunity to exhibit his literary talents. I have felt that this was all because of me and have always felt guilty.

Father helped the Crown Prince constantly with his studies. He

* During this period there were two major factions, the Noron and the Soron. In the not too distant past, enmity between these two factions had reached a point of frequent purges, executions, and banishments. However, Yŏngjo's policy was to somehow maintain a tenuous balance. For details, see JaHyun Kim Haboush, *A Heritage of Kings: One Man's Monarchy in a Confucian World* (New York: Columbia University Press, 1988), 117–65.

† The function of these offices was advisory or admonitory. Those who were appointed to these offices usually had a reputation for scholarship and moral integrity.

often chose useful and worthwhile passages from the classics and other books and wrote them out for the Prince. Soon the Prince routinely sent his compositions to Father, who returned them with comments. The Prince, of course, continued his formal studies with his tutors, but he also learned much from his father-in-law. For who among his subjects and officials could desire as sincerely as my father that the Prince would grow to be a sage king, whose peaceful reign would be remembered for ten thousand years? But how sad! How sad!

When I first married the Crown Prince, his talent and generosity deeply impressed me. He was also extraordinarily filial. He served his grandmother Queen Dowager Inwŏn most affectionately. Though he was somewhat afraid of his father, he was utterly devoted to him, and his affection for Queen Chŏngsŏng could not have been greater had she been his own mother. In fact, the love and devotion that Queen Chŏngsŏng and Prince Sado had for each other was something special that inspired admiration. One need not mention his dedication to his mother, Lady Sŏnhŭi. Her Ladyship was kind and affectionate by nature, but she was also quite stern. Maternal love did not temper discipline, which always remained strict. Consequently, her children stood rather in awe of her, a somewhat unusual thing between mother and child. When her son became the Crown Prince, she did not see fit to impose herself upon him as a mother, and so she treated him with deference. For instance, she used the most respectful level of speech when speaking to him. She did love him in a special way, but she still refused to let this affect the uncompromising way in which she educated and disciplined him. Thus the Prince was always formal and quite careful in her presence. These high standards to which Lady Sŏnhŭi adhered were not something that ordinary women could easily attain.* She loved me very much also, but she treated me exactly as she treated her son. I used to feel rather uncomfortable being treated so deferentially by a mother-in-law.

Upon entering the palace, I began to serve the Three Majesties. My parents constantly urged me to serve them with filial piety. I was barely ten, but I must have been built sturdily. An important

---

* Lady Sŏnhŭi compiled *Yŏbŏm* (Model women), a collection of biographies of exemplary historical women. Yŏngbin Yi Ssi, *Yŏbŏm* (Seoul: Hyŏngsŏl ch'ulp'ansa, 1988).

duty that I could not neglect was paying regular visits of greeting
to my elders. I was expected to pay respect to Queen Dowager
Inwŏn and Queen Chŏngsŏng on every fifth day, and to Lady
Sŏnhŭi on every third day, though, actually, I went to see her almost every morning. At that time palace regulations were strictly
observed. For instance, one could not visit the Queen or the
Queen Dowager in anything but formal robes, nor could one go if
it was too late. Lest I oversleep the greeting hour (that is, dawn), I
could not sleep comfortably. I repeatedly emphasized to my nurse*
the importance of waking for the visiting hour. I did not dare to
omit even one visit. If it was the day of visiting, whether it was hot
or cold, in snow or in rain, whether in a storm or a great wind, I
simply went. How strict the palace rules were during those days
compared to now! But I did what was expected of me without
finding it too difficult. Perhaps it was because I had been raised in
the old way.

The Crown Prince had a number of sisters, and they were all
very affectionate. But my position differed from theirs. Since I
could not really behave as they did, I tried to emulate Princess
Consort Hyosun. There was a big difference in age, but I modeled
my behavior upon hers and learned from her. In this way we developed a very special relationship.

There were two older princesses, Hwasun, who was warm and
mild-mannered, and Hwap'yŏng, who was very gentle and particularly kind to me. There were two more princesses, Hwahyŏp and
Hwawan, who were more or less my age. They were still young
and so they played a lot, though I did not join in. As befitted their
exalted station in life, they had every conceivable toy. But I did not
look at them. Taking pity upon me, Lady Sŏnhŭi urged me to behave more freely. "At your age, you must want to play. You are too
concerned with palace rules and proper behavior. Do not worry so
much about that and play with them whenever you feel like it," she
would say. Lest I become envious, Her Ladyship, citing anecdotes
and explaining the ways of the palace, guided and advised me. But
I was truly uninterested in those playthings, and I was aware that
my position—born outside and brought into the palace through
marriage—was quite different from that of the princesses. Thus,

---

* Lady Hyegyŏng brought her nurse and several maidservants with her to the
palace. See the postscript of this memoir.

though I saw and experienced many things around this time, I did not let them bother me. The court praised me for this. I think this resulted from my education.

My first pregnancy came quite early. In the *kyŏngo* year (1750) I gave birth to Ŭiso, but I lost him two years later, in the spring of *imsin* (1752). It was an unhappy time. The Three Majesties and Lady Sŏnhŭi grieved the death of this royal heir so deeply that I was guilt-stricken, feeling as though a lack of filial devotion on my part had brought about this terrible event.

But the present King was born in the ninth month of that same year.* One night in the tenth month of the previous year (1751), Prince Sado had dreamt that a dragon came into our bedchamber and played with his *yŏŭiju*, a mythical jewel with which one could attain one's wish. Waking from the dream, the Prince was convinced that the dream meant something quite extraordinary. At once, that very night, he called for a piece of white silk and on it he painted the dragon of his dream and hung it on the wall. He was only in his seventeenth year at the time, and so I thought it strange that, even if he had had an unusual dream, he would so joyfully interpret it as "an omen to get a son," like some wizened ancient. The Prince seemed quite inspired when he painted that night, and the painting was magnificent. After my son was born, I could not help thinking that the dream might indeed have been a portent.

Because of my extreme youth when I had my first child, I did not do well in my maternal duties. After that terrible springtime loss, however, the felicitous birth of the present King brought great rejoicing to the Three Majesties, far greater than the first time. Naturally, my entire family, especially my parents, were immensely pleased. Mother had moved into my quarters a little before the delivery, and Father had already been staying at the palace for seven or eight days. When the King was born, my parents were beside themselves with joy. My happiness was, of course, incomparable. At birth the new Prince had beautiful and heroic features. Though I was not yet twenty, perhaps it was natural that I should be happy and proud of my newborn son, but somehow I also felt that, in the rough sea of life that lay before me, this son would be

---

* Chŏngjo (r. 1776–1800) was born on the twenty-second of the ninth month, 1752. *YS*, 77:26b–27a.

my future security. Looking back, I wonder whether this feeling might have been a premonition.

Soon after my son's birth, there was a large epidemic of measles. A princess broke out first.* The Medical Bureau requested that the Crown Prince and the infant Prince be moved to other quarters. The infant Prince was not yet twenty-one days old, and so this posed great difficulty.[†] However, the order had to be obeyed; the Crown Prince went to Yangjŏng House and the newborn Prince was moved to Naksŏn Hall. Though he was a baby not yet twenty-one days old, the young Prince was so strong and big that I was not nervous about his being carried quite a distance. I had not yet been able to hire a nurse for him, and so I let my own nurse and one elderly lady-in-waiting look after him. Before the day was out, Prince Sado broke out. All the ladies-in-waiting had already been stricken, and this left no one to take care of him. Lady Sŏnhŭi moved into Yangjŏng House to look after him, and my father came to the palace to be near the Crown Prince. His symptoms were rather mild, but he ran a high fever. It is not difficult to imagine how anxiously my father attended his son-in-law.

When Prince Sado improved a bit, he often asked his father-in-law to read to him. Thus Father would read to him from various books. After listening a while, the Prince would say in thanks, "It refreshes me to listen to your reading." Father read rather a lot to the Prince. With no servants available, I nursed the Prince while Father tended him continually, and so Father was very frequently asked to read something. I cannot recall all the books that he read to the Crown Prince, but I distinctly remember him reading Chu-ko Liang's memorial [to the young Emperor of Shu Han] proposing a military attack on Wei.[‡] Afterwards he said, "Of all the relationships in history between the ruler and his minister, that between Emperor Chao-lieh of Shu Han and Chu-ko Liang stands

---

* Princess Hwahyŏp. After about six weeks, she died of measles. *YS*, 78:9a.

[†] Korean custom forbade both the mother and her newborn child to move about or go out until twenty-one days after the birth.

[‡] Chu-ko sent this memorial to Liu Pei's son in A.D. 227. In this famous memorial, Chu-ko recounts the aspiration to reunify China, which he shared with Liu Pei, who died in 223, and expresses his determination to devote his life to carrying out this plan. *San-kuo-chih*, ed. Chen Shou, in *Erh shih wu shih*, 50 vols. (Taipei: I-wen-yin shu-kuan, 1958), 35:15a–18b.

out as the best model for the ages.* Your servant has always admired this memorial for that reason." He also recounted many other anecdotes about virtuous rulers and wise ministers. Though still in feeble health, the Prince listened with rapt attention.

As soon as the Crown Prince improved a bit, I came down with the illness. Since I was exhausted from looking after the Prince and had not had time to recover fully from childbirth, my condition was quite serious. On the same day, the present King came down with red spots all over his body. His symptoms are said to have been very mild, and he is supposed to have taken it rather well, as though he were much older. However, lest I worry excessively, Lady Sŏnhŭi and my father kept my son's illness from me, and so I did not know about it. But Father was greatly burdened now that he had several people to tend to and nurse. Shuttling back and forth day and night for an extended period between his daughter and his grandson, he must have reached a state of total exhaustion. Someone later mentioned to me that one night he just collapsed with fatigue and could not get up to continue. I learned of these things only after I recovered. Nonetheless, I felt terrible for all the trouble it caused him. I could especially appreciate the nervousness he must have felt in caring for his infant grandson with no help from anyone but my nurse. It was a blessing that my son had such a mild case of the illness.

After the measles, the young Prince grew up healthily. By his first birthday he already recognized a number of Chinese characters. His precocity set him apart from other children. When he reached his third year, the officials of the Office of Guidance for the Young Prince† were selected, and in his fourth year, he began to study the *Classic of Filial Piety* (*Hyogyŏng/Hsiao-ching*). He displayed no childish immaturity at all. He always enjoyed reading, so teaching him was no trouble. Early every morning, he washed,

---

* After the fall of the Han dynasty in 221, Liu Pei, a distant kinsman of the Liu imperial family of the Han dynasty, made a bid to reunify China. As a first step in this attempt, he sought the service of Chu-ko Liang. Chu-ko agreed to serve him only after Liu Pei came to his residence three times. However, their bid was unsuccessful. Liu Pei died in 223, and Chu-ko died in 234. Ibid., 32:1a–41a, 35:1a–44b. Still, Chu-ko came to be regarded as the paragon of ministerial loyalty and wisdom.

† A Chosŏn institution for the future heir to the throne.

then immediately turned to his books. He played with them and read them. In every way, he was unusually mature, and I had no difficulty in raising him. In retrospect I realize that this was truly exceptional. At the time, however, I was concerned that he might not be so bright and scolded him harshly as though he were much older. This was because I was a young mother.

Then I had two daughters, Ch'ŏngyŏn, born in the *kapsul* year (1754), and Ch'ŏngsŏn, born in *pyŏngja* (1756).

With his exceptional talent and superior scholarship, Prince Sado would surely have achieved greatness. Of its own accord, however, illness seeped into his remarkable nature and, between *imsin* and *kyeyu* (1752–1753), began to manifest itself in strange symptoms. Who can even imagine the depth of my anguish and my parents' nervousness. During her visit to the palace, Mother noticed certain symptoms of his illness and became exceedingly worried. That she missed me became a matter of insignificance now; the Prince's illness emerged as a matter of utmost concern. In deep anxiety, Mother took to praying. There was no length to which she would not go in her devotion and prayers. Concerned that the Prince's illness might worsen, she was unable to sleep at night. She gazed toward the palace, her thoughts lost deep in despondency. She was frequently seized by the desire to die so that she would not know of it. All this because of her unfilial daughter. Indeed, what worse filial failing is there than to cause such worry to one's parents?

Prince Sado was always very respectful of my mother. This was not the attitude one might expect a Crown Prince to take toward a mother-in-law who was, after all, only the wife of a scholar. Though she did not dare approach him as a son-in-law, one need not elaborate upon Mother's devotion to him. Even when the Prince was terribly angry, if Mother happened to be at the palace, she would speak to the Prince thus, "Things do not work that way," and he would immediately lose his anger. During Ch'ŏngyŏn's birth in *kapsul* (1754), the delivery was expected in the sixth month but the baby arrived almost a month later. Thus Mother remained at the palace for over fifty days, and the Prince spent a great deal of time in close quarters with her. During this period there were many occasions on which she calmed him down.

Mother passed away in the eighth month of that *ŭrhae* year (1755). It may be that no one is spared the sorrow of losing one's mother. Nevertheless, I felt completely alone in the world. In the depths of my grief, everything looked dim and distant. I was strongly tempted to follow my mother. But the Three Majesties consoled me. Moreover, I had to think of Father, whose grief for his trusted spouse was deepened by concern for me. Thus I did not do away with myself, but inwardly my heart bled.

The day I went into mourning for Mother, Lady Sŏnhŭi came to see me and consoled me with the kindness of a mother. I have never heard of such affectionate and thoughtful solicitude by a mother-in-law. To respond to her, I tried my best to control my wretchedness. Queen Dowager Inwŏn and Queen Chŏngsŏng also extended very special and tender sympathies to me. When I paid respect to them after the funeral, they held my hands, tears in their eyes. Their Royal Highnesses conveyed their condolences to my family also. This was a great honor. My family was deeply moved; they did not know how to repay this kindness.

Ignoring the depth of my pain, I remained in this world but lost interest in the life around me. His Majesty remarked at one point that I was a bit excessive in my mourning. Eventually, Queen Dowager Inwŏn, Queen Chŏngsŏng, and Lady Sŏnhŭi each chided me, saying that in my desire to do my duty as a mourner to my parent, I was violating the sartorial codes of the court. Thus I could not even wear full mourning for Mother though I would have liked to. This saddened me still further.

In the second month of the *pyŏngja* year (1756), my father was appointed Magistrate of Kwangju.* His departure was bad enough, but filial duty required that he take his mother to accompany him at his post. Grandmother's absence, just when I had come to see her as a mother, left me isolated and dejected. The deep worry [for the Prince's illness], which burned in my heart like a flame, grew worse, and I really lost my desire to live.

In the intercalary ninth month of that year, I bore Ch'ŏngsŏn. During my pregnancy, the memory of my mother, who had always come to assist me in childbirth, returned with poignance. In this dejected mood, I did not give myself the care my condition demanded. I ate only vegetarian meals for some time, and as the delivery drew near, my health deteriorated visibly. Concerned with my state, His Majesty instructed Father to care for me appropri-

---

* Kwangju was and is located in Kyŏnggi Province.

ately,* and soon I was provided with a large quantity of restorative medicine. The child was delivered safely, but my longing for Mother was so sharp that I spent several days weeping. Perhaps because of my low spirits, I recovered from the delivery with great difficulty. Father fretted over the slow recovery. To put his mind at ease, I restrained my grief. Then, that month, Father was appointed Governor of P'yŏngan Province.[13] He was visibly troubled to leave me in such a state, but royal orders took precedence over private concerns. He departed quickly for the new post.

In midwinter of that year, Prince Sado came down with smallpox. Father had always been concerned with how little he was able to do for him. Now, in an outpost at a distance of a thousand *ri*,† he was terribly upset to hear that the Prince was stricken with a grave illness. He continually sent messengers to keep in touch with the capital. I later learned that he was so overwrought that his beard turned white. My anxiety at the time cannot begin to be described. Fortunately for the nation, the Prince weathered the illness, and soon the danger passed. Immensely relieved, my father sent congratulations.

But within a hundred days, Queen Chŏngsŏng passed away. The Crown Prince mourned her with the grief of a son and impressed the whole court with his filial devotion. This was not all. On the day of her burial, a huge crowd of commoners and scholars joined the funeral cortege, and I was told that the Prince's grief was so heartrending that he moved all to tears.[14]

It was a difficult time, however. Not having fully convalesced from his smallpox, Prince Sado was still weak. Yet he had to endure many stern admonitions from His Majesty. The situation was tense and fraught with worry. I would rather not discuss the depths of my disquiet and nervousness during this period.

In the fifth month Father was transferred to a post in the central government, and so he returned to the capital. Concerned as he was for the nation, he was profoundly troubled by the state of things at court. We spent our days in deep gloom. Things grew even harder. I longed for oblivion.

---

* Around this time, on the twenty-second of the intercalary ninth month, Hong Ponghan was appointed Director of the Relief Agency and transferred to the capital. *YS*, 88:16a.

† One *ri* is about one third of a mile.

In the eleventh month tension reached an unbearable point because of the Crown Prince's secondary consort. Deeply angered,
His Majesty repeatedly exploded at the Prince.* Unable to contain
himself, my father defended the Prince. He spoke out and said
things to His Majesty that were, given his position, rather impolitic.† This elicited royal wrath. He was promptly dismissed and
sent outside the city gate. Uneasiness pervaded the court. Royal
fury fell upon me as well, and I also received stern admonitions. I
simply did not know what to do and spent my days deeply agitated.
Ever since I had come into the palace, His Majesty had always
treated me with kind affection, and even in time of tension [be-
tween father and son], his attitude toward me had not shown the
slightest change. I naturally felt deeply grateful, but also uneasy.
On this occasion, having been severely reprimanded for the first
time, I went down to the servants' quarters and waited. After a
long fortnight, His Majesty reinstated my father[15] and called me
in, displaying his usual affection. It was a stressful time; myriad
things had gone awry. The royal grace bestowed upon me, however, was truly limitless. There is simply no way that I can repay His
Majesty's kindness. I have gone through so much in life. Yet these
experiences are not things that can be written down in detail, and
so I will omit them.‡

The fortunes of the nation were in decline. A month after
Queen Chŏngsŏng's death, Queen Dowager Inwŏn passed
away.[16] Their Royal Highnesses had given me the tenderest affection and guidance. Their deaths, coming so close together, left me
sad and utterly forlorn. My residence was near Queen Chŏng-

* Prince Sado had two secondary consorts by whom he bore children. The lady
in question on this occasion was Lady Pak, referred to as Pingae. See *The Memoir
of 1805* for details. Yŏngjo was also angry at Sado for having neglected to visit him
for several months. On the eighth of the eleventh month, Yŏngjo expressed his
irritation to his officials. Upon hearing this, Sado sent a memorial on the eleventh
expressing his remorse. Yŏngjo was not satisfied with this expression of remorse
from his son, and on that evening, he summoned Sado. It developed into a full-
fledged confrontation. He severely scolded Sado, who was deeply mortified.
Haboush, *Heritage*, 193–95.

† On the evening of the confrontation between Yŏngjo and Sado, four high-
ranking ministers were present. When Yŏngjo's criticism of Sado became too
overbearing, they pointed out his excessive severity to his son. Hong Ponghan
joined this criticism of the royal harshness toward the Crown Prince. *YS*, 90:28b–
29b. Also see Haboush, *Heritage*, 193–95.

‡ See *The Memoir of 1805* for details.

sŏng's funerary chamber. I was determined to express final devotion to her, and during the five-month vigil at the chamber, I never
missed a noon sacrifice or the morning's or the evening's wails. I
also tried to find some way to repay Queen Dowager Inwŏn's
kindness. In her last month as she declined rapidly, I had no one with
whom I could share my anxieties for her now that Queen Chŏngsŏng
was gone. My lone figure anxiously went about trying very hard to
be of help. His Majesty attended the Queen Dowager continually.
He looked after her medication himself and refused to retire or to
change his clothes at night. This left me still more restive. After the
Queen Dowager's death, when I had expressed condolences to His
Majesty, I was overwhelmed by a sense of emptiness and grief. The
growing difficulties of my life caused me to miss Their Royal
Highnesses even more sharply. I shed many tears in their memory.

In the *kimyo* year (1759), when the three-year mourning for
Their Royal Highnesses was completed, there was a royal wedding.
This was, of course, a felicitous event, but not knowing what lay in
store for us because of the situation at court, we were deeply apprehensive.* Lady Sŏnhŭi, however, remained calm. Seeing that I
was perturbed and anxious, she drew me aside, saying, "Now that
Queen Chŏngsŏng has passed away, it is only right that His Majesty should remarry. The country needs a new queen." She walked
serenely over to His Majesty's side and, with a joyful expression
and a pleasant voice, congratulated him. Then she took upon herself the task of overseeing the preparations for the royal wedding.
She did not overlook the smallest detail and seemed genuinely glad
that the court, with a new mistress, would regain its order. Lady
Sŏnhŭi's conduct, which was guided solely by her dedication to
her lord, was truly admirable.

Although his illness was growing worse, my late husband did
not at all resent his father's approaching marriage. In his audience

---

* Three-year mourning, the longest and heaviest, actually meant twenty-six
months. This mourning was required of Sado for Queen Chŏngsŏng and of
Yŏngjo for Queen Dowager Inwŏn, in both cases the mourning of a child for a
mother. During one's mourning for one's parents, one was not supposed to marry.
Thus Yŏngjo waited two years and three months after the Queen Dowager's death
before his remarriage. His mourning obligation for his wife, Queen Chŏngsŏng,
ended after one year. Lady Hyegyŏng was apprehensive because the relationship
between Yŏngjo and Crown Prince Sado had deteriorated, and Sado's condition
had worsened. The presence of a new queen complicated an already bad situation,
since it was possible she would give birth to a prince.

with the Two Majesties* after the wedding, Prince Sado was extremely careful and respectful lest he inadvertently err as he sometimes did. One could easily see by his behavior on such occasions
that he was remarkably filial by nature. When he uneventfully
completed paying respect to his father and the new Queen, he was
so pleased that he patted himself on the back with his own hands.
Everyone knew this of him. Ah! I would beseech Heaven over this
limitless grief, but it is no use.

Even when he neglected his duty to pay respect to his father,
Prince Sado was extremely devoted to his children. He treasured
and loved his son, the present King, beyond measure. He insisted
that the young Prince be treated with respect commensurate to his
exalted position. Not even his sisters, much less his half siblings of
lower status, were allowed to go near him. In retrospect, that he
maintained these strict distinctions seems to be a manifestation of
his true nature, which was quite extraordinary.

Prince Sado was also affectionate to his sisters. He was always
respectful of his elder sisters, the Princesses Hwasun and Hwap'yŏng.
Pitying Hwahyŏp for being slighted by His Majesty, he was particularly tender toward her. When she died, he mourned her with
real sorrow. In sharp contrast to what the Prince endured, His
Majesty's partiality and affection were showered upon Madame
Chŏng.† One might have expected, as is quite natural, that the
Prince might have been less than amiably disposed toward this sister. However, if he felt something of this sort, he never showed it.
Only on several occasions, when the situation reached an extreme
point and his illness went out of control, did he lose his temper at
her. An ordinary person in his position could not have behaved
with such restraint.

In the third month of *sinsa* (1761) the Grand Heir‡ began his for-

---

* Yŏngjo and the new Queen Chŏngsun.
† Princess Hwawan. Lady Hyegyŏng often refers to her as Madame Chŏng, or
more precisely, the Chŏng wife *(Chŏng ch'ŏ)*, a derogatory term, because in 1778
she was deprived of her royal title and attendant privileges and was exiled to
Kanghwa Island. *Chŏngjo sillok* (hereafter *CS*), in *Chosŏn wangjo sillok*, 5:68b.
‡ The Grand Heir *(seson)* was a son of the Crown Prince designated as next in
succession to the throne after the Crown Prince, provided that the Crown Prince
was the son of the king. Chŏngjo was formally appointed Grand Heir in 1759 (*YS*,
93:29). The Chosŏn custom of investing a Grand Heir began in 1448. JaHyun Kim
Haboush, "The Education of the Yi Crown Prince: A Study in Confucian Pedagogy," in *The Rise of Neo-Confucianism in Korea*, ed. by Wm. Theodore de Bary
and JaHyun Kim Haboush (New York: Columbia University Press, 1985), 183.

mal studies and, in the same month, performed his capping ceremony at Kyŏnghŭi Palace. The Crown Prince was unable to attend,
and so I could not go either. I felt motherly disappointment, but, of
course, I was profoundly preoccupied. How did I survive those
days?

In that winter the Consort for the Grand Heir was selected. She
was of the Ch'ŏngp'ung Kim, one of the most illustrious lineages
and one with a sterling reputation for virtue. Some years before
this, my father had been invited to the sixtieth birthday party
for Madame Kim, the mother of Minister Kim Sŏngŭng of the
Ch'ŏngp'ung lineage. My family had enjoyed friendly relations
with the Kim family for generations, and Father had gone to Minister Kim's home for the celebration. There he had seen the present
Queen when she was a young child and had informed us that
Minister Kim's granddaughter was exceptional. My older brother,
citing the examples of Queen Sohŏn and Queen Insu,* opined that
since the Ch'ŏngp'ung Kim family was so renowned for virtue, it
would be good to select a Ch'ŏngp'ung Kim as the future queen.
But I dared not voice this opinion. My husband noticed her name,
entered as the daughter of Kim Simuk, on the list of candidates and
was strongly inclined in her favor. She was selected and the wedding took place. Prince Sado treasured and loved his daughter-
in-law. So affectionately was she treated by her father-in-law that
when he died, she mourned him with genuine sorrow, young
though she was at the time. The passage of time only deepened her
fond memories of him. Even now, whenever Prince Sado is mentioned, the Queen becomes tearful. She never forgot the kindness
she received long ago.

After the second selection, the bride-to-be of the Grand Heir
came down with smallpox, and soon afterwards, the Grand Heir
broke out in smallpox as well. In both cases the symptoms were
mild. Still, it was exceedingly worrisome that, with the final presentation close by, both of them, one after another, were struck by
a serious illness. One can easily imagine my nervousness. Fortunately, the Grand Heir, having been struck around the end of the

---

* Queen Sohŏn (1395–1446) was the wife of King Sejong (r. 1418–1450), who
was considered the greatest of Chosŏn kings. She was also regarded as having been
virtuous and accomplished. She bore eight sons and two daughters. Queen Insu is
better known as Queen Sohye (1437–1504). She was the mother of King Sŏng-
jong, who, upon his accession, conferred the title of queen upon his mother. She is
known for the authorship of *Naehun*, a book of instruction for women.

eleventh month, recovered around the tenth of the twelfth month. This would have been a joyous occasion for an ordinary family; how much more this blessing was for the nation! His Majesty beamed with relief. Prince Sado, who was exceedingly worried, was exhilarated. At times like this, he did not seem ill. It was probably because his natural love for his son burst forth. How moving! Yet how sad! My anxieties and worries for my son's illness cannot be compared to those of an ordinary mother. One need not describe at length how I prayed to the gods and spirits for his recovery and how my father anxiously tended him day and night. With the silent help of Heaven and the quiet benediction of the royal ancestors, both the Grand Heir and the bride-to-be recovered in succession. This was indeed an unusually fortunate turn of events. The final presentation took place in the twelfth month as scheduled. The wedding followed on the second day of the second month of the *imo* year (1762). I cannot begin to describe, amidst this great felicity, how constantly and ceaselessly I had to fret and worry over the other matter. What a bizarre turn the course of my life was taking!

Father was also in a terrible predicament. He wished to repay His Majesty's kindness, but he also wished to protect His Highness, the Crown Prince, and to safeguard the Grand Heir so that nothing would happen to either generation. He became terribly overwrought. His beard and hair turned white. He suffered from a heaviness in the chest, poor appetite, and indigestion. Each time he saw me, he shed tears and wished that "With Heaven's help, the relationship between the father and the son might be harmonious and the Grand Heir protected." Heaven observed and the gods and spirits witnessed his wholehearted sincerity. Would I say even one word on his behalf just out of private affection?

Seeing my father, my older brother was just as concerned and as deeply grieved. When he had passed the preliminary examination in the *kyŏngo* year (1750), Prince Sado said to him, "We have many similar ideas." The Prince favored him greatly. In *sinsa* (1761) my brother passed the final examination and was appointed a tutor in the Office of Lectures for the Grand Heir. In that capacity, he frequently assisted the Grand Heir in his studies and thus contributed quite a bit to the King's education. When my brother was on night duty, we often saw each other and shared our most profound anxieties. Invariably, however, we grew distressed and felt that it would have been better if we had known nothing.

In the third month of *sinsa* (1761) Father was appointed to the State Council. At the time there was no minister on the State Council,* and His Majesty was in ill health. Responding to the call, Father assumed office quickly. The problem at court grew worse daily. He really had no desire to be in government, but he felt that he simply could not refuse this call. He decided to do whatever he could to repay his indebtedness to the throne. Now, more than ever, he spent each day in tumult and trepidation.

The *imo* (1762) year was very dry. As a minister, Father officiated at a sacrifice for rain at the royal ancestral temple. At the time, the Crown Prince was gravely ill.† The situation was just horrid. On the occasion of this sacrifice, Father shed tears over the grievous state of affairs and silently beseeched the ancestral spirits in the royal tablets to assist in maintaining peace at court. I learned of this when he wrote to me. How I cried reading that letter! My heart grew even sadder.

In the early summer of *imo*, things grew still worse. My desire to do away with myself, and thus to attain a blissful ignorance, became ever so strong and I thought of various ways to achieve it. I often had a knife in my hand, but the thought of my son always prevented me from actually killing myself. Days passed in this manner. Around the beginning of the fifth month, Father received a stern royal reprimand, and so he left for the eastern suburbs. I was even more at wits' end.

On the thirteenth day, Heaven and Earth clashed and the sun and the moon turned black.‡ When this calamity happened, how could I desire to live even one second longer! I rushed to stab myself, but those around me took the knife from my hand. Then I thought of my son. To inflict further pain on the ten-year-old Grand Heir seemed unbearably cruel. If I were to die, who would protect him and who would see him to maturity? Moreover, I wished to take on those filial duties that the Crown Prince, in his illness, had left unfulfilled. Wishing to repay the throne and to

---

* Hong Ponghan was appointed Minister of the Right on the twenty-eighth of the third month, 1761 (*YS*, 97:14b). All three high-ranking ministers—the Prime Minister, Yi Ch'ŏnbo; the Minister of the Right, Min Paeksang; and the Minister of the Left, Yi Hu—had died. They were thought to have killed themselves because they felt responsible for Prince Sado. *YS*, 97:2b, 97:7a–b, 97:9b. Haboush, *Heritage*, 201, 281 note 107.

† For Sado's symptoms of insanity, see *The Memoir of 1805*.

‡ The day when Prince Sado was placed in the rice chest.

protect the Grand Heir, I gave up the idea of killing myself. Nonetheless, how can I ever forget, even to the last moment of my consciousness, the shame of not having known the proper end and my regret for my long and slow life.

The Grand Heir, with his filial and benevolent nature, grieved. Ch'ŏngyŏn and her sister seemed to experience sadness only for certain things and not for others. I cannot bear to describe the scene.

Father returned to the court after things had reached an irrevocable point. His pain was incomparable, and he fainted. He came back to his senses, but how could he have any desire to live? Like me, his only thought and concern was to protect the Grand Heir, and so, for the sake of the nation, he controlled his sorrow and did not retire from office.

That night, taking the Grand Heir with me, I left the palace for my family's residence.* Heaven and Earth ought to have changed color at that terrible and pathetic sight! How can I say more.

His Majesty granted us a reprieve. Through my father, he sent royal instructions: "Protect the Grand Heir." Though it was a time of extreme pain, I felt deeply grateful for his sagacious grace. Tenderly stroking my son, I instructed him, "Sagacious grace is extended to mother and son. You must repay him. Preserve yourself and, in remembrance of your father's sorrows, be a good son to him." Relying on each other, my son and I thus preserved ourselves. My sorrow, however, spread endlessly. Who else has experienced such grief?

Before the burial, Lady Sŏnhǔi came to see me. How deep and limitless her pain and grief must have been!† She was so far beyond

---

* Prince Sado was stripped of his positions as the Crown Prince and Regent and was made a commoner in status before he was confined to the rice chest to die. This meant that his wife and children, now commoners, could no longer stay at the palace. Consequently, late on the night of the thirteenth of the intercalary fifth month, 1762, they went to Lady Hyegyŏng's father's house. For details, see *The Memoir of 1805*. Also see Haboush, *Heritage*, 210–30.

† It is believed that it was Lady Sŏnhǔi who, upon realizing the utterly hopeless state into which her son had fallen, urged Yŏngjo to kill him. See *The Memoir of 1805* and figure 9. By this time, Lady Hyegyŏng and her children had returned to the palace. When Prince Sado died in the chest after eight days of confinement, Yŏngjo restored him to the position of Crown Prince. This enabled Lady Hyegyŏng, the Grand Heir, and other members of his family to return to the palace and resume their previous positions and duties. *YS*, 99:25a.

consolation that I was forced to restrain my sorrow to comfort her. I entreated, "For the sake of the Grand Heir, please do not desert yourself." After the funeral, Her Ladyship left for her residence, and I felt even more alone and abandoned. I really did not have the heart to continue living, but I had decided to live to protect my son. I prayed that he succeed in his scholarship and attain goodness.

It was not until the eighth month that I had an audience with His Majesty. Understandably, I was seized by deeply grievous thoughts but dared not express my sadness. I just said, "That mother and son are preserved is due entirely to Your Majesty's sagacious grace." His Majesty took my hand and wept. He said, "Not thinking that you would be like this, I was troubled by the thought of facing you. It is beautiful of you to put me at ease." Upon hearing his words, my heart fell and I felt a great weight on my chest. The severity of my life grew suddenly vivid to me. I said to him, "This person humbly wishes that Your Majesty would take the Grand Heir to Kyŏnghŭi Palace to instruct him." He asked, "Do you think you could bear to part with him?" I answered in tears, "It is a small matter that I would miss him, but it is a matter of great importance that he be properly instructed by being near Your Majesty."

Thus I sent the Grand Heir to the upper palace. However, the parting of mother and son was indescribable. The Grand Heir was unable to tear himself from me. He finally left, soaked in tears. I felt as though my heart was being driven through by a knife, but I endured it.

As days passed, the kindness of his sagacious grace increased and His Majesty loved the Grand Heir more deeply. Lady Sŏnhŭi transferred to her grandson all of her love for her son. Her saddened heart was now completely devoted to the Grand Heir. Staying in his room, she took care of the most minute details of his daily needs including his meals. The Grand Heir was very diligent. He woke up early before daybreak and left for his study hall to read. When the Grand Heir arose, this woman of seventy also arose and looked after his breakfast in person. The Grand Heir was in the habit of not eating very early, but I heard that, in consideration of his old grandmother's devotion, he forced himself to eat.

The Grand Heir had been fond of books since he was four or five years old, and he routinely arose before dawn, washed himself, and promptly began his studies with his tutors. Thus I was not worried that he might neglect his studies even though we were living apart. But I did miss him more intensely each day. The Grand Heir's longing for his mother was acute as well. Attending His Majesty, he would retire to bed very late. When he awoke at dawn each day he sent me a note of greeting. Not until he received my answer just before the morning lecture could he put his mind at ease. It was natural for a child to miss his mother, but the Grand Heir was like this every single day during the three years we lived apart. He was a young boy of a little more than ten years of age, but I marveled at his uncanny maturity. I suffered a great many illnesses during this period. In fact, I was almost continuously ill during those three years. From a distance, the Grand Heir consulted physicians and had medicines formulated and sent to me. He did this as an adult would. This was an expression of his Heaven-endowed filial nature. How precocious he was in everything!

Whenever he came to the lower palace to perform mourning ceremonies for his father, he did grieve so. At the conclusion of the ceremony when the time came for him to bid me farewell, he invariably left in tears. I was concerned that his young heart might suffer too much.

On the occasion of the Grand Heir's birthday in the ninth month of that year, I felt poorly. But in compliance with royal orders, I went up to Kyŏnghŭi Palace. I must have cut a pitiful figure. During the period of mourning,* I stayed in a small house with a low ceiling to the south of Kyŏngch'un Pavilion. His Majesty conferred upon my residence the name Kahyo Hall, the Hall of Praiseworthy Filiality. He wrote the calligraphy for the plaque himself and said, "Today I am writing this as a repayment for your filial heart." I received his gift in tears. Yet I was uneasy about it, as I felt undeserving of encomiums. When my father heard this story, he was so profoundly moved that he adopted the name of the hall as a family motto to be used on correspondence.

The royal decree of the second month of the *kapsin* year (1764)†

---

* Lady Hyegyŏng's mourning for her husband, Prince Sado. A wife's mourning for her husband was the heaviest and longest, equal to a child's mourning for his father.

† Yŏngjo's decree that made Chŏngjo an adopted son of Prince Hyojang, who died in 1728. This meant that Chŏngjo was no longer legally the son of Prince Sado and Lady Hyegyŏng. See Introduction, 18, 24–26.

was truly devastating. I found myself no less tortured than I had been two years previously at the time of that tragedy. How sharp were my regrets! I would not have met that humiliation had I done away with this odious life of mine! Still, I could not kill myself. How grievous! Lady Sŏnhŭi was so deeply pained that I had to restrain myself to console her. The Grand Heir was just as profoundly afflicted. No one who saw him remained unmoved. In his tender years, he had borne terrible pain; yet again he had to accept an unbearable royal decree. He was heartsick. Concerned that the pain might pierce too deeply, I consoled him and endured my own grief as silently as I could. How sad! The world is full of mothers and sons, but I doubt that any mother and son experienced such profound sadness as the King and I experienced together.

In the seventh month of that year (1764) the ceremony ending the mourning for Prince Sado was performed.* Lady Sŏnhŭi came down for the occasion and saw that Prince Sado's tablet was placed in the shrine. Not long after her return to her residence, she passed away. For the sake of His Majesty, Lady Sŏnhŭi had not shown her sorrow outwardly. She carried the grief in her heart, which caused the illness that ended her life. I need not say how immensely grieved I was. I felt completely alone and without support.

After Lady Sŏnhŭi's death, the general sentiment and the atmosphere of the court gradually changed. Princess Hwawan, without benefit of her mother's instruction, grew imprudent and difficult. She tried to alienate my son from me. With cunning words, she tried to turn him against his maternal family. The situation became quite vexing.

I deeply lamented the tragedy that Prince Sado had faced. Given the situation at the court now, it was most improbable that further repercussions of a serious nature would occur.† My husband had no surviving brother. What remained were two lonely shadows—His Majesty and the Grand Heir—and it was these two who mattered. The important thing was to be loyal to His Majesty and to safeguard the Grand Heir. Thus, in my dealings with the Princess, I was always friendly in speech and manner. My late father was of the same mind as I. He always instructed the Grand Heir to be

---

* This ceremony, called *tamje*, was offered two months after the second anniversary of the death.

† Lady Hyegyŏng is implying that the Grand Heir was secure.

solicitous of this aunt, and he advised me to be sisterly to her. However it may have been expressed, the basis for his concern was, of course, his single-minded devotion to the nation.

The Princess had an adopted son, Hugyŏm.* Hugyŏm was not a child who enjoyed being overlooked. After all, he was a grandson of the reigning monarch. My father treated him with due respect. Father also cultivated the friendship of Chŏng Hwiryang, the brother of the father-in-law of the Princess, despite the fact that he was of a different faction.[17] Chŏng Hwiryang reciprocated and was very well disposed toward us. After his death, the Chŏng family had no other senior member, and so Father guided young Hugyŏm with special care. However, after Hugyŏm passed the civil examination,[18] he came under the influence of others and his ideas about us changed. Then the troubles began for my family.

Father was not one who could turn his back on the nation and retire to private life. Besides, he had a particularly close relationship to His Majesty. Even before he had passed the examination, His Majesty had held him in rather special regard. When Father passed the examination in *kapcha* (1744) soon after my wedding, there was no one else closely related to the royal family who was serving in office. Thus, from the first when my father held a relatively low post, His Majesty entrusted him with affairs of state, large and small. For the entire thirty-year span of his public career, except for the time he served in provincial posts or when he was in retreat to observe parental mourning, not one day passed on which His Majesty did not have an audience with him. At one time or another, Father served in all the important posts in both the civil and the military bureaucracies, including such positions as Commander of the Five Military Garrisons, Minister of Taxation, and Head of the Relief Agency. He was so preoccupied and burdened with his duties that he could rarely go home to rest in peace. Both His Majesty's trusting attitude and Father's single-minded loyalty to his lord could truly measure up to the lofty standards of the ancients. They really had no cause to be ashamed were they to be compared to the worthies of antiquity. Father looked up to his ruler as he would look up to a loving father. Though he was not

* When Princess Hwawan's husband, Chŏng Ch'idal, died young and without an heir, custom decreed that she adopt a child from the Chŏng lineage.

unaware that, given his situation,* it was more appropriate that he retire, he preferred to devote his entire self to the nation. My older brother shared the same conviction. Then my two younger brothers passed the examination in succession and entered officialdom. They did not do this for fame and riches. Rather my family, wholly concerned with the nation, could not forswear examinations and public service. This brought power and glory, but these, in turn, aroused envy and jealousy. Ghosts and spirits envied us, and the living resented us. I cannot record all the complicated and tangled affairs that my family suffered.

With the royal wedding of the *kimyo* year (1759),† Ohŭng became the father-in-law of the King. Suddenly catapulted into prominence from his position as an ordinary scholar, he found himself again and again in situations for which he was totally unprepared. In consideration of his indebtedness to the throne, and feeling a certain sense of kinship to this new royal affinal relation, my father offered to help. In the manner of an older sibling, Father coached Ohŭng and made certain that he did not misstep. For a while Ohŭng was grateful and eagerly followed Father's instructions. The two families formed a close friendship.

I served the new Queen with deep deference, not suggesting in the slightest that I had come into the palace earlier or that I was older. Her Highness also treated me with utmost care. There was not the smallest conflict between the two families, and we hoped that the harmony would continue for many years. Intent on doing our public duty, my father and I entertained no other thought. However, once Ohŭng and his family consolidated their power and grew familiar with the way of the world, they came to resent us for having been there earlier, and they betrayed our goodwill.

Before *kimyo* (1759) His Majesty had treasured and trusted Father not merely as an affinal relative but as his own relation. He entrusted him with military and civil offices, consulted him on important state matters, and esteemed him most highly. Upon the death of his parent in the *pyŏngsul* year (1766), Father retired from

---

* He was the father-in-law of the Crown Prince whom the reigning monarch had put to death.

† Yŏngjo's marriage to Queen Chŏngsun, the daughter of Kim Han'gu, who was given the title Lord Ohŭng.

public life to perform his mourning obligations. It was during this period that Kwiju, Hugyŏm, and the others who had been jealous of my family got together and allied themselves against us.* They incited [others] on the left and harmed [us] on the right. There were many perilous occasions. Those who joined this wretched crowd included many among Father's long-standing allies, intimate friends, and close relations. How limitlessly ugly human hearts can be! Hugyŏm and Madame Chŏng tried to alienate my son from me and they planted in him the dislike of his maternal family. Kwiju, who had been green with envy because he felt his family to be of a lesser stature than mine, slandered us on totally unfounded grounds. It seemed as though danger might overtake us at any moment, morning or evening.

However, His Majesty extended his grace ever more kindly. When Father completed his mourning, His Majesty reappointed him Prime Minister[19] and bestowed upon him the same royal trust and affection as before. The deeper this royal trust grew, the sharper the slanders directed against us became and the more the schemes hatched to injure us multiplied. None in or out of the court helped, but many wished to harm us. There is a saying, "There is no tree that does not fall after ten blows," and perhaps it describes my father's fall. Bit by bit, the daily onslaught on my father wore at His Majesty's sympathies. Then that slanderous memorial by that scum Han Yu arrived in the third month of *kyŏngin* year (1770).† It was an extremely calumnious and vituperative attack on my father, and we suffered incomparable mortification and chagrin.

Because of his advanced age, His Majesty often erred in his decisions. Thus there were occasions on which my father, serving as a high minister in the State Council, should not have complied with royal instructions. However, the situation at court at the time was such that ministerial admonitions would not have been effective.

---

* Kim Kwiju was Queen Chŏngsun's brother. Hong Ponghan was in mourning because his stepmother died. His mourning obligation was equal to that due a mother, and it was customary for an official to retire from office for the duration, usually twenty-six months.

† Han's memorial charged that Hong Ponghan was a cunning and evil minister and that he should be beheaded. *YS*, 114:13b. Han Yu was a scholar, so he had a nominal right to send a memorial to the throne. Once accused, even the most powerful officials were obliged to await a royal decision.

Situated differently from other officials, Father was most gingerly and cautious in his criticisms of the throne. There were many instances in which, failing to abide by the ancients' ideal of ministerial remonstrance, he obeyed royal wishes uncritically. This was because he knew that it was not possible to do otherwise in any meaningful way. Those ruffians who, had they been in Father's position, would not have been able to take care of state affairs half as well, formed a clique and began to plan an all-out assault upon him.

It was obvious that Han Yu did not send that ugly memorial of his own accord, but that he did so at someone else's instigation.* It simply made no sense for him to send so unspeakably calumnious a memorial. Bestowing a special grace, His Majesty ordered that my father retire from active service.† We were stunned. This decision left us terrified. My father remained unperturbed however. Thanking his sagacious grace, in tears, he received the royal gifts of an arm rest and a walking stick.‡ Then he left for Yŏngmi Pavilion.

In my widowhood, I looked up to His Majesty and relied upon my father. I hoped that their exceptionally cordial lord-minister relationship would last for a hundred years. Hated by the petty and maligned by the scurrilous, Father was forced to leave court. It was not that I regretted his departure; rather I was bitterly chagrined that his undivided loyalty might not have been properly appreciated. Helpless and impotent, I was there but could render him no assistance. Obviously, my family was approaching catastrophe. Racked by apprehension, I could not rest, even for a moment.

In that state, I approached Madame Chŏng and pleaded with her on Father's behalf. I pointed out to her that, given Father's wholehearted loyalty, his situation was exceedingly sad. I implored her, asking that he not be made to fall from royal grace. Swayed by her son, Madame Chŏng did not seem kindly disposed toward us

---

* Lady Hyegyŏng claims that Han's memorial was a part of Kwiju's and Hugyŏm's scheme against her father.

† This order came after Han's banishment. Though Yŏngjo relieved Hong of the post, he bestowed honors upon Hong and displayed gestures of appreciation. Hong was given the post of *pongjoha*, minister emeritus. According to the *Sillok*, Yŏngjo relieved Hong of the post because he had grown tired of Hong's heavy-handedness. *YS*, 114:14a–15a.

‡ Traditional gifts that the king bestowed upon a high-ranking official upon retirement. Yŏngjo came to Sungjŏng Gate in order to give them to Hong Pong-han in person. *YS*, 114:15b.

any longer. Each passing moment brought more ominous developments. Something had to be done to save my father. My older brother, with his considerable age and position, could not bring himself to do anything drastic, nor could my second brother. This left my third brother.

Since childhood my third brother had a noble character, high principles, and a clear vision. He was not one for devious or shabby intrigues, but, among my brothers, he was the one with the youth, the pluck, and the cleverness to engage in them. I wrote him a letter: "In the past, there were filial sons who died for their parents. The present situation demands drastic action: one option is to kill oneself to attest the innocence of Father and the family; failing that, the only way is to cultivate Hugyŏm to avert disaster." In this way, I urged him on repeatedly. He refused again and again, saying that he just could not bring himself to do what was asked. He had a deep distaste for improper or devious behavior, but I induced him to act against his principles. I sought to persuade him, arguing that since he was acting purely to save his parent, he need not feel shame before the gods or the spirits. Once he decided, my brother did not worry about his reputation. Engaging cleverly in the arts of deception as practiced by the ancients, he succeeded in gaining the good graces of Hugyŏm. That my brother came to be hated by the world, and that he was tainted by his association with Hugyŏm, were all this sister's doing.

What Father faced in the second month of the *sinmyo* year (1771) was quite beyond our imagination.* Like a noxious vapor, the threat of calamity enveloped us. Kwiju and his uncle schemed in secret to exterminate my entire family. Despite his superior intelligence, His Majesty was getting on in years; his powers of discrimination had rather weakened. Shadows of imminent disaster hung over us. My father was sent to Ch'ŏngju and confined there.[20] Anything could happen at any moment. Wishing to protect his maternal family, the Grand Heir pleaded with Her Highness the Queen. Then, when Kim Han'gi† suggested to Hugyŏm

* Hong Ponghan was suspected of having engaged in a plot to make one of Prince Sado's secondary sons, Ŭnŏn or Ŭnsin, the successor to the throne. On the third of the second month, 1771, Hong Ponghan was deleted from the official register, and Ŭnŏn and Ŭnsin were banished to an island. Ŭnsin subsequently died of natural causes in banishment. *YS*, 116:7a–b, 116:20b.
† Kim Han'gu's brother and Kwiju's uncle.

that, in accordance with their plan to annihilate the Hong family, they proceed with the accusations against my father, Hugyŏm balked. It is difficult to say what would have happened if Hugyŏm had still borne the enmity he had felt toward us. Perhaps because of his new friendship with my brother, he stalled in his joint scheme with Han'gi. Hugyŏm's mother had gone to see her son and must have spoken sympathetically about us to His Majesty. The threat of imminent calamity was lifted. Greatly relieved, we called her our benefactress.

The basis upon which Kwiju and his uncle slandered my father was this. After Ŭnŏn and Ŭnsin were born,* His Majesty was worried that they might grow up to sow trouble. Out of concern for the future, Father said to His Majesty, "They are young and have committed no crime. It would be better if we gave them the benefit of the doubt rather than anticipate the worst. Your humble servant is closely related to the Grand Heir, and so no one would suspect him of ulterior motives if he were to befriend these princes. It might be wise for Your Majesty to bestow grace upon them, and for your servant to treat them with kindness so as not to invite trouble."

Father's intentions were modest. He wished to ensure that these unfortunate children of my late husband not fall in with a worthless crowd. They were, after all, my husband's flesh and blood, and my father felt duty-bound to protect them. It was because of his loyalty to the nation that he concerned himself with them. But their nature was not good. They did not abide by his guidance. Then they were sent out to their own residence rather early.† They often behaved improperly, but they disliked instruction. Father thought it unfortunate and fretted over them. The entire family grew concerned with possible repercussions. But these children were lonely and unprotected and Father made allowances for them, hoping that they would not become entangled in difficulties.

Then, in the *pyŏngsul* year (1766), Father had to wear mourning garb. He returned to the State Council in *kich'uk* (1769), but he served only one year before he retired in *kyŏngin* (1770).[21] He simply had no time to instruct these children. As intrigues and

---

* They were born in 1754 and 1755, respectively.

† As a rule, a royal prince was sent out of the palace to his own residence in his eighteenth year. Princes Ŭnŏn and Ŭnsin must have been sent out somewhat earlier than the norm.

schemes by the thousands rose against him, it was not possible to look after these children. So precariously situated, it had become impolitic for him to be concerned with affairs of the world. These children had shown no indication that they had benefited from his instruction, nor did they show any promise of doing so in the future. Consequently, Father entertained no illusions about his usefulness. Thus it was not difficult for him to wash his hands of them.

Loyalty to the state had led him to take them under his wing in the first place. He wished to guide them away from trouble. Out of fair-mindedness, reasoning that his closeness to the Grand Heir would place him above suspicion, he risked association with these lowly creatures to offer them opportunities for self-improvement rather than prejudging them. But they did not respond as he wished. Though he was still concerned that they might create problems for the state, he felt he had nothing to offer, and so he broke off his relations with them. Born of a vulgar mother, these two boys received no parental guidance. They exercised neither caution nor restraint. They became thoughtlessly exploitative of the weak and simply took what they wanted from the powerless. Tales of their misbehavior, one worse than the next, circulated far and wide. It was truly worrisome when His Majesty caught wind of their exploits. He grew furious at them and banished them.

Completely unexpectedly, however, Father was implicated. Calamity was dangerously near and we were at wit's end. Because of the Grand Heir's intervention, this passed. By normal standards of human emotion and Heavenly principle, Father's devotion to the Grand Heir should not have been called into question. That the Grand Heir was his grandson was reason enough to hold him very dear or, at the very least, much more dear than Ŭnŏn and Ŭnsin. Yet that evil crowd questioned this! With untenable sophistry they sought to hurt him. How dreadful are the depths of human malevolence!

Father's confinement to Ch'ŏngju was quickly lifted.[22] Nonetheless, accusatory memorials continued. As the accused, Father could not return to his house at Samho, and so he spent a month at a strange place awaiting punishment. These memories of him helplessly stranded like that bring back the bitterness I felt at the time. In the third month Father was reinstated, and in the sixth month he returned to court. Father and daughter were very happy to see each other again. We felt vindicated and relieved.

In the eighth month of that year (1771) Han Yu sent in another memorial, this time accusing my father of an even more heinous crime.* Father was again in danger. This crafty maneuver to deceive His Majesty's discriminating intelligence was again the doing of Han'gu and his family. Could it be that they were bound to us by unrequited enmity from a former life? At the time, their deception was not uncovered, and His Majesty sent down a severe judgment against my father.† The charge was very heavy, so he secluded himself in a house beneath the ancestral shrine by the gravesite. My older brother and his wife accompanied him.

In the previous year, while Father had stayed at Yŏngmi Pavilion outside the East Gate, my older brother and his wife had remained in Seoul, tending the ancestral shrine. My third brother and his wife had accompanied Father to his temporary lodging. This third sister-in-law was extremely filial and served her parents-in-law with devotion. Soon after she married into the family, Mother died. She always spoke of her mother-in-law's absence with regret and was extremely attentive and respectful in serving her father-in-law, careful to always follow his intentions. She was also very loving to her husband's younger sister. As a third daughter-in-law, she was not expected to function as the primary person responsible for attending her father-in-law. Thus, when she was called upon to do this duty in the kyŏngin year (1770), she redoubled her efforts. In the second month of sinmyo (1771), when Father faced that threat, she was several months pregnant. In this condition, she often bathed in cold water and climbed to the top of a nearby hill to pray for her father-in-law. She did this out of extreme devotion. I was immensely moved by it. But she died in the ninth month of that year. I felt that this was caused by her bathing in cold water during pregnancy. I was deeply grieved by her death.

In the first month of the imjin year (1772) Father was granted a royal pardon.‡ His Majesty sent him tender messages summoning

---

* Han Yu's memorial accused Hong Ponghan of having provided Yŏngjo with the rice chest in 1762, suggesting that he confine Prince Sado in it. YS, 117:7a–b.

† Hong Ponghan was made a commoner. According to the Sillok, Yŏngjo was greatly disturbed that discussions over Prince Sado's death reemerged as a topic of discussion. Punishing Hong was an expression of Yŏngjo's general dissatisfaction over the whole business. YS, 117:11a–b.

‡ On the twelfth of the first month, 1772, Hong Ponghan was restored to his previous post of minister emeritus. YS, 118:7a.

him back to court. Unable to disobey, Father moved to Samho and returned to court. When His Majesty received him in audience, the sagacious countenance shone with delight. His Majesty's affection for his old minister did not seem at all diminished. Subsequently, His Majesty would summon Father periodically for consultation on important affairs of state.

On the twenty-first day of the seventh month, Kwanju and Kwiju presented memorials to the throne one after another. Not one word of theirs was true, nor was even one phrase unconnected to some vicious scheme.* Their situation was so different from ours. What rancor did they hold against us that they went to such extremes as these? How unfathomable are the incongruous ways of the world! How indiscernible are the evils hidden in the human heart!

With discernment as keen and as all-seeing as the sun and the moon, His Majesty cleared Father of the infamy. Then, on the twenty-third, he sent down a stern order to Kwiju. I shed tears of gratitude. Of course, every subject is in royal grace, but my family's indebtedness to His Majesty is truly unique. Even now, whenever I am reminded of his kindness, I become tearful. His Majesty was appalled by what passed between the two affinal families. He declared that, in this vicious struggle, Hong Ponghan was as virtuous as Lin Hsiang-ju or as brave as Lien P'o,[†] and he ordered Kwiju to apologize to my father in the most abject and humble manner. Then His Majesty dealt with him appropriately.[‡] I had gone down to a small house to await punishment. His Majesty summoned and consoled me. He said, "I asked the Queen to look upon you in the same way as before. She will listen to me. Would you also please no longer be suspicious of the Queen and change your attitude toward her?"

I had been feeling acutely the force of the fanatical hatred directed at my family and myself in each phase of the campaign they waged against us. I knew that I had to act in accordance with

---

* Kim Kwanju was Kim Kwiju's second cousin. His memorial charged Hong Ponghan with three crimes and asked for his execution. Kwiju's memorial was similar. *YS*, 119:6b–13a. For details of the three charges, see *The Memoir of 1802*.

† Lin was a famous minister of the Ch'ao state during the Warring States period in China. He served King Huai and is regarded as a paragon of ministerial wisdom and loyalty. Lien was the general of the Ch'ao state. The two were famous as devoted friends.

‡ Kwiju was dismissed from office, and an injunction was issued declaring that he should not be employed in government again. *YS*, 119:13a.

the great principle, but I was not quite sure how I could resolve my feelings about the whole affair. However, I was tremendously moved by His Majesty's appeal. I do not believe that I can ever forget Kwiju's relentless antagonism. When it comes to Her Highness the Queen, however, I dared not harbor a grudge. I have been serving her with the utmost devotion, as the whole court has witnessed. It is difficult to believe that Her Highness approved of what her brother was doing. Whatever her views of her brother's activities might be, he caused her much worry and great trouble. In this sense, Kwiju was not merely a traitor to the nation; he also sinned against Her Highness. Regardless of what the Queen may have felt, she displayed no change in her attitude toward me. I admired Her Highness's virtue, and I tended her respectfully as was demanded by my obligation as a daughter-in-law.

After the matter of Kwiju's memorial was settled, His Majesty treated Father with the same affection and trust that he had shown before *kyŏngin* (1770). Father periodically came up to stay at his city residence to thank his sagacious grace.

In the *kyesa* year (1773) Father attained his sixtieth birthday. He was, however, in a melancholy mood. He had always regretted that his father had passed away in his sixtieth year before he could celebrate his birthday.* Ever more regretful of this as he approached his own sixtieth birthday, he would not touch breakfast and refused the congratulatory winecups. He did not leave his Samho residence and spent the day in tears. I could not bring myself to offer him a feast, but I had a simple meal prepared and sent to him with a message urging that he partake of it. He forced himself, but he could not eat. My and my siblings' thoughts were of our late mother who, had she lived, would have celebrated her sixtieth birthday in the same month as Father. Her early death deprived her children of the pleasure of seeing both parents joyfully celebrating their sixtieth birthdays together. Father also seemed grieved by the absence of his worthy spouse. In our separate ways, we spent the day in sad remembrance. Several days later, in compliance with a cordial royal order, Father came into the court. Accompanied by the Grand Heir and his consort, I saw him. We exchanged thoughts and consoled each other.

Saying that Father had spent his sixtieth birthday too quietly,

---

* Honge Hyŏnbo was born in 1680 and died in 1740.

His Majesty gave him in the tenth month a huge birthday party complete with music at his city residence. In deepest humility, Father accepted it. Since *kyŏngin* (1770), however, Father had not permitted himself normal freedoms. He applied very narrow strictures to his way of life. Thus, though he received the feast and accepted the music to express his gratitude for boundless royal grace, he did not conduct himself like a man free to enjoy festivity. He did not relax into casual conversation and easy laughter, and the gathering did not take on an air of merriment.

In the *kabo* year (1774) my second uncle was appointed a minister on the State Council.* I had regretted that my father, unable to bring himself to retire from public life, had encountered defamation and slander from that evil clique. For the Hong family, the most natural thing, clearly, was to give up public office and, giving thanks for royal kindness, enjoy a leisurely private life. When national affairs were at their most difficult and delicate, my uncle was called to this highest of public offices. The news alarmed me. I was paralyzed by fear and apprehension. Perhaps my family's excessive prosperity might have offended Heaven and angered the spirits. For whatever reason, my uncle mysteriously committed a slip of the tongue in the winter of *ŭlmi* (1775).† This led to the ruin of the family. How can one fathom the way of Heaven? I just wail and wail.

My uncle's blunder was indefensible. Yet I hoped that the royal intelligence would penetrate into his intentions and magnanimously forgive him.‡ However, His Majesty passed away on the fifth day of the third month of *pyŏngsin* (1776). How can I begin to describe the grief and desolation I felt! I had served His Majesty since I was ten years of age and, for more than thirty years, had received the kindest of affection from him. Even in the most tense and trying of times, he had not in the slightest lessened his tender regard toward me. He even honored me with a most gracious re-

---

* Hong Inhan was appointed Minister of the Right in the twelfth month of 1774. *YS*, 125:1a.

† In the eleventh month of 1775, Yŏngjo, in failing health, wanted to appoint Chŏngjo regent. Hong Inhan, who was at the time Minister of the Left, opposed the regency, but a regency was enacted. *YS*, 125:18a–19b, 126:10a. For details, see *The Memoir of 1801*.

‡ Hong Inhan was charged with being disloyal to Chŏngjo. For details, see *The Memoir of 1801*.

mark—that I was his old friend and that we understood each other. He was also particularly loving of the present King and his two sisters. Considering what I have been through and how difficult the way of the world has been, I owe everything, including my survival, to His Late Majesty whose sagacious grace was as immense as Heaven. Ah, sadness!

Now my son, whom I brought up in the most difficult of circumstances, succeeded to the throne. The loving heart of a mother leapt with joy and pride at seeing him take the seat of the sovereign. However, my suffering was not meant to be ameliorated. Threats of disaster fell again and again upon my family and grew ever more ominous. My heart bled with pain. I longed to do away with myself so that I would not see nor hear these things, but I could not desert my son. My pain, though deep, was of a private nature. My public duty lay in acquiescing to the royal decision. Thus, with unspoken pain in my heart, I remained in this world. In the seventh month I had to endure the news of my uncle's execution.* This was the ruin of the family. How could this be! How could this happen! After all, wasn't I the mother of the King? Calling upon Heaven, I wailed and wailed, but my grief again had to remain private. Despite pain and bitterness, I did not forget that one had to always redouble one's devotion to the state. My public duty demanded that I behave as though I had forgotten my uncle. I only hoped that Father would be spared.

Father was in an extremely precarious position. But as a grandfather of the King, he was situated differently than the others. Wishing to decide upon his course in accordance with royal orders, he had remained at his Samho residence, awaiting the royal decision. Humiliating and vicious charges were continually hurled at him. It was as though the world had discarded cognizance of human relations and had determinedly set out to harm the grandfather of the King. Stupid though I may be, I was sitting as the mother of a reigning King, and in this position, I had to face a situation in which the evil clique sought to punish my father. I was tempted to kill myself to show once and for all how wronged he had been, but I prolonged this odious life of mine in consideration of my son's feelings. My conduct revealed first the weakness of my

* Hong Inhan was judged to have been a traitor and was executed by a cup of poison in 1776. *YS*, 1:79b.

will and second how unskilled I was in managing affairs. Ultimately, however, my decision was rooted in devotion to my son.
The subject of humiliating accusations, Father left hastily for the
family gravesite, followed by the entire family. How can I describe
the grief I felt?

Having received so much kindness from His Late Majesty, it was
unthinkable that I not attend the morning and evening offerings
and the six daily wailings for him. Through my uncle's exile and
even after his execution, despite the indescribable sadness in my
heart, I faithfully observed my mourning duties. However, as I saw
what Father had to endure, my pain and anger got the better of me
and I lost all desire to live. I decided that it was shameless and un-
civil that the child of a criminal conduct herself in a normal manner. From the eighth month, I shut the gate and took to bed. Determined that I would share life or death, calamity or fortune with
my father, I never once went outside. Only when the King came to
see me did I raise my head. The King had experienced deep pain in
his life and was greatly disturbed to see his mother thus aggrieved.
So uncomfortable and wretched did he seem to be whenever he
came to see me, I tried to maintain a cheerful mien to lighten his
anguish.

As if what Father was facing were not severe enough, my third
brother's name had appeared on the list of criminals.* That this
brother of mine was disliked by the world was all my doing! I beat
my breast in frustration. Evil fortune had more in store for us,
however. In the *chŏngyu* year (1777) my older brother passed away.
How virtuous he was in his conduct, how accomplished in his
scholarship! It seemed that profound vexation over family misfortunes prompted his sudden departure from this world. He had
an aged parent still living, and thus the tragedy was even more
sharply felt. My father was completely shattered by his son's death,
so contrary to the usual order of life and death between parent and
child, and coming to him as he lay prostrate with anxiety. The
family was encountering calamity amidst disaster. Gazing up to
Heaven, I silently wept.

It is perhaps true that one is rarely spared the loss of a sibling,
but I never dreamed that my older brother would die in his prime
and, worse, die of the grief in his heart. I had always looked up to

* Hong Nagim was accused of having been involved in a seditious plot.

him. I had assumed that this wonderful older brother of mine, as befitted the head of his generation, would continue to serve our parent with filial piety and would lead and guide his brothers as well as the next generation. Regret for his death is etched so deeply in my psyche that even now, several decades later, when I speak of him, my breast grows tight and tears stream down.

In the eighth month of *chŏngyu* (1777) my third brother's case took a turn for the worse. Losing hope, we were prepared for anything. But, by royal discretion, my brother's life was spared for a time. Then in the second month of the *musul* year (1778) the sun and the moon of royal intelligence penetrated into the case. The King succeeded in discovering that the charge against him was fabricated and established his innocence.* How immense was this royal kindness bestowed upon my brother. The King rescued my brother! How can I describe the gratitude I felt at that moment?

Father had come to the capital and was awaiting punishment beneath the palace wall. After my brother's trial ended, he came into court. He had an audience with the King and then he came to see me. Father had gone through many things in the past several years including the unexpected death of his oldest son. He had aged a great deal. He seemed feeble. When I saw him, strong emotions gripped my heart. My father said how thankful he was that his son had been proven innocent. He also expressed deep joy to see me once more in this life. Then he left. I prayed to Heaven that he would continue to enjoy health and that we would see each other again.

My sins, however, weighed more heavily with the passage of time. Heaven sent another calamity. Father passed away soon afterwards.† Thus we were parted eternally. How limitless was my grief. My pain rose to the Heavens and my bitterness penetrated the Earth. Judging by his physique and his endowments, my father could have easily enjoyed a life of seventy years. Because of his dedication to the state, he had spent decades in deepest anxiety. He encountered innumerable slanders and humiliations and witnessed the ruin of his family. How frustrated and anguished he was

* Chŏngjo delayed the interrogation of Hong Nagim. When Chŏngjo finally did interrogate him, he was most solicitous of his mother's feelings and maintained a respectful attitude toward his uncle. After the interrogation, Chŏngjo declared Hong Nagim innocent. *CS*, 5:23a–24a.
† Hong Ponghan died on the fourth day of the twelfth month of 1778.

that he could not once and for all establish his single-minded devotion to the King! All this took its toll. In the end it shortened his life. How sharply I felt his unrequited grievances!

But who was responsible for this? This was all due to this unfilial daughter. Had I not been born, my family would not have suffered so much. My terrible sin of unfiliality could not be redeemed, even if my bones were to be ground to dust. My utmost wish at the time was to end my life so that I might follow my father to the netherworld. Unable to forsake the King's filial devotion to me, I discarded my long-standing resolution to share with Father the fortune and calamity of life and death. My shame and grief at this failure was so deep that it penetrated into Heaven and Earth. Had I died, I would not have known this remorse. Because I lived, I have suffered unrelieved pain. My sins of unfiliality grew heavier, and this odious life of mine grew more ignoble still. Can there be anyone as stupid as I?

Unable to do away with myself, I let three years pass. At the conclusion of mourning for Father, my three brothers went their separate ways like shooting stars. The days when our family had enjoyed each other's company in attending Father disappeared like a dream. I cannot begin to describe the desolation I felt.

One might ask, "Who has not been loved by one's parents and who does not love one's parents?" Nevertheless, I feel that my case was unique. I had left my parents early, and this seemed to make them think of me always. Not long afterwards, I lost my mother. Taking upon himself the role of mother as well, my father did not forget me, even for a moment. Even in the smallest of matters, he was mindful not to go against my wishes. That fate held great sadness in store for me came to be a source of supreme pain for him, and he redoubled his efforts to please me. What he did for me was really far more than can be expected of usual parental attentions. He also helped me a great deal financially. Aside from regular tribute and normal provisions, the Crown Prince's establishment had no other source of income. When the Crown Prince's illness worsened, we constantly needed money. Indeed, there were innumerable occasions on which, to put it simply, finding money was a matter of great urgency.* Not wishing to place me in jeop-

---

* In Prince Sado's last years, his illness resulted in a need for an endless and prompt supply of new clothing. See *The Memoir of 1805*.

ardy, Father continually supplied me with what I needed. The total sum, though it has never been calculated, must have been a great deal.

Father was incorruptible and frugal. Aside from his regular salary, he never brought anything home. He headed the Relief Agency and the Board of Taxation for several years. He also served as Head of the Five Military Garrisons for a decade. Wherever he went, he made certain that there were enough provisions for times of need. He never wasted anything. He was particularly talented in financial management. Somehow, he was always prepared. Whenever the Prince's establishment needed something, he unfailingly, miraculously, came up with it. There were many critical moments, and Father's provisions saved many lives. He responded to my needs so promptly. I simply do not know what I would have done if I had not had my father to rely upon. It was not only I who felt Father's beneficence on these occasions. Bringing their hands together, the ladies-in-waiting in my service also silently expressed their thanks to him.

For my son's wedding in *imo* (1762), Father took care of a great many things, relieving me of most of the burden. He made sure that nothing was left unprepared. He also sent money to the Grand Heir's establishment. After that terrible tragedy, he supplied the funereal and mourning garments for all concerned. There were expenses that the Crown Prince's establishment was expected to incur in mourning its deceased master—those connected with daily and monthly offerings during the mourning period and the great sacrifices on the first and second anniversaries of the death. Father advised me against using the supplies with which the establishment was provided, as I would have to repay the sum to Yŏngdong Palace over the years. He then supplied everything. He was extremely careful in all the details as an expression of devotion to the late Prince.

My life was odious, and I did not die. The three-year mourning for my husband ended. Soon Ch'ŏngyŏn and her sister reached adulthood and married.[23] His Majesty gave money for his granddaughters' weddings, but it was not sufficient. Father again helped. Aside from things beyond human intervention, there was nothing that he would not do for me. I knew that he did this out of love, but naturally I was quite uneasy. I often pleaded with him, "Please do not be so lavish with me." However, I dared not refuse his gifts.

In a quiet moment I asked, "You are so good to me. Does this not mean that you are giving the other children less than their fair share? They will need houses and land. Because of me, you are not able to do something for them. What will happen to them?" Father said, "If the country is at peace, they will do all right. There is no reason that I should provide for them." As a military commander, Father left the coffer sealed and, unlike other commanders, never spent lavishly on himself. However, he had extraordinary financial acumen and was always ready to meet the needs of the Crown Prince's establishment. Altogether what he supplied must have amounted to several tens of thousands of taels. Only later did I realize the headaches it must have caused him to do this for me. There was not even one way in which I was not unfilial or troublesome.

Aside from the Hwagye Pavilion, which my grandfather had bequeathed to him, Father had not had even one house built for himself despite his several decades of service in the highest civil and military posts. In his last years he had no place of his own in which to seclude himself, and so he had to search out someone else's place to rent. It was I who was the cause of this. Was there anything that I was not responsible for? Once the family suffered misfortune, my brothers, not being the sort to seek office at such times, were all reduced to terrible indigence. I lamented in my heart that, if Father had provided for their livelihood in prosperous times, they would not have had to live in such penury. I do regret that I was the cause of their misery.

Considering how much Father helped me, one might think that he had nothing left with which to assist others. On the contrary, he was remarkably sympathetic and responsive to needy clansmen, however distant. Even during those periods when he kept a maddeningly busy schedule, he unfailingly came to the aid of destitute clansmen. I heard that many could make fires only when they received what he sent.

Father had lost his own mother at a very early age and this had led to an obsessive devotion to his maternal family. He had insisted on providing supplies for sacrifices to his maternal grandparents and was particularly attentive to the affairs of his maternal cousins. I remember him speaking frequently of them with tenderness.

Though I lived, the pain of not having followed my father to the netherworld cut to the bone. I was also deeply saddened that I could not have his innocence proven and declared. In this also I was failing in my filial duties. In the *kapchin* year (1784) the King at last promulgated an edict that cleared Father of all accusations and charges.[24] Then he offered him a posthumous title.* Speaking from my own point of view, I felt quite sad that recognition of my father's wholehearted loyalty and single-minded devotion came too late for him. But I knew that Father, even in the netherworld, would be most grateful and deeply moved by this. I shed tears of gratitude on his behalf. On this occasion Suyŏng, as the family heir, was given an official post.† I did not rejoice over this honor. It was not that I was unappreciative of royal grace, but I had no heart to see my family in service at court again.

I looked back upon my life. Many thoughts pained me—the immensity of my indebtedness to Father, the memory of his tender and unfailing love, the sad misfortunes of my family that seemed to be worsening daily. As these thoughts seized me, the allure of doing away with myself to redeem my unfiliality appealed to me with renewed force. Yet I could not bring myself to do it. The thought of my son checked me. It was because of him that I was unable to kill myself in *imo* (1762). Unable to forget the lonely figure of the King, I again failed to follow my father in *musul* (1778). Thus I sinned against conjugal duty and deserted filial obligations. So deeply ashamed was I that I blushed at my own shadow. I lay awake at night, guilty over the decline of my family. Sometimes I felt as though fire was burning inside of me, and on those occasions, my bedding became so hot that I rose and pounded the walls in utter misery. Indeed, for how many years was I unable to fall asleep in peace!

Since the *pyŏngsin* year (1776), many terrible events had occurred to the state. Of these, Kugyŏng's treacherous schemes were especially horrible. He was one of those rare, truly evil men. He recklessly implicated and vilified a great number of people with trumped-up charges and had them killed. Then he committed a colossal crime. His treachery was revealed in the so-called "tomb

---

* The title was Lord Ikchŏng. *CS*, 18:26a.
† It is not clear exactly what post it was, but it was a minor sinecure. *CS*, 18:18a.

attendant affair" of *kihae* (1779).* The vileness of this plot was unrivaled in all of history. He carried it out all on his own. How incredibly ugly! I gnashed my teeth in my fury.

Most distressing of all, the King had no heir. This was not merely the concern of a private family; the future of the nation was threatened. Finally, after much wringing of hands, the King was blessed with the birth of a son in *imin* (1782). The King was over thirty years of age, and this felicity, coming as it did, brought inestimable joy. My sad heart became attached to the infant Prince, for whose sake I prayed for many many years of peace and prosperity.

Misfortune struck the nation again. The young Prince died suddenly in *pyŏngo* (1786). The King seemed to be even more solitary and forlorn than before. A sense of the precariousness of the future of the state reemerged.

I had no words with which to console the King. Indeed, what would happen to the monarchy? In silence, I prayed and prayed, my gaze upon the Yellow Springs,† praying that a sagacious prince be given to the nation so that it could attain peace and security. With a blessing from Heaven and the assistance of royal ancestors, a prince was born in the sixth month of the *kyŏngsul* year (1790).‡ This was the greatest of all felicities! An incomparable joy between Heaven and Earth! It was impossible to give thanks enough to Heaven. I just brought my hands together and offered my sincerest thanks. Heaven must have been moved by the King's good deeds and his remarkable virtue and rewarded him in this way. In truth, I did not expect that I would see this happiness again in this life and, moreover, on my own birthday!

My birthdays used to bring memories of my parents. I used to acutely regret my birth, which was the cause of the decline and fall of my family, and I lamented the bottomlessness of my unfiliality. Unable to ignore the King's touching devotion, I had observed birthday formalities, but secretly I had wished that I would not

---

* Hong Kugyŏng's attempts to become the maternal uncle of the heir apparent. Hong Kugyŏng helped Chŏngjo consolidate his position in the early years of his reign, but he became very powerful and some of his activities were thought to be a threat to the royal house. For details, see *The Memoir of 1801*.

† *Hwangch'ŏn*. The East Asian netherworld.

‡ This new prince later reigned as King Sunjo (r. 1800–1834).

live to see another birthday. Very unexpectedly, however, the new Prince was born on my birthday. This made me believe that Heaven, in compassion for me, sent down this great blessing on this day so that the whole nation would realize the significance of this coincidence, and I would no longer hate the day. In appreciation, I hugged and stroked myself. I gave up my desire to end my life in the sixth month of *kyŏngsul* (1790) and embraced life. This deepened my unfiliality, but my happiness over this felicity was just too great. Humbly accepting this Heaven-sent blessing, I decided to live out my alloted time. The depths of my gratitude and the greatness of my joy are shown by this change of heart.

The King is truly remarkable in his filial devotion. He serves Her Highness the Queen Dowager* with utmost respect. No one could begin to see the depth of the pain hidden in his heart. Not being able to forget that terrible day, he still mourns his father. As the spirits will bear witness, I have not resented at all the miseries that befell my person. I grieve deeply for my late husband, yet I do so with resignation. But I especially mourn and pity my son's hidden sorrow. The way the King remembers and commemorates his father has moved the nation. He serves this living parent with true devotion, placing at my service all that he, the ruler of a nation, has at his disposal, leaving me with no unfulfilled wish. The King lives in harmony with the Queen and treats all his secondary consorts fairly and kindly. He is conspicuously warm and loving to his two younger sisters. In fact, he is more attentive to them than this mother is. I naturally have maternal anxieties about them, but I need not feel even the smallest pang of regret for their sake since their brother leaves no wish of theirs unattended to. The King's affection extends even to his half brother and sister.† The crimes they committed were of the sort that normally would result in forfeiture of their filial relationship to their father; yet the King, in his sagacious virtue, treated them most magnanimously. This act of grace, which has rare historical precedent, drew encomiums from all. While I could not somehow banish fear and uneasiness, I admired his outstanding virtue.

---

* Queen Chŏngsun.
† Prince Ŭnŏn and Princess Ch'ŏnggŭn. All three of Chŏngjo's half brothers were at some point implicated in seditious plots. One survived. *YS*, 116:7a–b; *CS*, 4:19b–29b.

The Queen is virtuous and benevolent. Having inherited the duty of overseeing the royal household, she maintains the highest standards of goodness and propriety. She serves the Queen Dowager and myself with sincere devotion. Lady Kasun* is also filial, frugal, and modest. She assists the King and rears and instructs the heir with inexhaustible love and devotion. She renders much commendable service to the state. Is she not a treasure?

I congratulate myself on the continuing fortune of the dynasty. The serene harmony in this court is something that has not been seen for a long time. I am also proud and gratified that the manner in which I serve the Queen Dowager informs the high level of decorum that reigns at court.

I have lived in gnawing regret that I did not follow my husband to death, and I have experienced a thousand twists and ten thousand turns in this life. But I have successfully reared the King to adulthood. He is resplendent in his sagacious virtue. I have also brought up two princesses. With none of the arrogance of highborn ladies, my daughters are utterly devoted to the King and extremely careful in their behavior. I look upon them with heartfelt approval, and I hope that everlasting fortune and joy will be their reward for their modesty, diligence, and sincerity, rare qualities in noble princesses. Their children are not bad either, some handsome and some elegant. I am pleased to see that, while still in their prime, my daughters already have daughters-in-law and sons-in-law. My only regret is that Ch'ŏngsŏn, with the accomplishments and virtue of a noble-born lady, suffered misfortune in her life and so suffers a fate similar to her mother's.

After the decline of our family, my brothers and uncles secluded themselves remotely in the countryside. I did not expect to see them again in this life. The King wished so greatly to please me with all that was in his power that he created an opportunity for me to see my brothers and uncles again in this life.† They were immeasurably moved by that royal concern. Despite their reluctance to reappear in society, they came to the court to see me. I was profoundly touched by my son's thoughtfulness. Seeing each other after all that we went through, my brothers, my uncles, and I said

---

* She was a secondary consort of Chŏngjo and the mother of Sunjo.
† To please his mother, Chŏngjo invited Lady Hyegyŏng's family to the palace as part of the celebration for the birth of an heir in 1790.

very little. We just shed tears. They sang the praises of the King, and they expressed their hope that they would live their lives out uneventfully amidst mountains and rivers. I just hoped that they would enjoy good health, remain affectionate to each other, and enjoy the benefits of the peace and prosperity of the King's reign. When you, Suyŏng, received your first appointment, the very word "holding office" frightened me. Then, in the *pyŏngo* year (1786), the King summoned your brother and cousins* and bestowed upon them posts reserved for descendants of the illustrious. These posts were sinecure in nature, minor and insignificant, yet four cousins in officialdom seemed excessive, and, in fact, quite alarming. Then suddenly Ch'oeyŏng died. The death of one so talented and intelligent at such an early age seemed to indicate that the misfortunes of the family had not yet ended. Ah, unknowable fate!

My family fell because we had enjoyed excessive prosperity. Thus, though my brothers have shown no inclination to seek office, I am still concerned lest they be tempted to do so. I am also constantly fearful and nervous that one of my nephews might neglect his duties or earn criticism whenever they are assigned to the provinces or even to the most insignificant of posts. I guess all this is rooted in concern for my family.

Entering this year (1795), my pain and regret for my husband has been immeasurable.† How can I describe my state! As the King was overwrought with grief in remembrance of his father, I could not think only of my own pain. Lest the King's excessive grief harm his health, I refrained from giving myself over to sorrow. At the start of the year I received a royal congratulatory visit, but I did not have the heart to enjoy it. On the sixtieth birthday of Prince Sado, accompanied by Her Highness the Queen Dowager, I went to his shrine to pay respect.

Myriad doleful feelings and memories, intermingled, came upon me. Facing the tablet of my husband, I cried as the vastness of my grief filled my heart. He remained so distant. I could neither see his face nor hear his voice. He did not acknowledge my presence. My

* Those summoned were Hong Ch'oeyŏng (Suyŏng's younger brother) and Hong Huyŏng and Hong Ch'wiyŏng (the first sons, respectively, of Hong Naksin and Hong Nagim).

† This year was the beginning of a new sixty-year cycle for Lady Hyegyŏng. Prince Sado was the same age as the author, and her pain was in memory of her husband.

unrequited bitterness was so profound that my breast felt as if it would burst. The King, fearing excessive grief on my part, tried to calm me. I returned to my residence not having given full reign to my emotions. All appeared as in a dream; I remained deeply agitated.

In *kiyu* (1789) the King, having selected a new tomb site for his father at Suwŏn, had Prince Sado's remains reinterred there. On that occasion I could not even see his coffin, and I was left with unfulfilled longing. As the King himself was obsessed with the memory of his father, he fathomed his mother's wishes. Earlier this year (1795), he suggested that I visit Prince Sado's tomb with him, and he took me. I feared that a female presence in the entourage might violate ritual propriety. Nonetheless, I decided to follow my son. It was not merely that I did not wish to refuse the King's filial devotion; I did not think it wrong for me to visit my husband's tomb this year. I so desperately wanted to see his place of eternal rest.

However, the King intended the occasion to be more than just a visit to his father's tomb. He also wanted it to be a celebration of my sixtieth birthday. Wishing to render glory to his parents, he planned things in exhaustive detail. I decided to accompany my son to visit my husband's tomb* because, for once, I wanted to let out my sorrow. But the occasion was turning into something much grander than I had suspected. I remembered that, on his sixtieth birthday, His Late Majesty, King Yŏngjo, in remembrance of his mother, had refused all celebration, forbidding even the preparation of one special dish.[†] I also recalled that because my father had so grieved for his father on his sixtieth birthday, our siblings were unable to wish him a long life with a cup of wine. Under the circumstances, I had no heart to accept a toast of long life or to partake of a specially prepared feast. I was exceedingly uncomfortable. I went to the tomb with a heavy heart.

When I viewed the tomb, though I had no knowledge of geo-

---

* There are a number of screens and paintings of this procession illustrating the magnificence of the occasion. See figures 4 and 5.

[†] Yŏngjo spent his sixtieth birthday, the thirteenth of the ninth month of 1754, commemorating his mother. He paid a visit to Yuksanggung, his mother's shrine, and then went to Ch'angŭi Palace, where he had spent his youth. Returning to his palace late at night, he asked commoners whether they suffered abuse from the powerful. He also ordered that food be distributed to city residents. *YS*, 82:17a.

mancy to discern whether the site was good or bad, I could tell that it was truly an exceptional site. The King had been obsessed with the reinterment of his father and thought of the project day and night for a long time. He finally did it after several decades of careful and exhaustive planning. At the time of the reinterment, the King was extremely nervous lest something go amiss. He devoted all of his energy and attention to it. In a way, he was fulfilling his filial duty. Nevertheless, his sincerity and devotion were so peerless that I was moved anew to know that Prince Sado had such a wonderful son. As I approached the tomb, it affected me deeply to notice that whatever met one's gaze, whether stones, carvings, or even small objects, all were most unusual and most appropriate. There was nothing that was not the expression of the King's utmost devotion. Despite my limitless sorrow, I could not but admire his dedication. On this occasion the King grieved much. The tears he shed wet the grass beneath him. So sharp was the unrequited pain he carried hidden in his heart! I then recalled my alarm on hearing that the King, on his last visit here, had been so overwhelmed by emotion that he was in a feeble state for many hours and that the officials in attendance had been quite troubled by it. I grew alarmed that this might recur. For his sake, I restrained myself and held back my limitless grief. The King also checked his grief for the sake of this old mother. Mother and son consoled each other and, in our concern for each other, completed our visit to the Prince's tomb without incident.

This visit mercilessly reawakened my consciousness of how utterly odious my own life had been. I felt the deepest shame and remorse that I had lived on. In the midst of this unbearable pain, it occurred to me that at the time of my husband's death, the King was a boy not yet ten. Ch'ŏngyŏn and her sister were young children, both well under ten years of age. I simply did not know whether I would be able to see them through to adulthood. However, I managed to bring them up without mishap. The King was past forty years of age, as were his two sisters. Coming to see my husband accompanied by the flesh and blood that he had left behind, I silently reported to him that I had protected them and had seen them through to adulthood. Perhaps one can say that in this one way, my decision to live has borne some fruit.

On the following day, at a detached palace in Suwŏn, the King arranged a splendid feast for me to which he invited my entire family.* This was so vastly different from my intention of the previous day to commemorate my husband in quiet that it gave me little pleasure. I did not want to throw cold water on the King's high-spirited mood, as he was doing this from the most sincerely felt filial devotion. Thus I pretended that I was pleased, but I was exceedingly uncomfortable.

In the magnitude and number of changes and in the peculiarities of fate, I do not believe that the life I have lived as a widow has a counterpart in recorded history. Now my sixtieth birthday was celebrated in an unprecedented manner.[25] I felt that the King had made this party so magnificent partly to console me for my troubled life. Wherever my eyes turned, I saw luxury and abundance. There was nothing that the King did not arrange with meticulous care. The extraordinary expenditure that I could see everywhere made me still more uncomfortable. But I knew that the King did not rely on the Ministry of Taxation for even one item and that he prepared everything with the funds from the Palace Supply Office. I marveled that he was as peerless in filial devotion as he was in financial acumen. In exquisiteness of taste, in refinement of display, and in harmoniousness of arrangement, this affair displayed such excellent leadership as could have come only from the King. Though troubled by unease and painful recollections of my husband, I could not but feel a certain gratification.

Suyŏng, your mother, born to one of the most illustrious families in the country, married into the Hong family. Since I had already entered the palace, I did not see her wedding. She was the great-granddaughter of Lord Yŏyang.† As a child, she had occasionally visited the palace, and the Three Majesties liked her. Thus they were pleased to hear that she was affianced to my brother. To express their delight, on the day the bride arrived at the groom's house, a high-ranking lady-in-waiting was sent to convey royal congratulations, and when this lady-in-waiting returned to the palace, Queen Dowager Inwŏn and Queen Chŏngsŏng summoned her to inquire how things had gone. One can see the royal concern for the affinal family.

---

* For a visual representation of the occasion, see figure 5.

† She married Hong Nagin, Lady Hyegyŏng's older brother, in 1745, a year after Lady Hyegyŏng's marriage to Prince Sado. Her great-grandfather was Min Yujung. See note 11.

After her marriage, my sister-in-law paid a visit to the palace. It was the first time I saw her, and I was struck by her elegant mien and her noble carriage. She was so beautiful, her manner was so perfect, that standing beside the young ladies related to high officials or to the royal house, she stood out conspicuously. The eyes of the court were upon her, spellbound by her beauty and elegance. My parents were justly proud of this oldest daughter-in-law and very fond of her. My brother relied upon her. The whole family came to entrust the future to her. She had lost her parents in her youth, but she had been reared with care by her paternal aunt. As the oldest daughter-in-law of my family, your mother lived amidst power and wealth for thirty years, a rare thing for a woman not of royalty. She bore three daughters in succession. My mother, though she was not yet old, anxiously awaited a grandson. Then, in the fourth month of the *ŭrhae* year (1755), Suyŏng, you were born. My parents were immeasurably happy. It was truly a felicitous event for the family. Everyone congratulated your birth. My mother saw your birth but did not live to see you grow up. I always remember how happy she was when you were born.

On your father's death in *chŏngyu* (1777), you entered mourning. Before you completed your mourning for him, my father died in *musul* (1778). The role of chief mourner fell upon you, the oldest grandson. Thus you were under a double mourning obligation. What a sad time it was for you! Since your birth, I have had a special affection for you as the oldest nephew. With the deaths of two older generations, the heavy responsibility of guiding and managing the family now lies squarely upon you. I do not have to elaborate upon the expectations and fondness I have for you. You have asked me to write something for you. I found it difficult to describe my life. But I wrote this to let you, and my other nephews, know of my experiences and to instruct you.

Our family has enjoyed power and fame for generations. Father reached the highest of official posts. My two uncles and my three brothers,* one after another, entered officialdom. The power and prestige that our family enjoyed for a time were truly immense. We did feel a certain trepidation, but, as affinal relatives, we did not think it possible to separate ourselves from the throne. Yet because

---

* The two uncles were Hong Inhan and Hong Yonghan. The three brothers were Hong Nagin, Hong Naksin, and Hong Nagim.

we did not reckon upon the jealousy of the world, our family fortunes reversed. The root of the calamity was that we were infected by power and wealth. What a fearful thing the holding of office is! At the time, though, it seemed all so natural to serve in office. My father did so because he felt absolutely obliged to. Then my older brother passed the examinations, and my two younger brothers followed in his footsteps by passing both the preliminary and final examinations. When my second brother passed the examination, I began to feel a certain apprehension, thinking that it was getting a little out of hand. By the time my third brother celebrated passing the examination in the *kich'uk* year (1769), despite the natural joy I felt for his success, I grew deeply fearful of this truly immoderate power that the family was enjoying. I did not rejoice over it. Before long, our family suffered ruin. How can one not attribute this to excessive prosperity?

Now none of my nephews holds even the low degree granted to successful candidates in the preliminary examinations. Living in obscurity, you are not usefully employed. While this occasionally brings pangs of regret, I most emphatically do not wish members of our family ever to hold high office again. My sincere wish is that Father's loyalty be recognized, that future generations of the family be preserved, and that each member enjoy a peaceful life as a loyal subject. Serve the ruler with utmost devotion. By choosing to live in discreet obscurity, you shunned examinations and high office. Nonetheless, remain good affinal relations upon whom the royal house can rely. Do not damage the virtuous reputation of your ancestors and do not behave arrogantly. Be conscientious and honest in the execution of your duties of office. Attend the ancestral sacrifices with care; serve your widowed mother with filial affection. Be harmonious and friendly with members of the lineage. Respect your third and fourth grand uncles as you would your grandfather; serve your uncles as if they were your own father. Be generous and compassionate to your paternal aunt as if she were your mother, and guide and love your many younger cousins as though they were your own siblings. From the closest members of the family to the most distant relatives, attend to their needs with utmost care and consideration. Manage family affairs in such a way that relatives will praise the generosity of the main house. This is how to follow the wishes of your ancestors and to be a good descendant.

You are not young or immature, and so you must know all this. However, out of my concern for the family, I have written down these instructions and am giving them to you. Please be mindful of what I have said and do not be negligent. Now that your child is growing up, instruct him to be harmonious with the family. Caution your wife and children to attend the ancestral sacrifices with care and to choose the cleanest and the best sacrificial offerings. Maintain a clear distinction between your wife and your concubines so that order will prevail amidst harmony. The roles and the duties of each must be made clear so that there will be no confusion in family customs and tradition. Continue the good work of my parents and my older brother and restore our fallen family. I pray that the King will enjoy a long healthy life, that sage sons and godly grandsons will inherit the mantle, and that the dynastic house will continue for millions and billions of years. I also pray that my descendants, and those of my son, may flourish for generation upon generation, and that the family and the nation might enjoy peace.

Postscript

My parents had my older brother when they were quite young, and so they brought him up with strict discipline. My father was still in his youth and instructed his son with youthful zeal. In my childhood, I witnessed all this. My brother came to possess remarkable literary accomplishments and was renowned for his virtue and his impeccable manner. He always seemed able to retain in memory everything he read and heard. Discussing history, for instance, he could advance an argument on any point, citing numerous examples. When he saw me, he instructed me with tales of ancient and recent queens and royal consorts.

My older brother was quite uneasy over the conspicuous prosperity of the family. He said, "For an affinal family, the best way to preserve itself is to remain in lowly and inconspicuous posts. Now look at *chubu* or *pongsa*.* They are lowly and harmless posts that

* They were junior sixth and junior eighth ranks, respectively, in agencies that were basically sinecures.

one can obtain through royal favor without having to take the examinations. Your Ladyship should not rejoice over the prospering of your family." Even before my family became royal affines, we had not heard of anyone taking such low posts, and so, while I knew that what he said was correct in principle, I still laughed at it. Now I realize that he was prophetic.

My older brother had a dignified carriage and a handsome mien. He resembled Mother quite a bit, and so after my mother's death, I was particularly happy to see him. His Late Majesty had regarded him as "an official of unusual ability employable for high office." The present King viewed this uncle as his teacher. He grieved deeply when my brother died. The King has continued to think and speak of him a great deal. Afterwards, the King had my brother's collected works published.* Thus the King's esteem for him is manifest. Yet, despite his superior virtue and his remarkable accomplishments, my brother did not have time to completely fulfill his promise. He died while his aged father was still alive, committing a sin of unfiliality.† I am pained by this as well as by his unfulfilled talents!

When I left my family in the *kyehae* year (1743), my second and third brothers were, respectively, in their fifth and third years. Both were rather precocious, and they frequented the wedding pavilion as though they were older children. When they visited the palace after my wedding, His Late Majesty found them lovable. Whenever he saw them in my quarters, he took them around, placing them at the head of his procession. My late husband was quite young himself at the time. Restricted by palace custom, he had little chance to be with other young male children, and he was particularly overjoyed to be with my brothers. Thus, when my brothers came to the palace, he did not let them leave his side, even for a short time, and he showered them with affection. My brothers reciprocated. Young as they were, they also knew how to be respectful and loyal. They idolized him and followed him everywhere. Delighted, the Prince took them around with him, one on each side.

* Chŏngjo offered a sacrifice to Hong Nagin with a eulogy of his own composition in which he praised his uncle's virtues and his scholarship (see Chŏngjo, "Ch'amp'an Hong Nagin ch'ijemun," in *Hongjae chŏnsŏ*, 20:5b–6a). Hong Nagin, *Anwa yugo*, 3 *ch'aek*, was published under royal auspices in 1787. Chŏngjo wrote the preface.
† Dying while one's parents were alive was viewed as unfilial.

Their Highnesses, Queen Dowager Inwŏn and Queen Chŏng-sŏng, also took to my brothers. They often summoned them and bestowed gifts and kind words upon them. During my brothers' visits to the palace, they were often thrown in with the children of Lord Kyŏngŭn's family and those of Lord P'ungnŭng's[26] family. Once my brothers met Queen Hyosun's nephew, who happened to be about their age. One assumed that since they were similar in age, they would play together. My second brother, however, said to the boy, "You are a Soron and so we cannot play with you." My brother returned home. Upon hearing this, my mother scolded him. "It does not sound like a young child." I remember another episode when my second brother was about six or seven years old. Prince Sado happened to have a Crown Prince's coronet next to him, since he had just returned from a ceremony at the ancestral temple. The Prince picked it up and teased, "Should I put this on your head?" My brother grabbed his head with both hands and pleaded, "Oh, no. Please. A subject cannot wear that." Surprised that a child of that age was aware of such things, the Prince immediately stopped. But I noticed that my brother was covered with sweat. Compared with the children of today, one must say that he was quite mature.

My parents used to express their opinions of my two brothers thus: My second brother was wise, flexible, and versatile, and so would enjoy wealth. But my third brother was lofty, inflexible, and principled, and thus, although he might attain fame, he would live in poverty. The following anecdote fits this characterization.

Palace regulations prohibited boys over ten from sleeping over in the palace. Once Prince Sado summoned my third brother. When he reached the inner gate, the eunuchs guarding it must have said something impolite to him. Angry, my brother would not come in. In the end the Prince had to go out and get my brother himself. The Prince chided him gently, "If you are so stubborn and inflexible, how will you be able to help me?" Then he wrote something on a fan and gave it to him. How vividly I can picture this scene, as if it happened only yesterday. Really, though, my third brother was always gentle, obliging, and warm to me. He was my favorite brother.

In due course, my two younger brothers got married. Their wives were both of the Cho family and, in fact, were cousins. They were fine young ladies. My second brother's wife was sensible and gentle, and my third brother's wife was mild and friendly. My parents were pleased with them. Soon afterwards, however, my mother died. At the time, my second brother was in his seventeenth year and my third brother in his fifteenth year. In the depths of sorrow over losing Mother, I also felt sorry for my brothers, feeling that their entry into manhood was clouded by this loss.

My second brother passed the preliminary examination in *imo* (1762) and the final examination in *pyŏngsul* (1766). With evident pleasure, His Majesty said to me, "That child who used to give me a long herald's yea just passed the examination." He went on, "The Prime Minister did a good job of bringing up his son." When my second brother, as an official, read aloud from the classics, His Majesty clapped his hands and called out, "Well done, well done."

My father used to evaluate his sons' qualifications to the Grand Heir—Naksin was employable as Minister of Taxation, whereas Nagim was more suited to head the Office of Special Counselors or the Office of Royal Decrees. Then they jokingly concluded that, by some luck, he had managed not to entirely ruin his children, and they laughed together. But because of subsequent family misfortune, my brothers have retreated into obscurity. It is a pity that their talents have been wasted.

My second brother has a decisive personality. At one point he resolved not to participate in politics, feeling that he would only be contaminated by it. In the *kyŏngin* year (1770) he left the capital and settled in Samho, unwilling to go out into the world. However, he remained extremely considerate of others' needs. For instance, his filial attention left nothing to be desired during my father's stay at Samho. In *sinmyo* (1771) when Father was confined to Ch'ŏngju, he accompanied him there.

My third brother has been well behaved since he was very young. When he was five, his oldest brother got married and brought the bride home. Curious, many young and old members of the family often went to the bride's room. One would imagine that, with the curiosity of a child, this brother, too, might have entered his sister-in-law's chamber. Knowing that relations between brother-in-law and sister-in-law should be governed by strict propriety, he did not once go into that room. He never assumed a familiar or disrespectful attitude toward his elder sister-in-law and was always courteous to her. I remember my mother saying these things when she visited me at the palace.

My third brother was fond of learning. Precocious in his studies, he quickly passed the preliminary examination. Then he passed the palace examination at the top of the lists [1769], repeating the family tradition set by Grandfather. Grandfather left some calligraphy to be given to any descendant who might pass the examinations at the top. It was given to my brother, and he treasured it. It seemed as though the most brilliant future awaited him. But things went wrong, and he could not fulfill this promise. He was deeply ashamed that, fearing misfortune for the family, he concealed his true heart and befriended Hugyŏm. How often do I recall the moment in *kyŏngin* (1770) when my brother, having been repeatedly urged by me to associate with Hugyŏm to save the family, pledged that, once the threat was lifted, he would hide from the world. My father spent increasingly more time in the suburbs. My third brother decided to sell his town house and move to a place in the eastern suburb to sequester himself there for the remainder of his life. When the family suffered misfortune, my other brothers had no place to go, but my third brother had this place in the country. After the three-year mourning for Father was over, he finally settled at this place.

In the autumn of *sinmyo* (1771), while my brother was fretting about family troubles, he lost his worthy wife. This death, coming as it did in the midst of declining family fortunes, filled his home with sadness. The motherless children seemed so forlorn and the widower so lonely. My sister-in-law had been filial and affectionate to her husband's family. I grieved deeply for her. Since he had two sons, my brother decided not to remarry. He received two daughters-in-law in two successive years, and the household acquired a semblance of normal life. I hoped that at last they might reap the benefit of virtuous deeds sown by their deceased mother.

In the winter of *kabo* (1774), however, my brother's second son died. This sudden death was the first of its kind that occurred in the Hong family, and we feared that it might be an ominous sign. Now, with his brother's death, Ch'wiyŏng was left alone, and I pitied his lonely shadow. Possessing talents and character, Ch'wiyŏng has always been the hope of the family. There was no question that he was a treasure and his value in the family was as great as that of my oldest nephew, Suyŏng. Yet, that my brother should remain unmarried with only one son was not right. It would be too precarious. Father urged him to remarry. I also wrote many times urging him to change his mind. In the autumn of *ŭlmi* (1775) he finally remarried. Despite the worry and sadness he had borne, he was in good health. He fathered three sons from the second marriage. It must be due to his parents' accumulated virtue that he can have young children about him in his graying years.

My fourth—the youngest—brother* was born in the *kyŏngo* year (1750). Earlier in that year I gave birth to a child, and my mother, seven months pregnant, came into the palace and assisted in my delivery. I was exceedingly concerned over her condition, but in the last month of that year, my mother safely gave birth to a son. As a child begotten by my parents in their late years, my young brother was much indulged. His siblings also adored him, and whenever he came to the palace, I showered affection upon him. In *ŭrhae* (1755) he lost his mother. My fourth brother was only five, the age at which my father lost his mother. In my grief, the thought of this five-year-old brother's lonely plight tore my heart. He grew up under his grandmother's affectionate care. Not long after his marriage, his spouse died young from a strange illness. Then later that year, Grandmother died. My brother had regarded her as a mother, and so he must have felt this second loss deeply. He seemed to grieve so profoundly. Thoughts of this young brother of mine, whom I regarded more as a son than a brother, never really left me.

My fourth brother was serious and thoughtful, and in his youth, he acquired erudition. He was so remarkably kind and mature that it seemed that no one could turn their back on him. As family fortunes declined, however, he did not even take the preliminary examination. It is not that I prize passing the examination; it is just that I regret seeing such remarkable talents as his being wasted on an obscure mountainside. It seems that this brother has not seen that many good days. Born to older parents, he lost his mother at a very young age. He grew up during the pinnacle of the family's prosperity, but he personally reaped no benefit from it. When he reached about twenty years of age, the family fortunes declined and its members scattered. In addition to the family's plight, he had to bear the hidden sorrow of his marriage, which denied him the

* Hong Nagyun.

simple and ordinary joys of life.* I always sympathized with him particularly for this. He had children from his remarriage, however, and now he has grandchildren. This is all due to the accumulated good deeds of my parents.

When Father died in the midst of family misfortune, each of the children suffered profound grief. None of us had a real desire to live on, but none of us could follow him to death either. In the final analysis, we were all unfilial. In our grief, we hung our heads in deep shame. My third brother had purchased a house at Pŏlli. It was far from where his older brother lived, and they seemed always to miss each other. My second brother moved to Pŏlli, and the brothers came to live side by side with only a small stream separating them. This is something easier said than done and must have offered great solace to them in their waning years. Then, this year, my fourth brother moved his family to Pŏlli. Separated by a stream, the three brothers' houses stand like pines. These houses, consistent with the fortunes of the fallen family, have little with which to impress the observer. Nevertheless, my brothers have achieved their wish that they not be separated. Living within walking distance, they take solace and comfort in each other's company. I take great pleasure in this.

I have lived through many difficult and painful experiences. In addition to that unbearably painful event,† I had to bear the bitter death of my father and the premature death of my older brother. All these left me with little desire for life. However, I have always thought of my younger brothers and prayed for their health and peace. The news of their being near each other brought me deeply felt joy such as I have not experienced for a long time. I trust that my brothers' devotion to each other and their children's affection for one another will continue and that the loving harmony of the Hong family will rival that of Chang Kung-i of the T'ang dynasty.‡ I will take as much delight in this as my brothers and nephews will.

I was the only daughter, and so when I left for the palace, my parents were left with three sons. Missing me terribly, my parents

---

* Before marrying, his wife acquired a strange illness that prevented her from consummating the marriage. However, the wedding still took place. She died in 1766.
† Her husband's death in 1762.
‡ Chang Kung-i was famous for his brotherly affection.

wished for another daughter to ease the pain of having sent me off at such a young age. In the intercalary third month of *pyŏngin* year (1746), my sister was born. People usually prefer a boy, but my parents were overjoyed that it was a girl, feeling as though they had been given a special gift. In the atmosphere of joy and celebration in which the entire family congratulated one another, my parents named the baby. I, too, was delighted; I felt that some part of me had been returned to my parents. Before her first birthday, my sister was brought to the palace. How I immediately loved her! My parents indulged their new daughter; they treated her as a treasure in their palm.

My sister was a beautiful child, as beautiful as precious jade. She was very filial and affectionate, and she had an open disposition. She was also extremely bright and intelligent. In appraising her person, I had to admit to myself that she was superior to me. My sister, however, never showed a trace of arrogance or snobbishness, even though, being the family favorite, she was treated by her parents and siblings with special love and attention. Always polite and friendly, she was the joy of the whole family. My sister often came to stay at the palace. Whenever she came, His Majesty, King Yŏngjo; Their Two Royal Highnesses, Queen Dowager Inwŏn and Queen Chŏngsŏng; and Lady Sŏnhŭi all loved her. She was so perfect that ladies-in-waiting often compared her visage to a clear unblemished mirror. The beauty of her person can be understood from these comparisons. When she reached four or five years of age, she began to express a great sadness when she had to leave me to return home. Whenever she left, she sobbed uncontrollably, and this made it harder for me to bid her farewell. My sister was endowed with a filial nature, and she was never once disobedient to her parents, nor did she do anything that might have caused them to worry. In addition, she was respectful and affectionate to her older brothers. They all loved their little sister and treasured her. My older brother loved her even more than his own daughter, who became Madame Cho.

My mother used to come to assist me in childbirth. In the *kyŏngo* year (1750) my sister was about four, and she came with Mother. She behaved quite maturely. She waited with the others for the baby to be born. While she slept, the baby was born and the talk of it awoke her. She immediately got up and said, "His Majesty will be pleased, and Mother and Father will be very happy."

She said this in the manner of a grown-up, and everyone who heard it was amazed. My mother stayed on for some time to look after me. My sister developed a severe stomachache, and so she went home for a while. After her recovery she returned to the palace. That year my older brother had another daughter. Mother asked my sister about the newly hired wet nurse for this infant girl. She replied that the new nurse did not look very kind, and so probably would not be able to bring up the baby. She also calmly reported to Mother upon the poor state of health of our older brother's wife. Listening to her young daughter's report, Mother did not stop smiling. Obviously she was quite struck by the adult manner in which this girl of four described these matters. Very soon afterwards, the wet nurse did something bad and was sent away. Remembering what my sister had said about her, I thought it strange that she, at such a young age, had made an accurate judgment.

My sister looked up to me. When she visited the palace, she seldom left my side. From the time she learned to walk and talk, it seemed as though she was already remarkably considerate of others. There are many stories to prove this. In her frequent visits to the palace, she became acquainted with almost all of its inhabitants. One day she paid a visit to Queen Hyosun, who gave her a pendant that she took to always wearing. Then, in the *sinmi* year (1751), Queen Hyosun died. I did not see my sister until the second month of *imsin* (1752) when, because of certain problems concerning the state, my mother came to the palace accompanied by my sister. I noticed that my sister was not wearing the pendant that Queen Hyosun had given her, and so I asked her, "Why are you not wearing that pendant?" She replied, "Her Ladyship who gave it to me passed away. Somehow it seemed too sad to wear it." This reply brought smiles to everyone in the room. They all exclaimed that she was really very thoughtful and that she did not at all sound like a child. In the third month of that year, a tragedy struck.* When she saw me several months later, she greeted me with silent tears. Then she did the same for the wet nurse who had cared for the young Prince, holding her hands and shedding tears. My sister was six at the time. The nurse must have been deeply touched by this manifestation of sympathy from such a young child. Afterwards, she often spoke of it. How strangely mature my sister was.

* The death of Lady Hyegyŏng's first son, Ŭiso.

When Mother came for the delivery of the present King in the ninth month of the *imsin* year (1752), my sister also came. While she waited in the maternal quarters, she behaved just like an adult. When the King was born, she looked at him and said, "This Prince is sturdy and large. He will not cause worry to Her Ladyship." Everyone burst into laughter, saying how right she was. Mother also smiled but chided her a little: "You have some sense, but you sound too much like an adult. You should be more like a child."

"She is right—please don't scold her," I said in her defense. My sister never once failed to accompany Mother on her visits to the palace. How extraordinarily attached she was to me. Admittedly, younger sisters as a rule admire their older sisters, but I never saw anyone show such sisterly devotion as she.

At the age of nine, my sister lost her mother. She and my youngest brother were the same ages as my second aunt and my father had been in the *musul* year (1718) when they lost their mother. Why was such tragedy visited upon my family for two successive generations? How sad! My sister grieved deeply and conducted herself as a mourner. She pitied her young brother and tended to him with the thoughtfulness of an adult.

After the funeral, Grandmother took care of the boy, and my older sister-in-law looked after my sister. So as far as their daily needs were concerned, they were in good hands. But the image of these lonely and motherless children never really left me. My sister learned to read at a very young age. She was fond of reading and always carried books around with her. She often wrote to me, and her letters were so sad and full of remembrances of Mother that for each word I shed one tear. In the winter of *chŏngch'uk* (1757) my sister came to the palace to see me for the first time after Mother's death. She brought our youngest brother with her. We spoke of Mother and our sadness over losing her. We cried a lot and consoled each other. On this visit my sister read the novel *Yu Ssi samdae rok* (The record of the Yu family for three generations).[27] She was strangely affected by the sadness of the book. I attributed her response to her general melancholy.

I hoped that my beautiful sister would marry into an illustrious and virtuous family. She married in the *kimyo* year (1759). Her husband's family, the Yi, were closely related to the family that the cousin of my maternal grandmother had married into. Mother had attended her mother's cousin's sixtieth birthday feast and on that occasion had seen the boy whom her daughter later married. He did not come up to her high standards, and she rejected the proposal as unsuitable. After Mother's death, the suit was renewed, and as fate would have it, it was accepted. Elegant and serious, Mr. Yi[28] left nothing to be desired. But whenever I heard of my sister, I wondered whether she might have been undermatched.

She had children and she and her husband moved to a house of their own. She continued to be on most affectionate terms with Father. Her parents-in-law also loved her very well, and thus her life was peaceful. Her husband was a private scholar and so she lived in extreme frugality, but there was every reason to expect that the situation would improve. She was my only sister, and it was hoped that her family, under royal grace, would live in comfort. Then unexpectedly my family suffered decline. However, the calamity that befell her husband's family was far worse.* My sister, beautiful as jade, was cast into the mud. Among my concerns for the family, my thoughts of her took first place.

The law was very severe. My father obeyed the law strictly. So after my sister left the city accompanied by the other female members of her husband's family, though she lived in the country not far from where he resided, he never asked to see her. Since her birth, I had always been kept informed about her. After that unfortunate incident, she was removed from her city residence, and I was left completely uninformed about her. Unable to hear one word from her, I could not help lamenting her fate. With renewed force, I regretted that she, with such beauty and accomplishment, had not been fortunate in marriage and had suffered such a terrible predicament. It was like throwing a jade ornament into the mud or casting a bright jewel into the sea. How keenly Father, in the midst of his own troubles, must have felt for his younger daughter! His sympathy for her could not have been any less than mine, nor could her own sadness have been less profound.

My sister had truly admirable feminine virtues. She carried out all the mourning rituals for her father-in-law. She devotedly served the older ladies of the family, sent regularly whatever her husband

---

* Her husband's father was implicated in a seditious plot. This meant that her husband, as the son of a traitor, was also banished. As a criminal's wife, Lady Hyegyŏng's sister had to live in seclusion, having no communication with the outside world.

needed at his place of banishment, and kindly looked after a number of her husband's younger siblings. In her devotion to her husband's family, she must have surpassed the legendary Madame Chen.* I never heard of anyone so devoted. Then, in *musul* (1778), we bid our eternal farewell to Father. He had been thinking of his unfortunate daughter for three years. That he died in unrequited concern for her caused me to grieve all the more. I was simply inconsolable and fell into a bottomless abyss of sorrow. Both my sister and I had received particular love and help from Father and had caused him deep worry and anguish. In this, we were both unfilial, but perhaps she was slightly less unfilial than I. Father's death must have left my sister completely forlorn and deserted. My older brother had died already. She must have wondered whether she could depend on anyone to receive further support.

My second brother was filial and affectionate to his siblings. He sought to manage the household just as Father had. Neglecting nothing, he supplied his sister with everything that he thought she needed. Granted, he did this for his sister, but such brotherly love is something rare in this age of decline. My sister-in-law was as compassionate as was her husband. Discerning her husband's thoughts, she did all she could for his sister as if she could never do enough. If not for this couple, my sister might not have been able to sustain herself.

Fortunately, on the felicitous occasion of the birth of the royal heir in *imin* (1782),† my sister's husband was released from banishment under a special amnesty. This was indeed a great royal kindness. The King did this solely to comfort his aunt. My sister must have felt the immensity of royal grace. I also felt an incomparable joy for her sake. The reunion of husband and wife is a principle as natural as Heaven and Earth. I wished them a peaceful and healthy life together. My sister became pregnant from that month and bore three children in five years. Her health had deteriorated during her years of adversity; her liver and stomach had problems and she had no energy. After her childbirths, she became gravely ill, traversing the space between life and death. Though far

---

* Madame Chen was an exemplary, filial daughter-in-law who lived during the Han dynasty. After her husband's death, she served her mother-in-law with devotion for twenty-eight years. See *Oryun haengsil to* (Seoul: Ŭryu munhwasa, 1972), 37–38, I:5–6.

† The birth of Chŏngjo's first son, Munhyo.

away, I was deeply worried. However, Heaven took cognizance of her accumulated good deeds, and she recovered.

Despite destitution and poverty, my sister is blessed in her family. Her children, one after another, reached adulthood and married. Her daughters-in-law and sons-in-law are as fine as they can be, and there are numerous grandchildren. If that one word of stigma* were to be removed from them, then she would be thought to be a person blessed by fortune. Stigmatized as they are, however, my sister's children cannot aspire to serve in office. This remains beyond their reach. How regrettable! On the other hand, the King did so much for them. Although the King let the name of my sister's father-in-law remain on the list of traitorous criminals, he nevertheless made a special provision that his aunt's family be treated with courtesy. The King knows that my sister is always on my mind, and out of respect for my feelings, he makes every possible allowance for his aunt.

This past spring, after our visit to Hwasŏng, the King bent the laws of the nation and allowed me a reunion with my sister. This was such an extraordinarily thoughtful and generous gesture, truly rare among the rulers of a thousand years. The sisters were moved and grateful beyond measure, but my private rejoicing was overshadowed by an apprehension that this might cause a slackening of the law. I even considered declining this favor, but I decided to make no protest. I knew that the King was determined to grant any wish his mother desired, and that he created the opportunity for this reunion of sisters because he wished me to have no regret. Thus, after twenty years of longing and dreams of my sister, I saw her.

When we had parted, the older sister was middle-aged and the younger sister was barely past thirty. Then there we were, a sixty-year-old woman gazing upon her fifty-year-old younger sister. Twenty years of life in difficulty had taken its toll. Her once young face had changed and her beauty was, for the most part, gone. Glad to see her, yet regretful of the changes, I clasped her hand, silently shedding tears. We rubbed each other's cheeks and cried again. We told each other our stories. Sad and joyful words were exchanged as if a tangled thread was being unraveled. Before we fully shared our experiences, five or six days had quickly passed and

---

* The word is *yŏk*, meaning traitorous. The descendants of those convicted of treason were not allowed to serve in government.

we had to part again. There had been times when we entertained little hope of a reunion in this life. But, knowing that this would mostly likely be our final parting, our farewell was harrowing.

After she left, I wondered whether I saw her in real life or in a dream. Then I thought of how she must have been feeling. She has passed her fiftieth birthday. Many scenes from her childhood came to me—my parents' delight at her birth, her happy days with them, her many visits to the palace where she was adored and loved by everyone. These days were but a dream. Now she lived in hiding in a remote village with very little hope of days in the sun. Acting in profound sympathy, the King has already established that her father-in-law's true intention [was not traitorous]. If the sun and moon of royal generosity were to shine upon her again and that one word, "traitorous," were to be erased from her family history, her wishes and my happiness for her will have been completely fulfilled. From the depths of my heart, I wish that Heaven will ascertain her virtuous heart, let her days of sorrow end, and permit her to live out her remaining days in conjugal harmony and familial joy so that her furrowed brow may be smoothed in contentment. I also hope that a time will come when she is referred to as one full of blessing.

I have two uncles, the third and the fourth brothers of my father, who are of an age near mine. We grew up together in the same house. Unlike most uncles and nieces, we were very close. The fourth uncle was but a year older than me, and I was particularly fond of him. When he read books aloud, I used to sit by him and do counting for him. My grandmother, as befit her virtue, did not discriminate between her sons and the sons by the first wife or between grandsons and granddaughters. She loved us all equally. My mother practically brought up her young brothers-in-law. Thus she felt a certain motherly tenderness toward them. I naturally felt sisterly affection for these uncles.

My third uncle was very fond of me and always gave me toys and playthings. His marriage took place after I left for the palace, so I did not have many occasions to see his wife. Nevertheless, I heard the whole family singing the praises of her excellent conduct. Unfortunately, she died in her prime. She was the third woman in the family to have met an early death since the *ŭrhae* year (1755).* The absence of a wise mistress created unhappiness and desola-

* The year Lady Hyegyŏng's mother died.

tion in my uncle's home. For a long time, I could not see my cousins. When I finally saw them last year and this year, I was struck by how each grew to be a beautiful scholar. I cannot describe the depths of my feeling in seeing close relatives after so many years of separation.

My fourth uncle had shown exceptional talent for scholarship since early childhood and was frequently mentioned as a man of great promise. This was not to be, however. The family met misfortune, and he turned his back on the world and spent his days sequestered in the mountains. Although, out of private affection, I feel a tinge of regret for this, my public spirit does admire his resoluteness. Though poor, my uncle and aunt have grown old together and have celebrated their sixtieth birthdays together. This was a felicity that my family has not known, and I look upon it as a true blessing. It is a little sad that their two sons, despite exceptional accomplishments, are not employed. But my cousins take pleasure in their parents' company. Blessed with sons of their own, they contentedly serve their old parents with devotion. I do not think my uncle and aunt can be freed of the sorrows of the Hong family, yet their private life is full. They can be called King Fenyang* of the mountains and forests.

My fourth aunt was my cousin on my mother's side. We had been playmates from infancy and developed a special affection for one another. Since those misfortunes befell the Hong family, members of my family have rarely visited the palace. Thus I did not see her for a long time, and her face and voice lived only in my memory. Then I saw her this spring at Hwasŏng. How happy I was to see her again! I was especially glad to see that, despite a life of poverty and difficulty, she showed no decline in spirit or in health.

My father's oldest sister died young and her children did not fare well. Remembering how devoted Father had been to his sisters, I was troubled by my cousins' bad luck. Then my male cousin, the last of my paternal aunt's children, died with no issue. I felt quite sad and empty to see my aunt's family come to an end like that.

After my grandfather, Lord Chŏnghŏn, died in *kyŏngsin* (1740), my family experienced difficulties making ends meet. My father's second oldest sister was very affectionate to her natal family. She

---

* Kuo Tzu-i of T'ang China. He was reputed to have had a hundred sons and a thousand grandchildren, and he became a symbol of familial happiness.

was devoted to her stepmother and was fond of my mother as if she were her own sister. She helped us on many occasions. I remember particularly one period of dire straits between *imsul* and *kyehae* (1742–1743), after the three-year mourning for Lord Chŏnghŏn. We frequently awaited provisions from my second aunt so that we could cook and heat the house. She dearly loved her siblings, and she loved their children as though they were her own. She was born with a generous spirit that rendered her unable to harbor resentment. Her blessings were also great. Indeed, her fortunes seemed to be without equal in this world. Even while my son was Crown Prince, she received honors and the special regard of the court. One morning a calamity befell her. The magnitude of the misfortune was truly great; her world disappeared like smoke.* I have always felt terrible for this aunt.

My father's younger sister lost her mother when she was barely a year old. Thus, when she lost her mother, she was even younger than any of us when we lost ours. Father was particularly solicitous of his little sister. Nevertheless, events occur and situations change. There were a number of incidents that could have led to the lessening of harmony between them, but Father showed no perturbation, remaining absolutely constant in his affection. She also responded with sisterly devotion. Then the fortunes of her family were in decline, and, for a period, my aunt suffered misery and difficulty. Then last year Lord Cho was posthumously cleared of all charges and declared innocent. My aunt, once again in royal grace, visited me at the palace. This spring she headed the list of woman guests attending my sixtieth birthday celebration at Hwasŏng. By now she was one year short of eighty, but she was incredibly strong and healthy. I was, of course, very pleased to see her in such good health. At the same time, she made me think of Father, who died before he was seventy, and I could not help but shed tears. My aunt was truly amazing. Her movements remained as nimble as those of a young woman. Her clear features, her thoughtful and understanding attitude, and her quick and clever wit had not at all diminished. I was all admiration.

My older brother and his wife had five children who reached adulthood, each more talented and handsome than the next. It

---

* The exact nature of this calamity cannot be ascertained. One assumes that it must have been a particularly sharp political misfortune.

seemed that my sister-in-law was the most fortunate of women. Then two daughters, Madame Pak and Madame Song, died in succession. Their deaths were followed by other sudden deaths.* Visited by such tragedies in her late age, how deep her grief must have been! She seemed to grow much older than her years in a short time, and the family was deeply concerned over her. With the main branch of the family so diminished, Suyŏng seemed so lonely. But Suyŏng and his sister, Madame Cho, have been extremely supportive of each other. Together they serve their widowed mother attentively. I do so wish for a healthy and peaceful old age for my sister-in-law.

As a child, Madame Cho used to come to the palace frequently in the company of my sister, and even now she comes rather often. Whenever I see this niece, I think of my sister and my heart grows sad. The King also displays a particular generosity toward her, and she feels deeply indebted to royal grace. My niece is warm and gentle, and in her elegant beauty, she resembles her mother. She cuts a figure superior to the other affinal women. The whole court murmurs in praise of her and does not think of her as an outsider. She is nearing her fiftieth year. Though she is not a man, she has assumed the role of leader of her generation in the family and has discharged her social obligations admirably. I believe that in her I have, at a distance, someone who understands my thoughts and feelings, and I feel a special kinship for her. She has not produced a son, and whenever I see her worried look, I am deeply touched.

When I was selected as the Crown Princess Consort, I brought several servants with me—grandmother's slave, Haenyŏ, and her younger sister, Pongnyŏ, and another slave belonging to the wife of my father's second brother. Pongnyŏ was a slave who had been awarded to Father by my great grandmother after he passed the preliminary examination. At the time, Aji and her sister were also awarded. Aji later became my wet nurse and breast-fed me until I was four. Although she was on my family's slave register, she did not do menial chores and acted more like a woman of a better station. After I was weaned, my mother, not particularly liking her manners, made arrangements for her to live out. At the time of my departure for the palace, it was thought proper to send the wet

---

* Hong Nagin, her husband, died in 1777. Then the wife of Suyŏng, her oldest son, died. This was followed by the sudden death of her second son, Ch'oeyŏng.

nurse along, and so she was made to accompany me. Her character was honest, sincere, loyal, and diligent. Though she was sickly, she looked after me during my several pregnancies and childbirths. She lived long and rendered the same service and care to my two daughters during their childbirths. She came into the palace and eagerly helped in the maternity ward as late as the auspicious occasion of the *imin* (1782) birth. The number of childbirths in my family at which she assisted comes to about twenty altogether. In recognition of her service, the King had her descendants settle in a village on comfortable annuities. He always treated her generously and cordially. Indeed, the royal favor bestowed upon her was far more than what a person of low station can usually hope for. She died in her eighty-first year. Remembering my indebtedness to her and her long service, I was deeply saddened. The King sent a very generous contribution toward her funeral to express his appreciation of the fact that she had reared me. In his filial concern, there is nothing that the King does not think of.

As for Pongnyŏ, she has not been separated from me since *ŭl-myo* (1735).* When I was a child, she played with me. During the first selection in the *kyehae* year (1743), she was eighteen. She came to the palace with me and carried me on her back up and down the stairs. She subsequently accompanied me to the wedding pavilion and became my lady-in-waiting. Despite her low birth, she has served me with total devotion. Indeed, she would even have suffered fire or water for me, if need be. After my marriage in *kapcha* (1744), there were endless difficulties manifested in a thousand ways. Pongnyŏ dealt with each at my side. Despite her low birth, she is bright, tactful, and sincere. I trust her and rely upon her. During my four childbirths, she took care of all my meals and medicines. If something troubles me, she notices it immediately. When my mother was alive, she relied on Pongnyŏ to see to it that I did not overexert myself and that I received enough rest. Pong-nyŏ's devotion extends to my children, the King, the two princesses, and their children as well. She still attends assiduously to the needs of all of us. This is quite an extraordinary show of loyalty. I find it moving and praiseworthy.

There was a case in the previous reign in which a lady-in-waiting had received an official rank. It was the lady-in-waiting whom

* The year of Lady Hyegyŏng's birth.

Queen Dowager Inwŏn had brought with her at the time of her marriage, and it was granted to her soon after Queen Dowager Inwŏn's funeral in *chŏngch'uk* (1757). This was the first time that this had happened and everyone remarked how great was that honor. As a reward for Pongnyŏ's faithful and diligent service during the felicitous birth in *imin* (1782), the King awarded her an official rank. This was truly an extreme honor. Then after the felicitous birth in *kyŏngsul* (1790),* the King elevated her to the position of Palace Matron. This was an honor far beyond what a lowly woman might expect. When Pongnyŏ was given the official rank, I was not too uncomfortable as there had been a precedent for this in the person of the lady-in-waiting to Queen Dowager Inwŏn. But I considered Pongnyŏ's elevation to Palace Matron rather excessive and asked the King to rescind it. Praising her loyal service, he confirmed his order. Now that the King thus commended the lowly person whom I had brought with me, and the Queen treated her generously, accrediting her with meritorious service, there was nothing she could do but accept the royal kindness in humble gratitude. There was nothing I could do either, except concur. I have not heard of a case in which a servant of the natal family who accompanied her mistress to the palace remained to serve till her death. As for Pongnyŏ, she has accompanied me from *kyehae* (1743) and saw me through until I reached sixty years of age. One must admit that she has rendered meritorious service.

* The birth of Sunjo.

The Memoir of 1801

Princess Hwap'yŏng was Lady Sŏnhǔi's first daughter and His Majesty loved her above all his other children. Of a mild and kindly disposition, the Princess showed not the slightest trace of arrogance. Uncomfortable and distressed that she alone was showered with paternal affection while her brother, the Crown Prince, was not, the Princess pleaded ceaselessly with her father, "Please do not be like that." Whenever the Prince was in dire straits, she could not rest, as if nothing else mattered to her until things improved for him. There were many occasions on which His Majesty's anger was appeased through the Princess. The Prince was deeply grateful to this sister and relied upon her in all matters. It is no exaggeration to say that, until her death in the *mujin* year (1748), the Prince was protected mostly by Princess Hwap'yŏng. Had she lived and had she continued to labor for harmony between father and son, much benefit would have accrued from it. Unfortunately, she died young. His Majesty was completely brokenhearted, even inconsolable, over her death.* He had always loved Princess Hwawan, that is Madame Chŏng, next to Princess Hwap'yŏng; disconsolate over Princess Hwap'yŏng's death, he shifted his parental affections to Madame Chŏng. The extraordinary care and

---

* Yŏngjo even changed his place of residence in order to be near the location of Princess Hwap'yŏng's funerary observances. JaHyun Kim Haboush, *A Heritage of Kings: One Man's Monarchy in the Confucian World* (New York: Columbia University Press, 1988), 164.

attention that His Majesty now showered upon this young daughter is more than I can describe.

At the time, Madame Chŏng was only ten years old, and as a young child shielded deep within the palace, she knew little more than children's games. Still, there was Lady Sŏnhŭi, her mother, who provided guidance. Moreover, her husband Chŏng Ch'idal, Lord Ilsŏng, was a man of honor, the offspring of a family of distinguished ministers that knew propriety. He was eager to express his devotion to the Crown Prince. I have a feeling that Lord Ilsŏng was embarrassed and uneasy over the royal affection that was so concentrated upon his wife but not upon the Prince. Thus he coached his wife in correct behavior; as a result, though Madame Chŏng behaved peculiarly later, she did Prince Sado no harm. She made it possible for the Prince to accompany royal visits to tombs and, using[1] every means available, succeeded in obtaining royal permission for the Prince's trip to Onyang. Many indeed were the perilous situations in which she came to her brother's rescue, concealing much on his behalf. My disaffection toward her and her later dishonor* should not prevent me from acknowledging the truth. Had Lord Ilsŏng not died so early and had Madame Chŏng borne several children and partaken of the joys of family life, it is quite possible that she would not have stayed on at the palace, engaging in those endless schemes and intrigues.

After she was widowed, His Majesty did not wish her to live outside the palace, and so he had her stay nearby. Father and daughter were inseparable and it seemed as though power flowed from her. After the *imo* year (1762) there was no one of any importance in the palace, and after Lady Sŏnhŭi's death, no one could provide guidance for her. Nor was there anyone in her husband's family but a young adopted son. This meant that she had no one to fear or to be careful of. Meanwhile, His Majesty's affection for his young daughter increased daily. Her ambitions grew and she became willful.

Madame Chŏng was of a rather exceptional disposition for a woman. She was fiercely competitive, jealous, envious, and very fond of power. She wrought much havoc, of which I will provide several conspicuous examples. Wishing to be the sole object of her father's affection, she was jealous even of her father's attentions to

* In 1778 she was punished for misdeeds during Yŏngjo's reign.

a lady-in-waiting. She kept the Grand Heir in her palm, not letting him out of her sight even for a moment. Wishing to act as his mother, she did not like the fact that I was the Grand Heir's mother. Envious that I might be a queen mother upon his accession, she concocted that royal decree of *kapsin* (1764).*

Jealous that the Grand Heir might enjoy the intimacy of his consort, she used a hundred slanders and a thousand invectives to turn husband against wife, and she succeeded in causing them to become permanently estranged. Nor was she pleased at the thought that the Grand Heir might become intimate with a lady-in-waiting; she did not allow him to look at a woman, lest a son be born to him. She shunned the Grand Heir's maternal relatives and, with evil and cunning schemes, sowed in him seeds of suspicion and mistrust so that he might be unkindly disposed toward them. This was the event of the *kich'uk* year (1769) concerning the palace servants. If the Grand Heir was fond of his father-in-law, then it was Lord Ch'ŏngwŏn of whom she was jealous; when he studied the *History of Sung Dynasty* (*Songsa*), then even that book became the object of her jealousy. The law she followed was this: in all things, she alone should have power, that all might be obliged to follow her. None were to have any say in the smallest thing. What kind of person was this? And all of this was bound up with the fortunes of the nation. It is impossible to fathom Heaven's design: how could Heaven let the calamity of that year occur?[†] It almost led to the ruin of the dynasty. Why did Heaven produce this strange woman, and why did it permit her to wreak havoc as ministers and officials were eaten like fish and meat?

The causes of the calamity of that year arose from the unnatural relationship between father and son, a relationship that worsened, drawing them to that end. That was the memory etched into my heart; that was the source of my bitterness and my deepest regrets. His Majesty had treated his own son thus; there was no way to know what he might wreak upon his grandson, who was still more distant.

Moreover, Kwiju[‡] showed every sign of wishing to harm me and

---

* The decree that made the Grand Heir, later Chŏngjo, an adopted son of Prince Hyojang.
  † Prince Sado's death in 1762.
  ‡ Kim Kwiju, the brother of Queen Chŏngsun.

my family. If, perchance, the Grand Heir failed to please His Majesty's sagacious heart, then what might happen? It was Madame Chŏng who held the key to the Grand Heir's safety and His Majesty's sagacious heart. Thus, when the Grand Heir and I lived in separate palaces, I entreated her that no matter what happened, she must see to it that the Grand Heir not contravene His Majesty's sagacious intentions. I also warned my son, "Look up to your aunt. Please be respectful and kind to her just as you would be toward me." Constrained as I was, my maternal anguish and pain must have moved her. For a time, she sympathized with me. She cooperated with me in every detail, speaking of the Grand Heir to His Majesty only in the best possible light. His Majesty unquestioningly accepted his daughter's opinions on everything. If someone had faults but she said that he was perfect, then His Majesty would follow her, and if someone were good and she reproved him, then His Majesty would cast him out. Thus, while His Majesty had loved the Grand Heir from the beginning, that he did not change in his affections toward his grandson after that year* may be attributed in great measure to Madame Chŏng. But in order to dominate the Grand Heir, as I have said, she displayed hundreds, even thousands of peculiarities. Had I not treated her with the utmost care and patience for my son's sake, there is no telling what might have happened.

Once, in the *chŏngch'uk* year (1757), a groundless rumor circulated to the effect that Prince Sado was about to kill Lord Ilsŏng. At the time, the Prince had no such intention. My father asked for an audience with the Prince and, recounting what he had heard, advised, "Please find a way to restrain yourself." The Prince assured him, "I never wished to do it." The Prince then wrote to Chŏng Hwiryang, Lord Ilsŏng's uncle, reassuring him that the rumor was utterly baseless and requesting that he put Lord Ilsŏng at ease. Chŏng Hwiryang was profoundly moved by this considerate gesture. Afterwards, in *sinsa* (1761), when the Prince made a trip to P'yŏngyang in secret without seeking His Majesty's permission,† Chong attended to his every need, and later, when the trip was discovered, he helped to calm the furor. At any rate, the two families became quite friendly. Chŏng Hwiryang now and

---

* 1762.
† For details, see *The Memoir of 1805*, 302–4.

then spoke to Madame Chŏng, his nephew's wife, saying how kind my father had been and advising her to serve me with sisterly affection. Madame Chŏng was particularly good to Father, often remarking on his kindness.

After Chŏng Hwiryang died, the family had no senior person, and Madame Chŏng said to me, "I trust that your honorable father will teach and guide Hugyŏm into maturity." She requested that, on her behalf, I ask my father to do this. In addition to being kind, Father was well aware that it was impolitic not to abide by her wishes, and so he regularly spent time instructing Hugyŏm. What he most feared for the boy was that he might fall in with evil companions. When he heard people speaking critically of Hugyŏm, or when he heard rumors that the boy, with no senior member of his family to guide him, had befriended rakish sorts, in sincere concern my father admonished him on several occasions. He also brought the matter to Madame Chŏng's attention, saying that he heard such and such and suggesting that it would be better if her son did not do such and such.

Hugyŏm was a frightfully audacious little thing from the time he was very young. Taking advantage of his mother's power, he grew arrogant and reckless. He would not heed my father's admonitions, since they came from one who was not even a kinsman. I suspected that he said terrible things about my father to Madame Chŏng because he resented my father for having disparaged him to his mother. Being extremely competitive, Madame Chŏng did not wish to hear anything uncomplimentary spoken of her son. I detected a noticeable change in her attitude toward us. Feeling that the enterprise was rather futile, I said to Father, "Though they say they want you to instruct him, they are not of the same family. Admonitions delivered with the best of intentions may cause bad blood. Perhaps it is better not to concern yourself with Hugyŏm any longer." Father ceased advising him. Not long afterwards, Hugyŏm passed both the preliminary and the final civil examinations in succession[2] and, as the son of a beloved daughter, instantaneously became a great favorite of His Majesty. Day by day, as royal affection for him grew, many sought him out and flocked to him. In fact, Kwiju went over to Hugyŏm and opposed my family.

Between *imo* (1762) and *kapsin* (1764), Lady Sŏnhŭi guided the Grand Heir with strict decorum and stern admonitions on every occasion, wishing exactly as did I, that he would grow to be good and virtuous. This bored the child. I, too, with the devotion of a mother, did mostly tiresome things to him—keeping watch over his conduct, pointing out unflattering things, and so on. By temperament, I am not good at saying pleasing words to people. When it came to my own children, what sweet words would I have spoken?

In the meantime, his paternal aunt was someone who had in her palm the power of life and death, disaster and prosperity. Whether one was favored and fortunate or condemned and cast out depended upon what issued from her mouth. Her wishes were carried out within minutes. How could the Grand Heir not fear her? Thus, in the course of following and fearing the powerful, he grew attached to his aunt. Madame Chŏng was not satisfied with this, however. She wished to alone dominate the Grand Heir and to be as a mother to him. Before *kapsin* (1764) the Grand Heir was under his grandmother's wing, so his aunt could not very well use her wiles. But when Lady Sŏnhŭi passed away, Madame Chŏng had no one to worry about. She could do as she pleased. After *ŭryu* (1765) she resorted to all sorts of schemes to destroy our familial love.

The first of her wiles was to greatly praise the Grand Heir to His Majesty so that royal affection would increase visibly. As she had intended, this impressed the Grand Heir so that he came to feel a particular regard for his aunt. Then she showered him with such things as beautifully quilted clothes, embroidered shoes, fine swords, and all kinds of delicacies. Many of these were not customarily available in the palace, and so they brought special delight to the young Prince. Beyond the food usually available at the palace, I had no special delicacies. My father, having no interest in such things, was even less acquainted with them. He never thought of offering clothes, food, or toys to his royal grandchild. Thus, in the Grand Heir's experience, his mother only criticized and admonished him, while his maternal relations did not display any affection in obvious ways by showering him with extravagant gifts. To the child's mind, his mother and her family appeared dull, and his affection for them gradually diminished, while his aunt gained proportionately in his esteem and affections.

From about the winter of the *ŭryu* year (1765), one could sense the strain. If, for example, the Grand Heir were sitting across the

dinner table from his aunt and partaking of delicacies and I happened to come in, he seemed to feel uneasy, wondering "What
would Mother say of my sharing this table?" or "What would
Mother think of this food?" It was not that he wished to conceal
things from me, but he was uncomfortable with what I might
think. He subtly but unmistakably expressed an inclination to ex-
clude me from some aspects of his life. The Grand Heir was a child
of twelve or thirteen at the time, and so he cannot be blamed. But
as for her, if she possessed a human heart, she would not have behaved in that way. The Grand Heir was the son of her late brother
[who had died so tragically], and the child, who was the only reason for my existence, had been entrusted to her because of a
unique and difficult situation. Had she acted in accordance with
the demands of human emotion and Heavenly principle, out of
sympathy for our pitiful plight and sharing my concern, she would
have instructed and assisted him in virtue. On the contrary, she
schemed and plotted to alienate son from mother. How evil-
minded and odious this was. Yet I behaved as if I were oblivious to
what was going on. I said nothing.

In the spring of *pyŏngsul* (1766), His Majesty was in ill health for
more than a month. He moved to the Queen's residence, Hoesang
Pavilion, and there Madame Chŏng and the Grand Heir tended
him day and night. I paid only brief visits to His Majesty, and so I
remained ignorant of what took place. It was at about this time
that Hugyŏm and Kwiju got together. The Queen treated the
Grand Heir quite nicely, and Madame Chŏng, wishing to scheme
against me, joined forces with the Queen. That Kwiju really wanted
to befriend Hugyŏm facilitated the matter. In this atmosphere,
words slandering my father were somehow spoken to His Majesty,
but these words could not make even a crack in the trusting and
affectionate relationship that His Majesty and my father had built
over so long a period. Then Father suffered the loss of his stepmother, and so he retired from court to observe a three-year
mourning for her. This was a long time. It certainly was not like
having a daily audience with His Majesty. Taking advantage of his
absence, venomous tongues wagged and countless calumnies were
hurled against him.

In the *muja* year (1768), Hugyŏm wanted to be appointed
Magistrate of Suwŏn. At the time, the Prime Minister was Kim
Ch'iin. I received a request [from Madame Chŏng] asking that my

father put in a good word for Hugyŏm with the Prime Minister. I wrote to Father, relaying the message. His reply was, "It is not that I grudge putting in a word for someone. But I feel that to recommend a youth not yet twenty* for a post which commands five thousand cavalry would be to fail in one's duty to the nation. Nor do I think it is the way to cherish the youth himself." Thus he refused to speak to the Prime Minister about it.

Now Hugyŏm was coming into his own.† He was sought after and wielded considerable power. Many things set him against my father—his previous dealings with Father, the story of the Suwŏn post, and various other things. Madame Chŏng grew very close to the Queen and they seemed devoted to each other. Thus Kwiju, his father, and Hugyŏm were all in one camp and together they wished to harm Father.

After Father had completed the mourning period, His Majesty recalled him to the State Council, displaying to his old minister the trust and affection he had always shown. Although this boundless royal grace was profoundly moving, it deepened the aversion that clique held for my father. Influenced by Hugyŏm and Kwiju, Madame Chŏng completely ceased making homage to my father. Instead, daily she spoke of him in invectives. As the common saying has it, "There is no tree that does not fall after ten blows." Gradually, royal trust lessened.

There was one incident through which they managed to turn the hearts of the people and to reduce my family to this current state. In the *pyŏngsul* year (1766), Hŭngŭn was chosen as the husband of my daughter, Ch'ŏngsŏn. He had a beautiful mien and an elegant carriage. The Grand Heir was quite taken by this new brother-in-law. Around *kich'uk* (1769), Hŭngŭn fell into dissolute behavior. Accompanied by palace servants, he frequented courtesans. He seems to have openly and heedlessly spoken of these things to the Grand Heir, who, with the curiosity of a young boy, accepted his brother-in-law's talk with alacrity. Since the Grand Heir's residence, Hŭngjŏng Hall, was very distant from mine, I was completely ignorant of these events. Hŭngŭn was serving in

---

* Hugyŏm was in his nineteenth year.
† Chŏng Hugyŏm was appointed Magistrate of Kaesŏng in 1769. *Yŏngjo sillok* (hereafter *YS*), in *Chosŏn wangjo sillok*, 113:6b.

office, and when he was on duty at the palace, he went to the Grand Heir's residence to pay respect and to amuse him.

At the time, Madame Chŏng controlled the Grand Heir as though he were a marionette. She did not allow him an inch of freedom. She made it impossible for the Grand Heir to be intimate with his wife. Jealous of the Grand Heir's generosity toward his wife's family, Madame Chŏng was eager to create a chasm between them. But it happened that Ch'ŏngwŏn's second cousin, Kim Sangmuk, befriended Hugyŏm and was in fact acting as the brains of that group. In consideration for Sangmuk, they decided to let the Kims alone for the time being and instead assault the Grand Heir's maternal family. Madame Chŏng naturally resented the Grand Heir's affection for his brother-in-law, Hŭngŭn. With cunning plans designed to shoot two objects with one arrow, one night she came to see me.

In a confidential and affectionate manner, she said, "The Grand Heir is so fascinated by Hŭngŭn that he is not himself. At the party the other day, for instance, the Grand Heir made Hŭngŭn talk about the beautiful courtesans he had seen outside and had him point out a courtesan with whom he had been intimate. Hŭngŭn also told the Grand Heir about the women with whom palace servants were keeping company. Many things of this sort are going on now. This cannot be! Think of what happened [to your husband]. It all began with the evil influence of palace servants who led him astray. The Grand Heir is still only a boy. If he constantly hears those stories, and if, admiring that foolish Hŭngŭn, he begins to frequent those quarters, where might it lead? Unless something is done to put a stop to it, His Majesty will hear of it. The incident of that year could recur. This humble person has been entrusted by Your Ladyship with the guidance of the Grand Heir, and it is her belief that we must put an end to it now. However, if it were known that it was this humble person who brought this matter up, she would have a problem [with the Grand Heir]. Her solitary child might even get hurt by it. Only because of her concern for the country and because she feels that duty dictates it, this humble person reluctantly informs Your Ladyship. So please pretend that Your Ladyship learned of this elsewhere. The best thing would be merely to banish those palace servants and to do it very quietly. Since the Prime Minister is the Grand Heir's maternal grandfather, he can, from his position, easily admonish the young Prince. It is also entirely in accordance with legal procedure for your honorable father to punish palace servants." Seeming genuinely concerned for the nation and sincerely anxious for the Grand Heir, Madame Chŏng went over things in minute detail.

My bitterest and most persistent regret over Prince Sado was the thought that he went astray because no one intervened and he was left under the sway of palace servants. How sincerely did I pray that the Grand Heir would be good! Now Madame Chŏng was saying these things. I took her completely at her word. I thought that she was voicing her concern for his sake because she loved him. I never suspected that she was scheming to alienate my son from me and to sow in him ill-feeling toward his grandfather. Those words, "the incident of that year could recur," were just too alarming. Moreover, knowing her as I did, I knew that if I were not to take her seriously enough and not to immediately attempt to correct the situation, it would be like her to stir things up just to show that she was right. Then His Majesty might hear of it, and that would lead to much turmoil.

Chagrined by Hŭngǔn, I declared that I would speak to my son requesting that he cease these activities. But she said, "Please don't rush in like that. Proceed slowly, making certain that it does not turn into a big fuss. Write to the Prime Minister asking him to punish the palace servants. Not even his children or his brothers should hear of it. It would be best to ask the Grand Heir Consort to hand the note to her father, Minister Kim, who could then pass it to the Prime Minister. But please do it secretly and cautiously and make certain that these scoundrels are gotten rid of." This suggestion was probably a scheme to involve Ch'ŏngwŏn as well. I had no inkling that she harbored evil intentions. Wholly preoccupied with that frightful image and terrified that the Grand Heir might start making outings, I did not follow her advice to give the note to Minister Kim. I wrote directly to my father, explaining the situation and pleading, "Please banish these palace servants."

Father refused, saying, "It will create a great commotion. It won't do." Other members of the family also strongly advised him against doing anything about it. It seemed that my heart had never completely recovered from the terror of that year. Haunted by those fearful words, "the incident of that year could recur," and driven by anxious devotion to my son, I repeatedly pleaded with my father, but he persisted in his refusal.

Madame Chŏng instigated me. She said, "Your honorable father may be concerned with the nation, but for some reason he certainly is not doing what is right. If he is like that, and if, perchance, the Grand Heir should start to frequent certain quarters, who will stop him?" She seemed truly distressed and worried. I became terribly agitated. I fasted for several days and sent my father a message. "If you do not punish these ruffians, and the Grand Heir winds up frequenting those quarters, then what is the point of my living? I have decided to starve myself to death." I begged and beseeched him with tears. Father demurred and hesitated a bit longer, but in the end he reluctantly concurred, saying, "Out of my devotion to the Grand Heir, I will act, discarding all concern for my own life and death, disaster and fortune." Subsequently, he consulted with Ch'ŏngwŏn [and acted].

At first Cho Yŏngsun, then the deputy minister of the Board of Punishment, resisted, saying, "Can't do." After Cho listened to my father's reasoning, however, he said, "Things are different with the royal family. There will be great repercussions. But I am moved by the fact that my lord, out of devotion to the nation, has decided on this course of action, disregarding his personal safety or fortune." He then arrested several palace servants and, without a word of inquiry, quietly banished them. Father wrote to the Grand Heir, saying, "Hŭngǔn is a flamboyant and frivolous lad. He is not someone that Your Highness should be so friendly with." Then he reported, "Because Hŭngǔn frequented certain quarters, I punished several palace servants." When he saw the Grand Heir, he also admonished him strongly on this point.

The Grand Heir was quite embarrassed and chagrined by the whole affair. His youthful mind did not quite grasp the whole-hearted loyalty of his mother and his grandfather, and he was rather miffed. With her incomparably evil heart, Madame Chŏng seized on this. It was she who had instigated this, insisting that she wished the Grand Heir to remain unblemished. For this reason, she had induced me to pursue the matter. But she did nothing to assist me with the Grand Heir. She did not say, for example, "It is natural for Her Ladyship, with the love and concern of a mother, to respond like that. Nor was it out of place for Your Highness's grandfather to take the matter into his hands. His loyalty to the nation makes him vigilant of Your Highness's superior virtue, lest it be harmed. Your Highness should not take it personally. Heed his advice."

Instead she said, "Was it something that they should have made such a big fuss over? Now that they stirred it up into such a big thing, letting the whole world know of it, where does that leave Your Highness? A grandfather should cover up his grandchildren's faults; instead he is announcing them. What sort of human feelings does that show?" Speaking thus, Madame Chŏng continually provoked my son. Completely dominated by her at that time, the Grand Heir listened to her every word. Now she was speaking ill of us daily. Hugyŏm also came frequently and fanned the young Prince's resentment, seizing every opportunity to cloud his superior intelligence. Instigated by his aunt and her son, the Grand Heir's young heart changed. He no longer held his maternal grandfather in high esteem and affection, and, although it did not go that far with me, he was no longer as open as he had been.

It was evident that the Grand Heir was deeply angered and embarrassed by the incident, and I felt pity for him. But, secure in our knowledge that we acted out of single-minded concern for his virtue, neither I nor my father worried too much about future effects. The Grand Heir, despite his anger, maintained the same outward attitude toward his mother and grandfather. This convinced us of the rightfulness of what we had done, and we gave no further thought to possible repercussions. Only much later, during the *ŭlmi* year (1775), upon hearing Kugyŏng say, "the *kich'uk* incident caused him to have serious misgivings [toward the Hong family]," did I realize the depth of my son's resentment.

Once he ascended the throne, I explained the circumstances to him. I said, "Madame Chŏng's prediction that the incident of that year might recur really terrified me. Even an ordinary mother wishes the best for her son, but imagine my situation. I lived through the tragedy of that year and was living entirely because of my son. With my private affairs so completedly vested in Your Highness, not to mention Your Highness's public responsibility, how could I not be overanxious for your goodness and perfection? I must say that Madame Chŏng's sudden prediction really agitated my frightened heart. And there was still something more that I had to take into account. She had already declared that, unless we did something to put a stop to the situation, His Majesty would hear of it and this would lead to the reenactment of that tragedy. I knew how fickle she was and I did not think that it was at all improbable that she herself would bring the matter to His Majesty's attention, creating a great deal of trouble. What would have happened to Your Highness then? This possibility bothered me even more. My father and my brothers all refused, but threatening to starve myself to death, I forced my father to take up the matter. I did this with the single-minded concern of a mother. I never imagined that I was falling victim to Madame Chŏng's vile scheme—advising me to take this step while she used it to instigate and arouse Your Highness's ire against us. She flaunted it as proof that your maternal family was exposing your mistakes to the world, opening a chasm between Your Highness and my family.

"Then that clique around Kwiju and Hugyŏm widely circulated words to the effect that as the Hong family had earned his displeasure, the Grand Heir would no longer come to their defense even if they were to come under attack. Thus it would be easy to thrash the Hongs. This led to wholesale assaults on my family from such people as the so-called ten scholars and other sundry groups.* They were flocking to those who recently acquired power and were swayed by rumors suggesting that the way to achieve recognition as reputable scholars was to attack the royal affinal family. One thing led to another and the situation of my family went from bad to worse until they were reduced to this state. In fact, it was I who, with my own hand, brought calamity upon my family. It is not that I am ashamed of what I did. After all, my father and I acted entirely out of loyal devotion to Your Highness. I cannot, however, redeem myself for my crime of unfiliality [toward my father]."

The King smiled and said, "It happened when I was a boy. What is the use of talking about it? I sincerely regret it." Whenever the conversation turned to this incident, he became shamefaced and said, "It has been a long time and I have forgotten all about it."

In the *kyŏngsin* year (1800), in celebrating the capping ceremony of the Heir Apparent,† the King posthumously restored Cho Yŏngsun to his former post. His face radiant with pleasure, he said, "That business with Cho Yŏngsun has been bothering me all these years, just as if something was caught in my throat. Today I took

---

* Memorials indicting Hong Ponghan started to arrive in 1770.
† Sunjo.

care of it. I feel so relieved." I replied, "It is truly fortunate. Cho was severely punished for doing what my father asked him to do. That family must have resented us deeply.* My sense of discomfort has been immeasurable. I feel so relieved that Your Highness finally restored him to honor. It is truly fortunate."

The King said, "Cho Yŏngsun committed no crime. At the time, the threat that Madame Chŏng made, 'the incident of that year will recur,' was circulating about and it somehow was attributed to Cho, who came to be blamed for the remark. It was completely unjust. Someone told me that it was His Lordship[†] who, while sitting at the Palace Provision Office, declared to many ministers and officials that 'the incident of that year will recur.' I investigated but found no one who heard him say it. Then the story changed and I was told that His Lordship did not say it at the Palace Provision Office but that Chŏng Kwanghan heard it second hand and spread it about. I discovered with certainty that the prediction originated with Madame Chŏng and not with His Lordship. Blaming His Lordship was unjust, but implicating Cho Yŏngsun was even more unjust. Now we are done with the *kich'uk* (1769) incident. I did this not for Cho Yŏngsun but to vindicate His Lordship."

I thanked him repeatedly on behalf of my late father. One could see from this that the King was remorseful over the *kich'uk* incident and that he was fully aware of the injustice of holding my father responsible for that terrible prediction. How ugly and evil was that duplicitous plot of Madame Chŏng. Imagine, trying to alienate the Grand Heir from his maternal family!

From the *kich'uk* year (1769), however, power changed and so did people's hearts. Hugyŏm and Kwiju in alliance worked in separate spheres to promote their schemes. In *kyŏngin* (1770) they produced that horrible Han Yu memorial followed by the *sinmyo*

---

* Cho Yŏngsun may have been involved in the incident in which the palace servants were punished in 1769. According to the *Sillok*, however, he served in office until 1772. In the fifth month of 1771, for instance, he was appointed Deputy Minister of Personnel. In 1771 he went to China as the deputy ambassador in the winter embassy. In 1772, after he returned from China, he sent a memorial requesting that honor be posthumously restored to Ch'oe Sŏkhang and Yi Kwangjwa, the Soron ministers. For this he was exiled and demoted to commoner, but in 1774 he was released from his place of exile. *YS*, 116:31b, 117:18a, 119:36a–37a, 122:11a.

† Hong Ponghan.

(1771) incident and the *imjin* (1772) memorial.* Thus it must be said that the root of my family's ruin was the incident of the *kich'uk* year.

By the time Kwiju's memorial came in the seventh month of *imjin* (1772), the Grand Heir was eager to save his maternal family. Madame Chŏng and Hugyŏm had also come to the conclusion that it was not possible to completely destroy my family. Thus they arranged for my father to be saved and for Kwiju to receive a stern royal admonition. The cordial relationship Madame Chŏng had enjoyed with the Queen since *pyŏngsul* (1766) came to an end. The alliance between Kwiju and Hugyŏm in opposition to my father ended. Hugyŏm adopted a new posture. Now he sought to save my family while he attacked Kwiju. Madame Chŏng now disliked the fact that her residence was close to the Queen's. Hence she moved to Yŏngsŏn Hall. By then the Grand Heir was older, and he was deeply engrossed in his studies. His dependence on Madame Chŏng, which had made it difficult for him to stay away from her even for a short time, appeared to have abated somewhat.

Madame Chŏng would extol Hugyŏm, speaking of how extraordinary his scholarship was and how impeccable his manners were. She spoke of the Grand Heir less favorably, as if he did not measure up to her son. Even she should have known not to talk like that! After the Grand Heir became more independent, she watched him with sharp eyes as quick as lightning lest he ogle some ladies-in-waiting or favor a eunuch. She made it impossible for the Grand Heir to enjoy a moment's peace. From the *kyŏngin* year (1770), she intruded into the relationship between the Grand Heir and the Grand Heir Consort. She harped on things of no import or significance, exaggerating them out of all proportion and declaring them to be great failures of the Grand Heir Consort. In hundreds of thousands of cases, she harassed and persecuted her relentlessly. It is impossible to record them all.

The Grand Heir was dispassionate by temperament and did not enjoy conjugal intimacy with his wife. However, even if he had wished for it, how could he attempt anything while that person controlled his fate, keeping him in her palm and doggedly oppos-

---

* Hong Ponghan was accused of making an alliance with Chŏngjo's two half brothers and scheming on their behalf. For Kim Kwiju's and Kim Kwanju's memorials requesting that Hong Ponghan be executed, see *YS*, 119:6b–12b.

ing and obstructing their conjugal relations? This meant that there was no hope for an heir. My father, praying day and night that the Grand Heir and his wife might live in harmony and produce an heir, earnestly advised him against continued aloofness. The other members of my family were also deeply anxious about the situation. While Madame Chŏng did what she could to tear the Grand Heir away from his consort, fearing that they might produce a son, Kwiju and his clique circulated rumors intimating that "the Crown Prince cannot have children." This furthur disturbed the hearts of the people. Recalling her malice makes one shudder even now.

Madame Chŏng's personality was such that she could not live without provoking havoc. Having attacked my family at length, she sought to eliminate the family of the Grand Heir Consort. She resented the Grand Heir's fondness for his father-in-law and his preference for his brother-in-law Kim Kidae, who was accomplished in scholarship and served as a tutor in the Crown Prince Tutorial Office. She slandered them incessantly and did all she could to persuade the Grand Heir to send his wife away from Hŭngjŏng Hall. In the seventh month of *imjin* (1772), Ch'ŏngwŏn died unexpectedly. Awakened by the news, the Grand Heir, who was so kind-hearted, was deeply shaken. He walked over to his wife's residence. He seemed dazed. His eyes brimmed with tears and he bore the most pitiful expression. I consoled him, thinking that it must have been quite a shock. All that concerned Madame Chŏng, however, was the possibility that the Grand Heir, in sympathy for his wife's loss, might feel kindly disposed toward her. So she said abruptly, "Is it such a big thing that Your Highness should grieve so? It is as if Your Highness has assumed the mask of that dead person."

I was appalled by what I heard. I was doing my best at that time not to hate her, but what she said was just too malevolent and unpropitious. Shuddering, I protested, "What words are these? Could it be that you are drunk today? Can't you be more discriminating in what you say? How can you bring one who has just died onto the body of our precious person?"

She realized how horrid her remark was. The Grand Heir was also rather taken aback by it. She immediately made motions of atonement. At first she said, "I made a blunder." But then she said that, even if her son were to be punished, her daughter-in-law and grandchild made into slaves, and she herself banished to a remote island under house arrest surrounded by hedges of brambles, she would not be able to sufficiently pay for her crime. It is strange that she should have so abruptly made that malevolent remark, but it is stranger still that the horrible things that she prophesied in the depths of that night about her own family have come to pass.* It is almost as though she was under the spell of ghosts or spirits.

Although Madame Chŏng was wicked and as changeable as a chameleon, she was still but a woman. Had it not been for Hugyŏm, she would have remained content to meddle in the affairs of the inner palace, thinking it impossible to interfere in the politics of the court and to wield power. I had occasion to observe the audaciousness of Hugyŏm's character. In *kyŏngjin* (1760) Prince Sado threatened his sister, Madame Chŏng, saying, "If you do not arrange for me to go on a trip to Onyang, I will kill your son." He took Hugyŏm and locked him up under guard. At that time, Hugyŏm was in his twelfth year, an age at which most children would have been frightened to death. Hugyŏm, however, showed no signs of fear; rather, he behaved haughtily. I felt that he was unusually bold. He was rather precocious, not at all dull-witted or slow. He did not aspire to virtue or dignity but, quite early on, seemed inclined toward arrogance and willfulness. Wishing to eliminate my father and to wield power, he sought to use his mother. Since he was so power-hungry, competitive, envious, and malevolent, and since his mother did everything that her son asked of her, between mother and son the innumerable cunning machinations and evil tricks they spawned wrought great havoc on the royal family and the state. I can only lament Heaven's will for permitting this.

I remain deep within the inner palace, and so I am not well informed about the details of the ways in which Hugyŏm dominated ministers and officials during his reign of power, ordering them about as though they were his personal slaves. Nor am I privy to the way in which he completely subjugated the whole world. I will just mention a few conspicuous examples known to the entire public.

---

* Chŏng Hugyŏm was banished in the third month of 1776 and was executed in the seventh month of the same year (*Chŏngjo sillok* [hereafter *CS*], in *Chosŏn wangjo sillok*, 1:7a, 1:79b). In 1778 his wife and children were separately banished to uninhabited islands (*CS*, 6:4a). In 1778 Madame Chŏng was punished. *CS*, 1:7b, 5:68b.

In alliance with Kwiju, he tried to harm my father in *kyŏngin* and *sinmyo* (1770–1771). This was a crime worthy of death. His attack on the Prime Minister Kim Ch'iin in *imjin* (1772) was another such crime. Kim was attacked for a recommendation he had made for a vacancy in the Censorate. After His Majesty adopted the policy of grand harmony (*t'angp'yŏng*),[3] it was a rule that no list of candidates for vacancies in the Censorate could be forwarded to the throne by the Board of Personnel unless it contained names of both Noron and Soron officials. Such lists were not permitted to contain names from only one faction. Chŏng Chon'gyŏm was the Minister of Personnel, and in submitting the names of candidates for the post of the Censor General, he somehow listed Kim Chongsu on top, followed by two others all of whom happened to be Noron. His Majesty did not notice it.

It may have been that when Kim Ch'iin and Kim Chongsu cooperated with Hugyŏm in attacking my father, they were not as submissive as he wished them to be. Perhaps Hugyŏm was not informed of the fact that the recommendation was being made, and that displeased him. Furthermore, Hugyŏm was Soron, as was his wife's family. Various Soron got together and convinced Hugyŏm that a recommendation list consisting entirely of Noron was an outrage, that it was nothing less than a display of power by Kim Ch'iin, and that this could not be tolerated. Hugyŏm told Madame Chŏng of the list, and she apprised His Majesty of it. His Majesty always regarded factional practices with bitter resentment. Thinking that Kim Ch'iin—the Prime Minister and the son of the former Prime Minister Kim Chaero, who had supported the policy of grand harmony—was practicing factionalism on behalf of his nephew Chongsu, His Majesty was provoked into a towering rage. He immediately banished Kim Ch'iin and Kim Chongsu to uninhabited islands, confining them to houses surrounded by hedges of brambles.[4] There was even discussion of putting Kim Ch'iin to death. What a horrible thing!

It happened that Chongsu was on bad terms with my family, and so there was some suspicion that my family—my father, my two uncles,* and my third brother—had coaxed Hugyŏm to punish the Kims. My third brother, Nagim, was singled out as their archenemy. This was, of course, baseless. My family was not with-

* Hong Inhan and Hong Chunhan.

out resources. Had we hated Kim Ch'iin, we could have trapped him for something else. Being Noron ourselves, we certainly would not have done it for submitting an all Noron list. The criminal charge against the Kims specified in the royal verdict was that they assumed the posture of pure scholars of great integrity and rectitude. It simply does not make any sense to punish someone for assuming the role of a pure scholar.* Not even a three-year-old would believe that my family instigated Hugyŏm in this affair. How laughable.

At one point, my family was nearly destroyed because of Hugyŏm's machinations, but later they were saved also through Hugyŏm and his mother. In the end, my family went down with him.† There just was no way for them to dissociate themselves from Hugyŏm for the duration of His Majesty King Yŏngjo's reign. With benefit of hindsight, I sometimes wish that, even in the adversities of the *sinmyo* year (1771), we had not associated with Hugyŏm. But, seeing one's parent deeply in trouble, how can one not try to save him? Madame Chŏng and her son must have been in my family's karma from a previous life. I can only lament!

The world seems to think that my second uncle attained high position only through his older brother's influence. This is not true at all. When he first passed the civil service examination, His Majesty remarked that he was marked for an important office. Later, His Majesty even said, "He is better than his older brother." My uncle always had his own special relationship to His Majesty. After *kyŏngin* (1770), when my father was deeply in trouble, royal trust in my uncle did not wane. The Grand Heir also liked him and felt close to him. So, during this period when my family was in a terrible state, my uncle served as the Governor of P'yŏngan Province and as a minister on the State Council.[5]

One must understand the difficulty of turning one's back on royal trust. Nonetheless, with his family in such misfortune, it was

---

* These two sentences sound vague. The *Sillok* reveals that Yŏngjo was extraordinarily sensitive to any move that might be construed as factional behavior on the part of his officials. What the king accused his officials of on this occasion was that they acted in the name of principle but did not transcend factionalism. For a debate concerning different positions on factionalism, see Haboush, *Heritage*, 117–35.

† Hong Inhan, for instance, was killed along with Hugyŏm for more or less the same charges. *CS*, 1:79a–b.

wrong of him not to sever his ties with the official world. If some-one had faulted him for having continued to serve while his older brother was in disgrace and for having sought wealth and prestige while Hugyŏm wielded power, he would have gladly accepted the censure. I must admit that I myself felt rather indignant about his keeping office. But it is grievously unjust that he was termed a traitor for his conduct in connection with the regency proposal and that he met such a cruel end.

When my second uncle served on the State Council in the *ŭlmi* year (1775), His Majesty was quite weak and feeble. Hugyŏm did not have much power but was very demanding, and so he created many difficulties. At the same time, Kugyŏng[6] emerged as the fa-vored confidant of the Grand Heir and acted arrogantly. My uncle had long since been on bad terms with Kugyŏng's uncle, Naksun,[7] and now he disapproved of Kugyŏng's frivolous behavior. He was not yet aware of the extent to which Kugyŏng was favored by the Grand Heir. He regarded him only as a young member of the Hong family. He despaired of what he saw in Kugyŏng, thinking, "Who would have known that, among the descendants of Lord Yŏngan, there should be such an odious thing! He will be the ruin of the family."* On several occasions, my uncle admonished Kugyŏng.

Kugyŏng's disposition was such that he killed anyone who touched so much as one hair of his. Once, Kugyŏng asked my father, "Either through your brother or through the Minister of Personnel, please see to it that my father[8] gets an official post." At first my father tried to desist, but after several visits and much urging he reluctantly wrote to his brother. Kugyŏng remained there waiting for a reply. But the answer was delayed for a long while, and so he took his leave saying that he would return. As he was leaving, he encountered outside the house the messenger bearing the reply. He intercepted and read it. My uncle's answer was: "How is it that you ask me to give a position to this madman? It won't do." As he read this, Kugyŏng turned white and assumed an expression of murderous rage. I believe that Kugyŏng trumped up those charges against my uncle partly in retaliation for that. He

---

* Hong Kugyŏng was two generations junior to Hong Inhan. Kugyŏng was his third cousin twice removed in the paternal line. Lord Yŏngyan is Lady Hye-gyŏng's fifth-generation ancestor.

must have resolved to kill my uncle and, at the opportune moment, created that charge.

The bill of indictment for my uncle charged that, in addition to attempting to prevent the regency, he tried to eliminate a faithful assistant to the Crown Prince, namely Kugyŏng.[9] But there is evidence to the contrary for the second charge. My uncle was a seasoned politician, unusually clever and quick in the ways of the world. Though at first he was unaware of Kugyŏng's power and so admonished him, he gradually came to appreciate Kugyŏng's position and kept careful watch lest he fall victim to Kugyŏng's vengefulness. In the tenth month of *ŭlmi* (1775), His Majesty wanted to send Kugyŏng to Cheju Island as a secret censor to investigate the local management of relief grain. The Grand Heir, however, asked my uncle to see to it that Kugyŏng not be sent to the provinces. In compliance, my uncle asked His Majesty, "Hong Kugyŏng has been serving in the Crown Prince Tutorial Office for a long time. Please send some other official." Thus my uncle succeeded in having Yu Kang sent in his place and in permitting Kugyŏng to stay in the capital. Had my uncle wished to eliminate him, why should he not have taken advantage of this golden opportunity, sending him to Cheju rather than persuading the throne not to send him to the island?

As for the first charge, it is very unfortunate. His Majesty was on in years, his asthma frequently acted up, and there were long intervals during which the royal judgment did not function adequately. Under the circumstances, it would have been proper for a minister of state to propose a regency. As the situation became more critical day by day, there was no one who did not have a regency in mind. As for me, I have always regarded the regency as my downfall. All the troubles [leading to my husband's death] originated with his regency, which had been initiated in the *kisa* year (1749). Thus just the word "regency" struck terror into my heart. Moreover, although the royal health was in critical condition, the Grand Heir, the appointed successor to the throne, was there keeping the foundation of the state firm and strong. It did not seem that the future of the state depended upon the establishment of a regency.*

When His Majesty discussed a regency, Madame Chŏng evaded

* For the delicate nature and history of the regency, see the Introduction, 21–22.

the issue, saying, "This is a grave decision concerning the state. I have no opinion." My uncle did not know that Madame Chŏng had not been able to speak quietly with His Majesty for a long time. He suspected that she was playing a trick using the regency as a trap. Thus he reasoned that, if he were to compliantly obey the royal order, then great problems would ensue. Once he decided that His Majesty's order for a regency was a test, he became terribly afraid and was at wits' end. He just groped for a way to muddle through the issue, taking no definite position. He settled upon accepted formalities, saying, "How could Your Majesty send down such an order? How could your humble servant, serving Your Majesty, comply with it?" His Majesty had been growing increasingly confused; over half of what he said was senseless. He would send down orders such as one calling for a special examination or a great festival in celebration of some imaginary event. On one occasion, he appointed as head of the Medical Bureau Kim Chin'gwi,[10] a minister long since deceased who had served under King Sukchong. When His Majesty came to his senses, he would laugh, saying, "We can't promulgate these orders." Thus royal orders were frequently canceled.

My uncle, though somewhat short in learning, had an unusually keen sensitivity to shifts in political power. Had he understood that His Majesty was serious about the regency, why would he not have at once complied, turning that to his merit? Because my uncle suspected that His Majesty in his heart did not truly want the regency or that it was perhaps one of those senseless orders that would be canceled later, or even a trap laid by Madame Chŏng, he acted fearfully to avoid getting caught. In the end, he was charged with hindering the regency.[11]

If he had been charged with failing to propose the regency while the royal health was in decline and affairs of the state were imperiled, and thereby failing to meet those standards of integrity and character set by the ministers of old, then no one could quarrel with it. Nor would he have felt so wronged, even though he may have had to face that extreme misfortune. He was, however, adjudged a traitor who had hindered the Grand Heir's regency because, fearing the Grand Heir's intelligence and virtue, he would no longer have been permitted to exercise power as he wished. How grievous and how unjust was this charge!

The crime my uncle committed was a lapse of speech. He made

this lapse in an audience with His Majesty on the twentieth of the eleventh month in the *ŭlmi* year (1775). His Majesty said, "The Grand Heir does not know about state affairs, personnel matters, or the factional business of the Noron and Soron. Isn't that worrisome?" My uncle replied, "Why does His Highness need to know about the Noron and the Soron?" This is the so-called statement of "the three things that [the Prince] need not know (*sam pulp'il-chi*)." My uncle was termed guilty for this reply because it was interpreted as saying that the Grand Heir had no need to know any of the three matters—personnel matters, the business of the Noron and the Soron, and, especially, state affairs. But in effect, His Majesty did not ask about these matters one at a time, going on to the next after waiting for my uncle's answer. His sagacious heart regarded the Grand Heir as very young and immature, and so he was saying that it was worrisome that his grandchild did not know state affairs, personnel matters, or the business of the Noron and Soron. My uncle seized on the last item, "the business of the Noron and the Soron," and replied "Why does His Highness need to know about the Noron and the Soron?"*

True, His Majesty Yŏngjo loved the Grand Heir. But the Grand Heir was concerned that if all the officials were to start voicing his praises, then His Majesty might become suspicious that, since he was old and feeble, all were flocking to the young Heir. And so the Grand Heir pleaded with my uncle, "Please do not praise me too much in His Majesty's presence." My uncle promised to comply with his wishes. Moreover, His Majesty abhorred any factional talk. He never brought up the topic of the Noron and the Soron and it was inadmissible for officials even to mention it. My uncle was afraid that, were he to answer, "How is it possible for the Heir Apparent not to know about the Noron and the Soron," His Majesty, having thus tested him, might burst out, "Do you mean to say that the Grand Heir knows of the factions that I have so resolutely forbidden?" His answer was an attempt to circumvent the issue, the course he thought most prudent.[12] What he thought

* The *Sillok* records of the day contain a different version of what Hong Inhan said. They record him as saying, "His Highness the Crown Prince does not need to know about the Noron and the Soron. He does not need to know about the administration of such personnel matters as the appointment of the Minister of War and the Minister of Personnel. He especially does not need to know about state affairs." *YS*, 125:18b.

was one clever answer turned into three answers to three questions, and considering the sentence construction, he can only be faulted for a lapse of speech. To be made a traitor for that, however, is a thousand times, ten thousand times, unjust and mortifying. My uncle met that cruel end. But how can he close his eyes in the netherworld? And how could he have accepted that verdict in his heart?

Had I kept my family better informed of the situation at the palace and the intentions of the Grand Heir as well as those of His Majesty, then my uncle would have known of His Majesty's sagacious intentions and would not have answered erroneously. Given my inflexibility, this was not possible. I always felt quite shame-faced and embarrassed to inform my family of palace affairs, and I seldom did anything of the kind. On the matter of the regency, I deliberately kept my family in ignorance because I wanted them to be completely above suspicion. I did not want to take any chances that they, as the maternal family of the proposed regent, might be accused of eagerness in accepting the regency, that Madame Chŏng might hear that they knew of the proposal, or that His Majesty's sagacious heart might be enraged that they knew of it. When I think over these events, however, there is not one that is not my responsibility and my fault. How sharp is my remorse and regret.*

That so many members of my family served in office and that they enjoyed such spectacular wealth and power were purely con-sequences of their position as the maternal family of the Grand Heir. Thus one might charge that, relying upon him, they wielded power and corrupted the court. As their power and wealth de-pended completely upon the young Heir, the foolish hearts of the affinal family would naturally welcome and rejoice in a regency or an accession of this Heir Apparent. To accuse them of hindering the Heir Apparent from assuming the regency makes no sense at all. Then upon whom would they rely in their pursuit of power and wealth? His Majesty was close to ninety and his health was already in sharp decline. Something might happen to him at any time.

---

* The *Sillok* records that Lady Hyegyŏng sent a letter to Hong Inhan begging him to accept the regency and that, despite this letter, Hong persisted in his ob-jection (*YS*, 125:19b). She may have sent a letter, but it is unlikely that anyone other than Hong Inhan knew what it said. For details, see the Introduction, 22–23.

Under the circumstances, who would alienate the Heir Apparent, who held the keys to future power, just for some immediate gain, no matter what it may have been? The Grand Heir displayed no sign of resentment toward his maternal family. I did not know of it myself, and there was no sense in which my uncle did. In fact, he just assumed that during my son's reign, he would wield greater power as the senior minister related to the king, and he eagerly looked forward to it. It is simply beyond human sentiment and heavenly principle to say that he attempted to harm the Grand Heir.

In that audience, His Majesty said, "My eyesight has become so poor that I cannot with my own hands put dots on the names of the persons I have selected for office;* I must rely on those around me for that. As for other administrative matters, I have delegated them to eunuchs. The situation is quite similar to the one in which my Late Royal Brother, King Kyŏngjong, cried out, 'Should it be the Crown Prince, my brother, or should it be the courtiers around me?'† In the same spirit, I would like to entrust state affairs to the Grand Heir." The Prime Minister Han Ingmo said in consternation, "There is no real need to worry about courtiers." Han's reply was in error as well. A memorial attacked him as much as it attacked my uncle.‡ Han must have replied in this way because he did not feel that a minister of state could comply without protest to a royal order of such great import and he wanted to get through the moment somehow. I doubt very much that he had other motives. If one were to speak of lapses in speech, however, Minister Han was as guilty as my uncle. If one were to discuss being guilty

---

* After receiving the recommendation list, the king dots the names of the persons he has chosen.

† In 1721 Kyŏngjong, because of his feeble health, considered making his brother, Yŏngjo, a regent. This remark—whether power should be in the hands of his brother, an heir to the throne, or in the hands of the people around him—is supposed to express the king's strong desire to see administration in the hands of his brother rather than the power-seeking officials around the throne. In other words, if an official were to oppose the proposal of a regency, then he would be understood to be unwilling to relinquish his power to handle state affairs in the name of the ailing king. The Noron accepted the regency with this logic, but Kyŏngjong changed his mind and the regency was not established. This incident catalyzed a large-scale purge of Noron officials.

‡ The memorial came from a minor censor, Sŏ Myŏngsŏn, on the third day of the twelfth month, 1775. It criticized both Han Ingmo and Hong Inhan for resisting the regency. *YS*, 126:1b–2a.

of not immediately complying with the royal order, the Prime Minister and the Minister of the Left were culpable in the same degree. It has come to pass that Prime Minister Han has become a man of unblemished honor* while my uncle alone remains on the list of the most heinous criminals. How can the state's ministration of justice be so unfair?

The Grand Heir openly resented my uncle; [when he ascended] he did want to get even. His edict banishing him to Yŏsan was merciless. It enumerated many crimes, enough to make certain that he would never again function as a guiltless person, but its concluding phrase said, "It is an extreme exaggeration and even an error to attribute to him seditious intentions or preparations for a coup. This is utterly preposterous."[†] Although the King, having resented his maternal family for quite some time, did wish to strike a blow, he did not really intend to completely ruin them, since his old mother was alive. As for Kugyŏng, he was not a sworn enemy. He just wanted to display his power. Persecuting the King's maternal family permitted him to feel that the world was at his feet. He knew, however, that my uncle was not guilty of a crime punishable by death. It is quite unlikely that he wished to go so far as to have him killed. I thought that by banishing my uncle, the King had finished with the case.

However, Kim Chongsu appeared in the fifth month of the *pyŏngsin* year (1776). Wishing to brand the Hong family as traitors, he persuaded Kugyŏng that, if he were to successfully implicate my uncle in a rebellious plot, he would be rewarded handsomely for his loyal service in uncovering sedition. Therefore my uncle's crime was adjudged to be heavier and heavier, even though each new verdict was based on the same charge with no additional counts. Within three months of his banishment, he met that cruel end.

Later, in the fifth month of *imja* (1792), discussing this incident in the Royal Lecture, the King said, "That remark 'He does not

---

* Shortly after Chŏngjo's accession in 1776, Han Ingmo failed to attend the interrogation of Chŏng Hugyŏm and Hong Inhan. For this he was stripped of his post and cast out of the city. On New Year's Day of 1777, Han was released from confinement and exonerated of all charges. *CS*, 1:71a–b, 3:1a.

† This edict refers to Hong Inhan's stupidity, his greed for power, and his predilection for scheming. It attributes all of these failings to his lack of learning. It denies the charges that Hong entertained seditious or rebellious intentions. *CS*, 1:17b–18a.

need to know' is as ambiguous as 'One can't say there isn't.'* It is not so criminal that one should be punished for it." This royal pronouncement must be contained in *The Records of the Royal Secretariat*. As the pronouncement was publicly available, all must have read it.[†] The saying "One can't say there isn't" was the phrase for which Ch'in killed Yueh Fei, the most unjust killing of an innocent in history.[‡] This incident is so famous that it appears in books written in vernacular Korean. Even we ignorant women feel bitter on Yueh's behalf. It is not possible that the King, with his excellent learning, did not know the origin of this phrase. When he described my uncle's situation by using this phrase, he must have meant that my uncle was unjustly punished. Who among those who read the King's pronouncement, even if they were unrelated to my family, could fail to see his intention? In that pronouncement, he also declared, "The remark 'He does not need to know' that he made in the *pyŏngsin* year (1776) was no crime. In fact, I punished him for the events of *imo* year."[13]

Afterwards, the King came into my residence and told me, "It has disturbed me that I have not been able to find a way to clear him of 'the three things that [the Prince] need not know.' I feel quite relieved that I shifted his crime to the events of *imo* year

* Yueh Fei was a Chinese general during the Sung who had fought valiantly against the Jurchen. Ch'in Kuei, on the other hand, argued for negotiation with the Jurchen. Ch'in had Yueh imprisoned under trumped-up charges, and Yueh died in prison. "One can't say there isn't" *(mo shu yo)* is the phrase that Ch'in used to implicate Yueh. Another general, Han Shih-chung, criticized Ch'in for this. See the remark in Yueh's biography. *Sung-shih*, ed. T'uo T'uo et al., in *Erh shih wu shih*, 50 vols. (Taipei: I-wen-yin shu-kuan, 1958), 365:20a.

† The discussion that the king had with his officials in the Royal Lecture was recorded in the *The Records of the Royal Secretariat* and was on public view so that any official could read it. Chŏngjo made this statement on the twenty-seventh of the intercalary fourth month, 1792. On that day Chŏngjo was quite disturbed at the mounting cries to examine the circumstances surrounding Prince Sado's death. On this occasion he evaluated the crimes of various people whom he had punished. What he said of Hong Inhan was, "The remark 'He does not need to know' is similar to 'One can't say there isn't.' As for Hong's being prosecuted for it, it was not only for this crime at the time.... It also had to do with the event of that month of that year [Prince Sado's death in 1762]." *Sŭngjŏngwŏn ilgi*, 115 vols. (Seoul: Kuksa p'yŏnch'an winwŏnhoe, 1961–1970), 90:506b–507c, esp. 506c. This is recorded verbatim in the *Chŏngjo sillok*. *CS*, 34:60b–63b, esp. 61b.

‡ Their biographies in the dynastic history make this point abundantly clear. Yueh's biography is included in the section on "loyal ministers" *(ch'ungsin)*, and Ch'in's is in the section on "evil ministers" *(kansin)*. See *Sung-shih*, ed. T'uo, 365:1a–24a, 473:4a–24b.

(1762) and that it will be easy to clear him." Surprised, I said, "That my uncle was punished for what he said in *pyŏngsin* (1776) was so unjust. But it makes even less sense to say that he was guilty in the events of the *imo* year. I do not understand what Your Highness is saying." The King answered, "If I said that he was guilty for a specific crime associated with the events of the *imo* year, it might be difficult to clear him. But I shifted his crime to the events of the *imo* year without naming any specifics. This means that in several years no one will be able to figure out what his crime was. Besides, in the *kapcha* year (1804) I intend to redress, on a large scale, those who have been unjustly judged guilty in connection with the events of the *imo* year. Now that his crime has been shifted to the events of the *imo* year, he is cleared of the crime of *pyŏngsin*. Let's wait until *kapcha* and he will be completely rehabilitated."

Lately, the King has felt even more remorseful. He has frequently said such things as "He was a wronged minister" and "Had he survived, he could have been the first among the venerable old statesmen." He also reminisced upon how devoted to him my uncle had been, how fond of my uncle he had been, and how he had consulted with him on everything. He reassured me, "There will be a better future." He also praised him: "He was equipped to function as a pillar of the world and the center of the court. He was really a hero. Today's ministers cannot approach him." The King then mentioned that he learned many things from my uncle, such things as how to deal with people, proper deportment, and even sartorial manners. Had his sagacious heart actually thought my uncle a traitor, he would not have spoken of him in this way.

Early in *pyŏngsin* (1776), when my uncle met that horrible fate, my bitterness and misery were incomparable. The thought of doing away with myself or taking some other extraordinary measures did occur to me.* My foolish maternal heart, which rejoiced at the accession to the throne of the son whom I had reared under such uniquely difficult circumstances, balked at the idea—if I did not preserve myself, then it would tarnish my son's reputation for filial

* To display her anger at the injustice of the verdict that her uncle was a traitor. Social custom did not require that she feel an obligation to share his fate.

piety and mar his virtuous image. I reckoned, "My son has just begun to rule. He does not see through Kugyŏng's maneuverings now, and so he is making this mistake. It will not be long before he will regret it." With such hope, I restrained myself. Instead of doing away with myself, I continued to behave as if nothing were amiss. People in and out of court criticized me for being weak and indecisive. I humbly accept that judgment. Indeed, the King did come to regret what he had done and firmly promised me that, inasmuch as he was planning to vindicate my family in *kapcha* (1804) for unjust accusations, he would also restore my uncle. Trusting his words as if they were as solid as gold or as firm as stone, I impatiently looked forward to *kapcha*. Once again, Heaven disfavored me, and as time passed, the fortunes of my family plunged to greater depths. The King died in the prime of his life. All his hopes and plans are now tossed away and deserted. How bitter, how lamentable!

Though I am only a woman, I have read a considerable number of unofficial histories of this dynasty translated into Korean.* I have never encountered a case in which an unjustly punished person was not vindicated in the end. My uncle's case was truly unjust. I await the day when the present King, my grandson, matures and learns to discern right and wrong. He will surely dispel this bitterness of his old grandmother. I have no idea whether I will live to see that day, though. I hope and pray that, when the young King reads this, even if I am no longer here, he will be moved to redress my uncle's thirty-year-old injustice. Formerly, during Myŏngjong's reign (r. 1545–1567), Yun Im was charged with having plotted to enthrone his son-in-law, Lord Pongsŏng.† In the trial at the State

---

* During the Chosŏn dynasty, all official histories and most unofficial histories were written in literary Chinese.

† Refers to the so-called purge of 1545 (*ŭlsa sahwa*). Yun Im (1487–1545) was brother of Queen Changgyŏng (1491–1515), King Chungjong's (r. 1506–1544) second wife. After Queen Changgyŏng's death, King Chungjong married Queen Munjong (1501–1565) and there was a constant power struggle between Yun Im and Yun Wŏnhyŏng (d. 1565), Queen Munjong's brother. When Injong (r. 1544–1545) succeeded Chungjong in 1544, Yun Im, his maternal uncle, wielded power, but when Injong died after eight months on the throne and was succeeded by Myŏngjong, Yun Wŏnhyŏng, the new king's maternal uncle, came into power. Yun Wŏnhyŏng accused Yun Im of sedition and had him executed along with his three sons.

Tribunal, witnesses testified against him. Yun was adjudged to have been guilty of sedition beyond a shadow of doubt. Later, Yun's crime appeared in the *Mujŏng pogam* (Precious mirror of pacification).[14] The description of Yun's crime there makes one think it the most dramatic and seditious plot in history, and no one dared to object to it for a while.* However, since the entire trial was sheer fabrication, it gradually generated public outrage until everyone expressed a sense that Yun had been utterly wronged. King Sŏnjo, however, felt the offense to be grave enough that it should not be reversed lightly. In compliance with the wishes of Queen Dowager Kongŭi, he did change his mind in the end. He reversed the judgment against Yun and posthumously restored him to his official post. Yun Im was the maternal uncle of the husband of Queen Dowager Kongŭi, and the Queen Dowager was, in turn, Sŏnjo's aunt. Queen Dowager Kongŭi longed for redress for her husband's uncle. King Sŏnjo, in deference to his aunt's wishes, took those measures. Even now there is no one who does not feel sympathetic to Queen Dowager Kongŭi's wishes and who does not admire King Sŏnjo for his filial consideration.[15]

My uncle's case is much more favorable than Yun Im's. The charge against him was much lighter than the one against Yun Im, and I am the King's grandmother. King Sŏnjo complied with his aunt's wishes to redress her uncle by marriage. No one could possibly object to my desire to clear my uncle, nor could anyone object to the King's accommodating his grandmother's wishes. Moreover, this was a case whose disposition the late King had come to regret, and he publicly declared on many occasions that he was planning to rectify it in the *kapcha* year (1804). Two pronouncements of the late King, one in *pyŏngsin* (1776) and one in *imja* (1792), clearly testify to this intention. It is not something that the young King should feel uneasy or hesitant about.

It is believed that Queen Dowager Kongŭi was so determined to restore Yun Im because her role in the Yun Im affair had been misconstrued in the first place. The royal edict of the seventh

---

* Lady Hyegyŏng remarks that Yun Im's case found its way into a book because her uncle had the same fate. Hong Inhan's crime and that of Chŏng Hugyŏm were described in the *Myŏngŭirok* (The record of clarifying righteousness), a book published in 1777 under royal auspices. See *Myŏngŭirok*, ed. Kim Ch'iin et al., 3 *ch'aek*, 1777, Kyujanggak.

month of the *pyŏngsin* year (1776) calling for the execution of my uncle says that I requested it.* In view of what is written, it seems as if I killed him myself. If people who did not know what went on were to point me out, saying that I am ethically equivalent to a criminal who cooperated in killing my uncle when I should have saved him, I would have no way to defend myself against this accusation. But who in all of history would cooperate in killing one's own uncle? Before long, my life will end. If I were to die without having cleared my uncle's name, then I would, in fact, become a person who had killed her uncle, and there would be no place for me even as a ghost. It would be far worse than Queen Dowager Kongŭi, who was for a time unfairly suspected. She was able to move her nephew. Though I may be shallow in my devotion, can I not move my grandson the King? My greatest frustration is the King's youth. Though he may wish to do it, he is not yet able to decide on his own, and my decrepit life is on the verge of fading away. Oh! Bleakness!

Kugyŏng passed the civil examination in the autumn of *imjin* (1772). As a child, he plainly showed his [devious] character. Suffering from insanity, his father, Nakch'un, could not instruct his son. Kugyŏng was wild and dissolute. He drank and womanized excessively. He behaved so recklessly that his family gave him up for lost and the world thought him a wastrel. He did have some talents, though. He made a point of showing off the little learning that he had reluctantly acquired. He was also witty, clever, bold, and ambitious, and he feared neither Heaven nor Earth. This crazy thing habitually announced that he would take the world in his hand. His cronies, who were at first astounded at this proclamation, laughed at him. After Kugyŏng succeeded in the examination, he served for several years as a historian in the the Office of Royal

---

* Just before King Chŏngjo agreed to the ministerial request for the execution of Hong Inhan in the seventh month of 1776, he said, "Every time I wished to make this decision, the thought of causing distress to my mother made me hesitate. Today I sent her a message expressing my concern. Her Ladyship instructed me, 'Though private affection is overwhelming, the laws of the state are supremely strict and cannot be bent. Ministers and censors have been pressing for his punishment continuously. It is not necessary, in worrying about my distress, to compromise the integrity of the state.' In compliance with Her Ladyship's virtuous words, I have made up my mind. The punishment will be enacted." (*CS*, 1:79b.)

Decrees. His duty required that he frequently remain in the palace.* His Late Majesty [King Yŏngjo] became quite fond of him and used to refer to him as "my grandson." The Grand Heir also found him very charming. Kugyŏng was about the Grand Heir's age. He was beautiful, witty, and quick. The signs of danger were already there. The Grand Heir first saw him once or twice. Then before long he grew very close to him and comfortable with him. In the beginning this fellow cunningly posed as a forthright critic, but his criticisms and admonitions were just disguised fawning, something pleasant to hear. When the Grand Heir, thinking Kugyŏng a man of rigorous principle, began to trust him deeply, there was nothing that Kugyŏng did not control.

The Grand Heir remained secluded in the palace at the residence of the Heir Apparent. Other than servants, the only persons with whom he had close contact were his tutors and his officials. They spoke to him of his studies and not much else, certainly not gossip or rumors from either inside or outside the court. Naturally, the Grand Heir felt bored and restricted. Then he met Kugyŏng, who did not hesitate to tell him everything he heard and saw. The Grand Heir was utterly charmed and thrilled by this new acquaintance. He gradually shied away from the officials to whom he had hitherto been close and came to regard Kugyŏng as his only confidant, incomparable to anyone else. It was as if a man were completely bewitched by a new concubine. If Kugyŏng found someone distasteful, or if someone did or said something remotely critical of him, then to the Grand Heir he accused this person of "slandering His Highness," offering no evidence for the charge. As the Grand Heir so conspicuously favored him, Kugyŏng would have been held suspect even if he had been discreet. But the Grand Heir loved this man of frivolity who was notorious for his fickleness. Of course, there were murmurings of criticism. There were those who lamented, "The Crown Prince is so close to that peculiar character," and there were those who said, "Even if the Crown Prince allowed him to be that way for a time, how dare he behave so impertinently?" During the *kabo* and *ŭlmi* years (1774–1775), every household buzzed with talk of Kugyŏng and all expressed dismay over his behavior. Kugyŏng must have heard quite a lot of

* The historian's duty was to follow the king and to record his every public activity and remark.

it himself. No sooner did he hear any criticism than he went at once to inform the Grand Heir, turning it all into defamation of the Heir Apparent. The Heir, deep in the palace with no access to anyone, heard only Kugyŏng. Devoted to Kugyŏng, he was unable to detect the ruffian's cunning schemes. He believed what he heard.

In this way, Kugyŏng managed to deepen the Grand Heir's trust in him. Then he was credited with having acted meritoriously in bringing about the regency. Within seven or eight months of my son's accession, he was catapulted into such positions as First Royal Secretary and Secret Censor. At the same time, he was Commander of the Palace Guard Garrison, and so he stayed at the palace, referring to his place as the Palace Guard Residence. Then he was placed in charge of the Five Military Garrisons; his title was Commanding General of the Five Military Garrisons and General of the Capital Detachment Regiment. The honors and royal favors bestowed upon him were simply unprecedented.

At whim, Kugyŏng killed innumerable people. My family was one of the first to suffer his blows. He resented my uncle for reprimanding him while his uncle, Naksun, and my uncle were longstanding enemies. It was rumored that Naksun was looking for ways to have my uncle killed. It does seem that Kugyŏng listened to his uncle. This contributed to the extremity of the disaster that befell my uncle. In the four years that Kugyŏng was in power, he did hundreds of thousands of faithless and reckless things. Living deeply secluded in the palace as I did, I was not informed in detail. According to rumors buzzing about, Kugyŏng lived openly with woman physicians at his official quarters in the palace as if it were his own private home; he had his meals prepared exactly like the royal meals and was incredibly arrogant in the royal presence and contemptuous toward ministers.* I simply could not understand how, considering the accumulated ancestral virtue of the Hong family, such a vile traitor could be born into it.

Though Kugyŏng was insolent, he was a man of small vision, and so at first one did not expect him to scheme for large things.

---

* The *Sillok* historians' comments are more scathing than Lady Hyegyŏng's. In addition to confirming everything she says here, the *Sillok* adds details recounting that Hong Kugyŏng used to recline on a high daybed in his room at the palace, requiring ministers to bow beneath him, that he insulted and screamed at the elderly, and so on. *CS*, 8:26b.

Then Kim Chongsu appeared on the scene in the fifth month of the *pyŏngsin* year (1776). He began to act like a son to Kugyŏng.* Together they practiced a thousand, even ten thousand, evil intrigues. Chongsu was none other than my second cousin, the son of my father's first female cousin.† My grandfather loved this niece and called her his adopted daughter. After her marriage, she had two sons, Chonghu[16] and Chongsu. They lived in the same neighborhood as my family. The two families were very friendly and the children grew up like siblings. After my royal marriage, however, my family rose to prominence while they, though descendants of ministers, posed as pure scholars devoted only to learning. The close and affectionate relationship between the two families thus changed. Still, regarding Chonghu and Chongsu as children of the family, my father occasionally admonished and instructed them. They grew strangely obstreperous and arrogant however. At one point, Father saved their lives. Seeing that they frequently behaved quite iniquitously, Father disapproved of them. Because of this, they seem to have harbored resentment. Since Father admonished them in order to instruct the youngsters in the family, he did not think about it afterwards. In addition, their mother was the oldest among the cousins of my father's generation. In consideration for her seniority and in memory of his father who had favored her, my father treated her as an older sister. Whether he served in or out of the capital, he unfailingly sent her gifts on holidays and on each change of season, expressing a particular devotion and affection. Who would have imagined that they were planning to kill their mother's cousin?

In the *chŏnghae* year (1767), Chonghu was being reviewed for a senior post.[17] Contrary to custom, the Minister of Personnel did not seek out the views of other ministers or scholars. He conducted the review in solitude. My father was in mourning at the time but, representing the scholarly consensus, disapproved of this deviation. Chonghu profoundly resented this and decided to seek revenge. In *imjin* (1772) when Chongsu was sent into exile for a

---

* Strictly figurative speech meaning that Chongsu was as obedient as a son to Kugyŏng.
† Their grandfathers, Hong Sŏkpo and Hong Hyŏnbo, were brothers. Chongsu's mother was the first daughter of Hong Sŏkpo and she married Kim Ch'iman.

time,* the Kim brothers insisted upon attributing that to my third brother, despite the transparent improbability of their claim. I also heard that they publicly declared that they would see to it that my family would be ruined. I was saddened that we were groundlessly suspected by our kin.

Their time came when Chongsu formed an alliance with Kugyŏng. Chongsu constantly prodded and instigated him to do things that Kugyŏng himself would not have thought of. Chongsu was deceiving the world. Kugyŏng was pleased that Chongsu was as friendly as a son or a brother, as submissive as a slave, and as obsequious as a concubine. He accepted Chongsu's word and participated in his plots. If it had been left to Kugyŏng alone, I do not believe that the calamities that my family suffered would have been so extreme. When that reckless Kugyŏng was indiscriminately killing people for nothing more than petty resentment, Chongsu joined in to wreak his own vengeance. When these two started to settle past scores, many, guilty or not, were killed. Since Kugyŏng fell precipitously, some in the younger generation know of his crimes, but very few know the crimes of Chongsu, who, chameleon that he was, quickly changed sides and thus was not implicated with Kugyŏng.† If one were to discuss and evaluate their crimes, there would be six or seven of Chongsu's for every three or four of Kugyŏng's. Often I would say to the King, "What Kugyŏng did was not entirely his fault; in fact Chongsu was more responsible for it." The King would smile, saying, "That's true."

When Kugyŏng was in royal favor, there was nothing he desired that he could not do to his heart's content. Not satisfied, he gave his sister to the King to ensure that, as a royal affine, he would enjoy unlimited power. At the time, because of Madame Chŏng's machinations, the Queen was not favored. Had Kugyŏng been a loyal official with the interests of the throne at heart, the right thing for him to do, as the confidant whom the King trusted as a brother, would have been to urge the King to form a conjugal intimacy with the Queen. The Queen was only twenty-six and had no

---

* Kim Chongsu was banished to a remote island. His crime was involvement in factional issues. *YS*, 118:27b–28a.

† After Hong Kugyŏng was dismissed from office in 1780, Kim Chongsu sent a memorial criticizing Kugyŏng's character and arguing for severe punishment. *CS*, 9:16b–17b.

abdominal ailment. However, Kugyŏng arranged for the Queen
Dowager to send out an official missive declaring that the Queen
had such an ailment,* deepening the estrangement between the
royal couple. If he came to the conclusion that it was not within his
power to bring them together, he should have urged the King,
who was without an heir at nearly thirty years of age, to select a
mature girl to facilitate the speedy birth of a son. Instead, he seized
upon a vile scheme, offering the King his very young sister, barely
twelve at the time. This meant a long wait before there would be
any hope of childbearing. She was given the official title Wŏnbin,
and her palace title was Sukch'ang.[18] The conferral of the title
Wŏnbin, meaning First Consort, was a flagrant act; it was, in fact,
an inadmissible violation of propriety in view of the fact that the
Queen was still present. The way of Heaven, however, manifested
itself clearly. His crimes had reached their limit, and so his sister
died suddenly in *kihae* (1779).[19]

Chagrined and overcome with anger, Kugyŏng dared to suspect
that the Queen had something to do with his sister's death. Having
planted seeds of suspicion in the King, he had many of the Queen's
ladies-in-waiting arrested, and with a big sword in hand, had them
interrogated with merciless beatings and other terrible tortures. He
was hoping to obtain a confession that would incriminate the
Queen.[20] Though he did not succeed, the confessions thus exacted
came rather close to inculpating the Queen. These bizarre goings-
on at the court led to threatening and frightening rumors circulating far and wide. Some fearful merchants at the city market even
closed their shops and ran away. One is hard put to find a worse
traitor than this Kugyŏng.

Once his scheme to perpetuate his power and wealth was
thwarted, one would expect him, if only out of fear of Heaven, to
temper his arrogance and, if only to atone for his sin, to suggest
that the throne select a lady of illustrious family. But, lest the royal
heart favor the family of the newly selected lady, Kugyŏng was determined to obstruct a reselection. He persuaded Tŏksang to sub-

* In the fifth month of 1778, Queen Dowager Chŏngsun sent instructions,
written in Korean, for King Chŏngjo to the effect that, since at the age of almost
thirty he had no heir, he should select a consort among the daughters of scholar-
official families. *CS*, 5:49a–b.

mit that horrible memorial.* Subsequently, Kugyŏng bestowed upon Tam, Ŭnŏn's son,† a prestigious sinecure as Guardian of Tombs and Shrines complete with the title of Prince Wanp'ung, and he made him the posthumously adopted son of his sister.[21] This made Tam a kind of adopted son to the King as well. What Kugyŏng was attempting was to become a maternal uncle to the Heir Apparent so that he could permanently enjoy power. The King was not yet thirty years of age and had no impediment to siring an heir, but Kugyŏng attempted to prevent him from having a son of his own. The King, temporarily blinded by his fascination with Kugyŏng and trusting his word, had followed his every suggestion uncritically, believing that each was motivated by devotion to the throne. But when it came to this matter, it was inconceivable that the King, with his clear intelligence, would not eventually awaken to the evil in Kugyŏng's heart. Kugyŏng took in the young Tam as his nephew and made him almost the King's son. He arranged it so that the King's own eunuchs would escort the child about as though he were in effect the Heir Apparent. Tam's father, Ŭnŏn, a frivolous and unstable man, gave himself airs, not at all suspecting that his son's present status might be the root of future troubles. He had his men employed in the office of the Guardian of Tombs and Shrines. His ignorance was simply pathetic.

My brothers wrote me, voicing outrage and astonishment over this turn of events. "What in the world is this measure? What is this step?" they wrote. At this point, my grief and rage reached such an explosive point that I spoke to the King, saying, "What is this

---

* Song Tŏksang (d. 1783) sent a memorial in the sixth month of 1779 that said it was extremely urgent to seek widely to obtain an heir. This was a euphemistic request that the King select an heir from the royal clan. As this memorial suggested a transfer of the royal line from the existing one to another, it could easily be construed as lèse-majesté and soon was taken as such. (CS, 7:49a–b.) As a great-grandson of Song Siyŏl (1606–1689), the great Neo-Confucian scholar and the founder of the Noron, Song Tŏksang had entered the bureaucracy in 1753 on recommendation and remained in inconspicuous posts until 1776, when his career, supported by Hong Kugyŏng, began to take off. In 1779 he was appointed Minister of Personnel. Upon Hong Kugyŏng's dismissal in 1779, he attempted to dissociate himself from Hong, but he could not eradicate the fact that he had sent in that notorious memorial. He was imprisoned in 1782 and died there in 1783. His two sons were separately confined to the countryside. CS, 9:25b, 11:67a–68a, 15:8a, 15:19a–b.

† Since Ŭnŏn was King Chŏngjo's half brother, Tam was Chŏngjo's nephew.

measure and what is the meaning of it? Please think of it. Is Your Highness old? Does Your Highness have an illness? The desire to have a son is shared by old and young, noble and base alike. With the dynastic mandate entrusted to Your Highness, it is surely a matter of concern that Your Highness, nearing thirty years of age, does not yet have a son. Under someone else's thumb, Your Highness is deciding not to have a son. What is the meaning of this?" I protested and lamented like this before him.

Kugyŏng's power, as imposing as Mount T'ai, was such that no one dared utter a word of criticism. Thus Kugyŏng's sister's funeral chamber was the room that had been used for Queen Chŏngsŏng; her grave was named Inmyŏngwŏn, her shrine Hyohwigung, and every official, from the ministers serving on the State Council down, wore mourning garb and burned incense. No official who served at the time could escape blame for acting improperly.*

I alone raged and lamented. My anger soared as high as Heaven. I gnashed my teeth. Unable to abide what was going on, I wailed and cried whenever I saw my son, and stroking him, I sorrowed and grieved. The King seemed gradually to realize that he had been duped by that ruffian Kugyŏng who called Tam his nephew, treated him as though he were the Heir Apparent, and slept and ate with him. Their schemes daily grew more cunning and vicious; the situation grew proportionately more precarious and perverse.

With his penetrating intelligence, how could the King not come to regret and resent it? Deeply anxious over the future of the state, he was in a quandary. In rage and sorrow, sincerely and repeatedly, I urged him, "Please think of a way to have a son." The King was by nature benevolent and filial. Moved by my pleas, he pondered my plight and his situation, and he decided that I was right. His attitude toward me grew even more considerate. As for Kugyŏng, the King had him resign from all his official posts in the ninth month of *kihae* (1779). Because of his long affection for him, he was determined to spare his life. But after his resignation, Kugyŏng's behavior grew so grotesque and atrocious that the King confined him to Kangnŭng, at which place he soon died.[22]

---

* For a description of Wŏnbin's funeral, see *CS*, 7:43b–44a. The *Sillok* historian comments that the arrangements were truly excessive, but, fearing Hong Kugyŏng, no one dared to dissent. One Chŏng Hongsun, then serving as a minister without portfolio, did not participate in the incense-burning ceremony for Wŏnbin and was dismissed from his post. *CS*, 7:50b.

Since ancient times, there have been countless vicious traitors and cunning power-seekers, yet I doubt that any were quite like Kugyŏng. Of the many crimes of which he was guilty, one was that he casually accused many of sedition, termed them traitors and rebels out of nothing more than private grudges, and indiscriminately killed them, staining the King's sagacious virtue. A second was that he obstructed the marital harmony between the King and his Queen and sought to monopolize wealth and power by giving his young sister to the King. A third was that, after his sister's death, he tried to prevent the King from having an heir and schemed by adopting Tam as his sister's posthumous son, planning to make his nephew the Crown Prince, which, had he succeeded, would have made him the maternal uncle of the Heir Apparent. A fourth was that he cruelly tortured the Queen's ladies-in-waiting, hoping to get a confession that would incriminate the Queen so that he could pursue his vile plots against her. In addition, when he was with other people, he is said to have made a great many impertinent, disloyal, and even blasphemous remarks about the King. Since I have not personally heard him saying these things, I will not record them. An official who is guilty of any one of these crimes would not be able to avoid the heaviest punishment. But even though Kugyŏng was burdened with a thousand crimes and ten thousand evil acts that one never heard of before, he ended his life peacefully in his own bed. One must lament the indifference of Heaven.

Chongsu posed as a high-minded, principled scholar. It is obvious from this anecdote that very early in his career he schemed to get a post by attaching himself to Hugyŏm. At the farewell audience before Chongsu left for his new post as Magistrate of T'aech'ŏn, His Majesty [King Yŏngjo] gave him a bolt of silk, saying, "Make your official robes of this." His Majesty had detested Chongsu for having engaged in factionalism. This sudden gracious generosity could not possibly have come about had it not been for Hugyŏm. Chongsu had a natural bent for anything by which he would profit, and so he ran after Hugyŏm. Hugyŏm, however, did not really take him in. Chongsu gritted his teeth at this rejection, but he soon joined Kugyŏng's circle.

Of Kugyŏng's thousand cunning intrigues and ten thousand evil acts, there were none that Chongsu did not assist in. When Kugyŏng was dismissed from office, Chongsu made Chonghu send in a memorial arguing that the decision be reversed. In his memorial, Chonghu declared, "[He] is the most loyal of ministers. As a tiger on a mountain quiets all lesser creatures, his presence at court quiets the lesser officials. He should not be absent from the court for even one day."* Chongsu and Chonghu later claimed that they had been deceived by Kugyŏng, but they sent this memorial from P'yŏngan Province in a great hurry away from all pressure, afraid only that others might precede them.† At the time, however, after Kugyŏng arranged for Tam's adoption, had Tŏksang send up that memorial, and obstructed the selection of another consort for the King, the unspoken consensus was that he was a traitor. Moreover, Chongsu and Chonghu sent in a memorial supporting Kugyŏng despite the fact that this meant going against their factional affiliation. Where is principle when one betrays one's faction?

Later, Chongsu sent a memorial to the throne attacking Kugyŏng, but he did this under pressure from the King. I said to my son, "Chongsu acted as if he were Kugyŏng's own son. Now he recriminates against him mercilessly. How can this be?" The King answered, "It is not his intention, but if he wants to survive, what choice does he have?" I said, "He must be a nine-tailed fox who is capable of a thousand changes and ten thousand transformations." "It is an apt description of him," the King answered laughingly. This shows that my son was not unaware of Chongsu's true character.

After Kugyŏng's fall, the way to follow the principle of Heaven and to soothe popular sentiments would have been to correct the mistakes made during his dominance and to rehabilitate those, such as my uncle, who had been wrongly punished. But Kugyŏng's crimes had not been clearly manifested, and the guiltless who were punished have not yet been cleared. This is because, though Kugyŏng was gone, Chongsu still perpetuated his devices.[23]

Not once in his life did Chongsu earnestly advise the throne or

---

* This memorial was sent by Kim Chonghu on the twenty-third of the tenth month, 1779. It expresses dismay over the dismissal of someone, but it does not name the person. Whoever it is, the person in question is praised for supporting principle and protecting scholars. Hong Kugyŏng was dismissed in the ninth month, but King Chŏngjo was still expressing his support for him. CS, 8:41a–b.

† The Sillok records that on the previous day Kim Chonghu arrived from where his brother Kim Chongsu was stationed and passed through the capital city. CS, 8:41a.

correct what was wrong. Rather, he applied himself enthusiastically, with his sleeves rolled up, to such things as attacking the Hongs and imprisoning people. In all of history it is difficult to find vapors as poisonous as those that surrounded Chongsu. But despite his knowledge of Chongsu's character, the late King remained constant to him to the end. Because of his frugal habits and his uncorrupted tenure in office, Chongsu did not alienate people. The King felt that, under the circumstances, he could maintain his old affection for him. But Chongsu's so-called frugality and incorruptibility were all posture. He also gained a reputation for filial devotion to his mother. However, had he been truly considerate of his mother's feelings, would he have killed her first cousin?* Even had her cousin been guilty, Chongsu was not the only living person in this world. He could have left the task of his cousin's punishment to others. But he took it upon himself to kill his mother's close relative while she still lived. How can one say that his filial devotion was genuine? People are cognizant of most of Kugyŏng's evil deeds, but not Chongsu's. Yet Kugyŏng was but a shell of which Chongsu was the core. I have written the details of what happened so that the truth might be known to the world.

My third brother was born in the *sinyu* year (1741), when I was in my seventh year. His appearance and character were pure and luminous; he was a boy of unquestionably superior endowment. It is hardly necessary to say that my parents showered their love on this son and that I was partial to him. When he came into the palace, His Majesty also found him beautiful and had him and my second brother accompany His Majesty around the palace. Prince Sado especially loved my third brother. My brother excelled in learning and passed all three stages of the civil examinations at the top of the lists, earning a reputation for scholarship and talent. I have always thought of him as a sibling and a friend, one with whom I shared mutual understanding. The family and I had great hopes for him.

Soon after his entry to officialdom, the family encountered problems. I felt quite sorry that he was made to feel discomfited and uneasy so soon. Between *kyŏngin* and *sinmyo* (1770–1771) the shadows of calamity cast upon my father grew deeper and more threatening daily. I thought that there was no way in which I could

---

* Hong Inhan.

appease Kwiju, nor did I feel that there was much sense in approaching Madame Chŏng, since she, influenced by her son, had long since changed her attitude toward us. As things stood, the only way to appease them was for someone in my family to befriend her son, but for some reason Hugyŏm disliked my older brother and my second brother. This left my third brother.

My third brother was refined in manner, indifferent to wealth and power, and averse to chasing after luminaries, and so he had few casual friends. He was not even well acquainted with our house guests. With this personality, he certainly was not willing to beg for favors or to do anything shameful. Yet, of the Hong brothers, he was fresh and young and was not hated by Hugyŏm. I wrote to my third brother, saying, "In ancient times, there were filial sons who died for their parents. Now the situation demands that, for your father's sake, you befriend Hugyŏm and save the family. Hugyŏm is just someone who, being the princess's son and assured of royal grace, enjoys displaying his power. He is not a eunuch nor a rebel. If you do not save your father because you fear being besmirched by Hugyŏm for a time, it would not be the way of a good son." I pleaded with him thus. At first he resisted fiercely, but as disaster approached and the destruction of the whole family seemed imminent, and as my urgings became more intense, my brother could not but enter the fray, casting thoughts of his own integrity to the winds. He befriended Hugyŏm and made it possible for my father to avoid the cruelest fate. But, in the estimate of some, my brother fell from grace because of this. All because of this sister.[24]

My third brother embarked on an official career in the footsteps of his father and brother, and with his scholarship and talent, his prospects seemed limitless. However, his lofty ambition had to remain unfulfilled. He was deeply ashamed that he did not keep his principles but befriended Hugyŏm in the face of adversity, even though it was only out of concern for calamities that might befall an aged parent. He pledged that "When the family attains stability, I will not go out into the world." At some point, he acquired a house in a district east of the capital and wrote to me, saying, "Your brother won't be able to go far away. In the near future, I will go to the countryside nearby and, thinking of the palace in the capital, live out my life in seclusion amidst the streams and rocks." To this day, I can vividly see the calligraphy of his letter.

My brother made sure that he did not derive the smallest benefit from his association with Hugyŏm. He befriended Hugyŏm for the sake of his father and brother. He felt that if he attained office through Hugyŏm, it would not represent his true intention and he would be no different from those who sought out the unworthy and corrupted the world. So between the seven years from *kich'uk* (1769), when he passed the examination at the top, to *ŭlmi* (1775), he did not accept posts higher than those he had already acquired before *kyŏngin* (1770). Thus he remained as a junior counselor in the Office of the Special Counselors or a lower-ranking tutor in the Crown Prince Tutorial Office. He adamantly refused to be promoted to fourth special counselor, a post only one step higher than what he had, not to mention anything in the senior echelons of the bureaucracy. Nor did he accept a post as magistrate even for a small town. When he was recommended for paid leave to pursue scholarship, an honor given to promising young scholar-officials, he also refused. That he accepted neither one penny more in salary nor one rank higher in his post since *kyŏngin* (1770) quite clearly shows that his association with Hugyŏm was not motivated by self-interest.

All my third brother did in his association with Hugyŏm was to see to it that Madame Chŏng's fickleness and Hugyŏm's explosive and uncontrollable cunning not be turned against the Hong family again. Aside from that, he did not even wish to know whom Hugyŏm employed, spurned, killed, or saved. Nor did Hugyŏm consult him on those matters. This fact is known to everyone. When people ally themselves with the powerful and create disruptions in society, they usually seek self-aggrandizement, and what aggrandizes other than wealth, power, prestige, and fame? Given his pedigree, his scholarship, and his astounding success as top candidate in the examination, my brother was assured of every desirable post in the government. Had he sought self-interest in befriending Hugyŏm, would he not have sought important posts and increases in salary and rank? By so scrupulously avoiding the smallest benefit, my brother wished the world to understand that it was his desperate concern for his father that had led to his association with Hugyŏm.

Sangun* was by nature vicious and cunning. He was the descendant of a family that had been punished and destroyed. He

---

* Sim Sangun (1732–1776). He was a faithful follower of Chŏng Hugyŏm.

pandered to Hugyŏm, using his talent as bait. My third brother met Sangun at Hugyŏm's place and they became acquainted. My brother was not pleased with Sangun, but his fear of Hugyŏm led him to remain on good terms with Sangun. In *ŭlmi* (1775) a special examination was held to celebrate the establishment of the regency, and the successful candidates included three persons descended from either Ch'oe Sŏkhang or Cho T'aeŏk, the rebels of the incidents of the *sinim* years (1721–1722).* This caused a public furor. One day Sangun visited my brother and said, "I am thinking of sending in a memorial requesting that Ch'oe and Cho be deleted from the list. What do you think of the idea?" My brother answered, "You are in a very delicate position yourself. Your appointment is not exactly without controversy. You'd better not send in such a memorial, nor should you interfere in affairs of this kind. Passing Ch'oe and Cho was preposterous, but public dissent is growing and someone will surely come forward with a denunciation. It does not seem to be your place to discuss it." Sangun was offended by this and left in a huff. On that very day, one Sŏ Yunyŏng sent a memorial on the same issue, depriving Sangun of the opportunity to be first on the matter.[†]

Several days later, my brother received a letter from Sangun. It said, "This morning, I sent in a memorial. The memorial is too long for me to send you a copy of the entire text. I just copied the list of issues that I discussed." Enclosed was a piece of paper on

---

* Ch'oe Sŏkhang and Cho T'aeŏk were two key Soron ministers involved in what is known as the *sinim sahwa* (the purge of 1721–1722), in which the Soron purged the Noron. Upon Yŏngjo's accession, the Noron repeatedly sought vindication. Because of Yŏngjo's determined effort to end bloody factional purges, a purge of Soron did not occur, but the Soron gradually lost ground. (See Haboush, *Heritage*, 117–65.) The special examination was held on the eleventh of the twelfth month, 1775, the day after Chŏngjo began his regency. Fifteen people passed the examination, including Ch'oe Suwŏn, Cho Yŏngŭi, and Cho Ugyu. (*YS*, 126:12a, 126:16a.)

† Sŏ's memorial arrived on the nineteenth of the twelfth month. This memorial pointed out that the answers on the examinations of the three candidates under discussion contained the same phrases. It warned that the examination should be better proctored (*YS*, 126:17b–18a). Another official, Yi Isang, had already sent a memorial on the sixteenth complaining about the selection of three descendants of Soron officials who had been responsible for the purge of 1721–1722 (*YS*, 126:16a). Thus Sŏ Yunyŏng's memorial was not the first on the topic of the examination. On the twenty-first day, the three candidates were removed from the list. *YS*, 126:18a.

which he wrote the first character of each item that he discussed. There were eight items altogether and the first characters included "faction," "office," and so on. The last one was "affines" and the gist of his argument was that they should not be given office. On this last item, he copied a fair portion of his discussion rather than just writing one character, probably because he wanted my family, royal affines, to see it. Though my brother could not tell what the memorial really said, he was surprised that Sangun, a member of a destroyed family, would send a memorial on issues so controversial that they would make the sender conspicuous. So he answered Sangun, saying, "Though you are convinced that what you have done is right, others who see the memorial will most likely criticize you. In that sense, I am not certain whether sending the memorial was a good idea."

That evening my brother saw the original of the memorial* and was greatly astonished. He at once wrote to the Inspector General Yun Yanghu urging him to arrest and interrogate Sangun. He also wrote to Yanghu's brother, Yun Sanghu, asking him to press the same point to Yanghu. But Yanghu did not comply. The whole story on this is well known since my brother told everything from beginning to end when he was interrogated in the *musul* year (1778).† He also submitted Sangun's letter to the King and the piece of paper on which Sangun listed the items in his memorial. Yun Sanghu was still living then, and so my brother requested that Sanghu appear as a witness to his contention that he had urged Yanghu to interrogate Sangun.[25] My brother found Sangun's memorial appalling and repugnant. He deeply regretted his association with Sangun and energetically and persistently, about a hundred times more than others, requested Sangun's punishment. It is clear that there is no truth to the allegation that he had something to do with Sangun's memorial.

---

* The memorial is written in very strong language lamenting the ill effects of factional practice and citing various contemporary examples. The memorial was taken as a veiled attack on the new regent, Chŏngjo. *YS*, 126:18a–19a.

† Sim Sangun was interrogated and banished (*YS*, 126:19a–26a). Later, in 1776, he was accused of sedition and was tortured to death (*CS*, 1:92a–b). Hong Nagim was accused of having been involved in the plot with Sim Sangun and was interrogated by Chŏngjo. He was adjudged to have been innocent and was released. See *The Memoir of 1795*, footnote on page 103.

When a seditious plot was discovered in *chŏngyu* (1777),*
Sanggil, one of the defendants, said in his interrogation, "When
we were planning to overthrow the dynasty, we discussed Hong
[Nagim] among ourselves, saying that he was not in office because
he was an affine. But he would, in the long run, control the
military [and so we should accommodate him]. Hong promised
that, in that event, he would aid us if we were to execute our
plan."[26] This made no sense at all and not even a three-year-
old would be persuaded by it. If they implicated my brother by
charging that he was resentful of the court because he was not
employed and therefore joined a seditious plot, then there would
have been a certain logic to it. But they charged that my brother
expected to attain a powerful position and control the army,
and that he assured them of help in that event. Why would anyone at the peak of success and in royal grace think of sedition? If
he were to control the army, then his family would prosper,
his power and wealth would reach ultimate heights, and he could
satisfy all of his desires. Under the circumstances, what would
anyone gain by joining in sedition? Even though these ruffians
said these nonsensical things about my brother, he had no idea of
what was going on, and there simply was no way to make him
guilty. But Kugyŏng somehow detested my brother and was determined to harm him. It seemed for a while that a disaster was
imminent.

In his sagacious virtue, the King wished to spare my brother's
life. Finally, in *musul* (1778), the King cleared my brother of two
accusations that had been brought against him and declared him
completely innocent. The royal edict announcing this was truly
wonderful. It detailed the event logically and analyzed the situation
impartially. Then it concluded, "When we evaluate this by the
standards of Heavenly principle and human affection, one comes to
the conclusion that it cannot be. Even if there were a trace of suspicion, we would forgive him. But there is none. Today we manifest how false was the accusation that was brought against him, and

---

* It was a plot to kill Chŏngjo and to enthrone Prince Ŭnjŏn. The principal
rebels involved were Hong Surhae (1722–1777), who had served as a governor of
Hwanghae Province, his brothers, his son Hong Sangbŏm (d. 1777), his nephew
Hong Sanggil, and several others. *CS,* 4:19b–29b.

we hereby declare that he was entirely wronged. Now we can face Her Ladyship, my gracious mother."* The King was truly pleased with what he did on this occasion. That my brother, the King's uncle, was arrested and interrogated as a criminal was unprecedented in either Chinese history or the history of our dynasty. When this happened, I was so aggrieved and frightened that it was as if I had gone through the experience myself. But I was moved by my son's sagacious filial piety. I was genuinely touched by the thoroughness with which the King exposed the complete fallacy of the allegations, exculpating my brother of the faintest shadow of criminality.

After Kugyŏng departed, the King came to regret many events. As years went by, he became kinder and more respectful toward his maternal uncles. He regarded it as a great pity that my third brother, with his accomplishments in scholarship and calligraphy, was not in office. He periodically sent paper to my brother asking him to write something on it and had it made into screens. These came to quite a few. He put some of them in his room and gave me several, too. He also pasted my brother's calligraphy of seasonal celebratory phrases on the walls. He even had my brother write his own poems and had them made into a hanging plaque. From *sinhae* (1791), the King began to collect my father's memorials, and his contact with my brothers became more frequent. After my second brother died, my third brother became his sole consultant. From the *chŏngsa* year (1797), the King began to edit my father's collected papers. He consulted with my brother on every detail, deciding which should be kept and which omitted and which corrected and which restored. They exchanged several memoranda every day.

Whenever the King saw my brother, he would invariably say afterwards, "In mien and bearing, he is truly remarkable. No one at the court today can match him. He is in retreat now, but eventually

---

* Chŏngjo said that he decided to go ahead with Hong Nagim's interrogation because Lady Hyegyŏng urged it. Lady Hyegyŏng was said to have maintained that if her brother had been guilty in plotting against the king, she would not mind if he were punished. She believed that there were no grounds for the accusation, so she wanted his innocence to be established through due process. Although Chŏngjo conducted the case, he expressed great solicitude for his mother's feelings. *CS*, 5:23a–24a.

he will attain a post at least as high as that of Yun Sidong."* The King also said these things of him: "He will be in his sixty-fourth year in *kapcha* (1804) and will have no trouble serving as a minister," "His prose is clear and pure. He is the best writer of his generation," "He is my friend," "He is a fellow scholar with whom I have a spiritual kinship."

In his later years, whatever the King composed he sent to my brother asking for criticism. If it was a poem, he asked him to write a poem in rejoinder using the same rhyme. On each of these occasions, the King displayed some gesture of generosity. He sent to him all sorts of gifts, but in particular, if he happened to taste something good, he wished to share it with his uncle and always sent him half of what he had. He said, "Your writing is worthy of transmission to later generations. I will see to it that your collected works are published." His treatment of my third brother was so special that they were like father and son in an ordinary family.

There is no member of my family, old or young, who was not indebted to royal grace. But my brother was particularly so. He was already indebted to the King for a new lease on life, but in addition he was treated so graciously. He was always profoundly grateful. He often shed tears of gratitude and said, "Even if I were to die for him, I could not repay one ten-thousandth of the royal grace I received." Everyone in the palace knows that the late King, my son, favored my third brother in this way. I am sure that the present King, despite his youth, is also very well aware of it and does not need me to tell him of it.

Aside from that ineradicable pain,† for one half of my life I have endured sorrows because of misfortunes heaped upon my family. Having received a firm pledge [from my son] concerning the *kapcha* year (1804), how could I fail to be relieved; how could I not rejoice? It was only to be a matter of a few years before my family would enjoy peace and security. How expectantly I hoped that my brothers could soon roam the mountains in a carefree spirit, bathed in royal grace and living out their remaining years without in-

---

* Yun Sidong (1729–1797) had a long, though checkered, official career that included banishment on several occasions. He served as the Minister of the Right in 1795. He was a descendant of Yun Tusu (1533–1601), an illustrious minister who served during the Japanese invasion of Korea in the 1590s.

† The pain of losing her husband so cruelly.

cident. How could I have imagined, even in my dreams, that I would lose my son and see my third brother meet that cruel end?

At the national funeral in *kyŏngsin* (1800), many members of my family were called upon to serve on the standing committee.* This did not augur well. My third brother was among those appointed to the committee. Prime Minister Sim Hwanji, who served as the interim caretaker of the government during the funeral,† several other ministers, and some royal secretaries objected to his appointment and sent [to the Queen Dowager] an odious, strongly worded memorial. While the late King was alive, no one voiced objections to my brother's visits, whether he was in office or frequented the palace in gratitude to royal kindness. But within a few days of the late King's death, this abomination! It was simply not true that my brother would accept any temporary post just because it was offered. But even if he were to accept one and regularly attend at the palace, what crisis could it have caused to the nation? Sim Hwanji, unable to wait even for a minute, felt compelled to criticize my brother's appointment as urgently as if it were a matter of the survival of the nation! He did this even before the late King's body was placed in a coffin.

I was beside myself. At seventy years of age, I had lost my only son. I cried out to Heaven, wailed and sobbed, not knowing whether I was alive or dead. At that moment, this evil man chose to incriminate my brother in that way. Had this man said that all members of my family were forbidden to come into the palace, it might have been easier to take, but he pointedly singled out my third brother. True, my third brother had been implicated in a truly awful case, but the late King, after personally conducting an interrogation, realized the falsity of the accusation and indisputably established my brother's innocence. The royal pronouncement on

---

* The funeral of King Chŏngjo, which lasted five months until the burial in the eleventh month, 1800. For details, see *Ch'ŏngjong taewang pinjŏn honjŏn togam ŭigwe*, 3 *ch'aek*, manuscript, 1800, Kyujanggak. Queen Dowager Chŏngsun ordered that Hong family members including Hong Yonghan, Hong Chunhan, Hong Nagim, Hong Nagyun, Hong Ch'wiyŏng, Hong Suyŏng, and Hong Huyŏng serve on the standing committee for the funeral. See *Sunjo sillok* (hereafter SS), in *Chosŏn wangjo sillok*, 1:3b.

† Though the Heir Apparent ascended the throne soon after the death of the king, he could not immediately take up administration because of his mourning duties. Some elderly minister, usually the prime minister, was empowered to take care of state affairs for the first twenty-six days.

this point was as plain as it could have been. The King had it recorded in the *Sok Myŏngŭirok* (A continuation of the record of clarifying righteousness),[27] so that everyone was made aware that my brother was cleared of all wrongdoing and declared completely innocent. After almost thirty years, my brother was censured again for an old charge. This meant that if a man had been unfortunately implicated in a disastrous case at some point in his life, even if he were proven and declared innocent beyond a shadow of doubt, he would have to live in ignominy for the rest of his life. Where in the world is there such a law and such an argument?

The late King completed editing my father's memorials, but he passed away suddenly before he could publish them. It is hateful that I did not at once follow him in death. Though I sustained my life by a thread, I felt as though I were dead and did not feel in my heart that I would live much longer. Perhaps to console my grieving heart for the late King or, alternatively, to push my family's fortunes even further to their lowest point, a person in charge of outside affairs at my palace informed me late in the eighth month,* "It has been decided that His Majesty is going to announce [the publication of Hong Ponghan's memorials] and the Kyujanggak will sponsor and publish it with a royal announcement."†

Not having yet understood that the way of the world could be so cruel and so wretched, I handed over the manuscript that the late King had edited. The manuscript contained, in addition to my father's memorials, about sixty prefaces written by the late King. Expecting that they would at least print it even if the publication might not be accompanied by a royal announcement, I gave them the original. Feeling that I was at the threshold of death, out of devotion to my father and wishing to honor the late King's painstaking labor, I desperately wished to see the publication of the manuscript.

* King Sunjo ascended the throne early in the seventh month.
† On the eleventh of the eighth month, 1800, the *Sillok* records the following instructions from the Queen Dowager Regent: "The collected memorials of Lord Hong Ikchŏng have been edited by our late King himself. His Late Majesty was about to print them and disseminate them to the world. Let the Naegak proceed with the printing. When they are printed, the book should be offered at the sacrifice at Lord Ikchŏng's shrine. This is to honor His Late Majesty's intentions." (*SS*, 1:17b.) "Naegak" was another name for Kyujanggak. Established by Chŏngjo, Kyujanggak was an institution devoted to scholarship and the preservation and publication of books.

Before they printed one volume, however, Sim Hwanji and several others strongly disputed the project and the printing was stalled. As I read their disputation, great shivers went through me. My heart took fright and my liver and lungs felt as if they were broken into pieces or completely crushed. Their argument, quite apart from insults to my father, was full of words and phrases intended to persecute and taunt me.* Although I had become a pathetic figure, almost an old palace woman with nowhere to go and no one to turn to, I was still the mother of the late King. Even though Sim enjoyed earthshaking power, he still had been the late King's subject and had served the King as his liege. He humilated me thus, all the while saying that I was the mother of the late King. Between Heaven and Earth, where have you seen such iniquity? The present King is still in his early youth; thus the nation is in a rather precarious state. The hearts of men and the mores of the world have degenerated so hopelessly that now the world does not even acknowledge motherhood. Anxiety for the state and despair for degraded humanity make me wish to weep.

While the late King was alive, I let him do as he wished in serving his mother, whether he did so only with filial devotion or by availing himself of the splendors that the throne could afford. After his demise, I was but a neglected widow with a dubious place in the royal hierarchy.[†] I did not feel that I deserved regular greetings from the court[‡] or visits by the Medical Bureau, and so even as I traversed the path between life and death, I was exceedingly uncomfortable at being tended by the Medical Bureau. Now that I

---

* On the twentieth of the eighth month, 1800, at a regular audience with the King and the Queen Dowager Regent, Prime Minister Sim Hwanji, Minister of the Left Yi Sisu, and Minister of the Right Sŏ Yongbo requested the discontinuation of the printing of Hong Ponghan's papers. They argued that Hong Ponghan was a criminal, as was clearly manifested by many memorials; that Chŏngjo wanted to print them only out of filial piety to please his mother; and that the present situation did not require the printing of the memorials of "a disloyal and abominable official." (*SS*, 1:19b.) It was not until 1815 that King Sunjo had this manuscript published (*SS*, 18:7b–8a). Both the Kyujanggak and the Changsŏgak have several copies of the *Ŏjŏng Hong Ikchŏnggong chugo* (The royally edited memorials of Lord Hong Ikchŏng). This publication consists of eighteen volumes.

† Lady Hyegyŏng, King Chŏngjo's mother, was treated as such by him. But Chŏngjo's adoption brought ambiguities to Lady Hyegyŏng's status vis-à-vis Chŏngjo. Her official status was that of the wife of Crown Prince Sado.

‡ The court sent greetings twice daily to the king, the queen, and the queen mother.

was persecuted and humiliated and others anxiously awaited my death, I felt that if I permitted them to continue their greetings and visits to me, the hatred in their hearts would grow yet more intense and I would invite further humiliation. I was certain that if the late King were cognizant of what was happening, he would not wish me to receive greetings after such terrible insults. I resolved to refuse all the greetings from the court and the visits of the Medical Bureau, so as to bring joy to their evil hearts and to seek my proper state. But I hesitated to carry it out before my son's funeral.[28]

After the funeral, memorials opposing conferral of posts and promotion of Nakp'a and Sŏyŏng* began to arrive. The grounds for opposition were that they were "the descendants of that rebel." Previously, when Han Yonggwi referred to Suyŏng as the descendant of that rebel, the late King thundered in a towering rage, "All grandsons are the same. If the term 'the descendant of the rebel' can be applied to a son's son, then the same appellation should apply to a daughter's son!"[†] By the same logic, if a secondary son or a grandson were to be termed the descendant of the rebel, a daughter would surely be one, too! There is no way of knowing whether such evil and reprehensible practices existed in old days.

Yi Anmuk's memorial came shortly afterwards. It was far worse, heaping upon my late father the worst possible abuse and the most intense invective.[‡]

I was placed in a completely defenseless position. There was no way to stop the entire palace from holding me in contempt. There arose in my heart a strong desire to cut myself off from everything and to know nothing. Thus I decided that, when the wailing cere-

---

* Nakp'a was Hong Ponghan's son by a concubine. Sŏyŏng was Hong Nagyun's son, Lady Hyegyŏng's nephew.

† "That rebel" refers to Hong Ponghan, Lady Hyegyŏng's father, who at one point was accused of having promoted Chŏngjo's two half brothers. Suyŏng was Hong Ponghan's son's son, and King Chŏngjo was Hong Ponghan's daughter's son.

‡ Yi's memorial arrived on the seventh of the eleventh month, the day after the burial of Chŏngjo. This memorial contained the words "descendants of the rebel" (yŏgŏl), but no one, neither Hong Ponghan nor anyone else, is specifically named (SS, 1:33b–34a). Two months later, on the sixth and sixteenth, Yi sent two more memorials extremely critical of Hong Nagim. SS, 2:2b–3b, 2:8b–15b.

mony for the late King was completed,* I would declare myself to have given up life, and I would go to Yŏngch'un Hall, the late King's residence, and lie there to await death. Life and death already seemed to me a dream. What was there for me to cherish that I should endure such aggrievement and humiliation?

In the eleventh month, I would finally carry out what I had always wanted. I wrote instructions in Korean, saying that I would no longer accept visits from the Medical Bureau. I dispatched the instructions and went to Yŏngch'un Hall. Upon reaching the residence that my deceased son had used, I searched for and stroked his traces and, grieving in my solitude, wailed and cried until I lost my senses.

At first Lady Kasun attempted to dissuade me, but later, pitying me, she did not forcibly stop me. The news reached the Queen Dowager and she was terribly provoked and angry. She sent down a number of instructions reproving me for my conduct. She also ordered that my message to the Medical Bureau not be forwarded to its destination. It was reasonable that Her Highness dissuaded me from carrying out my decision, but what followed was completely unexpected. I heard that Her Highness declared in bitterness, "There is someone behind her. I will punish him and put him in his place." Then, on the twenty-seventh of the month, she sent down an edict to the effect that my third brother was instigating me and that he should thus be banished to the distant district of Samsu.† This was exactly the way ladies-in-waiting were treated; when they are suspected of having committed a crime, either their brothers are locked up or the Palace Supply Office is made to deal with them. What depravity was this that the mother of the late King was treated in this manner!

Despite his youth, the present King was greatly shocked. Minister Pak,‡ also startled by this departure from decent practice, advised the King to seek an audience with the Queen Dowager and

* This ceremony was performed after three regular sacrifices. The wailing ceremony for King Chŏngjo was performed on the eighteenth of the eleventh month, 1800. *SS*, 1:35a.
† On the northern frontier of Korea and reputed to be extremely cold and unsuitable for human habitation.
‡ Pak Chunwŏn (1739–1807), the maternal grandfather of King Sunjo. At various times he had been Minister of Public Works and Minister of Justice.

to request the rescission of her order. Procedurally, the Queen Dowager's order had to go through the throne before it could be sent to the proper office and put into effect. Lady Kasun also asked the King not to send out the Queen Dowager's order. She then spread out a straw mat in the courtyard in front of Hŭijŏng Hall and prostrated herself upon it, pleading with the Queen Dowager: "Your Highness's instructions, which reached the throne, are deeply astounding. They seem truly excessive. Unable to comply with the order, this person is instead awaiting punishment." For my sake, Lady Kasun awaited punishment, prostrating her precious self on a straw mat in the freezing courtyard. This expressed her utmost devotion [to me] in memory of the late King's sagacious filial piety. I cannot express how this moved me, miserable though I was.

I was still lying at Yŏngch'un Hall, determined to end my life, when Lady Kasun came. She persuaded me to go with her, saying that the young King, not daring to come to Yŏngch'un Hall, was waiting for his grandmother in the cold mourning hut. Unable to bear to hurt his young heart, this weakling reluctantly followed her out. Once I came out, I felt it would be too awkward to ignore the Queen Dowager, who was in the same palace. So on that day I went to the Queen Dowager's residence and asked, "What is the reason for this terrifying order?" Her Highness answered, "You made this move not because you wished it, but because someone else instigated it. How could I not deal with it?" It seemed that in the course of my life, I was to be spared nothing. Difficulties of every nature and description seemed to await me. Had the late King been there, she would not have dared to treat me in this way. Barely containing my urge to burst out in a Heaven-piercing wail and shed bloodstained tears, I said forcefully, "It is too much. Please don't be like that." In addition to having to contend with the pressure from the present King and Lady Kasun, once she faced me, she seemed to feel that she had gone too far. Her expression became milder and she revoked the order.

Taking my life was not something I had suddenly thought of. During the late King's reign, whenever I had to contend with grievous events, I was invariably tempted by the idea, but trusting the late King, I contained myself. But when my son died, I was so racked with grief and pain that I longed to die. At that moment, I was again faced with an odious event that not only heaped humiliation upon my late father but also persecuted my own person. How could I desire to live a minute longer? Thus I decided to carry out the act.* Who among my family even knew of my decision? I may be deficient, but I am just as devoted to my family as anyone else. Would I, past seventy and in my dotage, be instigated by others to do that? Even supposing that I did it because of someone else's advice, why should they punish my brother for what I did? Where would that leave me? Besides, I had other brothers and nephews. Why did they single out my third brother?

There was nothing I could do but contain my anger and restrain my bitterness. Days passed. What I said in my instructions [to the Medical Bureau] and in my memorandum to the Queen Dowager was not something they could accept. So, since they could not kill me and vent their anger that way, they were determined to kill my third brother in my place. Beginning with his supposed role in my actions, other accusations were hurled at him. The scheme against him was pursued relentlessly until the eighteenth day of the twelfth month when there was that severe order.† The situation became daily more perilous for my brother, and there seemed no way that he could escape harm. From senior ministers down, all demanded that he be eliminated, and they sent memorials requesting that "the breeding ground for trouble (*wagul*)‡ should be rooted out." They clamored for the execution of my brother with no specific charge against him.§

In all history, beneath Heaven, can there have been such unreasonable and preposterous persecution? Since ancient times, many have suffered unjustly. Yet, to effect punishment, there must have been some involvement on the part of the victim that he could be charged with a crime—either he served in office, or he had power, or he interfered in the life or death of others, or he recom-

---

* Suicide.
† On this day, in a regular audience, Queen Dowager Chŏngsun strongly argued that there were people at court who were betraying the late King and asked that those who considered themselves to be guilty of this confess. *SS*, 1:44a–49b.
‡ *Wagul* literally means "den of thieves."
§ On the twenty-fifth, Queen Dowager Chŏngsun critic[...]
none had come forth either to confess to the crime of betra[...]
request the punishment of anyone. After this criticism the [...]
punishment of Hong Nagim (*SS*, 1:50a–50b). On the twen[...]
and the Office of the Special Counselors made the same r[...]
the following day, the Censorate requested Hong's executio[...]

mended or blocked candidates for office, or, alternatively, he made himself conspicuous by participating in some controversy. But why my brother?

They did not rehash the old charges. His testimony and the late King's conclusion made it clear that no criminal case could be based upon them. So the charges against him were a mixture of this and that, which they put together with no attempt at logic or truth. The first charge was that he acted for Ŭnŏn in the *sinmyo* (1771) incident. This was the incident in which my father had been unjustly accused of scheming for Ŭnŏn. Now, after thirty years, they were implicating the son as well. This was something unheard of. The charge itself made no sense. The late King was, after all, the most precious kin of my father and my brother. Why would they desert their grandson or nephew in favor of someone completely unrelated? For that matter, was there a single person in all of Chosŏn who preferred Ŭnŏn? How woeful that my brother had to be hurt along with Ŭnŏn.

Another charge was that my brother wished that a dynastic ritual be performed [for Prince Sado].* He never once spoke of such a dynastic ritual. He did not even mention it in passing when among family members. And so this charge was not based on any evidence or a report that someone had heard him discussing it, but rather on a supposition that he must have discussed it. The next charge against my brother was that he was a breeding ground for trouble because he allied himself with an unwholesome clique. The whole world knows that my brother, after the misfortunes that befell the family, had been living in retirement for almost thirty years with no contact with people outside our family. So this charge was again a complete fabrication. They wished to go so far as to accuse him of heterodox learning, but since there was no way to do this credibly, they implicated him enough to make people harbor suspicions. This was a most reprehensible deception.†

* This charge meant that Hong Nagim wanted to confer upon Prince Sado the title and rituals appropriate to a king. This was an extremely sensitive political issue. Hong Ponghan had been accused of wanting to do this.

† "Heterodox learning" refers to Catholicism. In 1801, the Korean court carried out the first large-scale persecution of Catholics, who had become quite numerous among disaffected intellectuals. Chou Wen-mu, a Chinese priest, and several dozen Catholics were executed. See Charles Dallet, *Histoire de l'Eglise de Corée*, (Paris: 1874), 1:120–45, which supports Lady Hyegyŏng's claim that her brother was not a Catholic. Throughout the nineteenth century, Catholicism became more popular despite repeated persecutions.

My brother concentrated on the classics and on composition, so he was not in the habit of reading widely. He did not read ordinary books, and never set his eyes on such books as the *Romance of the Three Kingdoms* (*San-kuo-chih yen-i*) or *Water Margin* (*Shui-hu-chuan*). As for heterodox writings, I doubt that he had even heard of the titles. He did not know that there was such a thing as heterodox learning until he heard it from the late King in a quiet meeting. I can still remember how surprised and concerned he was, and how strongly he urged the King, "Please forbid it." To begin with, that so-called heterodox learning is something that the alienated or the malcontented might pursue. It is not something that would interest the powerful, the wealthy, or royal affines. Certainly no member of my family would even look at such books!

Among those who turned to this heterodox learning, there were many Namin.* My family has known very few people for the past thirty years, and when it came to the Namin, we knew no one. We had no contact with Ch'ae Chegong, and my brother did not even have a nodding acquaintance with Yi Kahwan.† O Sŏkch'ung is supposed to have confessed that he associated with my third brother‡ and that it was due to my brother that his ancestor, O Sisu, was posthumously restored to his former post and rank.§ Sim Hwanji is the one who reported this in his memorial, and the falsity

---

* A faction that had been out of power since 1694. Chŏngjo employed a number of Namin during his reign.

† Ch'ae Chegong (1720–1799) was a leading Namin who served as prime minister under Chŏngjo. During the 1790s the Chosŏn court showed concern over the increasing number of converts to Catholicism. Ch'ae was a high minister on the State Council and proposed a policy of tolerance. While he was in power, Catholics were only mildly censured. Chŏngjo also adopted a policy of tolerance toward Catholics. Yi Kahwan (1742–1801), a great-grandson of the famous practical learning scholar Yi Ik (1579–1624), became interested in Catholicism when his uncle Yi Sŭnghun (1756–1801), the first baptized Korean Catholic, returned from Peking in 1784 with books on Catholicism. His interests remained scholarly until quite late. He continued to serve in the bureaucracy. At one point he was Minister of Justice. In 1801, during the persecution of the Catholics, he died under torture. For his trial, see *SS*, 2:38a–39a.

‡ O Sŏkch'ung was executed in the third month of 1801 for practicing Catholicism (*SS*, 2:49a–b). The *Sillok* records that it was Yi Kahwan who confessed that Hong Nagim was acquainted with O Sŏkch'ung. O Sŏkch'ung was then brought in, and he confessed to knowing Hong Nagim. *SS*, 2:38a.

§ O Sisu (1632–1681) was a Namin politician who, serving in a time of intense factionalism, had an illustrious but troubled official career. He was executed in 1680. His posthumous career was equally troubled. He was posthumously restored to his former post and rank in 1689, deprived of them in 1694, and again restored to them during Chŏngjo's reign.

of this remark proves beyond all doubt that the things said against my brother were all fabrication. The O family had for generations looked upon us as archenemies because, long ago, when O Sisu had been under censure, it had been my great-great-grandfather, serving as Inspector-General,[29] who succeeded in having O punished by staging a palace strike for three days. So even if an O wished to establish contact with us, he would have been prevented from doing so by this past relationship. Moreover, if, having been persuaded by my third brother, the late King had posthumously restored O Sisu's rank and post, that would suggest that my brother had considerable influence on the throne. If this was so, why was he unable to posthumously restore the rank and post of his own uncle?* Everything was a completely groundless falsification. None deserves any further discussion.

To execute any person is a grave matter for the nation. Even if my brother had committed a crime, the fact that he was my brother and the late King's maternal uncle should have prevented him from being carelessly harmed. Yet, though none of the charges placed against him could be proven, with threats of palace strikes and joint memorials demanding his execution, they eventually succeeded in causing him to meet that cruel end on that distant island a thousand *ri* away.†

Under Heaven, from ancient times until the present, can there

---

* Hong Inhan.
† Hong Nagim was spared interrogation. Thus we have no record of what Nagim himself said on the question. However, his verdict evolved so that during the twelfth month of 1800 he was under censure for other charges. Then, quite separately, in the first month of 1801, the question of Catholicism emerged as a pressing problem at court. The first incident occurred on the tenth of the first month, when Queen Dowager Chŏngsun condemned the spread of heterodox learning (Catholicism). Memorials requesting severe punishment for Hong Nagim continued to come in, but they still did not link him to Catholicism. Only after the twenty-sixth of the second month, when some defendants who had been accused of practicing Catholicism mentioned the name of Hong Nagim, did he come to be accused of being a Catholic (*SS*, 2:4b–39b). From the end of the second month until the end of the fifth month, when Hong Nagim was finally executed, the bureaucracy placed the Queen Dowager Regent under mounting pressure to execute Hong Nagim as well as Prince Ŭnŏn, Prince Sado's secondary son. Ŭnŏn was also accused of being a Catholic (*SS*, 2:39a–3:21a). Ŭnŏn's wife was an active and committed Catholic and gave aid and shelter to Catholics, including Chou Wenmu. She was also put to death in the 1801 purge. Her Catholic name was Maria Song. Ŭnŏn was also killed on this occasion. Hong Nagim was executed on the twenty-ninth day of the fifth month, 1801, on Cheju Island, where he had been banished. *SS*, 3:20a–21a.

have been such a bitter and painful case? Having lost my son in my feeble old age, I spent my days and nights grieving, wishing that death would come quickly. And right in the midst of this, my brother, out of the blue and without a single crime, was put to such a cruel death. Though I was alive, I could not save him. Can one find another as odious and as stupid as I?

I heard that the present King came and, seeing my state, left tearfully for a deserted place and cried abundantly. Because he was young, he could not save my brother, but he probably could not help being saddened because he knew that my brother was guiltless; he remembered how kindly and affectionately his father had treated my brother, and he pitied my sad plight. Though I was in extreme pain and grief, the present King's kind and filial heart kindled in me a hope for the future. I managed to stay alive. Were I to kill myself in grief, it would satisfy the impatient wishes of that evil clique. But there is no way that my unjustly killed brother can be brought back to life. My breathing grows weak and I am not confident that I will live another day. Yet were I to die without seeing my deceased brother's innocence proven and declared, I would have no face with which to greet him in the netherworld and my soul and spirit would remain eternally bitter. Oh! Heaven! I pray and beseech! Let me remain here to witness the restoration of my brother's innocence before I die. Day and night I pray in tears and blood.*

* In compliance with his ailing grandmother's wish, King Sunjo posthumously restored Hong Nagim to his former post in 1807. *SS*, 10:2b–3a.

英祖大王御眞
光武四年
庚子移摸

Figure 1. Portrait of King Yŏngjo dressed in formal red dragon robes.
This is an early twentieth-century copy of an eighteenth-century original
that is no longer extant. The Royal Museum, Seoul.

Figure 2. Lady Hyegyŏng's bethrothal palanquin, in which she was taken to her bride's pavilion from her home in 1744. She was carried and accompanied by palace servants, ladies-in-waiting, and her relatives. From *Changjo Hŏn'gyŏnghu karye togam ŭigwe*, manuscript, 1744, Kyujanggak.

Figure 3. T'ongmyŏng Pavilion in Ch'anggyŏng Palace. It was used for gatherings of either an official or a social nature. It is approximately 40 feet deep by 80 feet wide. The interior consists of one large room.

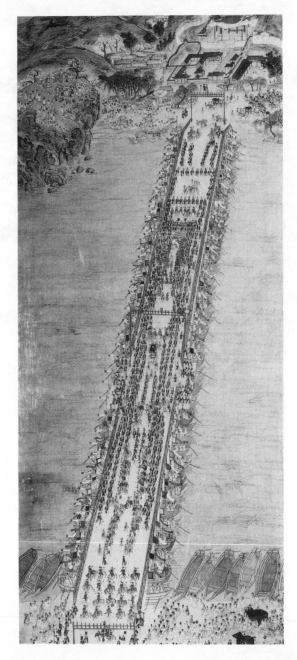

Figure 4. This is the first panel of an eight-panel screen depicting King Chǒngjo's famous visit in 1795 to the tomb of Prince Sado, his father, in commemoration of Sado's sixtieth birthday. This panel represents the beginning of the procession as it crossed the Han river on a temporary bridge laid across boats. Crowds of spectators are represented on the banks of the river. The Royal Museum, Seoul.

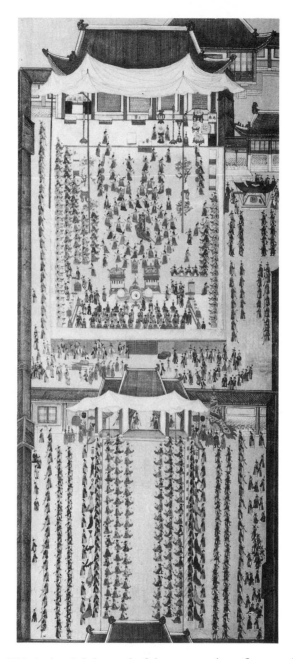

Figure 5. This is the eighth panel of the screen whose first panel is illustrated in Figure 4. This panel depicts the great feast King Chŏngjo held
in honor of Lady Hyegyŏng's sixtieth birthday at a detached palace
in Suwŏn a day after King Chŏngjo and Lady Hyegyŏng visited Prince
Sado's tomb.

Figure 6. Painting of a plantain tree by King Chŏngjo, who is well-known for his scholarship and his skill as a painter and calligrapher. Tongguk University Art Museum.

Figure 7. A painting of chrysanthemums by King Chŏngjo. Tongguk
University Art Museum.

Figure 8. A rice chest. This is essentially identical to the one in which
Sado was confined, though smaller. It measures $3\frac{1}{2} \times 3\frac{1}{2} \times 2\frac{1}{2}$ ft., whereas
the one in which Sado perished is said to have been $4 \times 4 \times 4$ ft. The rice
chest illustrated above is in the official residence of the Foreign Minister of
the Republic of Korea.

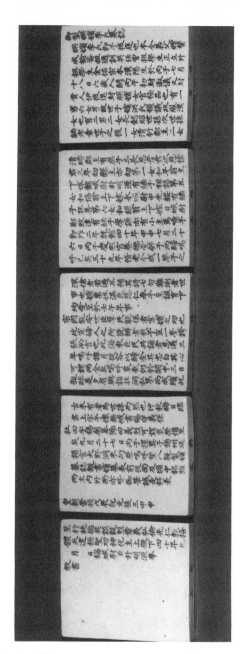

Figure 9. Epitaph tablets containing King Yŏngjo's necrology, written in 1764, of Lady Sŏnhŭi, his consort and the mother of Sado. The epitaph is poignant in its praise of Lady Sŏnhŭi for having advised him to take the necessary measures to kill Sado and thus save the monarchy. White porcelain with calligraphy in cobalt blue underglaze decoration. Yŏnsei University Art Museum.

The Memoir of 1802

It has been almost sixty years since I came to the palace as a child. During that period, my life has been extremely turbulent; I have encountered countless adversities. In addition to that incomparably painful event, I have suffered such an endless succession of devastating trials and tribulations that it is not logical that I should have lived. I sustained my life because, given the fact that the late King served me with utmost filial devotion, I could not bear to end my life. Heaven detested me more as time passed, however, and I suffered that truly unbearable loss. It would have been natural for me to follow my son in death, but this odious life of mine is as stubborn as the earth or a tree. I was unable to kill myself. In my heart, I cherished the young King, my grandson, and so I grasped this thread of life. Life, though, became insupportable.

Even if an ordinary woman of humble station had, at seventy, lost her only son, her neighbors would pity her and offer condolences and sympathy. However, within several months of my losing the late King, insults were heaped upon my late father. Then it was charged that my third brother had instigated my abortive attempt to end my life. Within seven or eight months, using absurdly false charges, they banished him to a distant island to be confined to a house surrounded by bramble hedges. Soon afterwards, they executed him. In this way they transferred to my brother the punishment they wished to inflict upon me for my attempt to end my life. In this sense, the killing was not directed at my brother but at me.

Evil cliques are ascendant; they have turned their backs upon late King. In disdain for the youthful ruler, they have persecuted the mother of the late King. The decline of human morality and failures of ministerial propriety have never reached such extremes. Weeping tears of blood day and night, I desperately long to follow my son and my brother in death, yet I remain. My recent losses have left me with no support or anchor. Whether I wish to live or die, I can do neither. All is due to my horrendous sin and my miserable fate. I can do nothing but beseech Heaven and curse the ghosts. Since time immemorial, no queen or royal consort has suffered what I have in my life; no other family has been put to the trials that mine has met. The way of Heaven is all-knowing. The present King is benevolent and filial. I trust that, even if I were to die without seeing it, he will distinguish right from wrong; he will avenge my suffering and bitterness.

If I do not record events as they occurred, there is no way in which he will come to know of them sufficiently. Gathering my spent wits and my remaining strength, I will begin by describing the sagacious filial devotion with which the late King served me and the discussions he had with me. I will then move on to other points to elaborate and to clarify the issues. Who but I knows of them? Who else can speak of them? My life might end at any moment, and so I will entrust these writings to Lady Kasun that they shall be given to the present King after my death. If he were, someday, to realize the sadness of my life and the unjustness of my family's plight, and if he were to appease my thirty years of accumulated bitterness, my departed soul would be able to meet with the late King in the netherworld; mother and son would console each other on our great good fortune in having a virtuous son and a godly grandson who has fulfilled our lifelong desire. If there is the smallest fabrication or exaggeration in these writings, I would be deceiving the late King and deluding myself by misleading the present King, and I would be indulging in favoritism on behalf of my private parent. How could I not fear the immediate retribution ~~~ ~nd Earth? I have experienced countless events in the
hared many thousands of intimate conver-
ng. In my decrepitude, however, I remem-
:n thousand. I will also gloss over irrelevant
of the state or family matters, and I will
or points. Thus I am afraid that this record
iuch detail. Seventh month, *imsul* year (1802).

Although the most common of human relations is that of mother and son, the mother-son tie between myself and the late King was like no other. If it had not been for the late King, I would not be here today; had it not been for me, the late King would not have been protected and preserved. Having experienced hundreds of trials and difficulties and having been each other's support through these stormy years, mother and son both awaited a blessed old age when, in retirement, we could enjoy the peace and prosperity of the nation. For reasons I cannot fathom, august Heaven has deprived me of my son in midcourse. Beneath Heaven, since history began, there cannot have been a loss so heart-rending as this. That I did not die during the tragic incident of the *imo* year (1762) was only to protect the late King. When Father, bitterly frustrated in his attempts to demonstrate the unjustness of the vile slanders and accusations brought against him, died prematurely in the *imsul* year (1778), I wished to follow him, but I was dissuaded from it by the sincere filial devotion of the late King. Then I lost my son. Soon afterwards, I let my guiltless brother meet that cruel end. Thus I have become one who failed in loyalty [to my husband], affection [to my son], filial piety [to my father], and sisterhood [to my brother]. With what face can I remain in this world for even one more day? Because of my affection for the young King and because this odious life does not of itself end, I linger shamefully in this world. Can there be another as muddled, as stupid, as irresolute, and as weak as I?

The late King had an innately filial nature. In his later years his filial attentions grew even more thorough and careful, and he served me as though he could not do enough. When he made excursions, even within the city, in recognition of his mother's anxious concern he repeatedly dispatched messengers bearing notes and greetings. Trips to his father's tomb took days, but, considering my nervousness, he stopped his entourage on the road every two hours to send me his messages. Where can I go now for even one letter from him? Ah! Sadness!

The late King was extraordinarily endowed. He had a beautiful and dignified face, an exceptional carriage, and a magnificent physique. He learned to speak and to read at a very early age. From childhood, he was diligent and hardworking; except when he slept and ate, he was seldom without a book in his hand. His accomplishments were superior to those of the wise rulers of old. There was nothing he did not know. Of all the rulers since the sage kings of antiquity, there was none to equal the late King in scholarship or composition, in sagacious virtue, or in wise administration. Even at nearly fifty years of age, burdened with myriad aspects of government, he finished a series of books each winter. In the winter of the *kimi* year (1799),* he finished the entire *Tso chuan* (Tso commentary). When he was a child, and he finished a book, I would prepare a special meal for him as a way of expressing delight and encouragement. On this occasion, recalling that old custom, I prepared a celebratory meal. The late King, appreciative of his old mother's gesture, ate and drank with abandon in the company of ministers and composed a piece to commemorate the occasion. It seems like yesterday. Who at that point would have imagined that the changes in the affairs of the world would reach such a point as they have at present?

The late King was peerless in benevolence and filial piety. It is impossible to satisfactorily record the faultless manner in which he complied with the wishes of His Late Majesty [King Yŏngjo] and the sincere filial devotion with which he served his parents. The thrust of his conduct in these matters is truthfully recorded in his official biography,[1] and so I will mention only several things. Before the *imo* year (1762), there were many difficult moments. Despite his youth, the late King comprehended the complexities of the situation. He took care of his conduct, never once causing dissatisfaction to His Majesty. So pleased was His Majesty with his grandson that, whenever he saw me, he sang his grandson's praises, speaking of his intelligence and his accomplishments. This would not have happened if the late King had been unable to touch His Majesty's heart with filial devotion and unimpeachable conduct.

From early childhood he was extraordinarily devoted to me. He ate only if I ate and slept only if I slept. On many tense occasions he was able to behave with the concern and maturity of an adult. He was of great help in many ways, much more than one would expect of a child. At the time of the tragic incident of the *imo* year (1762), he grieved like an adult. He was inconsolable. His sad bearing and his piteous cries moved bystanders; no one who saw him grieve or heard his wail could withhold tears. The pain of losing a father seems to have redoubled his devotion to his mother; he

* The last winter of Chŏngjo's life.

was unable, even for a moment, to relax his concern for me. When we were apart, he had difficulty sleeping. When we lived in separate palaces, he would not eat breakfast until he had received my letter of greeting. If I were slightly ill, he personally had medicine mixed and sent to me. These incidents revealed his extraordinary filial concern.

Oh! Grief! How can I bring myself to speak of that *kapsin* (1764) decision!* How can I record that pathetic scene—mother and son, stricken by dismay and sorrow, hugging each other desperately, wishing we were dead! The pain that the late King suffered has not been equaled by anyone in any ruling house. Out of his duty to the nation, he ascended the throne, but he was obsessed by the tragic image of his father, and as years went by that memory grew more intense. He had the Gate for Greeting the Sun and the Gate for Viewing the Moon constructed at the Kyŏngmo Shrine [for Prince Sado] and visited the shrine more than once or twice a month. Yet his longing heart still regretted that he could not pay respect to his father morning and evening. He served me with all the wealth and splendor available to the throne, yet he did not think it enough. With a pleasant expression and a joyous voice, he looked in on me four or five times a day and was always concerned lest he do something contrary to my wishes. In my old age, I have often suffered ill health and, on those two occasions when I was seriously ill, once in *kimi* (1799) and then during *kyŏngsin* (1800), the late King was so concerned and nervous that he completely gave up sleep, not even changing into bed clothes. He also personally tended to the medicine, boiling tinctures and extracts and, once done, offering them to me himself, not wishing to leave this to others. Though we were mother and son, my gratitude is inestimable.

The late King always had simple and plain tastes. In his later years, he grew even more austere and frugal in his habits. His residence had short eaves, his room was small and without polychrome decoration, and he did not permit frequent wallpapering or renovation. His quarters could not be distinguished from those of a poor, unemployed scholar. Except for the formal dragon robe of the sovereign, he did not drape silk on his person but chose roughwoven cotton instead, and he refused silk bedding. He lim-

---

* Yŏngjo's order making Chŏngjo an adopted son of Prince Hyojang.

ited the number of side dishes to three or four in his morning and evening meals and had them placed in small plates to regulate quantity. When I occasionally mentioned that he was a bit excessive in his frugality, he would eagerly denounce the vice of luxury, concluding that, "To uphold a frugal and simple life is not sparing wealth or foods but a way of cultivating good fortune." Thus, he chided me. I could not but admire him.

The late King was not blessed with a son until rather late. The absence of an heir caused concern for the dynasty. The birth of Munhyo in the *imin* year (1782) brought great joy, but the King suffered two terrible losses in *pyŏngo* (1786).* Grief-stricken and despairing, he suffered ill health; I became quite alarmed. Then, in the spring of *chŏngmi* (1787), he chose Lady Kasun as a consort.† She was benevolent and warm in her conduct, beautiful in appearance and carriage, and she possessed the style and restraint of a well-bred lady. Once she entered the palace, Lady Kasun served me with the utmost devotion and loyalty, and so I came to love her as my own daughter. She served the late King most beautifully and truthfully, not once going against his sagacious heart. The late King treasured and trusted her; often he seemed as if he were about to entrust her with a message of grave import. I now believe that he felt a certain presentiment.

With each passing day, I prayed more eagerly and ardently than the previous day that Lady Kasun would be blessed with a son. With Heaven's silent assistance and the invisible benefactions of ancestors, on the eighteenth of the sixth month of the *kyŏngsul* year (1790), at three o'clock in the afternoon, the blessed event took place at a house facing my residence. The present King was born. This was a blessing that consolidated the dynastic foundation for myriad years. Mother and son congratulated each other. We spent days in celebration and joy. Strangely, the newborn child

---

* Prince Munhyo died in the fifth month of 1786, followed by his mother, Lady Sŏng, who died in the ninth month of the same year. *Chŏngjo sillok* (hereafter *CS*), in *Chosŏn wangjo sillok*, 21:42b, 22:31b.

† Although Lady Kasun was definitely a secondary consort because Chŏngjo had a legal wife, Queen Hyoŭi, she was a *yangban* woman. Chŏngjo performed a formal marriage ceremony after a three-stage selection procedure. This made her different from the usual secondary consorts who, as a rule, started as ladies-in-waiting at the palace, were taken in without a wedding ceremony, and were not of *yangban* families. *CS*, 23:21a, 23:23b.

shared his birthday with me. The late King used to remark on it, saying, "The child's birthday is the same as Your Ladyship's. This is an extraordinary coincidence unprecedented in history. Your Ladyship's utmost sincerity and devotion have brought this on. Heaven did not casually produce this coincidence." I was not sure whether I deserved this encomium, but I was inclined to feel that when it came to devotion to the dynasty or the King, there was none more devoted than I. Would it not be wonderful if Heaven indeed made his birthday the same as mine out of sympathy?

In the spring of *kyŏngsin* (1800), the present King performed the capping ceremony and was invested as the Crown Prince. The late King counted the days to the arrival of the winter, when the three-stage selection procedure for his son's wife would be completed and he would gain a daughter-in-law, one of a virtuous and illustrious family. It saddens me to think that, with the late King's departure, I will witness the wedding alone.*

The late King had been aware all along that the site of Yŏngu Tomb† left something to be desired. Early in the *pyŏngsin* year (1776), my father strongly recommended reinterment, but because it was a matter of such grave import, the King could not come to a decision easily. In *kiyu* (1789) he had a geomancer select an auspicious site at Mount Hwa in Suwŏn city, and he carried out reinterment, changing the name of the tomb to Hyŏllyung Tomb.‡ The late King informed me, "According to the laws of the ancients, a plot of land such as this can be found only once in every thousand *ri*." He also said, "Now that I have moved him to a spot that had once been intended for King Hyojong,§ I have no regrets. In the two characters I selected, 'hyŏllyung' (illustrious eminence),

---

* The first selection in the three-stage selection procedure for Sunjo's wife took place in the second month of 1800. Five girls were selected. The second selection was completed in the intercalary fourth month of 1800, when three of the five were chosen. Chŏngjo's death led to the postponement of the final selection of his son's bride and his wedding. The third selection took place in the ninth month of 1802, and the wedding ceremony was performed in the following month. *CS*, 53:41a–b, 54:19b–20a. *Sunjo sillok* (hereafter *SS*), in *Chosŏn wangjo sillok*, 4:33b–34a, 4:37a–39a.

† Prince Sado's original tomb.

‡ The reinterment was carried out in the tenth month of 1789 in an elaborate ceremony. Chŏngjo was quite emotional on the occasion. *CS*, 28:15b–33a.

§ Hyojong (r. 1649–1659) was the eighteenth king of the Chosŏn dynasty and Chŏngjo's fifth-generation ancestor.

the world will ascertain my unspoken wish." I cannot begin to describe how wholeheartedly the late King devoted himself, day and night, to overseeing the reinterment.

After the reinterment, his remembrances of his father grew more intense. He had his own portrait hung in the pavilion beside the grave to symbolize his wish that he be there always, tending his father's grave. He made provision that every five days the grave would be thoroughly put in order. In the first month of every year, he visited the tomb and paid respect to his father. In addition, each spring and autumn, he sent out such exhaustively detailed instructions concerning the shrubbery and plantings that it was almost as if he himself had landscaped it. He asked the inhabitants of the old town to move to the new city of Hwasŏng.* Subsequently, as a way to protect the tomb and to maintain its glory, he had city walls and a splendid detached palace built.

In the spring of *ŭlmyo* (1795), he took me to the Prince's tomb and together we paid our respect. Afterwards he held a great feast at Pongsu Pavilion to which he invited male and female relatives and civil and military officials as well, causing them to enjoy themselves drinking and eating until the small hours of the morning. The aged were offered drink at Nangnam Pavilion and the poor were given rice at Sinp'ung Pavilion. Joyful spirits and the sounds of merriment filled the air from Hwasŏng to the capital.† All this was but to express his filial affection to this old mother. Who among the officials and subjects of the entire nation did not admire him and sing his praises?

Out of duty to the dynasty, the late King remained on the throne, laboring diligently in his role. However, with the ineradicable pain in his heart, he did not enjoy that position and resolutely refused honorary titles.‡ He always entertained a hope that one day

---

* Suwŏn city was renamed Hwasŏng. *CS*, 37:4b–5b.
† See figure 5 for a representation of this feast. Also see note 25 of *The Memoir of 1795*.
‡ Chŏngjo received no honorary title *(chonho)* while he was alive. Although this followed the pattern of many earlier kings of the Chosŏn dynasty, it set him apart from his immediate predecessor, Yŏngjo, who received five eight-character honorary titles while he was on the throne. See JaHyun Kim Haboush, *A Heritage of Kings: One Man's Monarchy in the Confucian World* (New York: Columbia University Press, 1988), 62.

he would be able to relinquish his throne. He then begat a sagacious son to whom he could entrust the dynastic mission. He built the city of Hwasŏng magnificently so that it was second only to the capital in splendor and conferred such names as Nonae Hall (Hall for approaching old age) and Mirohan Pavilion (Pavilion of leisure for the not so old) upon the new pavilions. He said to me, "I have occupied the throne not because I coveted it, but because I had to for the nation. In the coming *kapcha* year (1804), my son will reach his fifteenth year, and I will be able to abdicate to him. I will then be able to fulfill my greatest wishes. I will retire to Hwasŏng with Your Ladyship to the task of rendering to Prince Sado the supreme honors that I could not grant from the throne. I could not do this because of His Majesty's order.[2] It was extremely distressing [that I could not offer such honors to my father]. Nonetheless, that was the right way for me. The right way for my son is to comply with my request by honoring his grandfather as I could not, fulfilling my wish. Because of these considerations, the right way for the ministers and officials of my court is to refrain from honoring Prince Sado. Once the new King ascends, the right way for them will be to comply with the new King's wish. The right way is not unalterably fixed; rather it changes with circumstances and time. How would it be if we, mother and son, having survived what we did, were to receive such glory and care from our descendants in accordance with the way of filial piety?"

I felt a great surge of pity for my son. I thought of the overwhelming duties of rule and silently wept. He, too, grew sad. In tears, he said, "Were I to go to the netherworld to meet my father after accomplishing that task [of honoring him] through my son as I could not myself, what more could I wish for?" He often pointed at his son and said, "This child wishes to know about Prince Sado. He is quite mature. I could not bring myself to speak of that incident, and so I asked his maternal grandfather to tell him. But his maternal grandfather also said that he could bring himself to tell the Prince only the main points." The late King said of the present King, "This child was born to accomplish that task for Prince Sado. He came as an answer to that wish. It must have been an expression of Heaven's will."

In the early *ŭlmyo* year (1795), when he conferred honorary titles upon his ancestors, he was able to confer an eight-character honorary title on Prince Sado.* Afterwards he said to me, "Kim Chongsu, who has been so opposed to the measure, now says, 'Please offer him the jade scepter, a gold seal, and an eight-character title.' Now everything is done except for one character [the king (*wang*)]. For that let's wait for the new king." He then recited the eight characters of the title, "*Changyun yungbŏm kimyŏng ch'anghyu* (Manifest humanity, eminent pattern, fundamental decree, auspicious blessing)." Being an ignorant woman, I did not hear it correctly and asked, "*Kimyŏng ch'anghyo* (Auspicious filiality)?" The late King smiled and said, "As for the character *hyo* (filiality), it will be used in a title designating him as *taewang* (great king) some day, and so I have not used it. Besides, in our dynasty the custom is not to use *hyo* in honorary titles."†

I had in my possession a red cloth with gold thread woven into it, and he said to me, "At the conferral ceremony of royal titles, I expect Your Ladyship to wear the phoenix-embroidered robe of the queen.‡ So please don't discard this cloth. Take good care of it. With the filial piety of your grandson, you will someday use it." In his last years, the ceremony that he was planning for *kapcha* (1804) took on such central importance in his consciousness that nothing he planned, did, or said could escape being done with that event as a reference point. Though I remained somewhat incredulous that it would be realized, I could not help thinking what a splendid conclusion of rulership it would be. I half expected to actually see this unbelievably rare event realized in my long sojourn in this world.

My family has been slandered and vilified by the envious since *kyŏngin* (1770). By *pyŏngsin* (1776), that vicious calumny reached its peak, and my family suffered calamities and reversals of fortune. I cannot describe the depths of my bitterness and pain. I went down to a lower house§ and, determined to die, I wailed and cried night and day. The late King, however, consoled me with heartfelt sympathy. I thought that his Heaven-endowed benevolence and

---

* Chŏngjo had already conferred upon his father a four-character honorary title on two occasions, in 1783 and in 1784. *Chosŏn wangjo ŭi chesa* (Seoul: Munhwaje kwalliguk, 1967), 108.

† *Hyo* was used in honorary titles for queens, but not for kings.

‡ If the title of king was to be conferred upon Prince Sado, the title of queen would be conferred on Lady Hyegyŏng on the same occasion.

§ Quarters usually reserved for servants or those of low rank.

filial piety glowed with divine radiance, that a temporary occlusion of his intelligence by cunning ministers was like a darkening of the sky by fleeting clouds that pass without diminishing the true brightness of the sun and moon. Surely, he would eventually see the sincere loyalty of my father and the unjust treatment of my uncle. Lest his [reputation for] filial piety suffer if I were to give up life, I pushed myself and decided to continue this wretched life of mine. Ghosts and spirits were witness to the truthfulness of my sentiment, but I could not help but feel ashamed in my heart of hearts.

As expected, the late King indeed repulsed that evil crowd.* Deeply remorseful over the way he had treated Father, he admitted that he had been excessively harsh to him. He often said, "I told them that I had witnessed it with my own eyes. It was not Grandfather who had 'that thing'[†] sent in, but they insist that he was guilty. Isn't it ridiculous!"

I answered, "Their position, according to what I heard, is this. The first one, from the outer kitchen of the palace, had been brought in before Father entered. But they say it was he who suggested the one from the Palace Guard, the one that was used! What an unconscionable calumny this is!"

The late King replied, "What could they have known? That man from the Palace Guard also came in before Grandfather reached the palace. That thing from the outer kitchen was found to be unusable, and so they brought another one from the Palace Guard because it was nearby. Munjŏng Pavilion is inside Sŏnin Gate, and the eastern station of the Palace Guard is located just outside of Sŏnin Gate. The situation became terrible at about three o'clock and had turned utterly hopeless by five. His Lordship came to the palace only after the curfew gong was struck.[‡] I saw this myself and

---

* Hong Kugyŏng, who wielded great power in the early years of Chŏngjo's reign. In 1780 Hong was expelled to the countryside. He died in 1781.

† The rice chest in which Prince Sado was confined to die. During Chŏngjo's reign, the question of who suggested that Prince Sado be locked in a rice chest and who had the chest brought in became a heated political issue, giving rise to a witch hunt.

‡ The curfew gong was struck at 9 P.M. According to a historian's journal, Hong Ponghan came into the palace much earlier than Chŏngjo asserts here. But he was with several other high-ranking ministers and they were promptly ordered to leave the scene of the father-son confrontation. Hong came back, but he was with other ministers. See Haboush, *Heritage*, 219–30.

so I know it very well. Grandfather had nothing to do with the fact that those two things were brought in from different places. In my reply to Chŏng Ihwan's memorial, I reluctantly referred to the phrase that I find difficult to use in order to clarify [maternal] Grandfather's innocence.* The whole world knows of it."

I asked, "Then what is the charge against Father now?"

The late King said, "Perhaps it can be compared to Ch'oe Myŏnggil's criticism of those who held high positions under King Kwanghae†—at a time of national crisis, they, as senior ministers, failed to die. This is an extreme though logically tenable position. But His Lordship succeeded in protecting me, and he thus secured the dynasty. History will surely acknowledge the crucial service he rendered to the dynasty. However, propriety does not permit me to declare on the throne that his protection of me was right, when discussing right and wrong in the affairs of that time. So I am letting them do and argue as they wish. That is why I am unable to commend Grandfather. But when my son ascends the throne, how can he fail to praise and honor the loyal heart that protected his father and secured the dynasty?" The late King pointed to his son and said, "During the reign of that child, Grandfather will be exculpated and Your Ladyship will enjoy even greater filial devotion than during my reign."

From the winter of *sinhae* (1791), the late King collected my father's writings on the administration of government, his memorials, and his discussions in royal audiences. He entitled the manuscript "Collected Memorials" (*Chugo*) and personally edited it

* Soon after Chŏngjo's accession, Royal Secretary Chŏng Ihwan sent a memorial denouncing Hong Ponghan for three crimes. One was that Hong had suggested that the rice chest at the Royal Guard be brought in. In his reply, Chŏngjo defended Hong, saying, "This is something I find difficult to bring up between the ruler and the minister, and between the superior and the inferior. On the seventh day of the second month in the *sinmyo* (1771), His Late Majesty said to me, weeping, 'If someday an official were to bring up to you the issue of these two words ["that thing"], he would not only be disloyal to me but also impure to you. The reason I punished Han Yu and Sim Ŭiji was that they brought up the matter of these two words. Hong Ponghan had nothing to do with it. The thing arrived while Ponghan was still waiting outside. Outsiders don't know, but they think that Ponghan recommended it to me. But the truth is different.'" *CS*, 1:9a–10a.

† Ch'oe Myŏnggil was one of the key people who joined in the successful coup of 1623 that dethroned King Kwanghae and installed King Injo. The meritorious ministers of the new regime maintained a deeply critical stance toward those who served under Kwanghae.

piece by piece. In the twelfth month of the *kimi* year (1799), after almost a decade of labor, the manuscript was put in order. It contained about sixty pieces that the late King composed as prefaces to various writings of my father.[3] One day the late King came in accompanied by the present King and read some pieces to him. He showed him the entire collection, adding, "Only now have I repaid Grandfather's loyal service and done my duty as a grandson." He said to me, "I have sung unstinting praise of Grandfather's loyalty and his meritorious deeds. In describing him, I have employed words that refer to the Duke of Chou. At times he becomes the Lord of Wei, at times Han Fu-p'i, at times a sage or a worthy.* Once published, this book will be transmitted to a hundred generations. There will no longer be any cause to discuss his past sufferings."

In the fourth month of *kyŏngsin* (1800), the late King composed an introduction and a preface to the entire collection and wrote to my third brother, saying, "Grandfather's loyal service will be revealed by this." This letter is preserved by my family. The late King then said to me, "At the time of publication, I intend to include another piece on his most exceptional contribution." What he meant was that he could not suddenly praise my father's loyal service of protecting and saving him during that fateful year, and so he wanted to wait for an occasion when this service could be given full notice. I read the royal prefaces. The graciousness and the liberality of the tribute the late King rendered to his maternal grandfather was extraordinary. Indeed, it exceeded anything a son might have composed. Moved and grateful, I brought my hands together and said, "Today I feel the joy of having a ruler-son. This vindicates my life of shame."

However, my tormented fate is still not resolved! In the bottomless sorrow of losing my son, I had to see the clamor over my father's collected memorials. Some even insisted that the late King's compositions, which were interspersed among my father's writings, should be eliminated from the manuscript.[†] With this, the

---

* The Duke of Chou was one of the cardinal paragons of virtue in the Confucian tradition. Han Ch'i was a wise minister of the Sung dynasty. He pacified a rebellion and contributed to a peaceful succession. He was enfeoffed as the Lord of Wei. Han Fu-p'i was also a wise minister of the Sung dynasty.

† The implication is that a guilty person should not have the honor of having the King write prefaces for his writings.

humiliation of my late father reached an extreme; the persecution unleashed on my own person spun out of control. But the derision was extended to reach the late King himself! Though the late King is no longer with us, his son is the sovereign whom everyone claims as his lord. Yet they do this sort of thing. What times are these? How depraved!

The first royal edict [of 1776] that sent my uncle into exile said that he had "no seditious intentions or suspicious ambitions." In *imja* (1792) the late King declared that "The remark 'He does not need to know' is as ambiguous as 'One can't say there isn't.' The remark is not sufficiently incriminating that he should be punished for it. He will be cleared of guilt some day." In recent years he spoke of my uncle quite frequently, treating him as though he had already been declared innocent. Of his plans for his maternal family, the late King used to say, "As soon as we carry out the big task in *kapcha* (1804), I will also see to it that all the charges [against the members of the Hong family] will be nullified. Regrets of mother and son will be dispelled at once." In the second month of *kyŏng-sin* (1800), he reaffirmed this intention in an edict that said, "I want to exonerate one person today and another tomorrow so that none will remain condemned and no family ruined. In that way, we will live in great peace and harmony."*

But I was rather impatient with the way the late King was putting things off to *kapcha* (1804). I said, "That will be my seventieth year. There is no guarantee that I will live to that age. Besides, what if my lord does not honor today's pledge at that time?" The late King answered in anger, "Does Your Ladyship think that I will deceive a seventy-year-old mother?" Thus I could do nothing but to eagerly await the *kapcha* year. Because of my odious and miserable fate, none of these plans and pledges were to materialize. My miserable plight and my family's misfortune have reached this unbelievable point. I do not believe I have encountered such a case as this in any history book. Under the circumstances, what is the use of living even for a moment longer?

---

* Chŏngjo declared a large-scale amnesty when he appointed Sunjo as Crown Prince in the second month of 1800. Thinking the amnesty too extensive, officials including the Prime Minister requested that Chŏngjo rescind it. This was more or less how Chŏngjo reaffirmed his intention to exonerate as many people as possible. *CS*, 53:26a–b. For details on the 1776 edict and 1792 declaration about Hong In-han, see *The Memoir of 1801*, 162–63.

My only hope is the present King. Though young, he takes after his father in benevolence and filial piety. I pray day and night that once he reaches maturity, he will execute the unfulfilled wishes of his father.

The royal marriage of the *kapcha* year (1744) altered my family's position, and so my father did not wish to take the civil examinations. However, the scholars of the mountains and forests opined, "The father-in-law of the Crown Prince has a unique position. It is senseless to foreswear the examination." My father took it and passed it in the tenth month of that year. His Majesty King Yŏngjo had been anxiously awaiting the result and was pleased with the news. The Prince, though young, was delighted. "My father-in-law passed the examination," he announced happily. No one from the families of either Lord Kyŏngŭn or Lord Talsŏng had succeeded in the *munkwa* examination and so my father was the first royal affine who had passed it in quite a long while.* Pleased with their new in-law's successful candidacy, Their Royal Highnesses Queen Dowager Inwŏn and Queen Chŏngsŏng summoned me specially to offer congratulations. Queen Chŏngsŏng's family had suffered in the *sinim* (1721–1722) purge, and she was partial toward the Noron. Her delight at Father's success was as great as if it had been her own father's. I was overwhelmed and touched by her enthusiasm. How vividly I remember this scene as if it were just yesterday!

The world in its ignorance has assumed that His Majesty's trust in my father was due to familial relations. This was not true. In the spring of *kyehae* (1743) my father, as student representative at the Royal College, had a royal audience at Sungmun Hall. At the time, His Majesty was greatly impressed with Father—the way he offered his opinion and the way he carried himself in the royal presence. When he retired that day, His Majesty said to Lady Sŏnhŭi, "Today I have seen a [potential] minister for the Crown Prince." "Who is it?" Lady Sŏnhŭi asked. "The student representative Hong," he replied, adding, "I am offering a palace examination, hoping that this Hong will pass." This episode was later related to me by Lady Sŏnhŭi. Judging by this story, my father's relationship with the

---

* The *munkwa* was the highest of the civil service examinations. Lord Kyŏngŭn was the father of Queen Inwŏn. Lord Talsŏng was Sŏ Chongje, the father of Queen Chŏngsŏng, Yŏngjo's first queen.

throne began when he was a student-scholar, at which time His Majesty had already marked him as a future minister.

At the time of the final selection of a princess consort, there were other well-recommended girls; though I was the grand-daughter of a minister, Grandfather was deceased, and so I was the daughter of a mere student-scholar. This made their selection of me quite exceptional. His Majesty's sagacious heart favored me, but the decisive factor was that I was the daughter of one whom His Majesty was planning to employ in major capacities. Even if he had not been a royal affine, my father would surely have had a successful career given his talents and abilities, which had already impressed the throne. Because of me, he was placed under extreme constraints and subjected to unbelievably complex political situations. In the end, he faced mounting calumny, and his political fortunes plummeted. He died before his time with bitterness in his heart. The benefit he received from being a royal affine was small, but his suffering because of it was great. This was all because he had me. Thus I have lived my life in guilt and bitterness.

After his success in the examination, Father grew rapidly in His Majesty's esteem. He was appointed to a succession of offices, each with heavier responsibilities than the last. At various points, he was entrusted with currency and grain, military troops,[4] and finally the premiership. His absolute impartiality, his complete sincerity, his talent, and his wide knowledge pleased His Majesty's sagacious heart. Never once did he commit an impropriety or violate a rule. During the twenty years that Father headed parts of the military and civilian bureaucracy, he saw the benefits and losses of the populace, their pains and joys, as his own. No malfeasance or abusive practice that he noticed either in or out of the bureaucracy was left uncorrected. To this very day, those corrections are in force. Admittedly, this was possible mostly because of the remarkable compatibility between him and His Majesty, a rare and outstanding example in the annals of royal-ministerial relations. However, if not for his talents and extraordinary sense of loyalty, he could not have accomplished so much.

My father's political fortunes did take a dismal turn, and he fell victim to endless slander and calumny. But that was all because of variations on two baseless stories. Though he was in public service for thirty years, no one has remotely intimated that any course of action he took led to the decline of the nation or brought harm to the people. Not only educated scholars and officials but rank and file soldiers, ordinary residents of the city, and even ignorant people in rural areas remember his virtue and feel indebted to him. Their overwhelming consensus is that "were it not for Minister Hong, neither they nor the nation would have survived." This is not what I, out of private affection, say. If one were to ask anyone in the street, even a child or a soldier, one would hear that my father was a wise minister indeed. This verdict is certainly not what is accorded a person just for wielding power for a long time. His many accomplishments in office are well known. The late King enumerated them in his preface to the "Collected Memorials,"[5] and I do not wish to repeat them. Here I will only point out how utterly unjust the accusations against him were. A detailed account of how he fell victim to that vicious calumny is recorded elsewhere.* There is no need for me to go into it here.

Suppose that Prince Sado's illness had not reached that indescribably difficult state or that His Majesty had not become aware of it, and that Father for some peculiar reason had informed His Majesty of the Prince's illness and provided him with "that thing," advising him what to do with it. Of course he was my father, but after all, one's husband comes before one's father, and though I may be an ignorant woman, I know of this most basic of principles. Thus, had that been the case, would I not have had the discrimination to follow my husband in death at the time? Even if I had been unable to do that, would I still have maintained a daughter-father relationship? What of my son, the late King? Would he have interceded on behalf of his grandfather in the *sinmyo* year (1771)? Would he have gone to such lengths to defend his maternal grandfather, refuting that memorial [of Chŏng Ihwan] and citing His Majesty's words? Had Father been guilty, would Heaven have allowed his line to continue? Would I, even reduced to what I am at present, have survived for forty years and received the filial devotion of my descendants?

At the time [of Prince Sado's death], the future of the nation hung imperiled, sustained by no more than a thread. Had my late father mishandled the situation, the ruin of my family would have been but a secondary matter; the very survival of the late King

* See *The Memoir of 1801*, 150–55.

would not have been possible. Faced with that inexorable situation, my father wailed and cried, shed tears of blood, but, despite his grief, succeeded in protecting the late King and preserving this monarchy right unto this very day. Because His Majesty trusted my father and relied upon him, he preserved the late King. Otherwise, in that towering rage, pursuing such a course of action toward his own son, would he have considered his grandson? Had that happened, what would they say of him now? How censorious the judgment of later generations! Situated as he was, what, then, would have been the right course for my father? To beat his head upon those stones till he died, leaving the Grand Heir to perish as well? Or, seeing that the situation had gone beyond the reach of hope, should he not have acted to save the Grand Heir, continuing the dynastic line? One need not consult men of knowledge to find an answer.

The late King used to say to me, "Grandfather's loyalty was rare even among the ancients. To prevent official criticism, I have been unable to acknowledge either his loyalty or his merit. I have no one to blame for this. Thus I act as though muddled or duped, just marking time. Haven't I even [posthumously] exonerated that monstrous Han Yu of his crime! The pressure to do so overcame my resistance,[6] but I know that this is not a righteous principle for the ages. From the next reign, Grandfather's merit and accomplishments will be manifest. I wish to change his posthumous title to include the character *ch'ung* (loyalty)." He said this hundreds and thousands of times. Lady Kasun also heard it. I would not utter one word of exaggeration just because he is no longer with us.

Because of these desires, the late King labored ten years on my father's official papers. Oblivious to fatigue, he worked on them day and night, composing many pieces of his own for inclusion in the book. What he intended to do with this publication was not just to honor my father's long public service and his accomplishments; he wished to show the world the depth of his appreciation for his grandfather's loyal and admirable service in protecting him and stabilizing the dynasty. Who among the ministers who were close to the late King do not know of this? He still worried that Father's role in the incident of that year [1762] might not be fully understood. He searched for ways to declare him guiltless without having to resort to a separate explanation. For this reason, when editing the entry for the thirteenth day of the fifth month in the *imo* year (1762) in my father's life chronology, the late King carefully wrote down the precise time [when Prince Sado entered the rice chest]. He also added a long description of how devotedly and carefully my father attended to his duties as director of [Prince Sado's] funeral and how he took care that the minutest details of the funeral rites were properly observed.[7] The late King then asked my brothers, "His Lordship's memorial on the *imo* event, which he submitted to the throne directly,* is not included in his collected works.[8] What is the reason for this?" My brothers answered, "It is because we are still bound by the order prohibiting the circulation of public documents concerning the incident of that year."[†] The late King said, "That is not written in stone. Besides, that memorial reveals His Lordship's true intentions and the facts of the incident. Why don't you include it?" He urged them repeatedly. But before long, my brother met with calamity,[‡] and so this was not done.

How excited and pleased the late King was when he obtained His Majesty's handwritten letter of the *sinmyo* year (1771) exonerating my father! He said, "Let's include this in the Records of the Crown Prince Office." Including it in my father's life chronology,[§] he said to me, "I finally found a written account of what I witnessed myself. Now I have included this piece in Grandfather's life chronology. It is irrefutable evidence [of his innocence] that will stand for a thousand years to come. I have no regrets." Had my father been involved in the incident of that year even in the smallest degree, the late King would not have spoken of his grandfather in this way. Nor would he have even thought of working on his grandfather's "Collected Memorials" or his life chronology. In matters that allowed no deviation, the late King always upheld righteous principles, even if it meant leaving something unfulfilled

* According to Chosŏn court custom, memorials to the throne were received by the Royal Secretariat. In exceptional circumstances, high-ranking ministers were allowed to hand their memorials to the king directly.

[†] There was a ban on discussions of the 1762 incident.

[‡] This phrase must refer to the execution of Hong Nagim in 1801. It seems that with his death, the project to publish Hong Ponghan's collected works came to an end.

[§] Hong Ponghan's life chronology (*yŏnbo*) was compiled for the most part by Hong Nagin, his son. It was completed by someone else, perhaps Chŏngjo himself.

in the way he served his parents.* If he had felt that his maternal grandfather had not been an exemplar of righteous principles, he certainly would not have forgiven him just because he was his grandfather. Beyond that, the late King was not merely expressing the usual familial respect but an extraordinary encomium to his grandfather. Does one need more persuasion than this?

My father was exonerated of all three charges in the *kapchin* year (1784),† which one would ordinarily take to mean that he had previously suffered unfair accusations. But for some inexplicable reason, my father was yet again reviled for that same old charge of which he had been exonerated in *kapchin* (1784). What injustice!

Two opinions have emerged concerning the event of that year [1762]. One is that His Majesty's decision was an impartial and brilliant act of justice. Those who hold this opinion call it the most sagacious and admirable of His Majesty's accomplishments, one in harmony with all of Heaven and Earth. The other opinion is that Prince Sado was not ill but met that tragedy unjustly. Those who hold the former opinion assume the criminality of Prince Sado, that he harbored a truly evil intent. This renders an aura of righteousness to His Majesty's act. It makes it a meritorious deed of the same nature as vanquishing an enemy nation. But what kind of person does this view make of Prince Sado; where does it leave the late King? This view discredits Prince Sado and the late King. The second view, on the other hand, implies that His Majesty took that extreme measure against the Crown Prince on the basis of mere slander. This opinion might originate in a wish to console Prince Sado and to restore his honor, but it does so at the expense of His Majesty's virtue.

Both views are equally faulty. Both display terrible impropriety toward the Three Royal Generations‡ and distort reality. As my

---

* Not conferring titles of king and queen upon them, which was in adherence to his duty to Yŏngjo.

† Chŏngjo posthumously cleared Hong Ponghan of the three charges—that he gave Yŏngjo the rice chest in which Prince Sado was confined to die, that he begrudged the use of top-quality ginseng during Yŏngjo's illness, and that he discussed the possibility of offering a posthumous royal title to Prince Sado (*CS*, 18:17b–18b; Chŏngjo, *Hongjae chŏnsŏ*, 32:15b–18b). Hong was accused of the first crime by Han Yu in 1771 (*Yŏngjo sillok* [hereafter *YS*], in *Chosŏn wangjo sillok*, 117:7a–8a); the second and third crimes by Kim Kwanju and Kim Kwiju in 1772 (*YS*, 119:6a–12b). Afterwards Hong was periodically accused of these three crimes, including once by Chŏng Ihwan shortly after Chŏngjo's accession. For example, see *CS*, 1:9a–b.

‡ Yŏngjo, Prince Sado, and Chŏngjo.

late father said on several occasions, it was clearly an illness [on the part of Prince Sado], but, though it was illness, the safety of His Majesty and the dynasty itself were sustained by a mere breath. There was no way, despite his unfathomable sorrow and pain, for His Majesty to avoid that decision. As for Prince Sado, he could have been blamed only if he possessed his senses. As he grew more afflicted, he lost his true nature; he was unaware of what he was doing. What must be regretted is that he became ill; it had absolutely no bearing on his virtue.

As this was the truth, one must say that His Majesty's decision was made under irresistible pressures, that Prince Sado could not have been helped, and that the late King knew his duty even as he suffered deep grief. Only when this complete picture is presented can the truth be told and justice achieved for all. The first opinion describes His Majesty's decision as sagacious, making Prince Sado a criminal, while the other, seeking to benefit Prince Sado, makes His Majesty an unfeeling parent. Both are unjust to the Three Royal Generations.

And then there are those who maintain that His Majesty was right but are intent on placing all the blame on my late father. In total ignorance of what happened, they insist that my father offered "that thing." How can this be? Are they trying to be loyal to His Majesty King Yŏngjo or are they trying to be loyal to His Highness Prince Sado? They are merely turning the incident of that year into a pit in which to ensnare people. That incident, in whose shadow I have lived in unbearable pain and sorrow for every minute of these forty years, has become the center of a cunning scheme with which they harm people, a foothold with which they advance themselves in the world. Oh! I wail in bitterness.

After the demise of the late King, that evil clique has risen in the world.* Dissatisfied and angry that they could not completely eliminate me, they brought calamity to my brother and made my father a leader of traitors. It even came to pass that a royal decree was issued with my father's name heading the criminal list. Though I am ignorant of the history of the ages, I do not believe that, even in the most venal and depraved of societies, there can have been such an evil clique as the one that, in the presence of the late

---

* Because Sunjo was underage in 1800, Queen Dowager Chŏngsun acted as regent. Her family and those who were opposed to Lady Hyegyŏng's family were in power. Lady Hyegyŏng is referring to them.

King's mother, listed the late King's maternal grandfather as a head traitor and disseminated the decree to the whole country. Moreover, their written recommendation to persecute my brother, which was sent to the throne in the sixth month of the *sinyu* year (1801), contained a passage saying that a "certain sibling" of my brother was "incomparably traitorous."* Who could they have been referring to as my brother's sibling? Who but me? They were openly calling me an arch-traitor. This shows how the world has changed, how precipitously ministerial integrity has fallen. There is an old saying that it is not enough to wail and shed tears. Still, even that does not adequately express my state of mind.

Because my father was so unfortunate as to have lived in difficult and precarious times, he remained in office for a long time. Graced by a profound royal trust that held him in a very special regard and burdened with the cares of the nation and anxieties for the young Grand Heir, he could not, despite a constant and acute longing to retire, disengage himself from the duties of office. Shamefully, under the influence of events, he remained and thus failed to live up to the [standards of] loyalty and integrity of the ancients.† If a man of rigorous principle and honesty at court or in private life could not fathom my father's true intentions and had criticized him, saying that he lacked solemn loyalty and the integrity of a high minister, my father would have smiled and accepted it as he certainly should have. Nor would I have minded that criticism.

My family, which had served in office for generations, seemed for a while to have entered a period of unobstructed fortune. Men of the younger generation passed the civil service examinations one after another; the glory of the family overflowed and its power grew excessive. It is not odd that people grew angry at us and that ghosts and spirits shunned us. Reflecting upon this after falling into ruin, I find it ten thousand times regrettable and bitter that my family did not depart from the paths of power, but instead remained immersed in the flow of examinations and official posts. Yet it is truly unjust that my family reach this extreme point, maligned

* The recommendation they sent late in the fifth month requesting the execution of Hong Nagim and Ŭnŏn and the edict they sent early in the sixth month announcing their deaths are couched in vicious and condemnatory language. But I could not find this exact phrase in the *Sillok* version. SS, 3:19a–21a, 3:24a–b.

† By this standard, Hong Ponghan should have retired from public life upon the death of Prince Sado.

by slander and calumny. How vividly do I see that prosperity and decline, calamity and fortune, join in a circle. As my family has declined after having flourished, I beseech Heaven in tears and blood that perhaps someday this bitter injustice will be known to the world and that calamity shall turn to fortune.

Kwiju's family, catapulted out of poverty and obscurity[9] into sudden prominence by the royal marriage in *kimyo* (1759), exhibited the inevitable awkwardness and inexperience. My late father decided that it was in the best interests of all parties concerned that the two royal affinal families maintain a cordial relationship. Thus he instructed them and, with inexhaustible care and attention, arranged to conceal their rustic and unrefined manners. In the beginning the Kim family was grateful and even moved by his concern, but as their power and influence increased, their hearts grew more wicked, and eventually they became our sworn enemies. How incredible!

Kwiju's father was a man of suspicious and devious nature, but Kwiju was even worse, a truly depraved, vicious, and violent character. Had they modeled themselves after Lord Kyŏngŭn,* who would have faulted them? They were originally from Ch'ungch'ŏng Province and were on friendly terms with those who espoused distorted and peculiar theories. Kim Hallok, Kwiju's first cousin once removed, the father of Kwanju, was a disciple of that Namdang.[†] He acted as though he were engaged in the business of scholarship. Thus those scholars from Ch'ungch'ŏng Province looked up to and relied upon Kwiju and his family as though they were gods and spirits. By promoting and supporting these scholars' theories, however, Kwiju and company deviated from their proper place as royal affines.[‡] Nor did they manage to maintain a consistent position throughout, as they dropped their support halfway through. What distinguished them was their arrogance, absurdly pretending to be

---

* Kim Chusin. Like Kim Han'gu, he held no official post at the time of his daughter's enthronement, but after his daughter's marriage, he maintained a low profile.

† Namdang was the nom de plume of Han Wŏnjin (1682–1751), a very well-known Neo-Confucian scholar. His famous debate with Yi Kan, known as the "Horak debate," concerned human nature. Lady Hyegyŏng seems to be disdainful of this debate and the scholars involved in it. None of them served in office.

‡ Royal affines were expected to support the royal house. As a rule, they were not expected to present themselves as "pure scholars" who shunned office.

something that they were not and behaving in such an altogether ludicrous manner that they became laughingstocks.

Since my family was an illustrious one that had produced high ministers for generations and had become royal affines earlier than the Kims, they resented us, suspecting that we might scorn and look down upon them. During *kyŏngjin* and *sinsa* (1760–1761), when Prince Sado's illness reached an irreversible point and His Majesty showered special favor upon them as new relatives, the evil hearts of Kwiju and his clique emerged into the open. Conferring, they agreed: "Now that the Crown Prince's loss of virtue has reached this point, something decisive will befall him soon. In that case, it would be only right if his son were not to be preserved either. If this were to happen, as there is no other prince, the throne would have to adopt a son. We, as [adoptive] maternal relatives to the new Crown Prince, would enjoy power and glory for a long time to come."

While they indulged in these daydreams, they feared that, because His Majesty so completely trusted my father, the Grand Heir might be preserved and so their dream would vanish. Thus in *sinsa* (1761), when Kwiju was little more than twenty, he dared to send His Majesty a letter in which he criticized my father and implicated Chŏng Hwiryang.* His Majesty was astounded by his behavior and in no uncertain terms warned Her Highness the Queen that this simply would not do. In intimating that my father failed to admonish Prince Sado and that Chŏng Hwiryang failed to report to the throne Prince Sado's [secret] trip to P'yŏngyang,† Kwiju's intention could not possibly have been simply to harm my father; he was ensuring that His Majesty would be informed of the missteps of His Highness the Crown Prince. It is impossible for a person in his position to be more nakedly evil and covetous than this. During this period, one Palace Matron Yi, a sister of Yi Kyehŭng, was in royal favor. She often waited upon His Majesty and mediated certain things between His Majesty and Prince Sado. She saw Kwiju's letter and was flabbergasted and chagrined. She protested to the Queen, "How dare Your Highness's family engage in that kind of behavior?" and demanded, "Please wash it out with water." My

* Sending such a letter to the king was a breach of public conduct in the Chosŏn court.

† Prince Sado made this trip incognito in 1761 without his father's permission. For details, see *The Memoir of 1805*, 302–3.

father came to be aware of Kwiju's intentions from this incident and was deeply concerned though he mentioned it to no one, not even to Prince Sado. One can gather from this that he did not want a confrontation with the Kims.

Just as they were most envious, feeling that the father-in-law of the King should be more important than the father-in-law of the Crown Prince, and just when their scheme to eliminate us was ripening, that tragic event* occurred. They must have been over-joyed, thinking that the Grand Heir would be swept aside. There would be an adoption; they would become maternal relatives of this new prince while the Hongs would be annihilated. Instead, the Grand Heir became the Crown Prince, my family was preserved intact, and my father served as minister of the State Council. Overwhelmed by chagrin, they made that unprecedented, vicious blasphemy. This was a scheme to sow seeds of confusion and doubt in His Majesty's sagacious heart in order to eliminate the Grand Heir. Though they uttered this evil phrase, I can scarcely bear to write it with my brush. If I were not to write it clearly, however, I fear that later generations might be perplexed by its content, and so I will push myself to record it.

Shortly after that terrible event, Kim Hallok declared at a meeting of the Kims of Hongju, "The Grand Heir is a criminal's son and thus cannot possibly succeed to the throne. Who among the descendants of T'aejo[†] would not do as well as he?" This is what the world refers to as the sixteen-character blasphemy (*simyukcha hyungŏn*). All the Kims present at the meeting heard it, and as they repeated it, it reached everywhere—though no one could really repeat such a horrid phrase verbatim out in the open. But I heard it, and so did the Grand Heir. Each of us thought it unbelievably hideous. At the same time, we only half believed its authenticity.

Not so long ago, the late King said to me, "I was always in-credulous of that blasphemy attributed to the Hallok and Kwiju group. But I recently verified it."

I asked, "How did you find out?"

The late King said, "Rumor had it that this phrase was spoken at a family gathering of the Kalmi group of the Hongju Kims. One night Kim Isŏng of the Office of Special Counselors was on duty.

---

* The death of Prince Sado in 1762.
† The founder of the Chosŏn dynasty.

He is a Kalmi Kim, and so I thought he might know. I urged him, 'Don't hide. Tell me the truth.' I alternately cajoled and pressed him. At first he was rather hesitant and was not forthcoming. But after all, wouldn't I be able to handle someone young and inexperienced like that? Finally he came out with everything. He told me that he had actually heard Hallok utter that phrase, as had many other Kims. They immediately went to Kim Sich'an, the head of that branch of the Kim family, and reported to him what they had heard. Kim Sich'an was greatly alarmed and deeply incensed. He felt that the statement left no doubt as to the traitorous intentions of Kwiju and Hallok, and he warned the youngsters of the family that they should firmly distinguish between what was loyal and what was traitorous. Kim Isŏng also mentioned that the phrase did not just come from Hallok, but that it had originated with Kwiju. After all these years, I have the proof that it was true. Isn't it incredible! Yet if I were to bring it up now, there is no telling what the repercussions might be. It is best to say nothing for the moment and to have a long look at the future. That group should still be feared. Better to accommodate and soothe them rather than to call for terrible incidents that might cause deep resentment."

The late King continued, "I also heard that after that year they even settled upon someone they would recommend to the throne for adoption. This was all part of the scheme that began with that blasphemous phrase. Just imagine! Some fool placed on the throne as the lord of the nation and, perhaps, in all pomp and grandeur, receiving the humble obeisances of the entire bureaucracy! What a repulsive picture! The more I think about it, the more deeply I shudder at their treacherous hearts and vicious words."

When the late King appointed Kwanju[10] the Magistrate of Tongnae, he told me that he was doing "something that cannot be easily explained, something extremely complicated and difficult." Of course, the late King cannot have failed to observe that Kwiju and his clique were vicious traitors. He had, in fact, known this for a long time. In the *pyŏngsin* year (1776), for instance, when he dealt with Kwiju's case, he listed only his minor offenses and left the rest of his crime unspecified, saying that it was "something truly unmentionable."* This unmentionable crime was none other

* Upon Chŏngjo's accession in 1776, Kim Kwiju was banished to Hŭksan Island. On this occasion, Chŏngjo bitterly condemned Kim Han'gu, Kim Kwiju, and Chŏng Hugyŏm for their intrigues against Hong Ponghan. *CS*, 2:27a–31b.

than that blasphemy. From this one can see that the late King had been informed of this crime before *pyŏngsin*, but when he spoke with Kim Isŏng, he obtained indisputable proof. Since ancient times there must have been many traitors and rebels who pushed some fool onto the throne and betrayed the rightful heir. As for our royal house, the six-generation line descending from King Hyojong has but one royal descendant, the Grand Heir.* Nonetheless, blinded by greed for wealth and power, Kwiju's clique wished to do away with this one true blood line, placing some total stranger on the throne as "a descendant of King T'aejo" and taking this country as if it were their own. There cannot possibly have been more depraved and monstrous villains than these traitors.

This blasphemy was also the reason why the Kims came to regard my family as their enemies and to persecute my father with such determination. As word of the blasphemy spread, they realized that they could neither carry out their schemes nor deny what they had said. It was at about this time that the Kims, acting as men of learning, began to befriend so-called scholars and to participate in scholarly debates. They gathered around them those who were reduced to poverty nearly to the point of death, either from Seoul or from the countryside. These were the sort who, lacking literary or martial accomplishments, enjoyed idle talk and delighted in schemes and gossip. Obviously they were covetous of material gain, but the Kims bent over backward to attract them, pretending that they were associating with them in the spirit of loyal friendship. These rustics were the lowliest and most lawless of malcontents. Not one of them in all their lives had even glimpsed the courtyard of a rich and powerful family. Now suddenly they were treated to fine food and sturdy clothes. If they asked for money, they got money; if they asked for rice, they got rice. If one among them fell ill, ginseng and deer horn were provided. If

* King Hyojong had an only son, King Hyŏnjong, who in turn had an only son, King Sukchong. Sukchong had three sons who survived to adulthood. The first, Kyŏngjong, died without issue, and the last, Prince Yŏllyŏng, died at the age of twenty, leaving no heir. The middle son was King Yŏngjo. Yŏngjo's first son, Prince Hyojang, died leaving no heir. His second son was Prince Sado. Prince Sado's heir by his legal consort, Lady Hyegyŏng, was Chŏngjo, referred to as the Grand Heir. Prince Sado had three other sons by secondary consorts. Thus, as Lady Hyegyŏng observes, only Sado's descendants are in the direct line unless one goes back more than six generations. However, she is overlooking the fact that Sado had sons by secondary consorts. Yŏngjo and Sado were themselves sons by secondary consorts.

one married or died, nothing was withheld for the wedding or the funeral. They were completely overwhelmed and felt eternally indebted to the Kims in life and in death. They went about singing the praises of the Kims, declaring them to be true sage scholars among royal affines, and making it possible for the Kims to continue with their reckless plans.* This was the evil scheme once used by Wang Mang.† Indisputably, Kwiju's intention was to eventually crush my family.

The late King often remarked that my father saved several tens of thousands of taels out of regional tributes as emergency funds in the Office of the Palace Guard and that Ohŭng together with Kwiju spent it all on those they hired in their plan to kill Father. He felt this to be such a bitter irony that once he mentioned it to an official to whom he felt close. The late King told me that this official's response was "A true description, indeed." It was truly odd that Kwiju's group was so single-minded in their determination to annihilate my family. Even if Father had erred against them, they should not have been so antagonistic, since the two families were bound by special relationships. Had we done something disadvantageous or hostile to them, then under the rules of normal human sentiment, they could have hated us. But from the beginning, we had treated them with kindness and without even one iota of hostility. No matter how long I search for a possible explanation for their hatred, I just cannot find it.

No matter how they tried to undermine the Grand Heir with their evil words and schemes, His Majesty's affection for him stood unchanged and royal trust in Father continued undiminished. Moreover, as the Grand Heir matured, his position grew even more secure. They were in dismay. Then, so entirely unexpectedly, that *kich'uk* (1769) incident involving those palace servants occurred.‡ The late King was still quite young at the time and he could not have been fully mindful that his maternal grandfather and this old mother were so completely and totally devoted to his welfare. His passing anger cooled his affection for his maternal family.

---

   * *T'anghwa rŭl p'ich'i anihage mandani* literally means "causing them not to avoid boiling water and fire."

   † Wang Mang was the interloper who, in the view of his overthrowers, usurped the throne from the last emperor of the former Han dynasty.

   ‡ For details, see *The Memoir of 1801*, 144–49.

Hugyŏm was not kindly disposed toward my family either, and through him, Kwiju noticed this change in the Grand Heir. Thinking that he finally had what he needed, Kwiju, in the manner of a thief turning on his master with a club, now assumed the role of a loyal and devoted follower of the Grand Heir, whom he flattered and cajoled. He insinuated to the Grand Heir that my father, fond of Ŭnŏn and Ŭnsin, wished to turn things against the Grand Heir. He also announced to the whole world that "Hong is making things difficult for the Heir Apparent who, in turn, is slighting Hong." Those who wanted an official post overnight and those who cultivated self-interest and changed with the times joined in at once. The so-called "ten scholars" and many other such groups all rolled themselves into one big clique scheming against my father. In the third month of *kyŏngin* (1770), they finally found that wretch Han Yu from Ch'ungch'ŏng Province whom they could persuade to send that evil memorial. It was Kwiju who planned the whole thing. This Han Yu could not boast of even a modicum of learning or a modest standing among the gentlefolk of the countryside. He was just a foolish wretch from some remote backwater, an ignorant, vicious, and foolhardy person who did not belong in the company of gentle-mannered people.

Some years previously, His Majesty King Yŏngjo had been deeply angered by Song Myŏnghŭm and Sin Kyŏng. Lamenting what he felt to be criticism by scholars of his policy of grand harmony, on which he had expended so much effort over the forty years of his reign, His Majesty punished Song and Sin.* Then he published the book called *Yugollok* (Instructions for later generations), the gist of which was that scholars were leading the

* In the fifth month of 1764, Yŏngjo ordered that Pak Sech'e (1631–1695), a renowned scholar-statesman who had served under Hyŏnjong and Sukchong, be canonized at the Confucian temple. Pak Sech'e had been a member of the Soron, and Yŏngjo's measure was meant to demonstrate to the increasingly Noron-dominated bureaucracy his commitment to the policy of grand harmony. In the tenth month, Sin Kyŏng, a grandson of Pak Sech'e, sent to the throne Pak's writings accompanied by his own memorial saying that the way the policy of grand harmony was being pursued by some powerful ministers was inconsistent with his late grandfather's hopes. In the eleventh month, when someone criticized this memorial, Sin sent another one in which he reaffirmed that Pak Sech'e's usage of the term "grand harmony" was being misrepresented by the present court. Sin was banished, and Song Myŏnghŭm and others who expressed agreement with Sin were demoted to commoner status. *YS*, 103:24a, 104:21b–22a, 104:32a–b, 104:33a–b.

country astray and that his successors should not employ them.[11] This was truly excessive, and there were none who did not think it a pity. Nevertheless, since it was an octogenarian ruler doing this in a moment of excess, my father—much in the way in which younger members of a family, in response to complaints of ingratitude by a respected elder, seek his forgiveness to appease him—decided that he, an old and trusted minister, should do nothing that would further enrage his sagacious heart. Trusting that all would understand, he complied with His Majesty's promulgation of royal instructions. He just wanted to smooth things over. He was serving in a time of genuine complexity and difficulty. His only true concern was to protect the Grand Heir so as to leave the foundation of the nation firm and strong. As for the rest, he took a rather philosophical approach; that is, he just decided that nothing could or should be done about an aging king's excesses and that there would be a time when all would be worked out. This was, indeed, a case of erring by acting from one's humanity. It was rooted in his devotion and concern for the Grand Heir.

Soon word circulated that sending a memorial to the throne criticizing *Yugollok* would bring fame.* Someone persuaded this wretch Yu, saying, "If you send a memorial about *Yugollok*, then you will achieve fame. You will get an official post in the future and become a *yangban*."[†] This stupid wretch believed it. Having some characters tattooed on his arm as a way of expressing his loyalty, he came to Seoul, set to present a memorial. He happened to be friendly with one Sim Ŭiji, who knew that Kwiju was searching for someone. Ŭiji and Kwiju conferred with each other and coaxed Yu. He should by all means bring up the issue of *Yugollok*, but they also said, "Right now, Hong has been a minister for so long and he wields so much power that His Majesty is tired of him. He did something wrong by the Heir Apparent, too, and so the Heir Apparent no longer cares for him either. The whole world knows about this, and yet people are unable to bring themselves to attack

---

* In fact, the protest was gathering momentum. In the fifth month of 1769, 1,800 students sent in a joint memorial requesting that the *Yugollok* be abrogated. Yŏngjo's response was to compose a continuation, *Sok Yugollok* (Continuation to *Yugollok*) (*YS*, 112:22a–b). *Yugollok* and *Sok Yugollok* are listed in *Munhŏn pigo* (3 vols., Seoul: Tongguk munhwasa, 1957, 245:11a–b), but they do not seem to be extant.

† *Yangban* is the colloquial term for a member of the hereditary aristocracy.

him. If you were to criticize him in your memorial, then not only would you get an official post, but you would be considered one who undertook a great and meritorious act." They tempted him endlessly in this fashion. They also turned to other inducements. Kwiju sent servants to the inn at which Han Yu was staying and ordered them to inquire loudly, "Is there a Mr. Han from Ch'ŏngju here? His Lordship the Prime Minister ordered the wretch be seized. He is here to make trouble by sending a memorial." On other occasions the servants covered their faces and heckled, "We are ordered to chase this person out of Seoul." Thus they baited Yu. His temper rose and he grew chagrined. Ŭiju then cajoled Yu with thousands of sweet words and promises. He said, "If you send this memorial, you will acquire a reputation for uprightness and integrity. You will enjoy power and glory." He gave Yu a memorial that he himself composed, and this wretch, not discerning whether he might die or live or whether what he was doing was right or wrong, sent in that vicious memorial.

Under the sway of Hugyŏm, Madame Chŏng was convinced that only by eliminating my family could she and her son consolidate their power. Allied with Kwiju, she tirelessly and ferociously slandered my father to His Majesty until his sagacious heart was seven- or eight-tenths turned against him. My father was relieved of his post for a rather insignificant issue in the first month of *kyŏngin* (1770).* He was soon recalled, but as a minister without portfolio, while the Prime Ministership went to Kim Ch'iin, who continued in this post till the third month. One could clearly detect in this a lessening of royal affection toward my father. When His Majesty saw Han Yu's memorial, he was deeply chagrined. However, influenced by those who maligned Father, His Majesty had Han Yu interrogated with rather light corporal punishment and banished him to an island.† Then His Majesty accepted my father's resignation. The royal intention was, of course, to shield my father from further attack. Nonetheless, considering the affec-

---

* On the eighth day of the first month of 1770, Hong Ponghan, serving as Prime Minister, led the bureaucracy in requesting severe punishment for a censor, Yun Hongnyŏl, whose recent memorial was deemed factional. Yŏngjo was angered by this and dismissed all the bureaucrats who had joined in this demand. *YS*, 114:2b–3a.
† Han Yu was expunged from the scholars' roster and sent to Hŭksan Island. *YS*, 114:13b.

tion and trust between them in that long relationship, this measure was totally unexpected. After that, my family was out of favor and my father was not at court. Kwiju alone wielded power. With Hugyŏm inside and with all sorts of faction-minded cronies outside, he schemed day and night to harm my father. I cannot begin to describe the precarious state in which we lived during that period.

In the winter of *kyŏngin* (1770), Ch'oe Ingnam sent a memorial that said, "It is embarrassing that the Heir Apparent is not paying respect at Prince Sado's tomb. Prime Minister Kim Ch'iin should be held responsible." The implication that the Grand Heir visit Prince Sado's tomb was not wrong but, given the extremely delicate issues that surrounded it, was not something that a subject might casually suggest. Moreover, the incumbent Prime Minister had nothing to do with it. This Ingnam, who sent the memorial, was an ill-mannered person with a reputation for shallowness and recklessness. He was a relative of Madame Chŏng's in-laws. Through this connection, my family had the misfortune of having made his acquaintance. Kwiju sent one Ku Sang to persuade Hugyŏm to insinuate to His Majesty that it was my father who had inspired Ch'oe Ingnam's memorial. His Majesty's sagacious heart was easily influenced by their explanation of why Father might have wanted such a memorial written. To wit, he wished to portray the incident of that year as having been His Majesty's fault and to use this to get rid of Kim Ch'iin. Because of this suspicion, His Majesty conducted a thorough and extensive personal interrogation of the suspects, torturing many severely,[12] hoping that someone would confess that Hong was behind the memorial. But because my father did not know about it, no one implicated him, although several people including Ingnam were beaten to death.[13] His sagacious heart, however, was not appeased. The murderous hearts of that evil clique were still inflamed. Thus after only several months, in the second month of *sinmyo* (1771), a terrible incident involving Ŭnŏn and Ŭnsin occurred.

When Ŭnŏn was born in *kapsul* (1754) and then Ŭnsin in *ŭrhae* (1755), I was afflicted by that feeling that attacks us women regardless of birth, high or low, and was not pleased. The Prince's illness, however, was getting quite awful, and he was not particularly enamored of the mother of these children. Moreover, these children were already born, unintended though their births may

have been. Even if I did wish to express jealousy toward my husband, the situation just did not allow for such a display. Of a weak
and indecisive nature, I felt that these children were, after all, my
husband's flesh and blood, lowly though they may have been.
Unable to ignore them, I made suitable arrangements for them.
His Majesty regarded them as a potential source of trouble and
harshly reprimanded Prince Sado. This caused me to bear the situation with greater fortitude than I would have otherwise. I felt
that, if I were to display jealousy under these circumstances, it
would increase the Prince's misery. His Majesty thought my acceptance of these children with no show of jealousy quite odd.
"You are acting contrary to human feelings," he scolded.

After that terrible event [1762], I felt even more pity for these
forlorn children. I had the duty of a legal mother—they were, after
all, flesh and blood that my husband had left behind. I looked after
them and made their lives as comfortable as I could. Then they
came of age and the time came for them to leave the palace and
take residences of their own. His Majesty was quite worried about
them. "What will they do?" he kept saying. My father, who, out of
fair-mindedness, always took the view that they were the flesh and
blood of Prince Sado no matter what, suggested to His Majesty,
"As they have grown and gone, one must be concerned that these
youngsters, still green and hot-blooded, might be seduced by
something or enlisted by someone into a dangerous involvement.
There is no telling what horrendous trouble they might fall into.
This would be extremely unfortunate. I, your servant, am so closely
related to the Grand Heir that no one will suspect me. If I were to
watch over and instruct them and educate them to be responsible
adults who cannot be seduced by dangerous things, it would
not just benefit them; it would be a blessing for the nation." His
Majesty replied, "I am truly grateful and moved by my lord's concern. Please do that." His Majesty added, "I wonder whether
they would listen to my lord's instruction."

The younger members of the family had a different opinion.
They said to Father, "That was a mistake. They will be the seeds of
trouble." They advised, "Please have nothing to do with them."
When Ŭnŏn and Ŭnsin came to the house, everyone including
very young children avoided them. My late father scolded the
household, "It's all misconstrued, unnecessary fear. Out of public

duty, I just want to instruct and guide them so that they will not be led into some terrible error." He then assured them, "Who would suspect me? Would the Grand Heir suspect me? Who would not understand my intention?" If someone were to say that Father, not discerning the mentality of this age of decline, did a foolish thing, let him. He received the same criticism from his own children. That a huge disaster would be concocted out of it was, however, beyond our wildest dreams. It was simply too incredible! Neither my father nor Lord Ch'ŏngwŏn was in any way guilty. But Ch'ŏngwŏn also rendered service to Ŭnŏn and Ŭnsin and gave them such things as palanquins. Should one also suspect Ch'ŏngwŏn?

My father's repeated attempts at instruction and guidance were wasted, however. Ŭnŏn and Ŭnsin were clods. Dull-witted and muddleheaded, they did not at all apply themselves to studying. The first, and perhaps the only, thing they learned was to assume the haughty airs of royal princes. In this way, they associated with an unseemly element from the palace and went about making trouble. They turned a deaf ear to my father and increasingly distanced themselves from him. Father then realized the futility of his effort. Fearing that further attempts might elicit only resentment, he gradually dissociated himself from them. When Father went to the countryside in the kyŏngin year (1770) after meeting that trouble, they completely ignored him, and he made no move toward them.

As he did every year, toward the end of the first month of sinmyo (1771) my father sent chestnuts harvested from his estate to each establishment of the royal family, including that of Prince Sado's daughters. Chestnuts were also sent to Ŭnŏn and Ŭnsin. This somehow ignited royal fury. In the beginning of the second month, His Majesty went to the Ch'angŭi Palace.* Acting as though he was anticipating an uprising, he had the palace and the city walls guarded by soldiers† and banished Ŭnŏn and Ŭnsin to Cheju Island. Imminent danger hung over my father.‡ The Grand Heir did

---

* Ch'angŭi Palace was Yŏngjo's residence when he was a prince. After accession, his visits to Ch'angŭi Palace usually signified displeasure with something. On this occasion, Yŏngjo went there for nine days. YS, 116:5b–8b.

† Yŏngjo also ordered that Ŭnŏn's and Ŭnsin's mother's house be guarded by soldiers. YS, 116:7b–8a.

‡ Hong Ponghan was also punished. For details, see The Memoir of 1801.

not accompany the royal carriage to the detached palace, and only Han'gi and Hugyŏm attended His Majesty. This was a result of their elaborate plan to induce a royal decision [to kill Father] at once. Kwiju was in mourning and so he sent his uncle, Han'gi, in his stead. From the beginning, his sagacious heart had felt great displeasure with us concerning Ŭnŏn and Ŭnsin. He did not like my taking them in without much ado, nor did he think it necessary for my father to bother with them. Furious at us, thinking that my family had conspired to induce Ingnam to write that memorial blaming the event of that year on him, and provoked by the trusted Kwiju's slanders and his beloved daughter Madame Chŏng's incitement, His Majesty was about to carry out the act.

The late King was astounded by the news and went to Her Highness the Queen to protest. "There is no evidence that His Lordship has planned to place royal grandchildren* on the throne. Accusing him of that, they are about to kill him. It just won't do to indict and kill someone for no other reason than that you hate him. Your Ladyship, you should put a stop to this." With these words from the Grand Heir, Han'gi and Hugyŏm relented, and thus the most immediate danger was lifted. My father, who had been confined to Ch'ŏngju for several days, was released.† Upon his return to the palace, His Majesty realized that the episode had occurred because of private animosities and trumped-up charges. He said to the Grand Heir, "The attacks and counterattacks between the two affinal families are causing a great deal of trouble for the country. I will have to think of a way not to be deceived by this crowd." His Majesty's sagacious intelligence had been only briefly clouded. In the end, he could not fail to recognize the machinations of those wretches and the fallacy of those accusations! That was why His Majesty spoke to the Grand Heir as he did.

Although the imminent danger passed because of the Grand Heir's intervention, their blood thirst grew stronger day by day. Now that they had shown their hand, it became harder for my father and his opponents to coexist—his detractors became more apprehensive than before of future consequences if my father were to live. For instance, in the second month, they succeeded in per-

---

* Ŭnŏn and Ŭnsin.
† Yŏngjo's comment on releasing Hong Ponghan was that he was doing this not for the sake of Hong but for the sake of Lady Hyegyŏng. *YS*, 116:10b.

suading His Majesty to release Han Yu, noting that he had shown perspicacity. This fool Yu obviously had been persuaded by the sweet talk of others that he would attain high office and gain advantage if he were to send in that memorial. Instead, he was beaten and banished to an uninhabited island. He felt that what he had done was not his true intention, and he composed "an essay of remorse." Kim Yakhaeng had been exiled to the same island earlier than Yu* and so talked to Yu. Kim Yakhaeng asked Yu why he sent that memorial. Yu said, "I did it because I was deceived by Sim Ŭiji and Song Hwanŏk and their crowd. It seems that Ŭiji and company were enlisted by Kim Kwiju. But I am just a scholar from the countryside who went up to Seoul to speak of the *Yugollok*. How could I have known the details? Only after I came here and heard many things did I realize that I was deceived. I felt so remorseful that I composed an essay called 'Remorse.'" He then showed the essay to Kim Yakhaeng. Thus the essay came to be known to the world. My family saw it and I heard about its contents. I do not know whether Kim Yakhaeng is still alive or not, but this essay makes it all the more clear that the whole thing was Kwiju's doing.

Once that wretch Yu was set free, Kwiju's clique coaxed him again. They said, "Hong Ponghan is definitely under siege. His Majesty released you because you showed understanding. Were you to do it again, you would surely get something better." The wretch sent another memorial in the eighth month. In this memorial he finally mentioned "that thing," saying that my father "gave [the rice chest] to His Majesty and suggested its use."† His willingness to engage in calumny knew no bounds. As punishment for bringing up "that thing," His Majesty sent Yu down to the Ch'ungch'ŏng provincial court and had him executed. Ŭiji was also interrogated. Asked what "that thing" referred to, he arrogantly retorted, "Your Majesty truly does not know what 'that thing' is?"[14] His Majesty termed this crime *lèse-majesté* and meted out punishment harsher than what had been imposed on Han Yu. Not only was Ŭiji executed, but his wife and children were separated from each other and exiled to distant places. His Majesty

---

* Kim served in the Censorate but was banished to Hŭksan Island from 1768 to 1771.

† Yŏngjo interrogated Han to see what he meant by "that thing" and how he learned about it. *YS*, 117:7a–b.

dealt Yu and Ŭiji the heaviest of punishments for having brought up the issue of "that thing," and certainly not for criticizing my father.[15]

Although His Majesty imposed capital punishment on those wretches, he was also deeply irate at my father. "Who is the one who has been stirring up that *imo* (1762) business* since the spring?" he raged. His Majesty ordered, "He will be deprived of every post and made a commoner."[16] What His Majesty meant when he said "stirring up that *imo* (1762) business" was that he was still suspicious and resentful of my father in connection with Ch'oe Ingnam's memorial. The royal pronouncement mentioned that my father "has been stirring up that *imo* (1762) business" and that he "helped to create it." One could very well interpret these phrases just as Yu did in his memorial—that my father offered "that thing" to His Majesty, asking him to "please use this to put an end [to Prince Sado]." Now, because a royal pronouncement said that Father "helped to create it," some people took it literally. In the face of this, what can be done about the suspicion and who can establish his innocence? What I say would probably sound like defense by an interested party. However, there is one proof that can stand in witness for the ages.

In disgrace, my late father shut himself up in the country in the ninth month of *sinmyo* (1771). One day he received a letter from the late King. It said, "In truth, the spirits and ghosts will stand witness to Your Lordship's wholehearted loyalty. That Your Lordship has nothing to be ashamed of in comparison to ancient men of principle is no mere private homage from a grandson to a grandfather. It should be publicly recognized by the age, a recognition that will stand for one hundred generations. Unfortunately, his sagacious intelligence is momentarily clouded and so he has meted out this measure placing Your Lordship in this plight. However, I heartily agree with Your Lordship that, despite life's thousand anomalies, hundred oddities, and limitless varieties of the unexpected and the amazing, there is one fundamental, unchanging truth—the importance of dedication to the nation and public welfare. Although the royal order was rather unexpected, Your Lordship's loyalty and devotion will long be remembered, for ten thousand generations. There should be no worry."

---

* Here it means creating an issue over the Sado incident of 1762.

The letter also said, "On the thirteenth day of the fifth month of that year,* at three o'clock in the afternoon, I heard that that confounded thing was ordered to be brought in from the outer kitchen. Realizing that something ominous was about to happen, I went into the Munjŏng Pavilion. His Majesty ordered me to leave, and so I did. I sat beneath the eaves of the Crown Prince Tutorial Office. Long after three o'clock I heard that Your Lordship had arrived outside of the palace and was having a fainting spell. So I sent out the heart-clearing pills that I was going to take myself. The timing of the events of that day makes it clear that 'that thing' was thought of by His Majesty himself and not suggested by Your Lordship. Because the measures His Majesty took that day were solely for the sake of the dynasty and because his sagacious heart was forced to make that decision, I have sustained my life until now. I am alive today because, though I am Prince Sado's son, I have to separate duty from grief. If, however, the situation had been, as that recent royal pronouncement seems to be saying, that a minister had suggested 'that thing' to His Majesty and that His Majesty, persuaded by the minister, had carried out that incident, then not only would it attribute insufficient virtue to His Majesty, but it would also obscure the righteous principle. If principle were to be obscured, then the fact that I am alive today would not be right either. Wouldn't it be distressing?" It then said, "I have spoken to Kim Han'gi about this." The late King thus clarified the timing of the events of that day—which came first and which came later—by recounting what he himself saw. With this one sheet of paper, it becomes clear that my father had not offered "that thing."† If this was the case, on what ground was he being censured?

It was not strange that uninformed people in the remote countryside, hearing nothing more than rumors, suspected my father. But Kwiju and company were royal affines. Besides, the Grand Heir spoke to Han'gi specifically about it. Yet they slandered my father. Had Kwiju not been so bloodthirsty, they could not have behaved in such an extreme fashion. Close though Kwiju's relationship

* The day when Prince Sado was confined to a rice chest.
† To my knowledge, this letter is not extant. However, as noted earlier in this memoir, Chŏngjo publicly declared very early in his reign that Hong Ponghan had nothing to do with Yŏngjo's use of the rice chest. He quotes Yŏngjo on this. CS, 1:9b–10a; Chŏngjo, *Hongjae chŏnsŏ*, 42:1a–2a.

to the throne was, he could not have succeeded in causing so many depraved incidents without the collaboration of Madame Chŏng and Hugyŏm. Outside, Kwiju plotted and schemed with his cronies; inside, Hugyŏm conspired with him, and thus they joined forces.

Then my third brother, urged by me to think of a way to save our parent, befriended Hugyŏm. Hugyŏm colluded with Kwiju partly because he was persuaded by Kwiju's crowd that he would wield great power if he eliminated Hong and partly because he did harbor some resentment toward my father. However, he did not seem to have set his heart irrevocably upon massacring the Hongs. As my third brother pleaded with him, Hugyŏm began to respond with some feeling. A marriage had just been arranged between the two families.* Hugyŏm was aware that, as the Hongs were the maternal family of a Crown Prince who would, in all likelihood, reign, there was the future to worry about. As for Madame Chŏng, she was fickle, changing from morning to evening. I ingratiated myself with her to the utmost in order to gain her favor. Furthermore, she did not hold a deep grudge against us. Gradually, they came around and, in the first month of *imjin* (1772), managed to have my father expunged from the criminal register.†

Now that Hugyŏm had slighted him and no longer responded to his plans, Kwiju no longer had a collaborator inside the court. In his anger, he sent a memorial to the throne in the seventh month. Kwanju, Hallok's son, followed suit.[17] Between Heaven and Earth, the brother of the Queen did this horrendous thing with no thought for its effect upon Her Highness or how it would affect her relations with her daughter-in-law. In this sense, Kwiju was not only the bitter enemy of my family but also a traitor to the nation, a betrayer of the late King, and a criminal to Her Highness.

Kwiju's memorial faulted my father on three counts. The first concerned a failure to use only top-quality ginseng during His Majesty's illness in the *pyŏngsul* year (1766), the next concerned pine-flavored tea, and the last concerned certain words my father said. During royal infirmity, it is not unusual to use two or three

---

* It is impossible to determine who the betrothed were and whether the marriage took place. If it did, which is likely, it involved the children of Hong Nagim and Chŏng Hugyŏm.

† Hong Ponghan was restored to the post of minister emeritus. The *Sillok* says that Yŏngjo took this measure to console Lady Hyegyŏng. *YS*, 118:7a.

yang of ginseng a day. In *pyŏngsul* the Director of the Medical Bureau was Kim Ch'iin, and my late father was Prime Minister. The medicine offered to His Majesty was made from a mixture of half top-quality ginseng and half more ordinary ginseng. One day Kwiju's father walked into the attendant's office and summoned a physician. He asked, "His Majesty does not seem to be doing well. How is it that his potion is not made entirely of top-quality ginseng?" My father was sitting with the Director at the Medical Bureau. Hearing this, he said to the deputy director, "We have so little top-quality ginseng left that, if we were to use only top-quality ginseng now, we would soon run out of it. Then we would have to use ordinary ginseng exclusively. That would be even worse." Then he said, "The affairs of the Medical Bureau are not something that the royal father-in-law should bother about." The matter should have ended there.

However, the Kims, father and son, were incensed at Father's suggestion that the royal father-in-law had interfered in the Medical Bureau. They turned the matter into something quite different, portraying themselves as paragons of loyalty and my father as one who prohibited the use of top-quality ginseng for His Majesty. How evil-hearted this was! As for the pine-flavored tea, it is even more ludicrous, so much so that it does not even deserve description. As for their accusation concerning certain words that Father said, here is the story.

When my father was in retirement during his mourning between *chŏnghae* and *muja* (1767–1768), Ch'ŏngwŏn paid him a visit. Ch'ŏngwŏn mentioned that the Grand Heir seemed intent on conferring a posthumous royal title [upon his father].* Ch'ŏngwŏn, who was related to my family by marriage, was on very friendly terms with my father and the two families were bound by the same interests. Since this was a matter of grave importance and since Ch'ŏngwŏn felt close to Father, he came to speak to him about it. So, after his term of mourning, when Father saw the Grand Heir at my quarters, he gingerly broached the topic in the course of a long conversation. He advised the Grand Heir, "On this matter, please do not be swayed by emotion; firmly adhere to the precedent." He warned the Heir of the danger and treachery in

---

* The discussion centered around what title Chŏngjo, upon his accession, would confer upon his father, Prince Sado.

the ways of the world and in the hearts of people. He said, "Even if the conferral were consistent with the law, there are still groups of malcontents who resent the government and who seek opportunities to stir up trouble. Just to name a few, there are the descendants of *kisa* (1689) and the remnants of the *musin* (1728) rebels.* It would be most tiresome if these groups, taking issue with the conferral, were to stir up trouble. I am quite bothered by this thought." The Grand Heir also concurred, "There is indeed that worry. How frustrating!" I was also worried about those problems, and the three of us all expressed concern.

The Grand Heir was still a boy at the time, and so he related this to Her Highness the Queen. Kwiju heard of it and brought this out in his memorial. What an odious wretch he was! Even if Father had been in the wrong, how could Kwiju send a memorial to His Majesty about something that had gone on in the inner court and he had heard at the Queen's residence? If His Majesty had been enraged at the Grand Heir for discussing the possibility of offering a posthumous royal title [to his father], there is no saying where the calamity might have reached. It is evident that Kwiju's scheme was not just to vilify my father but also to harm the Grand Heir. Can there be in this whole wide world another such devious, cruel, evil traitor?

In my father's position, what was there that he could not say to the Grand Heir, his grandson, in private conversation? Even if Father had said such things as "Please do offer a posthumous royal title" or "If Your Highness were not to offer the title, then you would become such and such," he would simply have been regarded as imprudent. But he said, "Don't offer the royal title. Please don't be swayed by emotion; firmly adhere to precedent." As for the rest, he was merely expressing his long-term concerns and worries for the nation, cautioning the Grand Heir on the limitless changeability of the hearts of men, living as they did in an age of decline. How could this be a crime? If this was a crime, then all warnings to their rulers by the ancients, such warnings as "the ruin of the country is imminent" or "thieves would arise," should also

---

* The descendants of *kisa* are the Namin, who were out of power since 1694. The *musin* rebels are the rebels of the 1728 rebellion. The 1728 rebellion, though pacified with relative ease, played an important role in shaping Yŏngjo's policies and in setting the mood of his court. Haboush, *Heritage*, 136–46.

be construed as threats to the ruler. Were this the case, who could have said anything at all? What sheer nonsense this is! The details concerning this matter are recorded in court documents and also in the *kapchin* (1784) royal instruction that exonerated my father, so I will only touch on the gist. The terrible memorials by Chŏng Ihwan and Song Hwanŏk in *pyŏngsin* (1776)[18] took up where Kwiju left off [in his memorial of 1772]. What need is there to speak of them?

If one carefully analyzes Kwiju's attempts to harm my family since *sinsa* (1761), a pattern emerges. In the beginning, it started with the hope that, once Prince Sado was eliminated, the Grand Heir would also be put aside, which would lead to an adoption that would make Kwiju's family the maternal family of the new heir. The next phase evolved after the event of that year [1762], when he realized that things did not turn out as he had hoped. Together with Hallok, he uttered the sixteen-word blasphemy. This was intended to confuse his sagacious heart and to replace the Heir Apparent, so that an adoption would be made and they would become the maternal family of the heir. However, His Majesty's sagacious heart remained firm, and the Grand Heir reached maturity. There was no likelihood that there would be a change of heir apparents, though their blasphemous phrase circulated far and wide, making it increasingly difficult to hide their intentions. But then, seizing upon the moment when the Grand Heir was feeling displeased with his maternal family, they pretended to be his most loyal subjects and accused the Hongs of engaging in activities disadvantageous to him. Although they adopted this tactic in order to get rid of the Hongs and to ingratiate themselves with the Grand Heir, their real motive was to conceal their own treachery. I feel that this blasphemy was the root of many calamities.

There must be people who are alive today who witnessed these events, and so they must have a general idea of what those times were like. But I doubt that there is anyone who knows them in such detail as myself. One cannot deceive even small children three feet high with the accusation that my father, short of losing his mind because of some disease, would have done something disadvantageous to the late King in order to benefit Ŭnŏn and Ŭnsin. Nor can one deceive three-foot-high children by arguing that Kwiju was a loyal subject and my late father was a traitor to the late King. What Kwiju said in his accusation of my father violates human feelings and Heavenly principles. Thus one need not seek a man of erudition to distinguish who was right and who was wrong and who was loyal and who was traitorous. Yet the curse that was uttered in the crowd around Kwiju and Hallok—that they would see to it that the dynasty came to an end—has not yet, to this very day, come out in the open. Kwiju has even been termed a loyal minister.* On the other hand, my family, who never dreamt of saying even half of a remotely disloyal word, is receiving ever harsher maltreatment and greater persecution as time goes by and has been declared the most heinously traitorous of families. There cannot have been, in the entire history of the human race, such ways and such decrees! Vomiting blood, I regret that I have not yet attained the bliss of unawareness.

* Kim Kwiju was banished in 1776 upon Chŏngjo's accession. In 1784, in a general amnesty celebrating the appointment of Prince Munhyo as Crown Prince, Kwiju was moved to a closer place, but he subsequently died. In 1801, when Queen Dowager Chŏngsun acted as regent for the young Sunjo, Kwiju was posthumously honored with the post of Minister of Personnel. *SS*, 2:2a–b.

The Memoir of 1805

The tragedy of the *imo* year (1762) is unparalleled. Early in *pyŏngsin* (1776) the late King [Chŏngjo], who was then still Crown Prince, sent a memorial to his grandfather, His Late Majesty King Yŏngjo, requesting the destruction of those portions of the *Records of the Royal Secretariat* [pertaining to that incident]. Once royal permission was obtained, those sections were washed away. The late King did this in filial affection; he was mortified that just anyone could read descriptions of the event in an atmosphere quite devoid of respect or solemnity.

Much time has elapsed. Those who know the details of the incident are growing fewer and fewer. This has provided ample opportunity to those who seek profit and enjoy wreaking havoc by twisting facts and fabricating rumors. Some have said, "Prince Sado had no illness. His Majesty did that to the Prince because he was deceived by calumnies against his son." Others have said, "His Majesty could not possibly have conceived of doing that terrible thing by himself. It was his officials who led him to that horror."

The late King was intelligent and clear-sighted. Though he was a child, he witnessed how the event developed, and so he was not deceived by these arguments. But lest he be perceived as wanting in filial devotion, he accepted far-fetched arguments about Prince Sado and the event of that year, refusing to distinguish true and false, right and wrong. Bearing a deep pain in his heart, he could not but be that way.

The late King Chŏngjo acted this way in unrequited affection for his father, but he knew the facts. It is different with the present King [Sunjo]. I feel that it is against heavenly principle and human affection that he, a grandson, be kept ignorant of an incident of such immense consequences, one involving his direct ancestor. He wanted to know of the incident, but his father, the late King, could not bring himself to speak of it to him in any detail. Now, who else would dare bring it up to him; who else even knows the intimate facts? When I am gone, there will be no one left who knows of it, and so the King will have no way of inquiring into it. To spare him this shameful ignorance, I have for some time wished to write of the incident from its beginnings to its very end and to present it to him, so that after reading it, he might destroy it.

Whenever I took up the brush, however, I could not bring myself to write about it. In this way, day after day passed. After countless adversities and misfortunes both public and private, my life seemed a frail thread about to break. I could not die without telling my grandson what I know of his ancestors; it would have been outside normal human sentiment. And so, resisting death and weeping blood, I wrote this record. Nevertheless, I omitted many things of which I could not bear to speak. I also fear that I was unable to eliminate many long and tedious sections.

I am deeply indebted to His Late Majesty. Not only did I receive from him kindness and affection each day as a daughter-in-law, but I also owe to him the reprieve of my life after that incident. I am, however, the wife of Prince Sado, and devotion to my husband reaches as high as the Heavens. Were I to say one unjust word against either father or son, I would not be able to avoid the most cruel death by the gods of Heaven. What others have said of the incident of that year is all false and groundless, none of it based on fact. I hope that this record will show a clear and coherent picture of the incident and how it unfolded from its beginning to its end.

It is true that, in the early days, His Late Majesty was not as loving of his son as he could have been, but in the end, he was left with no choice but to do as he did. As for Prince Sado, though his extraordinarily generous and benevolent nature was admirable, he became hopelessly ill, and because the nation hung in the balance, he suffered that terrible end. The late King and I had to live with our sorrows—we, his child and wife, survived the truly tragic death of a father and husband; we did not follow him. But our duties have hung just as heavily. Torn between grief and duty, we have always known that we could not confuse them and that we had to attend separately to the demands of each. And this is the point that I particularly wish my grandson, the King, to understand in detail.

To denounce His Late Majesty King Yŏngjo, insisting that Prince Sado was not ill, or to blame the ministers of state for the incident, will only distort the truth, failing to do justice to His Late Majesty, to Prince Sado, or to the late King. If one understands this basic principle, it is not too difficult to be just to all concerned.

In the spring of *imsul* (1802) I made a draft of this record but could not prepare it for the King. Recently, prompted by Lady Kasun to finish it for him, I have forced myself to complete it. Now I am offering it to the King, my grandson, that he may read it. My heart and my blood are in this record. While I wrote it, the pain and terror returned. My heart grew heavy, my spirits fled in fright, and my innards felt as if punctured. For each character, a tear fell; because of these tears, characters could not be completed and because of these wasted characters, sheets of paper were spoiled. Can there be another such as me in this wide world? Ah! Grief and sorrow. The fourth month, *ŭlch'uk* year (1805).

After the death of Prince Hyojang in *musin* (1728), the dynasty was without an heir for some time. This was an endless source of anxiety to His Majesty King Yŏngjo. Thus, when Lady Sŏnhŭi bore him Prince Sado in the first month of the *ŭlmyo* year (1735), His Majesty, Her Highness Queen Dowager Inwŏn, and Her Highness Queen Chŏngsŏng were overjoyed. With the birth of the heir, the future of the throne was secured. The delight of the Three Majesties was beyond compare. The whole country rejoiced; every subject danced in delight.

From the moment of his birth, it was apparent that Prince Sado possessed extraordinary intelligence and remarkable beauty. The records kept at the palace describe many unusual things in his first hundred days. At four months, he walked; at six, he responded to his father's call; and at seven months, he pointed out the four directions. In his second year, the Prince had already learned to write about sixty characters. Once in his third year, the Prince was presented with some sweets and cookies. He ate only those decorated with characters for "longevity" and "fortune" and avoided those with hexagrams. When his attendant urged him to take those with hexagrams, the Prince is said to have answered, "I don't want to eat them; hexagrams are not meant to be eaten." Afterwards, he requested that someone hold up a book with a portrait of Fu Hsi* and bowed to it.

There are many other stories of the same kind. When Prince Sado came to the letters "luxury" and "wealth" in the course of studying the *Thousand Character Classics*, he put a finger on "luxury" and, with the other hand, pointed at his clothing saying, "This is luxury." Once, given a cap studded with seven kinds of jewels, one that His Late Majesty had worn in childhood, he thought it too luxurious and declined to wear it. He also refused to wear the clothing that his father had worn on his first birthday, again saying, "I don't want to wear them. I would be ashamed to be seen in such luxurious clothing." Thinking this a most strange response for a child entering his third year, his attendants decided to test him. They placed a piece of unpatterned white silk and a piece of cotton cloth before him and asked, "Your Highness, which is luxurious and which is not luxurious?" The Prince answered, "This silk is luxurious and that cotton is not luxurious." More intrigued than before, they asked, "Which would you prefer your clothes to be made of?" Pointing at the cotton, he answered, "This. This is better." One can see from these stories that Prince Sado was exceptional even at this early age.

Prince Sado was endowed with a strong and fine bearing, a filial and affectionate nature, and extraordinary intelligence. Had he been kept at his parents' side, receiving their close guidance and their love, he would surely have fulfilled the promise of his virtuous nature. But he was separated from them at a very young age. Small mishaps grew into catastrophic problems, and finally they became unspeakable horrors. This was his ill-starred fate, a predetermined misfortune for the nation; thus it was beyond human control. Yet my grief and bitterness are inestimable.

His Majesty's excitement and relief at having produced an heir after a long, anxious wait seem to have eclipsed more personal considerations for his son. Now that a son had arrived, His Majesty was impatient to formally establish him as the Crown Prince with legal status and attendant pomp. Within a hundred days of the birth of his son, His Majesty moved him from Chippok House, where he was born, to a large building called Chŏsŭng Pavilion

---

* The legendary inventor of hexagrams.

that had lain empty for some time and where the Prince would grow up in the exclusive care of nurses and governesses. Chŏsŭng Pavilion was a residence intended for the Crown Prince. In addition to Chŏsŭng Pavilion, the compound included Naksŏn Hall, where daily study sessions were to be held, Tŏksŏng House, intended for informal and unscheduled scholarly discourse with his tutors, and Simin Hall reserved for the Prince's monthly plenary sessions and formal audiences with his officials and tutors. The Crown Prince Tutorial Office and the Office of Guards for the Crown Prince were located just outside the gate to the compound.

It is not difficult to guess what His Majesty had in mind in moving Prince Sado to Chŏsŭng Pavilion in such haste. He wished his son to be the actual, rather than the future, master of the Crown Prince's establishment since this would create the impression that the nation already had an adult heir. Unfortunately, Chŏsŭng Pavilion was located far from the residences of His Majesty and Lady Sŏnhŭi.* I have heard that His Majesty and Lady Sŏnhŭi visited their son daily regardless of bitter cold or extreme heat, frequently staying overnight at his residence. Still, it could not have been the same as bringing him up in their own establishment, seeing him morning and evening and guiding him constantly.

I have always been mystified by this decision taken by His Majesty. One would think that, since he had begotten a son only after much difficulty and since this was the son to whom he hoped to entrust the throne, he would have placed such considerations as legal status second to the more important one of rearing his son under his own supervision. Since Prince Sado lived far from his parents, they somehow spent less and less time with their son as he grew older. Away from parental view, he spent most of his time in the company of eunuchs and ladies-in-waiting, hearing gossip and tales of scandal. This clearly was the seed of the trouble. I cannot help but feel bitter over it.

I was told that at a very young age, Prince Sado was dignified in his deportment, serious in expression, and reticent of speech. This made people careful and respectful before him as though they were speaking to an adult king. Given this disposition and talent, the tragedy could easily have been avoided if he had been allowed to

* Yŏngjo's and Lady Sŏnhŭi's residences were each at most two kilometers from Sado's residence.

stay close to his parents. This would have enabled His Majesty, amidst his busy public schedule, to oversee his son's scholarly progress and to help him to understand his princely duties on a more personal basis. If this would not have been possible, then at least Lady Sŏnhŭi, to whom the successful development of this son was a primary purpose of life, could have kept him at her side and provided him with discipline and love. I feel strongly that if some sense of intimacy between parents and child had been maintained and if the Prince had not been left completely to the care of strangers, the situation would not have developed to that extreme.

In my opinion, there were two grievous and regrettable decisions made in those early years. The first was moving the infant Prince to Chŏsŭng Pavilion. The second was bringing in those peculiar and unpleasant ladies-in-waiting to care for him. One might say that this is just the narrow and prejudiced view of a woman. However, I mention it because I wish to trace actual causes. It happened that the previous occupant of Chŏsŭng Pavilion had been Queen Sŏnŭi. The Prince was moved there soon after she died.* Facing Chŏsŭng Pavilion was a house called Ch'wisŏn Hall where Lady Chang had resided after her dethronement in *kapsul* (1694) and where she had practiced black magic to bring death to the saintly Queen Inhyŏn.† It is really strange that His Majesty placed the infant Prince, still in his cradle, in a desolate palace and turned the cursed former residence of Lady Chang into the kitchen in which food for the Prince was to be prepared.

But this was not all. After the three years of mourning for Queen Sŏnŭi, the ladies-in-waiting in her service were all sent out of the palace. When His Majesty was preparing the Crown Prince's establishment, he was very concerned with maintaining his image,

---

* Queen Sŏnŭi, King Kyŏngjong's second wife, died in 1730, and so five years had elapsed.

† Queen Inhyŏn was the wife of King Sukchong (r. 1674–1720), Yŏngjo's father. Although she was universally admired for her virtue, she could not bear Sukchong an heir. When Lady Chang, a secondary consort, bore him the long-awaited heir, Kyŏngjong, Sukchong banished Queen Inhyŏn in 1690 and made Lady Chang his queen. Sukchong came to regret this and reversed the situation in 1694, demoting Lady Chang to the rank of secondary consort and restoring Inhyŏn to the queenship. Queen Inhyŏn died in 1701. Her death was allegedly caused by Lady Chang's practice of black magic against her. After several accomplices confessed to having participated in sorcery against Queen Inhyŏn, Lady Chang was put to death.

and so he ordered a search for ladies-in-waiting and servants who had been previously employed in any residence in the palace. For some inexplicable reason, His Majesty hired back those women who had been in the service of King Kyŏngjong and Queen Sŏnŭi, from Palace Matron Ch'oe down, and thus filled the five departments of Prince Sado's establishment. Returned to the very residence where they had served King Kyŏngjong and restored to the company they had kept in days of old, these women may have felt that they were still serving their old master King Kyŏngjong. At any rate, they were arrogant and hostile to the new people, and this seemingly small matter contributed to the trouble.* How regrettable!

His Majesty was extremely devoted to this son whom he had produced so late, and until the Prince reached his fourth or fifth year, he visited Chŏsŭng Pavilion regularly, often staying over. There was no laxity in this affectionate care for his son, with whom he spent long hours. Possessing a filial nature, Prince Sado responded with the natural love of a child for his parents. Thus, for a while, the distance between the residences caused no problem. If this constant care and guidance had continued as would have been likely in an ordinary family, there would have been no strain.

However, the fate of the nation was not to be so fortunate. His Majesty's sagacious heart became irritated with small things at the Prince's quarters, mostly imperceptible and of an unspecified nature. Consequently, without really knowing why, he visited his son less frequently. This happened just as the Prince began to grow; that is just when a child, suffering some inattention or relaxation of control, might easily fall under other influences. As the Prince was often left to himself at this stage, he began to get into trouble.

Of all his children, Princess Hwap'yŏng was by far His Majesty's favorite. In *muo* (1738) Lord Kŭmsŏng[1] was chosen to be Princess Hwap'yŏng's husband. Before the wedding, he was invited to come to the Crown Prince's residence to play with Prince Sado. As the designated spouse for his beloved daughter, His Majesty treated him with particular consideration.

I have noted that the ladies-in-waiting at the Crown Prince's

* Yŏngjo had a complicated relationship to his half brother Kyŏngjong. He repeatedly endured charges that he had murdered his brother. It is possible that he reemployed these ladies as a way of expressing his loyalty to his brother. See JaHyun Kim Haboush, *A Heritage of Kings: One Man's Monarchy in the Confucian World* (New York: Columbia University Press, 1988), 122–25.

residence had previously served King Kyŏngjong. Of these, Palace Matron Ch'oe, the head governess, was very straightforward and loyal but overly stern and excitable, lacking in warmth and serenity. Palace Matron Han, the next in rank, was capable and quick but deceitful and envious. Though she now served the Crown Prince, she had not forgotten the old days when she had served a king, and so she was conspicuously lacking in her devotion to His Majesty.

In their ignorance of high principle, these lowly women did not show Lady Sŏnhŭi the respect she deserved. They remembered her insignificant days; rather than treat her according to her exalted status as the mother of the Crown Prince, they were often insulting, using impolite language. At times they went so far as to make snide or cutting remarks. Though she tried not to show it, Lady Sŏnhŭi was disturbed by this, and His Majesty came to notice it as well.

It came out into the open one day during the New Year's season. It was the day on which a chant to bless the house for the new year was scheduled. His Majesty and Lady Sŏnhŭi came, and Lord Kŭmsŏng came also. Somehow things were delayed. Rather late in the day, the table and other necessary utensils for the ritual had to be arranged for. The ladies-in-waiting, who had been discourteous to begin with, became annoyed and criticized Lady Sŏnhŭi, saying something offensive that angered her. His Majesty sensed what had happened. He thought them terribly obnoxious, yet he refrained from punishing them for fear that if he were to punish them before Lord Kŭmsŏng, their resentment might be directed toward his daughter or son-in-law. Nonetheless, he was disgusted by these women. Not wishing to see them, he did not go to the Crown Prince's residence even when he wished to see his son. It is exasperating to think that, rather than let them go, he continued to entrust his precious son to these horrid women and, out of his dislike for them, ceased his visits to him.

Meanwhile, Prince Sado was growing. As is natural for a child of that age, he wished to play. Noticing that His Majesty's visits had become infrequent, Palace Matron Han said to Palace Matron Ch'oe, "If everyone admonishes and restrains His Highness, he will be depressed and low-spirited. After all, he is only a child. Why don't we do it this way: You guide him correctly by being strict. I, on the other hand, will once in a while let him play so that he can vent his frustration."

Palace Matron Han was deft of hand; of wood and paper, she made great swords in the shape of the crescent moon and bows and arrows as well. With Palace Matron Ch'oe, she took turns attending the Prince. She arranged it so that as soon as Palace Matron Ch'oe took leave, young apprentice ladies-in-waiting secreted behind the door would leap out bearing toy weapons, shouting and shrieking some semblance of martial sounds. How could the young Prince not grow fascinated with these martial games? True, the Prince had the nature of a sage. But as the famous story of the three moves of Mencius's mother tells us,* children, even the likes of Mencius, are intrinsically susceptible to their surroundings. Once Prince Sado became involved in those martial games, he began to worry that he would be scolded if his father came and caught him at it. His open and forthright attitude toward his parents began to change. For instance, anxious that his mother might learn of the games, he was watchful and hostile even toward the ladies-in-waiting who visited him from Lady Sŏnhŭi's residence. The Prince had the physique of a martial hero. Now that this baneful woman had introduced him to martial games just as he was beginning to learn and to get interested in things, he found them very much to his liking. Gradually, however, this interest became an obsession. It was the direct cause of his downfall. One shudders to think of the havoc that Han woman wreaked. Ah! The unpredictability of fate.

Three or four years went by in this way. It was only in *sinyu* (1741), when Prince Sado reached his seventh year, that His Majesty became aware of Palace Matron Han's perversity and sent her away. On this occasion several other women were punished as well. This measure was completely justified. But it would have been so much better if, after this discovery, His Majesty had completely replaced the staff in service at the Crown Prince establishment and, taking this episode as a warning, arranged for the Prince to be kept under parental supervision. With his filial nature, the Prince would surely have followed his parents. However, except for the dismissal of Palace Matron Han, His Majesty left things as they were. The same women were kept, and the Prince was left on

---

* Mencius's mother was reputed to have moved three times until she found the right environment for her son. Uno Seiichi, ed., *Shōgaku* (Tokyo: Meiji shoin, 1965), 177.

his own at a large establishment with no authority figure and no companions but eunuchs and palace ladies. What could he learn in these surroundings?

At about this time, a barrier imperceptibly began to grow between father and son; Prince Sado began to fear his father, while His Majesty started to feel apprehensive over the way his son was developing, fearing that the Prince might be acquiring traits of which he did not approve. To make matters worse, their personalities differed drastically. His Majesty was articulate, bright, benevolent, and kind. He was penetrating in observation and quick of comprehension. Prince Sado, on the other hand, was reticent and slow, deliberate of movement. His vessel of virtue was immense; yet he was in every way as unlike as one could be from his father. For example, when His Majesty asked him the most ordinary questions, the Prince answered very slowly and hesitantly. In exchanges on more weighty matters such as fatherly questions on the book that the Prince was studying, the Prince was far worse. It was not that he did not have opinions or views; he was just too worried that his answer might be wrong or foolish. He deliberated upon all the alternatives, and so it took a long time before he said anything that resembled an answer. This tried His Majesty's patience and certainly contributed to the growing tension.

When it comes to rearing and educating children, even the most highborn such as Prince Sado should be made accustomed to commands and instructions from their parents so that they will feel close to them rather than uncomfortable and fearful. However, this manner of growing up was denied to Prince Sado.[2] Still in his cradle, he was taken from his parents and cared for by ladies-in-waiting who indulged rather than disciplined him. They did everything for him, even including such small tasks as tying the sashes of his robe and knotting the laces of his socks. Thus he grew up with altogether too little restraint and too much comfort.

In his study sessions with tutors, however, Prince Sado was a serious and attentive student. He read the texts in a clear voice and unfailingly grasped the meaning of the passages he read. Those who taught him were impressed, and his reputation as a scholar soon spread. Thus it is all the more sad that, in his father's presence, the Prince grew inarticulate and hesitant out of fear and nervousness. His Majesty became more and more exasperated with him during these encounters in which the Prince was hopelessly tongue-tied. He was alternately angry and concerned about his son. Nonetheless, he never sought a closer relationship with his son, never sought to spend more time with him or to teach him himself. He continued to keep the Prince at a distance, hoping that his son would become on his own the heir he dreamed of. How could this not lead to trouble? When, after a long interval, they did see each other, the father would find fault with his son even before he could express fatherly affection; the son, increasingly uncomfortable with his father, came to regard these encounters as something of a hardship. Sadly, though no one spoke of it, the barrier between them soon became a reality.

Prince Sado was formally invested as Crown Prince in the third month of *pyŏngjin* (1736)* and began to hold study sessions with his tutors from the Crown Prince Tutorial Office in *sinyu* (1741). In the first month of *imsul* (1742), when he had reached his eighth year, the Prince was presented to the Ancestral Temple, and in the third month, he performed the ceremony of entering the Royal College.† I heard that he won the admiration of the multitude present at the ceremony.

The Prince's capping ceremony was held in the third month of *kyehae* (1743),‡ and our wedding followed in the first month of *kapcha* (1744). When I came into the palace, I was struck by the strictness of life at court. The Three Majesties presided over the palace; laws were severe and rituals elaborate, with no allowance for private sentiment. I became fearful and exceedingly cautious,

---

* Prince Sado was fourteen months old at the time. The formal investiture usually took place when the prince had reached his eighth year. Sado was the youngest of the Chosŏn Crown Princes at the time of designation. JaHyun Kim Haboush, "The Education of the Yi Crown Prince: A Study in Confucian Pedagogy," in *The Rise of Neo-Confucianism in Korea*, ed. Wm. Theodore de Bary and JaHyun Kim Haboush (New York: Columbia University Press, 1985), 177–88.

† This ritual marked the formal beginning of the Prince's studies. It consisted of a bowing ceremony at the shrine of Confucius at Sŏnggyun'gwan College and a ceremony of presenting dried meat to the professors. The former signified reverence to the sages and scholars of the past, while the latter symbolized a ritual request for instruction. Haboush, "Education," 179, 182.

‡ This ceremony marked passage into adulthood. During the Chosŏn dynasty, it often took place just before the wedding ceremony. In the case of royal princes who married quite young, sometimes in their ninth or tenth years, the capping ceremony was divided into two parts performed at an interval of five or six years. The ceremony Prince Sado performed on this occasion was the first part. For the wedding, see *The Memoir of 1795*.

unable to relax even for a moment. What surprised me was that Prince Sado, too, seemed to feel awe rather than affection for his father. For example, though he was only in his tenth year, he did not dare to sit in front of his father except in a prostrate position just as the officials did. I thought this extreme.

Then I noticed that Prince Sado never finished his morning toilet on time. Only after the tutors arrived for the morning lecture did he hurriedly wash himself. On those days that we were supposed to visit the Majesties, I arose very early, washed myself, put on a formal coiffure and ceremonial robes, and was ready on time, but the Prince seldom was. According to palace regulations, the Princess Consort could not go unless the Prince led the way, and so I was routinely made to wait for a long time. My childish mind found it very peculiar that the Prince was taking so long to get ready. I secretly wondered whether he was somehow ill.

Sometime around the *ŭlch'uk* year (1745), the Prince's behavior became strange indeed. It was not just the behavior of a child playing excitedly or loudly. Something was definitely wrong with him. The ladies-in-waiting became quite concerned, whispering to each other of their fears. In the ninth month of that year, the Prince fell gravely ill, often losing consciousness. As he was in such a peculiar and serious condition, what could I do but consult diviners for the cause of his illness? They all had the same answer— Chŏsŭng Pavilion was an inauspicious place and the Prince was suffering from its harmful effects. Using most of our financial resources, I had prayers offered and incantations read to the gods and spirits to cleanse the place of evil influence, but the Prince did not improve. Finally it was decided that the Prince had to be removed from Chŏsŭng Pavilion. He moved temporarily into Yunggyŏng Hall, one of the two houses adjoining the Queen's formal residence. I went to stay at Chippok Hall with Lady Sŏnhŭi.

In the first month of *pyŏngin* (1746), the Prince moved to his new residence, Kyŏngch'un Pavilion, and I followed. He had reached his twelfth year. Kyŏngch'un Pavilion was located near Chippok Hall and Yŏn'gyŏng Hall, the residence of Princess Hwap'yŏng. Lady Sŏnhŭi often visited her son, and Princess Hwap'yŏng, who was exceptionally kind and gentle, warmly welcomed her brother, often inviting him to her place. Being particularly fond of this daughter, His Majesty was much more kind to his son when he found him there with the Princess. Prince Sado was overjoyed at this change in his father. He became visibly less afraid of him. Had Princess Hwap'yŏng lived longer, she could have helped to bring father and son closer together. The benefit would have been immense.

In the *chŏngmyo* year (1747), Prince Sado held his lecture sessions regularly. Things went well until the tenth month when a fire damaged many buildings near the Main Hall in the Ch'angdŏk Palace, and we all had to move to Kyŏnghŭi Palace. Prince Sado's new residence was Chŭphŭi Hall; Lady Sŏnhŭi and Princess Hwap'yŏng settled respectively in Yangdŏk Hall and Illyŏng House, both of which were quite far from Chŭphŭi Hall. The distance put an end to their frequent get-togethers. In his solitude, Prince Sado returned to his games.

In the sixth month of *mujin* (1748), Princess Hwap'yŏng passed away. His Majesty was so utterly stricken by the death of the daughter whom he had loved beyond all else that he seemed ready to give up his own life. Lady Sŏnhŭi was as grieved. Immersed in their sorrow, they went into a state in which everything seemed a dream. Oblivious of what was going on around them, they paid little attention to their son. Not having to heed anyone, Prince Sado plunged further into his games. There was nothing he did not experiment with; he became excellent in archery, swordsmanship, and the other martial arts.

When he was not engaged in one of these activities, he painted. He also grew interested in occult texts and asked the official diviner, Kim Myŏnggi, to write down some magic formulae for him. He studied these, memorizing them. With his attention thus diverted, how could his studies not suffer? Judging by these examples, it is clear that his behavior depended upon the attention his parents paid to him. When he saw them frequently, he exerted himself in his studies and did not indulge in games, and there was no friction between father and son. But when he was left alone, he went back to his games and neglected his studies, and the tension between father and son increased. If only his parents had kept him under their supervision, the situation would not have reached that terrible extreme.

There is one thing that His Majesty used to do that aggrieves me to this day. Whatever his sagacious intention might have been, His Majesty did not find a quiet time to sit down with his son and teach and advise him affectionately. Rather, unconcerned with what he was up to, he left him to others. But at large gatherings, His Majesty invariably turned to the Prince in a scornful manner. I remember one such occasion. His Majesty was not feeling well and many people came to see him. Queen Dowager Inwŏn, various princesses, his two sons-in-law, Lord Ilsŏng and Lord Kŭmsŏng, and many others were there. Suddenly His Majesty turned to a lady-in-waiting and ordered, "Bring those things that the Crown Prince is playing with." Then he had the Prince's playthings displayed to all. This embarrassed the Prince deeply.

The same principle applied in testing the Prince on his studies. His Majesty always chose either regular audiences or those occasions on which many officials were present. In front of all, he asked the Prince to explicate the meaning of passages of a book that he was studying. Even if it was a passage that children could not easily comprehend, he kept inquiring with unrelenting sharpness. As it was, Prince Sado was already given to hesitation and stammering before his father even concerning things that he knew very well. Publicly tested and asked one difficult question after another, the Prince grew even more frightened and nervous, answering less and less well. This led to scolding or sometimes even derision. Of course, it is not right to resent one's father, but after numerous embarrassing scenes of this sort, the Prince grew bitter and angry at his father, who he felt was not instructing him with love. And this anger, coupled with his terror of his father and his sense of rejection, eventually led to his loss of mind.

While Princess Hwap'yŏng was alive, she sided with her brother. Whenever His Majesty found fault with him, she pleaded with His Majesty to be lenient, explaining how the situation might have looked from the Prince's point of view. She made a great deal of difference in her brother's favor. After her death, whether His Majesty was excessively harsh or conspicuously lacking in love for the Prince, no one advised him against it. The relationship only deteriorated. The father loved the son less and less, and the son, increasingly fearful of the father, became more and more negligent in his filial obligations. Had Princess Hwap'yŏng lived longer, she might have enabled them to be a loving father and a filial son, fulfilling their human duties to each other. In this sense, one cannot but feel that the early death of this kindhearted Princess adversely affected the fortunes of the country. Even now, I am chagrined by her untimely death.

Prince Sado was by nature generous and forgiving, open and magnanimous of spirit. But most of all, he was trusting and loyal and adhered to these principles in his dealings with all, even those who served him. Though he was terrified of his father, he would not deceive him, and so when he was questioned, even concerning those things that he clearly knew he should not do, the Prince answered him truthfully, hiding nothing. His Majesty also knew that his son would not lie to him.

I have said that Prince Sado was exceptionally filial by nature. He was also very affectionate to his sisters. He always looked up to Princess Hwap'yŏng. She was so conspicuously favored by His Majesty that one might say that his friendliness to her had something to do with this. In truth, the Prince did not follow power but was genuinely attached to her. He was also respectful and attentive to Princess Hwasun, his oldest sister. He felt sorry for her for having lost her mother very early.[3] The Prince's favorite, however, was Princess Hwahyŏp,[4] who was born in the *kyech'uk* year (1733). She was exceptionally beautiful and devoted to her parents, but His Majesty was very cold toward her, probably because of his disappointment that the child was not a boy. He did not change this attitude as she grew, and he even forbade her to stay in the same house with his beloved daughter Princess Hwap'yŏng. Princess Hwap'yŏng, distressed and uncomfortable over this open favoritism, entreated her father to be kind to her sister, but to no avail. When Princess Hwahyŏp got married, His Majesty was as cool toward her husband, Lord Yŏngsŏng, as he was to his daughter. Prince Sado seemed to feel a special affinity with this sister. They were close in age* and similarly disfavored by their father. He often commiserated with her and was particularly affectionate toward her.

In *kisa* (1749) Prince Sado reached his fifteenth year. His capping ceremony was scheduled for the twenty-second day of the first month, and our nuptials for the twenty-seventh.† It would have been a happy occasion if His Majesty had quietly enjoyed the satisfaction of seeing his late-begotten son attaining adulthood and

---

* Prince Sado was two years younger than Princess Hwahyŏp.

† Since Prince Sado and Lady Hyegyŏng performed the wedding ceremony before puberty, their nuptials and consummation did not take place until they reached their fifteenth year. As a prelude to this, the couple performed the second part of the capping ceremony that marked the passage into adulthood.

consummating marriage. However, for some strange reason His Majesty sent down a decree appointing Prince Sado the Prince-Regent. The royal decree was announced on the day of my capping ceremony. It was a sad, sad day. Myriad troubles came with the regency.*

In his abundant kingly virtues—filial devotion to his parents, the proper service of his ancestors, reverence for Heaven, and concern with the welfare of the people—His Majesty was truly outstanding among rulers of history. Based on what I have seen and what is recorded of him, no other sovereign can equal him. However, His Majesty experienced too many harrowing events: the purges and intrigues of the *sinim* years (1721–1722) and the *musin* (1728) rebellion, to name a few.[†] In the course of these events, he adopted numerous taboos and a peculiar gravity that were severe enough to be considered a sickness. I cannot go into specifics, but I will mention a few.

His Majesty was fastidious in his choice of words. He avoided using words that connoted death, such as *sa* (to die) or *kwi* (to return). He entered his living quarters only after changing from the clothes he wore at his regular audience or other public functions. On those occasions when he heard or discussed inauspicious things, he did not return to his chamber until he had brushed his teeth, washed his ears, and summoned someone to say at least one word. He returned by separate gates when he attended to pleasant things and unpleasant things. He forbade those whom he disliked from staying at the same house as those whom he loved. Nor did he permit those whom he did not favor to use the same road as those whom he favored. It is extremely disrespectful of me to say this,

---

* The regent was to be treated as a ruler. He was empowered to make decisions on administrative matters other than appointments, punishments, and the use of troops. The king reserved the right to veto any of the regent's decisions. Haboush, *Heritage*, 177. For Yŏngjo's reasons for enacting a regency, see ibid., 158–65.

† The Soron's purge of the Noron in 1721 endangered Yŏngjo, who with the support of the Noron had just been made Heir Apparent. He weathered this crisis with the help of Queen Dowager Inwŏn, his stepmother. The Soron remained in power for the remainder of Kyŏngjong's reign, and Yŏngjo felt a constant threat, though he did not face anything as serious as the one in 1721. The rebellion of 1728 was carried out by extremist members of the Soron who felt that, with Yŏngjo's enthronement in 1724, their days were numbered. They used the charge of regicide as a rallying cry. Though the rebellion was pacified within a short period, its effect on Yŏngjo was immense. Haboush, *Heritage*, 30–31, 136–42.

but I will never understand his demonstrativeness in manifesting love and hatred.

Even before the regency, His Majesty often asked Prince Sado to attend the trials of political criminals,* trials at the Board of Punishment, or trials that required personal interrogation by the king. These events to which the Prince was invited were all grim and inauspicious affairs. But this was not all. When His Majesty visited Princess Hwap'yŏng or the Princess who was born in the *muo* year (1738), who is now referred to as Madame Chŏng, he first changed from the clothes that he wore while tending to official business. When it came to his son, however, it was a different matter. On his way to his residence after attending to official business, he would stop at the Prince's residence and, standing outside, call him out. When the Prince appeared, he would ask, "How are you?"† As soon as he heard the answer, His Majesty would wash his ears right then and there and throw the water he used into the courtyard of Princess Hwahyŏp's residence, which adjoined the Prince's. Perhaps one should not make too much of this. Nevertheless, he would not allow himself to enter the residences of some of his children if he had not changed from the clothing that he had worn outside. But he came over and washed his ears after hearing an answer from his precious son. Whenever Prince Sado saw his sister Hwahyŏp, he said laughingly, "You and I are people upon whom he washes off his inauspiciousness." But the Prince was aware that Princess Hwap'yŏng did everything she could to make things easy for him and he deeply appreciated her help. He was not even slightly suspicious or jealous of her and was always affectionate. Everyone at court knew and admired his devotion to her. Lady Sŏnhŭi grieved over His Majesty's uneven treatment of his children, but there was nothing she could do about it.

His Majesty had an aversion to criminal cases, especially trials for murder or other serious crimes conducted at the State Tribunal or the Board of Punishment. He often sent eunuchs with instructions while he remained at the residence of one or another of the princesses. The edict enacting the regency cited his reasons as grief over Princess Hwap'yŏng's death, his ill health, and the need for a

---

* Persons who had done something that could be construed as subversive or disloyal to the monarchy.
† Literally, "Did you have dinner?" A conventional greeting.

rest, but His Majesty's true intention was to let the Prince-Regent take care of those cases that he detested but that were too serious for eunuchs. Once he became regent, Prince Sado looked after these administrative matters, assisted by eunuchs. Of the six regular audiences each month, His Majesty presided over the first three with the Prince in attendance, while the Prince-Regent alone officiated at the last three.

From the beginning, the regency was ridden with problems and conflict. For instance, when the Prince-Regent received memorials criticizing government policies or discussing factional issues, he would send a memo to His Majesty asking his opinion rather than taking care of them himself. Despite the fact that these memorials came from officials and despite the fact that the Prince had nothing to do with their arrival, His Majesty would grow furious at his son, blaming him. He declared that it was the inability of the Prince-Regent to lead the officials to harmony that caused the appearance of such contentious memorials. If the Prince-Regent were to send a memo asking His Majesty's opinion, His Majesty would rebuke him. "You cannot even handle matters of such insignificance. What is the use of having a regent?" But if the Prince-Regent did not seek his views beforehand, His Majesty would reprimand him just the same. "How dare you make decisions on such weighty matters without consulting me first?" he would scold. In everything, if the Prince did thus, His Majesty reproached him for not having done so, but if the Prince did so, then His Majesty criticized him for not having done thus. There was nothing that the Prince-Regent did that His Majesty found satisfactory. He was constantly discontented and angry with his son. It reached a point where the occurrence of cold spells, droughts, poor harvests, strange natural omens, or calamities caused His Majesty to denounce "the Prince-Regent's insufficient virtue" and to reproach the Prince most severely.

Thus if the weather was cloudy or if there was thunder on a winter day, the Prince-Regent instantly grew nervous and fearful lest he receive yet another berating from his father. Before long, he was frightened and anxious over everything; the illness developed gradually as his sense of terror spawned unwholesome imaginings and strange notions. How sad that His Majesty, an extraordinarily virtuous and supremely benevolent king and a remarkably intelligent and observant man, did not realize that his precious heir was growing ill. Alarmed by his father's criticism and stung by his fury, and despite his manly and gallant disposition, Prince Sado could not do one thing with ease or peace of mind. Not invited even once by his father to the grand spectacles held at court, such as celebratory palace examinations, archery competitions, or displays of the martial arts, he was asked to do only such grim things as the year-end reevaluations of criminal cases. The Prince simply could not maintain equilibrium or feel unhurt.

Truly, the situation required extraordinary forbearance from at least one party—either the son had to try ever harder in his filial duties though he felt his father to be excessively harsh or, alternatively, the father had to be more loving of his son even when he seemed rather untoward. But, as it happened, their relationship worsened steadily. There was no turning point, but it nonetheless proceeded toward that unspeakable end. Perhaps one should attribute this to the will of Heaven or to the nation's fate, something beyond the control of human powers. Nevertheless, I can relive scene upon scene, each vividly alive, with pain deep in my heart. Writing of these things now, I am overcome by guilt, feeling that my descriptions might in some way cast a blemish on their virtue. But I cannot withhold the truth. Filling each page places a great weight upon my chest.

Though Prince Sado reached his fifteenth year, he had never been permitted to accompany His Majesty on a visit to an ancestral tomb. As he grew older, the Prince became very curious to see the countryside, and so whenever the Board of Rites included his name in the royal entourage for a procession in the city or for a visit to a tomb in the country, he held his breath, anxiously hoping that his father would accept it. Invariably, however, he discovered that he was again eliminated from the list.

In the beginning, Prince Sado was merely disappointed and hurt, but after a while, it became a source of deep irritation; sometimes he even wept in frustration. Though he was deeply devoted to his parents, his deliberate manner would not allow him to express one-hundredth of his devotion. Not grasping this, His Majesty was constantly dissatisfied with him. He conceded nothing, nor did he make any accommodation for him. The Prince's terror of his father gradually turned into a disease. When he became furious, having no other way to release it, he vented it on eunuchs or ladies-in-waiting or sometimes on me. This happened so many times that I cannot keep count.

In the eighth month of *kyŏngo* (1750), I gave birth to Ŭiso. It was unlikely that His Majesty would not be happy to have a grandson. My safe delivery, however, seemed to have revived painful memories of Princess Hwap'yŏng, who died in childbirth in *mujin* (1748). He plunged into depression, lamenting anew that his daughter had died while others gave birth with no problem. Thus, while he was happy to obtain a grand heir, this happiness was overshadowed by rekindled grief for his daughter. His Majesty did not offer so much as one commonplace word of congratulation to his son, not even something like "You already have a child, eh?"

His Majesty had always been extremely kind to me, really much more than I had any right to expect. I was sincerely grateful, though somewhat uncomfortable, that I alone was favored. After Ŭiso's birth, though, His Majesty ignored me completely, refusing me even the smallest word of acknowledgment such as "You have safely delivered a son. I salute you." I was in my early youth.* I did not know the joy of having a child, and I felt terribly ill at ease. Overcome by renewed sadness, His Majesty frequently lost his temper and was generally in an ill humor. Lady Sŏnhŭi, on the other hand, was genuinely happy over the birth of a grandson, though her memory of her daughter could not have been less intense than His Majesty's. She regarded it as a great blessing upon the Altar of State, and until seven days after my delivery, she stayed near my maternity quarters and took care of me. His Majesty one day reproached her, "You are all happiness, Lady Sŏnhŭi; you must have forgotten all about Princess Hwap'yŏng. How cold-blooded you are!" Lady Sŏnhŭi laughed it off, but she lamented that his sagacious heart was so obsessed.

Prince Sado, who was rather mature for his age, was happy that a son had been borne to him and that he had thus strengthened the foundation of the nation. He did not dare complain of his father's indifference, but it was apparent that he was hurt by it. He said to me, "I, by myself, was enough of a problem. I now have a child. I wonder whether it will be all right?" It was heartbreaking to hear him say that.

Perhaps I should not speak of this, but I feel compelled to write of it. When I was pregnant with Ŭiso, I often dreamt of Princess Hwap'yŏng. In these dreams, she came into my bedchamber, sat

* Lady Hyegyŏng was in her sixteenth year.

next to me, and sometimes smiled at me. Whenever I awoke from these dreams, I felt quite apprehensive. I had heard how tenacious the ghosts of those who died in childbirth were, and in my childish mind, I felt a terrible fear for my life. When I bathed Ŭiso for the first time, I noticed a blue mark on his shoulder and a red spot on his abdomen, but I thought nothing of them.

Then, suddenly, on the eleventh of the ninth month, the day before His Majesty was scheduled to leave for a trip to Onyang,* he came into my quarters with Lady Sŏnhŭi. Both had strange expressions on their faces, a mixture of sadness and joy. They went directly into the room where Ŭiso was sleeping and loosened his shirt to examine him. Upon finding the marks they were seeking, they seemed stunned and shaken. They decided right then and there that Princess Hwap'yŏng was reincarnated in this child. His Majesty's attitude toward Ŭiso changed at once. He became affectionate to him in the same way that he had been to Princess Hwap'yŏng. When the child was first born, His Majesty did not even observe his taboo about changing clothes and came into the maternity room wearing the same clothes he had worn at official functions. From this day on, however, he meticulously observed it. I guessed that His Majesty must have seen Princess Hwap'yŏng in his dream. Whatever the reason, it was something so unreal and bizarre that one could not easily comprehend it.

When Ŭiso was about a hundred days old, His Majesty moved him to Hwan'gyŏng Pavilion, where he formerly held audiences but which was now refurbished for the infant Prince. He treated him as the most precious thing in the world and showered love and affection upon him. Prince Sado secretly hoped that his father's love of this grandson might extend to him and that he might be held in higher regard. In reality, however, His Majesty's affection for Ŭiso was based on his belief that he was a reincarnation of Princess Hwap'yŏng. It had nothing to do with who his parents were. Thus his attitude toward Prince Sado remained as cool as ever. So unknowable are human feelings! In the fifth month of *sinmi* (1751), when Ŭiso was barely ten months old, His Majesty formally designated him Grand Heir. He did this out of love for his

---

* Aside from visits to ancestral tombs, Yŏngjo very seldom took trips. He made the trip to Onyang in 1750 for political reasons. For details, see Haboush, *Heritage*, 102–14.

grandchild, but it was rather excessive. Ŭiso died in the spring of *imsin* (1752). His Majesty grieved beyond measure; he was simply inconsolable.

With the silent assistance of Heaven and the hidden aid of royal ancestors, I became pregnant again toward the end of *sinmi* (1751) and again gave birth to a son in the ninth month of *imsin* (1752). The newborn was the late King. Given my poor luck, this was more than I had expected. At birth, the late King had brilliant features and an excellent physique, indeed a True Man sent by Heaven. One night in the twelfth month of the previous year, Prince Sado awoke from sleep, saying, "I dreamt of a dragon. This suggests that I will receive a noble son." He asked for a piece of white silk cloth, painted upon it the dragon he had seen in his dream, and had it hung upon the wall of the bedchamber. It is, of course, to be expected that the birth of a sage would be foretold by a supernatural omen.

His Majesty, who had been distressed over the loss of Ŭiso, was immensely pleased to have another heir. He said to me, "This is an extraordinary child. This must be a blessing from the royal ancestors. As a descendant of Princess Chŏngmyŏng, you became the Crown Princess Consort, and now you have again brought forth an heir. How felicitous! You have made a great contribution to the nation." He advised me, "Please bring him up with special care. I would also like to add that bringing up a child frugally and simply invites luck." I listened to his sagacious instructions in deep gratitude and always obeyed him.

There are no words to describe Prince Sado's joy and happiness. The rejoicing by subjects and officials throughout the country for the birth of the late King was a hundred times greater than for the birth in the *kyŏngo* year (1750). How delighted my parents were! Whenever they saw me, they congratulated me for having such a remarkable child. I was still under twenty, but I felt happy and proud. I also somehow felt that this son was my future support. I prayed that I would receive his filial care for a long, long time.

In the tenth month of that year, an epidemic of measles broke out. Princess Hwahyŏp was the first to come down with it. Prince Sado was evacuated to Yangjŏng House, and the infant Prince was removed to Naksŏn Hall. He was only several weeks old, but because he was so strong we were not nervous about moving him a considerable distance. I had not yet had time to select a nurse for him, and so I left him in the care of an elderly lady-in-waiting and my wet nurse. Before the day was over, Prince Sado had broken out in measles. When he was over the worst of it, I came down with it, and then my son was struck. My condition was quite serious, perhaps because I was anxious over my husband's illness and had not yet completely recovered from childbirth. So, though my son's case was not too grave, Lady Sŏnhŭi and my father kept his illness a secret from me lest I become too concerned. Prince Sado was still running a high fever. Father had to divide his time three ways, between Prince Sado, myself, and the infant Prince. He became so exhausted that his beard turned white.

Princess Hwahyŏp died of measles. Prince Sado had always been particularly affectionate toward her. He felt sympathetic that she, like himself, was disfavored by His Majesty. During her illness, he sent one servant after another to inquire after her. When she died, he was overcome with grief. This shows that he was truly kind-hearted by nature.

In the last month of that year, His Majesty was deeply provoked by a memorial sent by Hong Chunhae, a censor.[5] In his fury, he prostrated himself at Sŏnhwa Gate, repeatedly denouncing the Prince-Regent.* It was a very cold winter with unceasing snow.[6] Though Prince Sado had just recovered from a great illness, he awaited punishment prostrate in the open air. Snow covered him over completely. One could not tell the Prince from the snow, but he just remained where he was. Queen Dowager Inwŏn came and attempted to persuade him to go inside, but he refused to move. Only after His Majesty's anger calmed a bit did the Prince get up. His thoughtful nature shined through on occasions such as this.

But the royal anger did not cease. On the fifteenth day, His Majesty left for Ch'angŭi Palace, his former residence where he had stayed as a prince. He declared to Queen Dowager Inwŏn, "I would like to abdicate." She was hard-of-hearing and so, misunderstanding what the King had said, she replied, "Do as you wish." "Now that I have the permission of Her Highness, the

---

* Yŏngjo was angry over the resurgence of the rumor that he had killed his older brother Kyŏngjong (*Yŏngjo sillok* [hereafter *YS*], in *Chosŏn wangjo sillok*, 78:10a). Although Sado was not responsible for the rumor, Yŏngjo blamed him in his disappointment that Sado's regency did not ease, as he had hoped, the virulent factional tension that he believed was at the root of this rumor. Haboush, *Heritage*, 178–80.

Queen Mother," His Majesty announced, "I will abdicate." Prince Sado was stunned and terrified. He immediately summoned his tutors and dictated a memorial begging his father to rescind the order. He did this so proficiently that those who took dictation were dazzled.[7]

His Majesty showed no inclination to leave his old residence and stayed on. This made the Queen Dowager exceedingly ill at ease. She announced, "Because of my poor hearing, I answered the King wrongly and committed a grievous error to the Altar of State." She then went to stay in a small and narrow house and wrote to His Majesty requesting that he return to the main palace. Meanwhile, Prince Sado had remained prostrate on the straw mat in the ice-covered courtyard before Sonji Pavilion near Simin Hall. After a while, he walked all the way to Ch'angǔi Palace* and, reaching there, again lay prostrate on the straw mat in the courtyard. At one point, he banged his head repeatedly against the stone pavement until his cap was torn and his forehead bled. He hurt his own precious body quite a lot. It is clear that the Prince did all this out of deep loyalty and genuine filial concern and that none of it was an affectation. Needless to say, the Prince bore severe reproaches from His Majesty during this period, yet he carried out his duties in complete composure and docility, gaining a reputation for being able to conduct himself under pressure.

His Majesty ordered that all officials of second rank and above be banished to distant places. Father was among those under censure, and he went to await the written royal decree outside a city gate. What weighed most heavily on his mind, though, was how Prince Sado was doing. He sent numerous letters of inquiry and advice. I kept them all, and when my son grew up, I showed them to him. He was touched by my father's loyalty to Prince Sado and took the letters, promising that he would find a way to pay homage to his grandfather for his devotion to his Prince.

After several days, His Majesty returned to the main palace. He rescinded his order dismissing the officials and conducted a formal audience with the entire bureaucracy. Afterwards, my father came

---

* It is about one and a half miles from Sonji Pavilion to Ch'angǔi Pavilion, which was located at present-day T'ongǔi-dong, Chongno-gu. This must have seemed distant to upper class Koreans of the eighteenth century, as they seldom walked any distance.

to my residence. He saw the wounds on Prince Sado's forehead and stroked them gently, tears upon his cheeks. They spoke to each other about what had just taken place. How vividly do I remember this scene! I can see their faces and hear their voices. It was so incomprehensible that the Prince seemed to be not one person, but two. When he was not suffering from illness, he was benevolent, filial, clearheaded, and mature; indeed, he left nothing to be desired. As soon as that illness got hold of him, however, he was utterly transformed, so different in fact that one could hardly believe that he was the same person. How strange and how sad!

Prince Sado was always fond of Taoist scriptures, magic formulae, and things of that sort. One day he said, "I have heard that if one were to master the *Jade Spine Scripture (Okch'ugyŏng)*,* one would be able to command ghosts and spirits. I think I'll try." Every night he pored over this book. One night very late, his mind seemed to slip into hallucination. "I see the thunder god," he said in terror. After that, his illness grew much worse.

Since entering his tenth year, he had begun to show signs that he might have been touched by this illness. The way he ate and moved was not entirely normal. After the *Jade Spine Scripture*, however, his personality itself seemed to metamorphose. He was now in perpetual terror. He could not touch anything that contained the word "Jade Spine." For instance, he even became fearful of the charm we wore on the fifth day of the fifth month† because it was named the Jade Spine charm. When it was offered to him on that day, he refused it in horror. The Prince also became exceedingly fearful of the sky and could not bear to look at the characters *nwe*, meaning thunder, or *pyŏk*, meaning thunderclap. Though he had always disliked thunder, his dislike had never been so pronounced. After the *Jade Spine Scripture* though, when it thundered the Prince lay on the ground on his face, his hands covering his ears. Only after the thunder completely stopped would he raise himself. His parents did not realize the extreme state into which their son had fallen. It was an indescribably distressing and unnerving situation. This terrible state began in the winter of the *imsin* year (1752) and the Prince remained in this

---

* A Taoist recantation text that was favored by blind fortune-tellers.
† A spring festival day.

condition all through *kyeyu* (1753). These symptoms seized him from time to time in *kapsul* (1754). But by then the Prince had fallen hopelessly into the grips of his illness. That *Jade Spine Scripture* was truly an accursed thing.

Sometime in *kyeyu* (1753), Prince Sado took in a secondary consort,[8] and she became pregnant. Terrified of what his father might say once this was known, the Prince had her resort to various methods of abortion. Since the child, a seed of trouble, was fated to come into this world, none of these worked. Thus Ŭnŏn was born safely in the second month of the *kapsul* year (1754). Even in periods when nothing out of the ordinary occurred, His Majesty found much fault with the Prince. After Ŭnŏn's birth, His Majesty sent down one severe admonition after another. The Prince spent days in terror and depression. Worried about the Prince being under fire, my father pleaded and reasoned with His Majesty until the royal anger subsided somewhat.*

I also did what I could to ease the tension. First of all, palace custom made it futile to be jealous of this sort of thing. From the beginning, Lady Sŏnhŭi repeatedly advised me, "Do not mind such things." Second, I was not so hard-hearted. Besides, as the Prince showed no sign that he was particularly enamored of that secondary consort, I had no cause for jealousy. Her time of delivery drew near, but no one made any arrangements. Prince Sado did nothing because, now that his casual intimacy with a woman had led to a pregnancy, he was frightened by what his father might say. Ignoring the whole thing, Lady Sŏnhŭi did nothing. I felt that if I, too, did nothing for her, things could get out of hand. I was not very experienced in these matters, but I did what I could to see her through the childbirth.

Later, His Majesty reproached me. "You just follow your husband's wishes. You don't even become jealous as other women do." This was the first time that I had been reprimanded since my marriage in *kapcha* (1744), and I was deeply mortified. It is so

---

* Hong Ponghan was the first person to broach the question of burying the umbilical cord of the new prince in accordance with royal custom. On the fifth of the second month, 1754, Hong said to Yŏngjo that five days had passed since the birth of the new prince and that the burial of the umbilical cord should be done. Yŏngjo did not permit it. On the eleventh, both the Bureau of Astronomy and the Prime Minister made the same request, but Yŏngjo again refused permission. *YS*, 81:7b, 81:9a.

ironic. A woman's jealousy is one of the seven heinous crimes,* and not being jealous of one's husband's interest in other women is considered a great feminine virtue, yet I was being criticized for not being jealous. This, too, must have been my fate. If the father-son relationship had been normal and either His Majesty or Lady Sŏnhŭi had welcomed the newborn as a grandson, or if Prince Sado had been partial to that consort, no matter how broad-minded I might have been my feminine heart could not have remained totally undisturbed. As it was, His Majesty and Lady Sŏn-hŭi completely ignored the child, while Prince Sado, overcome with fear, was simply at a loss for what to do. In this situation I was compelled to consider that if I, too, were to be excessively jealous, Prince Sado, in his confused state, might grow even more distressed and his illness might worsen.

In the seventh month of that year, I bore Ch'ŏngyŏn. His Majesty was very pleased. He said, "This is the first time in more than a hundred years that a princess had been born of a primary consort."

In the first month of ŭrhae (1755) Ŭnsin, Ŭnŏn's brother, was born.[9] Since he was the second son born of a secondary consort, royal reproof was less stern than it had been for Ŭnŏn.

Prince Sado's illness spread through him just as water soaks into a piece of paper. His ceremonial visits to his elders grew rarer; cancellations of his lecture sessions more frequent. As his mind was afflicted, he groaned often and assumed the wasted appearance of one incurably stricken. Whenever His Majesty summoned him with a tutor and asked him about his studies, he said nothing; he just shrank in terror.

In the second month of ŭrhae (1755), a seditious plot was uncovered,† and until the fifth month, His Majesty personally conducted the trials of the rebels.[10] Whenever a rebel was condemned to death in the presence of the entire bureaucracy standing by rank, His Majesty sent for the Prince, requiring that he witness the scene. During this trial, His Majesty ended the daily interrogations between seven o'clock in the evening and midnight or one in the morning. Each night on his way home, His Majesty stopped at the

---

* In Confucian countries, a wife's jealousy of other women was traditionally one of the seven permissible reasons for divorce.

† Rebellious posters appeared in the Naju district, Chŏlla Province. For details, see Haboush, *Heritage*, 188–90.

Prince's residence and asked for the Prince. When the Prince went out to greet him, he asked, "How are you?" As soon as he heard the Prince's reply, he turned and left. This was clearly intended so that the Prince's word might wash off all the terrible things associated with the trials of the day so that His Majesty might enter his own quarters cleansed.

As if it did not suffice that His Majesty did not invite his son to felicitous or auspicious gatherings, calling upon him only for inauspicious occasions, he came to the Prince every night regardless of the hour for the sole purpose of using his son's reply to clear away the day's bad luck that he did not wish to bring home with him. Had His Majesty tried to converse a bit by saying a few words, it would not have appeared so blatant, but he did not bother to add even one word. Even the most filial of sons and the most sane of persons would have been deeply hurt by such treatment. Knowing the symptoms of his illness, one would have expected that the Prince might say in anger, "What is it this time, Your Majesty?" However, Prince Sado managed to control his illness. Each night he awaited his father's call, and without fail he answered him. How can one deny his truly filial nature?

Prince Sado's illness was really an odd one. Its symptoms were such that his wife would be deeply worried and the eunuchs and ladies-in-waiting in his service would be in terror day and night, but his own mother, not to mention his father, did not know how badly off he was. In the presence of his father or in his dealings with officials, Prince Sado behaved quite normally. It was frustrating. Sometimes, especially on those occasions when things turned really bad, I wished that his illness in all of its aspects would become apparent so that all, from His Majesty down to the tutors, would become cognizant of the situation and seek a way to deal with it.

During this trial, there were many troubled incidents between His Majesty and the Prince-Regent. I cannot record all the worries and heartaches that I suffered.

Toward the last month of that year, Lady Sŏnhŭi became ill and Prince Sado went and stayed at Chippok House for a while to be near his mother. His Majesty was furious when he learned that the Prince was staying there. He disliked the idea that his son might stay near the residence of Princess Hwawan, his favorite daughter. He ordered the Prince, "Go at once." Prince Sado left in haste by jumping through a high window. A stern royal message followed, ordering the Prince to remain at Nakson Hall, not enter Ch'onghwi Gate, and read the T'ai-chia chapter of the *Book of Documents* (*Shu-ching*)* on that day. Humiliated thus for wishing to see his ailing mother and having done nothing wrong, Prince Sado was beside himself with grief and mortification. In rage, he screamed, "I will kill myself." After a while he took control of himself, but relations between father and son deteriorated further.

On New Year's Day of the *pyongja* year (1756), an honorary title was presented to His Majesty in a grand ceremony.† Prince Sado was again not invited. Deeply ill, the Prince now frequently canceled study sessions. He decided that Ch'wison Hall, which was being used as the outer kitchen, was quiet and peaceful, and he spent long hours in that place. Oh, was there anything not a cause for worry, not a reason for anxiety?

One day in the fifth month, after an audience with his officials at Sungmun Hall, His Majesty suddenly went to Nakson Hall to see Prince Sado. The Prince did not look very tidy—his face was unclean and his clothes were unkempt. It was a period during which a strict ban on drinking was in force.‡ Suspecting that the Prince was drunk, His Majesty commanded angrily, "Find out who gave him something to drink." He then asked the Prince who had given him drinks. But in truth, Prince Sado never drank. Oh, bitterness! It was so strange! Whatever His Majesty suspected and accused him of doing, he would invariably do just that. This happened so consistently that it seemed that Heaven was making him do it all.

On that day, His Majesty made Prince Sado stand in the courtyard and questioned him sharply about his drinking. The Prince was in fact completely innocent, yet, as was his wont, terror of his father rendered him unable to deny the accusation. Pressed relentlessly, the Prince said helplessly, "Yes, I drank." "Who gave it to you?" His Majesty asked. Unable to back out at this point, the

---

* This chapter was believed to have been written by Yi Yin to advise T'ai-chia, a king of Shang China who lacked benevolence.

† Yongjo received an eight-character honorary title. It was *Ch'ech'on kon'guk Songgong sinhwa* (Substance of Heaven, establishment of the ultimate, sagacious merit, divine influence). *YS*, 87:1a. For Yongjo's honorary titles, see Haboush, *Heritage*, 59–62.

‡ Yongjo waged a strong temperance campaign during his reign. For details, see Haboush, *Heritage*, 78–9.

Prince said, "Hŭijŏng, the lady-in-waiting in charge of the outer kitchen." Banging the doorway, His Majesty roared, "In this time of prohibition, you are drinking and behaving like a ruffian? What abominable, rank behavior!" At that point, Palace Matron Ch'oe said, "It is most unfair to say that His Highness drank. Would Your Majesty please see if he smells of alcohol?" She defended the Prince because she could not bear to see him unjustly accused when she knew perfectly well that not only did he not drink, but also no alcoholic beverage of any kind had come into his residence.

Prince Sado, however, admonished her, "Whether I drank or not, I said I did. How dare you speak out like this in the royal presence? Retreat to your place." This was not like the usual hesitation that he routinely fell into in his father's presence. He must have done this because, having been groundlessly accused, he was provoked enough to have lost his fear. Though I was deeply agitated, I thought it fortunate that the Prince could speak like that. His Majesty reprimanded him angrily again, "Now you are scolding a woman in my presence. Do you know that before elders, one must not scold even a dog or a horse? What arrogance is this?" "I did it only because she dared to defend me to Your Majesty." Prince Sado quickly changed his expression and assumed the humble and respectful manner of a younger person.

His Majesty banished Hŭijŏng to a distant place for her alleged crime of having supplied wine to the Prince. He ordered that the Prince hold remonstrative sessions first with his tutors and then with the ministers. Prince Sado was utterly mortified. All his grievance and resentment burst out in a towering rage. Hitherto, his public behavior had shown no indication that he was suffering from an illness. But on this occasion, for the first time, the Prince made a scene when two tutors arrived for the session. He shrieked in a fury, "You rascals! You do nothing to bring harmony between father and son. Though I am falsely accused, you cannot say one word in my defense. You think you can come in now? Get out! Just get out!" I do not remember who the other tutor was, but one was Wŏn Insŏn. Wŏn said something to the Prince and did not immediately leave. Furious, the Prince screamed, "Out at once!" and chased him.

In this turmoil, a candlestick overturned and the rice paper in the southern window of Naksŏn Hall caught fire. Before anyone could do anything, the fire had spread in full force. Meanwhile, the

Prince was chasing Wŏn Insŏn, who was running from Naksŏn Hall through a gate leading to Tŏksŏng House. Whenever His Majesty chose Sungmun Hall for an audience, the officials going to the audience entered the palace by Kŏnyang Gate. Since Chiphyŏn Gate was always locked, they passed Simin Hall and Tŏksŏng House, the Prince's lecture hall, and entered Sungmun Hall through Pohwa Gate. Just when the tutor Wŏn Insŏn was running toward Tŏksŏng House, several officials happened to be passing by on their way to an audience. Prince Sado shouted at them, "You do nothing to bring peace between father and son. You pocket your salary but you don't advise the throne. You are now going in for an audience? What for? What use are the likes of you, you rascals?" He chased all of them out. It was truly an embarrassing scene.

Now Naksŏn Hall was fully ablaze.* My son was staying at Kwanhŭi House, which was located only about four meters away, directly across from Naksŏn Hall. Seeing the fire engulfing Naksŏn Hall, I was in a panic. Though four or five months pregnant with Ch'ŏngsŏn, I ran to my son, jumping on the stepping stones that were about one meter apart. I woke up the sleeping young Prince and had his nurse carry him to Kyŏngch'un Pavilion. I thought that the fire would surely spread to Kwanhŭi House, but strangely, the fire passed around Kwanhŭi House and engulfed Yangjŏp House, which was located at a considerable distance from Naksŏn Hall. Can it be that Kwanhŭi House was saved because it was the residence of the future King? It was quite strange.

Upon learning that a fire had broken out, His Majesty quickly assumed that his son had set it in a tantrum and became ten times angrier than he had been. He summoned all the officials to Hamin Pavilion and called the Prince there. "Are you an arsonist? Why did you set the fire?" he roared at Prince Sado when the Prince appeared. The Prince's sense of grievance reached an extreme point. Instead of explaining to his father that the fire broke out because of an accidental toppling of a candlestick, he pretended, just as he had when he was accused of drinking, that he had intentionally set the fire. It was so sad and frustrating to watch him behave in that way. When this meeting was over, Prince Sado collapsed. Only after-

---

* This fire is recorded to have broken out at about one o'clock in the morning. *YS*, 87:34a.

wards, when he took some heart-clearing pills, did he regain consciousness. "I just don't see how I can live," he said mournfully. He then went to a well in the courtyard in front of Chŏsŭng Pavilion and was about to jump into it. I cannot really describe the scene—our shock and grief, the imminent danger to the Prince, and everything else. We barely managed to prevent him from jumping into the well and brought him to Tŏksŏng House.

My father had been serving as Magistrate of Kwangju city since the second month of that year. The Prince seemed lonelier with his father-in-law away in a provincial post. After the incident of the fire, His Majesty summoned my father back to the capital. When he arrived, His Majesty talked to him about what the Prince had done in the interim and expressed profound apprehension. Prince Sado told my father how deeply injured he had felt about the incidents concerning drinking and the fire and concluded his sad tale by saying, "I probably won't be able to live." It must have been heartbreaking for my father to hear this. He pleaded with His Majesty, "Please be patient and loving with the Prince." He cajoled Prince Sado, "Please try harder in your filial devotion." Even when the Prince was really upset, his father-in-law's advice usually had a soothing effect upon him. On this occasion, too, the Prince calmed down somewhat after being assuaged by my father.

I was still grieving for my mother, who had died the previous fall, and I was acutely troubled by the Prince's deepening illness. I had not yet recovered from the shock of those harrowing scenes on the day of the fire. Thus when I saw my father, I broke into tears, sobbing uncontrollably. We stood there, holding each other and crying endlessly.

That incident in the fifth month adversely affected the Prince's already worsening condition. From then on, the Prince not infrequently behaved quite intemperately in the presence of officials and held far fewer lecture sessions. He forced himself to attend regular audiences, but with no interest or spirit. Unable to overcome his depression, Prince Sado took advantage of His Majesty's periodic absences from the palace to engage in military games. He went to the rear garden and shot arrows and rode horses. With weapons and banners, he played with the ladies-in-waiting. He wanted the eunuchs to form a military band. They played wind ˗˗˗uments and beat drums.

seventh month the Queen Dowager turned seventy. To

celebrate the occasion, His Majesty held a palace examination for elderly scholars. Then, in a magnificent feast held in the rear garden, he offered his congratulations to his stepmother. Somehow, His Majesty invited his son to this feast. The Prince offered his congratulations with no mishap.[11] Thus when he returned from the feast, he seemed very pleased. This proves that, had His Majesty shown some sympathy for his son and had he treated him with some consideration, the Prince certainly would not have reached such a tragic state. Some unknown forces seem to have been driving father and son apart, however. They seemed to act toward each other almost against their wills. What can I attribute this to but Heaven? Oh! Cruelty!

Until Prince Sado reached his twenty-second year, he was not once permitted to accompany the royal procession to the ancestral tombs. Each spring and fall, he waited anxiously to be included in the royal entourage, only to be disappointed again. In fact, this was a great source of sadness and distress for him. On the first day of the eighth month of *pyŏngja* (1756), the Prince was permitted for the first time to take part in the royal visit to Myŏngnŭng. Informed of the news, the Prince was elated. He bathed and prepared himself meticulously for the visit. Fortunately, he encountered no mishap on this trip.* While he was on the road, he wrote letters of greeting to Queen Dowager Inwŏn, Queen Chŏngsŏng, Lady Sŏnhŭi, and even to his children. I have in my possession some of the letters he wrote on this trip. On such occasions his conduct showed no sign of illness. When he returned home without having experienced an unpleasant incident, he seemed to feel that he had been blessed with exceedingly good fortune.

For a while after this visit, Prince Sado did not encounter any harsh criticism from his father. His Majesty's sagacious heart was delighted that, in the eighth month, his favorite daughter, Madame Chŏng, had safely given birth to a girl, and he left his son alone. In view of this obvious discrepancy—His Majesty showering so much affection upon this daughter, though he had so little for the Prince—one might expect that the Prince would be resentful. He showed no displeasure, however. He was very happy that his

* Myŏngnŭng was the tomb of King Sukchong, Yŏngjo's father. The royal entourage also visited several other tombs after Myŏngnŭng and returned to the palace quite late at night. *YS*, 88:7b.

sister had safely given birth. Incidentally, I had come to learn that it was Lady Sŏnhŭi who had been responsible for the Prince's first visit to a royal tomb. Convinced that people might feel it peculiar that the Prince-Regent had not once been permitted to join the royal entourage, she had asked her daughter, Madame Chŏng, to plead her brother's case. Thus permission was obtained.

In the intercalary ninth month of that year, I bore Ch'ŏngsŏn. How happy Prince Sado would have been had he been his former self! As it was, he did not even come to see his newborn daughter. One could see how deeply ill he was.

Before long, my father was appointed Governor of P'yŏngan Province and left immediately for his post. His departure, which came at this critical time when the Prince seemed to be deteriorating daily, made me even more fearful and concerned.

In the twelfth month, Prince Sado came down with smallpox at Tŏksŏng House. His symptoms were very mild, but he was covered with lesions. I was terror-stricken, but luckily the lesions abated. Stricken with smallpox at twenty-two, he ran an incredibly high fever. It was truly fortunate that he came through safely and unscarred. Lady Sŏnhŭi came to our quarters to nurse him and spent night and day in deep anguish. I had moved the young Prince to Kongmuk House and stayed in the same small room as my husband to tend to him. It was an unusually cold winter; the walls of the room became frozen and turned into solid sheets of ice. It was truly an immense blessing for the nation that, despite the odds, the Prince-Regent emerged from this disease safely. His Majesty, however, did not once come to see his son during the illness. Furthermore, my father was stationed far away in that northern post. It is hard to describe the depth of my loneliness during this period when there was so little support available to me. When the Prince weathered the crisis, he was moved to Kyŏngch'un Pavilion to recuperate.

On the thirteenth day of the second month in *chŏngch'uk* (1757), Queen Chŏngsŏng's protracted illness* suddenly took a turn for the worse. Her fingernails turned blue and she vomited enough blood to fill a chamberpot. The color of the blood was not red; it was strangely dark and black. It looked as though something had come out that had been accumulating since childhood. We

---

* The text does not previously mention her illness.

were frightened. I had gone to the Queen's quarters first, and Prince Sado arrived very soon afterwards. By then, the Queen had just vomited and appeared to be in critical condition. Holding on to the vessel that contained what Queen Chŏngsŏng had vomited, the Prince wept, tears streaming down his cheeks. Everyone who saw him grieve in that way was deeply moved. Without losing any time, and before sending word to His Majesty, the Prince went to the administrative office of the Queen's residence with the chamberpot and showed its contents to the physicians. I heard that he was still crying when he consulted with them. Although he received boundless affection from his stepmother, one might assume that since he was not her natural son, he might have felt some residual distance. But his filial and kind nature responded spontaneously to her. Seeing him so grieved for her, no one would have known that he was diseased.

Queen Chŏngsŏng insisted that Prince Sado should not stay up late so soon after a major illness and repeatedly urged him to return to his room. Finally, around eleven o'clock at night, the Prince obliged and returned to Kyŏngch'un Pavilion. At dawn a lady-in-waiting came and said, "Her Highness went into a coma and does not respond." Prince Sado went at once to the Queen. She was indeed in a deep coma. She did not respond to him. Ten thousand times, he called loudly, "Your servant is here, your servant has come." Yet she remained silent. How he wept.

Having heard the news, His Majesty came after daylight on the fourteenth. The Two Majesties were estranged from one another, but the Queen's critical state brought him there. When the Prince caught sight of his father, he became so terrified that he could not cry or raise his head. It would have looked so much better if, despite his fear of his father, he had continued to do what he had been doing. Had he not cried, calling his stepmother and expressing such concern and sorrow as to move even bystanders to tears? Why could he not cry or put ginseng broth to the patient's mouth or speak of Her Highness's condition to His Majesty? Instead, at this critical moment, he crouched in a corner of the small room. As a result, it was impossible for his father to know that his son had grieved deeply until then.

As I feared, His Majesty began to criticize the Prince. He found fault with what his son was wearing, right down to the way the bottoms of his trousers were tied. Then he said, "How can you behave in this way when the Queen is so critically ill?" What was frustrating, so unbearably frustrating that I wished Heaven and Earth should burst open, was that every expression of the Prince's filial sorrow that he had displayed was now completely hidden by his terror. I could not explain to His Majesty, "He was not like this until Your Majesty came." Not knowing what had been going on, His Majesty was quick to assume that the Prince was unfilial and that he had no decorum. Lady Sŏnhŭi's vexation and my torment were simply excruciating.

By coincidence, Lord Ilsŏng, Madame Chŏng's husband, was also critically ill at this time. His Majesty had sent the Princess to her husband and was terribly agitated. Meanwhile, Her Highness grew worse, breathing her last at three o'clock in the afternoon of the fifteenth day. Prince Sado went down to Kwalli House to formally announce the death, and I, too, was prepared to begin mourning by calling upon Her Highness's departed soul and announcing the death. Yet His Majesty would not lead the way. He told ladies-in-waiting gathered there about his first encounter with Her Highness and reminisced at length about his life with her until her death. Darkness approached. The Prince was inconsolable. He wept and beat his breast. It was acutely embarrassing that the announcement of Her Highness's death was delayed that long. Finally, news of Lord Ilsŏng's death came. His Majesty then began to wail sorrowfully and, at once, began the mourning procedures for the Queen. I must say that it was extraordinarily out of form that the Queen's death was announced after dark though the death had occurred at three o'clock in the afternoon. Since it was so late, we had to wait until the following day to wash and prepare the body for the coffin. Then, after His Majesty's return to the palace from a visit to Lord Ilsŏng,* we put the burial garments on.

Prince Sado was plunged into grief. He called upon Heaven, he heaved and sobbed; his whole body shook with grief. He wailed constantly, calling the Queen as tears streamed continually down his face. A natural son could not have been more sorrow-stricken than he. I was hoping that His Majesty might see him in this state and regard him in a better light. However, when His Majesty re-

* The *Sillok* says that Yŏngjo did not return from Lord Ilsŏng's house until one o'clock in the morning. *YS*, 89:5a–b.

turned, the Prince again crouched in a corner and could no longer cry. How strange!

Queen Chŏngsŏng ordinarily stayed in the main room of the Great Pavilion, the official residence of the Queen. If she had a slight cold or even a bit of fatigue, she went to a side room. When her condition became serious, she said, "I cannot die in so sacred a place as the main hall of the Great Pavilion." The Queen moved hurriedly to Kwalli House, which was in the western wing of the palace, and died there.* After due preparations, her coffin was placed in Kyŏnghun Pavilion, which became her funerary chamber. A mourner's tent was erected at Okhwa Hall in which Prince Sado, as the chief mourner, was to stay for five months. The Prince attended the morning and evening offerings without fail and the midday ceremony as well. Some days he was present at all six wailings. I stayed at Yunggyŏng House across from Kwalli House.

Queen Dowager Inwŏn was over seventy and in extremely frail health. Although she mourned Queen Chŏngsŏng, she seemed in a daze, not grasping the full significance of the event. Toward the end of the second month, the Queen Dowager's health suddenly took a turn for the worse and she hovered near death, improving a bit now and then. She had removed herself from her regular living quarters to the secretarial office of the Queen Dowager residence and there she passed away on the twenty-sixth of the third month. Her death was sad, but what made it all the more poignant was that His Majesty, himself approaching seventy, grieved for his stepmother so deeply.

Queen Dowager Inwŏn's virtue had been truly outstanding. Under her supervision, the traditions and regulations of court life were carefully maintained and observed. She loved Prince Sado wholeheartedly and unquestioningly. When I entered the palace, she treated me with special regard. Her boundless affection for her grandson was expressed with warmth and solicitude. She regularly sent delicacies and specially prepared food to Prince Sado. Of all

---

* It was Chosŏn royal custom that only legal consorts, not secondary consorts, were allowed to die within the palace precincts. Secondary consorts were moved out of the palace when they became seriously ill. But even legal consorts were supposed to die in an inconspicuous place rather than in their main official living quarters. This custom was based on the idea that death polluted a living space. However, this custom did not apply to male members of the royal family.

the kitchens at the palace, Queen Dowager Inwŏn's was most highly regarded for its unusual and delicious food.

Learning of the growing tension between His Majesty and Prince Sado, the Queen Dowager had become deeply concerned. Whenever she saw me, she said pensively, "Isn't it disconcerting?" When Prince Sado donned full mourning garb* as chief mourner for Queen Chŏngsŏng, she said, "He looks so pitiful. He was already in a terrible state. Now he seems so sad." Frail as she was, she was moved by deep pity for him. She inquired frequently about his health. She had always insisted on strict adherence to decorum and had forbidden the princesses to sit casually next to me, shoulder to shoulder. Princess Hwasun was staying at the palace, but she was bedridden most of the time. Left unaccompanied, a young princess, Hwayu,[12] followed me around everywhere. So it must have happened that in a small room she sat next to me, her shoulder rubbing mine. Her Highness Queen Dowager Inwŏn, seeing this as a breach of decorum, grew incensed. "How dare she behave so casually to you? You are the Crown Princess Consort!" she fumed indignantly. We marveled that her sense of propriety had not diminished at all even though she was weak and racked by illness.

Queen Chŏngsŏng also had been very devoted to Prince Sado. Her sagacious heart had been genuinely troubled by His Majesty's unkindness toward him. Whenever news of the Prince's misbehavior reached her, she would become anxious and concerned over the future of the nation. She often visited Lady Sŏnhŭi and shared her profound concerns over Prince Sado.

The Two Highnesses' passing in as many months left the palace empty and desolate. Palace rules, which had been clearly delineated and strictly adhered to, fell by the wayside. Things became chaotic. How deplorable!

Having received much love and care from his grandmother, Prince Sado was particularly despondent over the departure of Queen Dowager Inwŏn. If only the relationship between father and son had been good, everything would have been fine.

The Queen Dowager's body was bathed and dressed in burial garments at Yŏngmo Hall. Then it was moved to Kyŏngbok Pavilion. T'ongmyŏng Pavilion was chosen as her funerary chamber.

---

* Hempen clothes, disheveled hair, and a walking stick.

On the last day of the third month, the body was placed in the coffin. The coffin, covered with white silk and placed on a white litter, was borne by her ladies-in-waiting to the funerary chamber through Yosŏ Gate, which the Queen Dowager had so often passed through to visit the rear garden. The grandeur of the procession equaled that accorded her at her wedding. His Majesty's mourning hutch was erected in Ch'ewŏn House.*

From the time Queen Dowager Inwŏn had become seriously ill, His Majesty had discarded all else to wait upon her day and night. He had administered her medications himself with the greatest care. Staying in the mourner's tent for the five months until the funeral, he never missed even one ritual from the morning offering to the six wailings. He was in his sixty-fourth year at the time, but his filial devotion and energy were simply incomparable. Since he was this way, and since he did not know his son's true heart, he found the Prince wicked and wanting. After the deaths of the Two Highnesses, the situation at the palace deteriorated rapidly.

There was a reason for the father-son relationship to decline further during this period. Several years earlier in the winter of *sinmi* (1751), Princess Consort Hyosun, the widow of the late Crown Prince Hyojang, had passed away. His Majesty, saddened by the death of his filial daughter-in-law, meticulously observed the mourning rituals for her, spending many hours in her funerary chamber. Attending a wake, he happened to notice a lady-in-waiting, a woman named Mun, who had been in Princess Hyosun's service. His Majesty took her in after the funeral, and soon she became pregnant. She had a brother named Mun Sŏngguk who was a high-ranking servant in the Office of Palace Management, and His Majesty became fond of him as well. By the time she gave birth to a daughter in the third month of *kyeyu* (1753),[†] His Majesty seemed quite enamored of this Mun woman. People were disquieted at this turn of events and, just before her delivery, many unsettling rumors circulated. According to one, "They are scheming to produce a boy. If she were to have a girl, they are going to secretly exchange her with someone else's boy." Another had it that "Her mother is a former nun and she is going to come into the palace for her daughter's delivery."

* This was for the chief mourner.
† The newborn was Princess Hwanyŏng.

I do not know why Sŏngguk harbored such evil intentions toward Prince Sado, but he was certainly a cunning and vile creature. These Mun siblings were clearly enjoying their power. He was promoted to the post of keeper of the keys and locks in the palace. Having served His Majesty since the winter of *sinmi* (1751), his sister was now the favorite. She was established in a house called Kosŏ House, just below Kŏn'guk Hall. Kŏn'guk Hall was the place where His Majesty had stayed as a young prince. He had given it to his first son, Prince Hyojang, and after his death his widow, the Princess Consort Hyosun, had remained there until her death. At any rate, the Mun woman had her first daughter at Kosŏ House and another was born there in the *kapsul* year (1754).*

The administrative office for the Mun woman's establishment was set up just outside Chungjŏng Gate in the rear garden, and a eunuch, Chŏn Sŏnghae, was placed in charge of it. Sŏngguk frequented this place. He knew that the King and the Prince-Regent were not on good terms. Hoping to use this to his advantage, he spied on the Prince and reported to His Majesty on the Prince's comings and goings. No one dared speak of the Prince-Regent, but Sŏngguk, emboldened by his newfound power, was undeterred. The Prince's servants were his cronies, and so he had no trouble finding out in detail what the Prince was up to. No sooner would he catch wind of something about the Prince than he would report it to His Majesty. What was circulating among women, the Mun woman reported. His Majesty was suspicious of his son even when he did not know what his son was doing, but now that he heard every detail of his activities, his sagacious heart grew more apprehensive and displeased. It was the misfortune of the nation that such a cunning woman and such a scheming thief achieved power.

Though I was well aware that the Muns were informing on the Prince, I was not so sure of what was being reported. I soon found out. Sometime in the *pyŏngja* year (1756), we needed ladies-in-waiting, and so I thought we should get daughters of those in our service. One was the daughter of Kim Suwan, who was in charge of keys and locks, and the other was the daughter of the second person in the Management Office of the Establishment of the Crown Prince and the Crown Princess Consort. This was not the Prince's

* Princess Hwagil.

idea but mine. We were terribly short of help, and so I settled on these two girls and arranged for them to enter our service. This happened one morning, and that very afternoon His Majesty, already informed of what had happened, summoned the Prince and scolded him angrily, "How could you select ladies-in-waiting without consulting me beforehand?" I was astonished. What must have happened was that Kim Suwan, a close crony of Sŏngguk, did not want his daughter to enter into service at the palace, and so he asked Sŏngguk to intervene on his behalf. Judging by how quickly His Majesty came to know what had happened at his son's residence, there was no doubt that it was Sŏngguk who had told him.

Prince Sado's illness grew worse. Before he had completely recuperated from his recent bout of smallpox, the Two Highnesses passed away. He was saddened by these losses. He was also heavily burdened by the ritual duties of mourning. This affected him adversely. As his illness tightened its grip, his behavior often fell short of propriety. Since Sŏngguk reported to His Majesty each little misdemeanor of the Prince that he heard of, the father-son relationship suffered even more. During the five-month wake, after a wail at Kyŏnghun Pavilion His Majesty would invariably drop by at Okhwa Hall to scold his son for whatever he happened to find irritating. Then, when the Prince went to T'ongmyŏng Pavilion, the same scene would be repeated. How angry this made the Prince! His rage was kindled like a well-constructed fire. It was His Majesty's habit to rebuke his son in front of a large crowd. It was at T'ongmyŏng Pavilion, before all the ladies-in-waiting, where the Prince went to honor his grandmother's memory despite the relentless summer heat of the sixth and seventh months, that His Majesty's sharpest and most humiliating derision awaited him.

No longer able to contain his rage, his mind helplessly seized by disease, Prince Sado began to beat his eunuchs severely. Beating servants in the mourning period was, of course, grievously wrong. How precipitously the Prince had fallen since the beginning of mourning when, sincerely and with all his heart, he had grieved for the Two Highnesses. From that year [1757], his "phobia of clothing" asserted itself. I cannot begin to speak of the hardships and heartaches this terrible symptom wrought.

After an exceedingly difficult five months, in the sixth month of *chŏngch'uk* (1757) Queen Chŏngsŏng's burial day arrived at last. Prince Sado's grief on this occasion was no less deep than it had been immediately following her death. He followed the funeral procession beyond the city gate. I heard that his sorrowful wail moved all to tears, whether participants or onlookers, officials, soldiers, or commoners.* When the Prince recovered his normal self, he was always like that. His Majesty, however, never understood this of his son. I do not remember the specific causes for that royal rage toward his son upon the Prince's return from this procession or just before his departure to meet the returning procession that bore the tablet of the deceased after the burial, but on both occasions the Prince had to endure great outbursts of reproof from His Majesty. Things were hard for His Majesty also. There had been a drought and other troubles. Nonetheless, he was too sharp and too unsympathetic to his ailing son.

That night, standing in the courtyard of Tŏksŏng House, gazing toward Hwinyŏng Shrine in which Queen Chŏngsŏng's tablet had just been placed, Prince Sado cried endlessly. He wished aloud to die and to leave behind the pains of this life. It is not possible for me to write of the pathos of this scene.

In that month, Prince Sado began to kill. The first person he killed was Kim Hanch'ae, the eunuch who happened to be on duty that day. The Prince came in with the severed head and displayed it to the ladies-in-waiting. The bloody head, the first I ever saw, was simply a horrifying sight. As if he had to kill to release his rage, the Prince harmed many ladies-in-waiting. I suffered so for this and soon decided that I had to speak to Lady Sŏnhŭi. I told her that the Prince's illness had grown much worse, indeed, so much so that he had taken to killing, and that I just did not know what to do. Lady Sŏnhŭi was utterly horrified. She was, in fact, so pained at this that she at once gave up food and took to bed. She then asked me whether she should speak to the Prince. Suddenly I was seized by fear for my own safety, for that would have led the Prince to search furiously for the informer and, given his frenzied state, it would make little difference that it was I who had told. In tears, I pleaded with Lady Sŏnhŭi. "I mentioned this to Your Ladyship because I was so troubled and because I felt it wrong not to keep Your Ladyship informed, but now Your Ladyship is so distraught I don't know what to do." She calmed down somewhat. I cannot

---

* For details about this day, see note 14 of *The Memoir of 1795*.

describe the anguish and helplessness that I felt. Suffice it to say that I longed for death so that I might pass into oblivion.

Queen Dowager Inwŏn's burial took place in the seventh month.* There were torrential rains that day. Yet His Majesty followed the funeral cortege to the place of burial and returned bearing her tablet. There was nothing even slightly remiss in his filial devotion. The Prince-Regent, though not unfilial, was in no condition to express such feelings. His illness seeped deeper and deeper. Now that he was killing people, our quarters became a house of horrors in which no one could be certain they would not fall victim.

My father had returned to the capital from the northwestern provinces in the fifth month. His Majesty was glad to see him and shared his grief with him. My father, of course, came to see Prince Sado. While my father was away, the Prince had gone through a great deal—smallpox, the Two Highnesses' deaths, and the deterioration and illness that had caused such anguish and terror. Father and daughter embraced each other, grieving together.

In the ninth month of that year, Prince Sado took in Pingae,† a lady-in-waiting who had served in the sewing department of Queen Dowager Inwŏn's establishment. She later bore the Prince a son.‡ The Prince had fancied her for several years. Now, mad with rage and with nothing to soothe his troubled heart, the Prince took her. He reasoned that, with Queen Dowager Inwŏn gone, no one would dare say anything of it. He had her place decorated with beautiful furniture and lovely objects and made certain that she lacked nothing. Before this, he had been intimate with many ladies-in-waiting. Whoever resisted him in any way he beat until he rent her flesh and consummated the act afterwards. Needless to say, no one welcomed his advances. Despite the many women he had been intimate with, he neither cared for anyone for long nor showed any particular fondness while it lasted. This was true even of the secondary consort who had borne him children. It was different with Pingae. He was mad about her. She was shrewd and de-

---

* The funeral cortege left the palace on the eleventh, and the burial took place on the twelfth. She was buried at Myŏngnŭng beside her husband, King Sukchong. For details, see *Inwŏn wanghu pinjŏn togam ŭigwe*, manuscript, 1757, Kyujanggak; *Inwŏn wanghu honjŏn togam ŭigwe*, manuscript, 1757, Kyujanggak.
† Lady Pak. She was later awarded the title Kyŏngbin.
‡ His name was Ch'an, and he later received the title Prince Ŭnjŏn.

manding. The Crown Prince's residence had limited financial resources, and so soon the Prince began to use things from the Office
of Palace Supply. This was very embarrassing. Though the officials
in charge remained silent, His Majesty could not have been ignorant of it. After all, would not Sŏngguk have reported it?

Several months later, on the winter solstice, His Majesty learned
of Pingae. He was highly provoked. He summoned the Prince to
question him. "How dare you do that?" Even when the Prince had
not erred, His Majesty was unrelenting in his criticism. One can
imagine how harsh he must have been on this occasion. In a towering rage, His Majesty commanded, "Bring that woman here at
once." Being infatuated with her, Prince Sado refused to send her
no matter what the consequence might be. Between repeated royal
urgings, "Bring her out quickly!" and the death-defying refusals of
the Prince, the situation seemed destined to explode. Since I knew
that His Majesty did not know what Pingae looked like, I chose a
lady-in-waiting about her age who was serving in the sewing department of my establishment and sent her out as Pingae.

From the time of my arrival in the palace in *kapcha* (1744), His
Majesty had shown nothing but kindness and affection to me. One
might expect that, since he was disenchanted with his son, he would
find the wife and children of that son disagreeable too, but he was
always tender toward me and loving toward my children, as if, in
his mind, we had no relation to his son. I was always deeply grateful for this royal kindness, but at the same time, it caused me a great
deal of uneasiness and discomfort. At any rate, on this occasion His
Majesty reprimanded me sharply for the first time in fourteen years.

He complained, "When the Crown Prince first took Pingae, you
must have known of it. But you did not tell me. Now even you
deceive me. How can you? At the time of the affair of the other
secondary consort, you were all sympathy for your husband. You
never expressed jealousy and took care of her child. I considered
this extraordinary, beyond what one can expect of a woman, and
really felt bad for you. But this time, he dared to take in a lady-in-
waiting who had served the Queen Dowager. This is completely
against the law.* Mind you, he is openly living with her, yet you

* During the Chosŏn dynasty, royal princes were forbidden to take as their
concubines ladies-in-waiting who had served in the establishment of their elders.
This was understood to be an extension of the incest prohibition.

said nothing. Having already been informed, today I asked you. Still you said nothing. I did not expect that you would behave so to me." He banged the ground with his fist while lashing out at me. Tremulous at being thus upbraided, I protested, "How can one inform on one's own husband? This humble person's duty demands otherwise." His reproofs grew sterner. Accustomed to his kindness, I was petrified.

Then I arranged that Pingae, disguised and accompanied by another lady-in-waiting, be taken to Madame Chŏng's residence outside the palace, where Madame Chŏng happened to be. I sent Pingae there with a message asking that she be hidden for a while.

That night His Majesty again summoned Prince Sado to Kong-muk House, where he was staying for the duration of the mourning for Queen Dowager Inwŏn. There he mercilessly berated his son. Unable to contain his grievances any longer, the Prince went directly to the well in front of Yangjŏng House and leaped into it. What a dreadful sight! The guard at the House, one named Pak Segun, climbed into the well and managed to bring the Prince out on his back. This was possible only because the well was frozen and there happened to be very little water in it. The Prince was saved, but he was dreadfully soaked and bruised. Already furious at his son, the sight of his son's unseemly jump into the well enraged him totally. The bureaucracy from high ministers down to minor officials happened to be in attendance. They, too, saw all. The Prime Minister at the time was Kim Sangno,* a devious character. Facing the Prince-Regent, he gestured as if he was sympathetic, but turning to His Majesty, he quickly assumed an expression of repugnance. It was really repellent.

My father was also present through all this. He was there when Prince Sado was rebuked and when he jumped into the well. Unable to suppress his concern for the country or his sympathy for the Prince, he threw caution to the winds and pleaded with His Majesty, "According to an old saying, 'when one loses the ruler's favor, one can grow so anguished as to run a high fever.' If the ruler-subject relationship produces such a response, then how much more intense it must be in a father-son relationship, which is, after all, given by Heaven. His Royal Highness arrived at this state be-

---

* Kim Sangno (1702–?) was regarded as having been supportive of Yŏngjo's punishment of Prince Sado. He held high ministerial positions during Yŏngjo's reign.

cause he suffered so long from the loss of his father's love. Your servant a thousand times and ten thousand times begs and entreats that Your Majesty please give this a thought."

My father had enjoyed an exceptionally cordial and trusting relationship with His Majesty and had not once been censured before this. But His Majesty was provoked by this piece of advice that my father ventured to offer, and since he was already angry at me, his displeasure at my father was compounded. So His Majesty immediately stripped him of his post and sent him a stern admonition. Father withdrew hurriedly and awaited his punishment at a place called Wŏlkwagye outside the city. This unsettled people who, at that time of disturbing rumors concerning the Prince-Regent and his difficulties with the King, were counting on my father. It was a precarious time; there was no telling what might happen next. Exceedingly distraught and uneasy over having elicited royal anger, I went to stay at the servants' quarters. After a while His Majesty reinstated my father and summoned me to show his usual affection. Though it was a difficult time for me, this royal grace was more than I deserved. I felt that I would not be able to repay his kindness even if my bones were ground to dust.

In the beginning of *muin* (1758), His Majesty was in poor health. But Prince Sado, because of his illness, did not once visit his father. It was most embarrassing. The situation grew increasingly tense, and as the days and months went by, things became harder and harder for me. Whenever I faced His Majesty my soul and spirit fled in fright. I cannot really describe the state I was in.

In the first month, Princess Hwasun's husband, Lord Wŏl-sŏng,[13] passed away. Having no children, the Princess held to the great principle with simple but unshakable determination and cut herself off from all food until, after seventeen days, she, too, passed away.[14] This was indeed the noblest thing ever to have come to pass in the royal house, but His Majesty, hurt that she had ended her life while her aged father still lived and that she had done it against his wish, declared that she had been unfilial and refused to permit the erection of a red gate.* Prince Sado was moved by his

* During the Chosŏn dynasty, the government erected a red gate to honor those deemed to have been exemplary in one of the cardinal Confucian virtues—loyalty to the ruler, filial piety to parents, and devotion to one's husband. Yŏngjo had gone to his daughter's house to dissuade her from fasting. When she died of that fast, he expressed profound sadness and disappointment. But the *Sillok* is full of praise for her act. *YS*, 91:4a, 91:6a–7a.

sister's faithfulness. He spoke of her at length with admiration. Afflicted as he was, I wondered how he could still respond so sensitively.

Prince Sado had been at Kwanhŭi House since that day in the twelfth month.* Once, in the second month of *muin* (1758), again disturbed over something, His Majesty went to see him at his place. He could not possibly have been pleased with the state in which he found his son. He then went to Sungmun Hall and summoned the Prince. This was the first meeting of father and son since their encounter in the twelfth month. His Majesty criticized the Prince for many things. Then, probably wanting to see whether the Prince would tell the truth though he knew that the Prince had been killing people, His Majesty ordered him to confess to all that he had done. Although the Prince was in mortal fear that his father might find out what he had done, it was his nature to invariably tell the truth when asked directly by his father. It was indeed strange that his inborn character would not allow him to tell a lie.

In his replies that day the Prince said, "When anger grips me, I cannot contain myself. Only after I kill something—a person, perhaps an animal, even a chicken—can I calm down."

"Why is that so?" His Majesty asked.

"Because I am deeply hurt."

"Why are you so hurt?"

"I am sad that Your Majesty does not love me and terrified when you criticize me. All this turns to anger."

Then he reported in detail the number of people he had killed, hiding nothing. At that moment, His Majesty—perhaps for a time responding to his natural instincts as a father or perhaps allowing his sagacious heart to be overcome with pity—said, "From now on I will not be that way."

His trembling rage somewhat abated, His Majesty came to Kyŏngch'un Pavilion. He told me of the exchange and asked whether his restraint would help. This was the first time he had spoken of his son in this fatherly way. This quite unexpected question caught me by surprise at first, but surprise turned to joy, and I replied tearfully, "Of course it would, Your Majesty. He behaves like this because ever since he was a child he has so wanted

---

* The day Prince Sado jumped into the well after being reprimanded by his father.

your love. He was frightened once, twice, and again until he came to acquire an illness of the mind."

"He actually told me as much—that his behavior had arisen from deep hurt," His Majesty said.

"Yes indeed, Your Majesty. One cannot begin to talk about his hurt. If Your Majesty were to guide him with love and care, he would not behave this way anymore." As I said this, I was overcome with emotion and began to cry.

With a tender expression, His Majesty said, "Well, then, tell him that I have inquired after him. Tell him that I asked how he has been sleeping and how he has been eating." This was on the twenty-seventh day of the second month, the *muin* year (1758).

Earlier, when I saw His Majesty going toward Kwanhŭi House, my soul had flown in fright lest something terrible happen. This solicitous remark from His Majesty, so completely unexpected, moved me deeply. Simultaneously laughing and crying, I said, "How wonderful it would be if Your Majesty in this way could lead him to take control of his mind again!" I bowed and brought my hands together as if in prayer. His Majesty must have pitied me. There was no trace of sternness when he answered, "That's what we will do." Then he left. What wonderful words! I felt as if in a delirious dream and remained stunned for some time.

Soon Prince Sado summoned me and I went to see him. I said, "His Majesty did not question Your Highness about killing, but you told him all about it. You say these things yourself, but afterwards you blame others. It is quite frustrating to deal with."

"He already knew everything when he asked me, so I had to tell him," the Prince replied.

"What did His Majesty say?"

"That I shouldn't do it again," he answered.

I mentioned what His Majesty had said and asked, "Doesn't Your Highness think that perhaps your relationship with your father will now improve?"

But at this, the Prince lost his temper. "Just because you are his beloved daughter-in-law, do you believe everything he says? He may say things, but don't trust any of it. In the end, I will wind up dead."

At times like this, the Prince did not appear to be ill at all. His Majesty had spoken out of genuine fatherly concern, and even though I had not really believed him, and even if it were only the feelings of the moment, I had been moved to tears by gratitude.

Now, seeing the Prince so astute despite his illness, I was again in tears. It must have been Heaven that parted father from son. Try as the father did to suppress it, he was soon overcome with distaste for his son, as if someone else controlled his feelings. As for the son, when he was with his father he concealed nothing and never tried to hide his transgressions. One sees that his true nature was good. Had he been treated in a normal fashion, he would never have come to this. What was Heaven's intention in inflicting such unheard-of sorrow on this land of Chosŏn! Only pain and grief remain.

It was at about this time that the Prince's clothing phobia became so very intense. It was inexplicable. I say "clothing phobia," but it was beyond description—a strange and mysterious affliction. For him to get dressed, I had to have ten, twenty, or even thirty sets of clothes laid out. He would then burn some, supposedly on behalf of some ghost or other. Even after this, if he managed to get into a suit of clothes without incident, one had to count it as great good luck. If, however, those serving him were to make the slightest error, he would not be able to put his clothes on, no matter how hard he tried. In the process, people were hurt, even killed. It was truly dreadful.

There were times when the Prince had to have so many sets of clothes made that the limited allowance of the Crown Prince's establishment could not cover the cost of that much cloth, even if it was all cotton. But when we did not have enough on hand, or if we ran out of cloth, people's lives hung on a breath. Thus I was desperately concerned to have enough clothing ready. News of this somehow reached my father, who was immeasurably pained by it. Out of sympathy for me and concern for people's lives, he kept me constantly supplied with cloth. The Prince suffered from this phobia to a varying degree for six or seven years. Sometimes it reached a terrible extreme; at other times it abated somewhat. When the Prince, with great difficulty and the luck of Heaven, succeeded in getting into a set of clothes, he himself was so boundlessly relieved that he wore them until they were filthy. Was there ever a disease like this? Among the hundreds and thousands of illnesses, I had never heard of one involving a difficulty in wearing clothes. I called upon Heaven to ask why, of all people, a person as noble as our Crown Prince should have been stricken with such a disease, but I never found an answer.

The first anniversaries of Queen Chŏngsŏng's and Queen Dowager Inwŏn's deaths were observed with no mishap. Thus two months passed rather uneventfully. Since Queen Chŏngsŏng's funeral, Prince Sado had not been allowed to visit her tomb, Hongnŭng. Finally, on one occasion, His Majesty reluctantly permitted the Prince to accompany him. That year we had an especially long rainy season. On that day there were torrential rains. His Majesty blamed the weather on the Prince. Just after the procession reached its destination, he ordered the Prince to return to the palace. Only his own carriage would continue to the tomb. Thus the Prince's desire to pay respect to Queen Chŏngsŏng at her tomb was frustrated. This must have seemed quite peculiar and incomprehensible to the officials, soldiers, and others present.

I was with Lady Sŏnhŭi when the news came. I had been praying that the Prince would carry himself well enough until his return. I was dismayed, even stupefied, to hear what had happened. The thought of the Prince, of his anger upon his return, made me dizzy with fear. He came in soaking wet from the pouring rain. How miserable he must have felt! On the way, he had found it necessary to stop at a military station in Seoul to wait until his bloodcurdling rage—rage that almost made him faint—had subsided. How grim and dejected he looked. As I looked at him, I realized anew that there was no way that he could have avoided his affliction. Unless possessed of filial piety that equaled that of the Great Shun,* no one could escape great grievance after treatment of this sort. Lady Sŏnhŭi and I could do nothing but hold each other, tears streaming down our faces. Prince Sado said simply, "It's becoming harder and harder for me to live." Later he brooded over this event and suspected that perhaps his clothing might have been a cause for his father's displeasure. His clothing phobia worsened afterwards. I could only lament.

His Majesty fell seriously ill toward the end of that year, and on New Year's Day of the following *kimyo* year (1759) he could not attend the sacrifice at the shrine of Queen Dowager Inwŏn. Uneasiness hung over the court concerning Prince Sado's duty to pay respect to his ailing father. Even when the Prince did visit, His Majesty did not look upon him kindly. The Prince, grievously ill and terrified of his father, avoided him at all cost. Whenever I vis-

* One of the legendary sage kings in China, Shun was a paragon of filial piety.

ited His Majesty, I felt the full strain of this awkward situation. Kim Sangno was Prime Minister at the time, and Prince Sado had asked Sangno to mediate things for him. Sangno quickly made an exaggerated show of concern. He was so skillful with his sorrowful face and his glib tongue that he convinced the Prince that he was on his side, that he had his interests at heart and was wholly sympathetic to the Prince's plight. After that day, in the twelfth month of the *chŏngch'uk* year (1757), the Prince repeatedly referred to Sangno as his savior.

Bedridden and unsure of recovery, His Majesty frequently voiced grave concern over the future of the state when ministers came to pay him respect. They were in an uncommonly delicate spot, caught between the King and the Prince-Regent. It was exceedingly hard for them to find the right thing to say. Sangno, however, experienced no such difficulty. He offered comforting words to the Prince as easily and fluently as a flowing river. While in His Majesty's presence, Sangno made a point of agreeing with His Majesty's apprehension for his son and assumed a most disapproving expression, reinforced by falling tears. When Sangno paid His Majesty a sick call, he refrained from speaking, lest he be overheard by Lady Sŏnhŭi who waited upon His Majesty day and night in the adjoining quarters or by the ladies-in-waiting in attendance.

His Majesty's quarters at Kongmuk House, his place of residence for the duration of his mourning for Queen Dowager Inwŏn, consisted of two small rooms.* His Majesty lay in the inner room before a door. The three head officials and the physicians of the Medical Bureau were in attendance in the outer room. Since the inner room was so small, when a minister came and prostrated himself, his head almost touched that of His Majesty, and so Sangno could have safely whispered secrets to His Majesty if he so desired. Suspicious character that he was, Sangno was still afraid of being overheard. Rather than speak, he wrote words with his finger on the floor. Reading them, His Majesty burst out wailing, banging the doorsill with his fist while Sangno, with a grieving face, crouched deeper. Of course, the situation was bad, bad enough to make any responsible minister want to weep, but Sangno's conduct, saying one thing to the Prince and another to His Majesty,

---

* During the Chosŏn period, the chief mourner was expected to reside in a rudimentary dwelling for the duration of the mourning period.

was, to say the least, most unbecoming. Lady Sŏnhŭi, who saw him fingering words whenever he came, was incensed and declared that it was truly a revolting sight.

In the midst of all this, Ch'ŏngyŏn came down with smallpox. Her symptoms were very serious at first, but after a while they abated and soon her illness was under control. Soon after the New Year, His Majesty recovered completely and kindly came to see her. I was grateful for these turns of events.

In the third month of that *kimyo* year (1759), His Majesty decided to formally designate my son the Grand Heir,[15] and so he ritually reported his decision at Hyoso Shrine, the shrine of Queen Dowager Inwŏn, and also at Hwinyŏng Shrine, the shrine of Queen Chŏngsŏng. Despite his illness, Prince Sado beamed with pride and joy. Except for those periods of acute illness when he became incognizant of his wife and children, he prized the Grand Heir above all else. He strictly enforced the distinction among his children in accordance with their status and would not let his daughters, not to mention his lowborn children of secondary consorts, vie with the Grand Heir. His management of such matters seemed untouched by his illness.*

The mourning periods for the two Sagacious Queens came to a close. On the sixth day of the fifth month, the *kimyo* year (1759), Queen Dowager Inwŏn's tablet was placed at the Ancestral Temple. Now that this was completed, I was overwhelmed by a sense of emptiness.

Just before the emplacement of Queen Dowager Inwŏn's tablet, the Board of the Rites had recommended the selection of a new queen. His Majesty reported his acceptance of this proposal at his late stepmother's shrine and chose a new queen through the three-stage selection process. The royal wedding took place in the sixth month.[16] By this time, Prince Sado was declining rapidly and a profound, unspoken, anxiety pervaded the court. Lady Sŏnhŭi, however, said to me, "Now that Queen Chŏngsŏng is no longer with us, it is only right that His Majesty choose a successor so that our kingdom will have a queen." She congratulated His Majesty and devoted herself to the preparations for the ceremony. Her

---

* Implicit in this is criticism of Yŏngjo, who did not maintain proper distinctions and did not treat Crown Prince Sado with consideration appropriate to his unique position.

thoughtful and virtuous conduct in the service of His Majesty was admirable. The Crown Prince and Princess Consort's ceremony of greeting for the new Queen was scheduled for the day after the wedding, and we made obeisances to the Two Majesties. Prince Sado carried himself with utmost deference and care on this occasion lest he inadvertently commit a disrespectful blunder. His exceptionally filial nature showed itself.

The formal investment ceremony for the Grand Heir finally took place at Myŏngjŏng Pavilion in the intercalary sixth month. The young Prince was in his eighth year. His serious and dignified manner won the admiration of all. Viewed from outside, Prince Sado's position would have seemed free of trouble. He was not only the Crown Prince but the Regent as well, and now his son, at seven, was formally invested as the Grand Heir, strengthening the future of the throne as securely as a large mountain or a founding rock. Yet the court was pervaded by a sense of foreboding, a sense that everything might just collapse at any moment. As the days passed, each with its own new difficulties, I found no way to fathom the will of Heaven.

That autumn and winter His Majesty was preoccupied with his private life, as was natural for a newly wed man. This left him with little time to check on the Prince's comings and goings. The year ended.

From the beginning of *kyŏngjin* (1760), Prince Sado's illness grew markedly worse. His Majesty renewed his criticisms, which daily became ever more scathing. The Prince's explosions of rage grew more violent, his clothing phobia more intense. He began to hallucinate, imagining that he was seeing people. Before he went anywhere, he sent someone ahead to clear the road of people; if someone for some reason was unable to remove himself in time and was seen by the Prince, however indistinctly, then the Prince could not continue to wear the clothes that he had on and had to remove them. But to change his military uniform, he had to burn many before being able to get into one. The quantity of silk that I provided for military uniforms during *kimyo* (1759) and *kyŏngjin* (1760) alone would have filled countless chests. Ordinary silk cannot be used to make military uniforms. I had to keep enough of the right kind on hand. My digestion fell into ruin over this.

On the twenty-first of the first month, Prince Sado's birthday arrived. How fortunate it would have been if the day were spent peacefully. But on his son's birthday His Majesty invariably held a formal audience or summoned the Prince's tutors to discuss and criticize the Prince. This hurt the Prince deeply. As it was repeated year after year, it became a source of deep sorrow. Never once was he permitted to sit at his birthday feast with peace of mind. Something always went wrong. Thus the Prince inevitably fasted on his birthday. This caused the whole court to buzz with tension. Each year, I lamented his pitiful fate.

On his birthday in *kyŏngjin* (1760), something upset the Prince terribly. His outburst was particularly violent. He simply could not say one respectful word to his parents. Rage and grief drove him into a state of total madness in which he was, as they say, "unable to distinguish Heaven and Earth." He ranted and raved; again and again he screamed, "What's the use of living?" and said many rude things to his mother. When his children came into his room to offer congratulations, he shouted at them, "How can one who does not know his parents know his children? Get out at once!" These young children, in their ninth, seventh, and fifth years, had adorned themselves respectively in a dragon-embroidered robe and formal blouses to make congratulatory bows to their father. Heartlessly rebuffed as they were, it is easy to imagine how astonished and frightened they must have been.

Though deeply ill, until then the Prince was able to confine his most vexing behavior to me, sparing his mother. But on that day, he was no longer able to conceal his illness from her. Lady Sŏnhŭi had, of course, heard of his illness, but she may have entertained doubts as to how much of it was true. Seeing it herself for the first time, she was aghast, just speechless. His conduct showed that he was so gravely ill that he did not recognize his seventy-year-old mother or remember his love for his children. Lady Sŏnhŭi's astonished expression and the children's fearful faces turned as pallid as cold ash. Ah! What an unbearable sight! I wished to turn into a stone and die on the spot. This was not possible. I lived on, but shrank to something less than human.

The spring brought a continuing deterioration in Prince Sado. My nervousness reached new heights. When the summer brought a drought, His Majesty, in his anxiety, blamed the Prince. "It is all because the Prince-Regent neglects to nurture his virtue." He fumed and sent down many caustic admonitions.* Hopelessly ill, the Prince could no longer withstand it. My despair passed all measure. I did not feel that I could live a minute longer. Each moment, I had no desire but to die.

Though Madame Chǒng later behaved peculiarly toward the Grand Heir and though one might fault her, if one is so inclined, for not having gone far enough on her brother's behalf in pleading his cause to His Majesty, the Princess out of fear never once refused a request that the Prince made of her. Sometime in the *kyǒngjin* year (1760), when the Prince's illness grew really bad, he began to place great demands upon her. Not only did he press her for financial contributions, but he announced that he expected her to smooth things over for him. Even before this, the Prince had asked her to intervene with His Majesty, but he always did it gently, almost pleading. Now, driven by rage and bitterness, he was out of control. It was as if his accumulated resentment for this sister, who had been so favored by their father while he himself had received nothing but scorn, and his suspicions that she was in some way responsible for the situation—both of which feelings he had hitherto suppressed—now exploded with irrepressible force. At one point he snarled menacingly, "Just make everything right, exactly as I tell you." The Princess stood there petrified and ashamed. I trembled with fear, expecting that he might become violent at any moment. But to our tremendous relief, he let it go at that.

According to what Madame Chǒng said, she did everything within her power for her brother but in ways that might not be obvious to him. Rather than directly intervene with His Majesty, since she was unsure whether that tactic would succeed, she kept a close watch on how events developed and tried to turn their course to the Prince's favor by maintaining constant contact with the people involved and attempting to influence them. This, she said, was why her brother might have gotten the impression that she was negligent in protecting him. In any case, now the Prince commanded that she arrange to stop His Majesty from having informal

---

* Sado apparently tried to respond to this criticism. On the third of the sixth month, 1760, he sent down an order to the effect that, since Yǒngjo was avoiding the main hall and taking a reduced portion of medicine as an act of penance for the drought, he would do the same. *YS*, 95:21a.

audiences with ministers. He knew that in these audiences the discussion would inevitably turn to his problems. The Prince also forbade Madame Chŏng to leave the palace for the Chŏng residence, fearing that something might happen to him during her absence. If she did, he threatened, "You won't see me again." She even had to cancel her plan to attend her adopted son Hugyŏm's capping ceremony, which was held on about the tenth of the sixth month at the Chŏng residence.

The seriousness of the Prince's illness and the harshness of the royal criticism it elicited made it increasingly difficult for father and son to remain in the same palace compound. The Prince was seized by a desire to have his father move to another palace so that he might be left alone to play military games in the rear garden and thus to release his pent-up feelings. Once he was struck by the idea, he grew obsessed by it. At the beginning of the seventh month, the Prince said to Madame Chŏng, "I simply can't live in the same palace with him any longer. You had better think of some way to make Father move. Maybe you can coax him into it by saying that you want to see what the other palace is like. I don't care how you do it, but make sure that it happens and fast!" Every day he badgered me to press Madame Chŏng "to make the move happen." It is no exaggeration that my life hung in the balance.

Finally, Madame Chŏng succeeded in persuading His Majesty to move, though by what method I cannot imagine. The move was scheduled almost immediately, on the eighth of the seventh month. On the sixth, two days before the scheduled move, Prince Sado summoned his sister. Grabbing the sword with his hand, he threatened her, "If anything happens to me, I will kill you with this sword." Lady Sŏnhŭi had come with her daughter, lest he harm her. How terrible she must have felt witnessing this scene. The Princess pleaded with him in tears, "I promise I will do anything Your Highness wishes from now on. Please spare my life." Prince Sado said, "I feel so constrained staying in the palace all the time. How about letting me take a trip to Onyang? You know that my legs are in bad condition from skin disease. Get Father's permission for my trip!" "As you wish," the Princess promised. She was allowed to leave.

No sooner did His Majesty move than royal permission arrived granting the Prince leave to travel to Onyang.* Madame Chŏng must have been forceful and persistent. Otherwise, both the move and permission for the trip would have been unthinkable.† I was impressed and amazed by how efficiently the Princess had managed to bring these things about. I could not help wondering whether the father-son relationship might have been made closer had the Princess used this forceful method of intervention from early on. But that was idle speculation. Things came of the will of Heaven and it was Heaven that brought forth this situation.

At one point, the Prince threw a *go* board (*Padukp'an*) at me because he was angry that I had done nothing to cause His Majesty to move. The board hit my left eye and almost hit, but fortunately just missed, the pupil. But my eye became terribly swollen. Thus when His Majesty moved, I was unable to pay him respect or to bid him farewell. Nor could I see Lady Sŏnhŭi off. I just grieved the parting in solitude. I felt cornered at the edge of a precipice with no way out but death. This solution—to end my life—beckoned with ever stronger appeal, but the thought of my son, the thought that I would have to leave him behind, kept me from actually doing away with myself. Yet my life was nothing but endless danger, perils of every sort. What use is there enumerating them?

Preparations for the Prince's trip got under way as soon as His Majesty had moved. The Prince set out for Onyang on the thirteenth of the seventh month. From the moment of his departure, Lady Sŏnhŭi was terribly anxious. This was partly due to concern about how her son would conduct himself on the road, and partly due to maternal concern for his well-being on his trip away from home. She regularly sent food that she prepared. She also sent a messenger to her nephew, Yi In'gang, who was the commander of the Kongju Military Division, asking him to inquire after the Prince or at least find out what rumors were circulating concerning him,

---

* Permission came on the eleventh of the seventh month, 1760 (*YS*, 96:2a–b). Yŏngjo had moved to Kyŏnghŭi Palace on the eighth of the seventh month. The *Sillok* tersely says that this move caused concern within and without the palace (*YS*, 96:2a). Kyŏnghŭi Palace was located in Sŏdaemun-gu at the site of present-day Seoul High School. This is about three miles east of the Ch'angdŏk-Ch'anggyŏng Palace compound.

† Another source attributes Yŏngjo's permission to ministerial counsel. Haboush, *Heritage*, 201.

and to report them to her. Before the Prince's departure, probably because of Madame Chŏng's intervention, His Majesty sent an order that the Prince begin his trip without the customary ceremony bidding farewell to the King. The Prince's entourage was anything but impressive. He wanted to go in proper splendor, a long line of soldiers before his carriage, heralds shouting animatedly, and drums banging majestically. But His Majesty had acquiesced to his son's trip under duress and was in no mood to send him out in great pomp.* It was simply unrealistic to expect that any official would dare to open his mouth about anything that suggested interference between the King and the Prince-Regent.

For me, the Prince's trip was a relief, though a temporary one. Supremely important as one's husband is to a woman, the situation was so difficult that I was in constant danger, to the point of not knowing when my life might end. This made me, or rather part of me, long to be somewhere far away from him. His absence offered a welcome respite. My father, too, had been feeling overwrought. The anxieties he felt and the difficulties he experienced being placed between father and son were beyond description. Suffice it to say that both of us fell victim to the sensation that our livers and stomachs were twisting and burning. I trust that people of later ages will be able to imagine our state of mind.

During Prince Sado's absence, the Grand Heir requested, "Please have my fourth uncle and cousin Suyŏng† come." Since I did not know what might happen to me from day to day, I also wished to see my family for what perhaps might be the last time. I asked my brothers and their wives to come to the palace.

At the time of his departure, Prince Sado seemed to be near death. Outside of the city gate, however, his rage must have subsided. He warned his entourage against abuse of peasants or farmland they might pass through. I was told that every subject who came to see his carriage pass by was so impressed by his princely dignity and consideration that they danced with joy, hailing him as an exemplar of sagacity and wisdom. After Prince Sado settled into the royal quarters at Onyang, his behavior remained exemplary,[17]

* Still, Sado's entourage consisted of close to a thousand people and included a military band. *On'gung sasil*, manuscript, 1760, Kyujanggak. Also, Haboush, *Heritage*, 201.

† Hong Nagyun, Lady Hyegyŏng's youngest brother, and Hong Suyŏng, her oldest nephew.

and I heard that the entire town of Onyang took on an air of serenity and peace and that the townspeople came to praise his gracious virtue. It must have been the sense of liberation that he experienced that prompted his illness to retreat and his senses to return.

Though Prince Sado had gone to great trouble to take this trip, once he arrived he found Onyang a small provincial town. It offered no unusual scenery, magnificent buildings, or monuments. After ten days at Onyang, he tired of it, and so he left for Seoul, arriving at the palace on the sixth of the eighth month. No sooner had he returned than the Prince said, "Onyang was so dull. I'd like to go to P'yŏngsan." But there was no way to request that His Majesty permit another trip, and so we all joined in persuading the Prince that P'yŏngsan was even smaller and duller than Onyang. The Prince did not insist on it, but it was evident that he was suffering from a sense of suffocation within the palace walls. His tutors and other officials were sending memorials urging the Prince to pay respect to His Majesty. The Prince was in no condition to do this. The matter remained a source of tremendous tension.

His Majesty had been sending frequently for the Grand Heir, having him stay near him. Now that his concern for the Prince had become grave and all-consuming, His Majesty seemed always to be referring to the problem, lamenting it and going over its various aspects in his encounters with officials, particularly in royal lecture sessions. Naturally, he vested his hopes for the future of the monarchy in the Grand Heir, and he often declared that he had no one but the Grand Heir to whom he could entrust the royal mandate. The Grand Heir was mature and bright, and, as his sagacious heart took great satisfaction in his grandson's manners and responses, His Majesty frequently expressed affection for him and faith in him.

Prince Sado had the habit of having recorders copy the contents of the royal lecture sessions and then reading them over. How would he respond to His Majesty's frequent avowals of affection for the Grand Heir, particularly such remarks as "I entrust the heavy burden of state to the Grand Heir." Though Prince Sado loved his son, the father-son relationship in the ruling house is known to have been difficult all throughout history. Besides, in his illness the Prince was intensely bitter about the fact that since childhood he had never been loved by his father. If he were to read that his father had great regard and praise only for his grandson, what, in his rage, might he do?

The survival of the dynasty depended entirely upon the Grand Heir; his safety alone ensured its preservation. Moveover, his safety depended on finding a way not to let Prince Sado see those remarks of His Majesty. But there was no way to stop the Prince from reading proceedings of the royal lecture sessions. What I did was to ask the eunuchs to keep an eye on the copy that was brought in for the Prince's view. If the copy contained problematic passages, they were to delete these passages and rewrite them before submitting them to the Prince. Sometimes, when I knew that the situation was particularly urgent, I went to the eunuch in charge on that day and had him omit the passages in my presence. I also wrote to my father explaining the situation and asked, "Please find some way to ensure the Grand Heir's safety." Out of his devotion to the country, my father used his influence and contacts to see to it that when the recorders copied the lecture sessions for the Prince, they omitted the problematic phrases.

During this perilous and troubled time, my father was constantly torn between his wish to repay His Majesty's kindness, his desire to protect the Crown Prince, and his duty to help and safeguard the Grand Heir. On those occasions when he had just too many things to worry about, his nerves acted up. He was unable to eat or to digest what he did manage to eat. Whenever my father saw me, he beseeched Heaven for the tranquility of the state. Given that the safety of the Grand Heir and the preservation of the dynasty rested on preventing the Crown Prince from seeing His Majesty's remarks in the royal lecture sessions, it was only natural that my father and I were anxious about it. How assiduously we put ourselves to the task, though! To anyone who wishes to find out, gods and spirits will confirm our efforts and devotion. If we had let Prince Sado see His Majesty's praise of the Grand Heir, I shudder to think what terrifying things might have happened to the young Prince.

In this atmosphere, the *sinsa* year (1761) began and Prince Sado's illness grew even worse. From the time His Majesty moved to the upper palace, the Prince was, as he had hoped, free to spend his time riding horses and playing military games in the rear garden. Since the seventh month of *kyŏngjin* (1760), he had spent a great deal of time there. But as the novelty wore off, he tired of it and, totally unexpectedly, began to leave the palace in disguise. When I first discovered this turn of events, I was completely overwhelmed by fear and consternation.

By this time, whenever he was seized by his illness the Prince invariably hurt people. For some time now, Pingae had been the only one to attend the Prince when he dressed. Hopelessly in the grip of the disease, he grew oblivious even of his beloved. One day in the first month of *sinsa* (1761), as he was getting dressed to leave for one of his outings incognito, he was suddenly overwhelmed by a fit of rage and beat her senseless. No sooner had he left than Pingae drew her last breath there where he left her. How pitiful her end was! There were her young children;* their plight seemed even more cruel and pathetic.

There was no telling when the Prince might return. It was imperative that the body be removed from the palace immediately. After the night was over, I had her removed to Yongdong Palace, which I chose as the place of her funeral. I took care of the expenses and procedures of the funeral and saw to it that, within the limits of my ability, the funeral procedures were correct and the materials used generous. Upon his return, Prince Sado heard of what had happened, but he said nothing. He was not in his senses. One after another, unspeakable difficulties continued. Throughout the second and third months, the Prince constantly came and went, presumably spending much of his time roaming somewhere outside the palace. The terror and agitation I experienced in this period is better left to the imagination.

In the third month the Grand Heir formally began his studies,[18] and in the same month he performed a capping ceremony at Kyŏnghŭi Palace. Needless to say, I longed to attend this ceremony celebrating my son's coming of age, but since Prince Sado was not in a condition to attend, I did not have the face to go alone. So I stayed away, pleading illness. How cruel I had to be.

In the second and the third months of that year, the three ministers of the State Council, Yi Ch'ŏnbo, Min Paeksang, and Yi Hu, who were serving respectively as Prime Minister, Minister of the Right, and Minister of the Left, died in succession.† His Majesty was not in the best of health, and the deaths of these three ministers depleted the State Council of its chief ministers. In the third month my father was appointed to the council. The delicacy of his

---

* Prince Ŭnjŏn and Princess Ch'ŏnggŭn.
† They were suspected of having committed suicide. See *The Memoir of 1795*, footnote to page 85.

position, the troubled state of affairs at the court, and his true desire made him deeply wary of accepting this post.* It was, however,
a decision that challenged him to measure himself by the principle
of holding forth in time of hardship, not merely in comfort or
convenience, and by choosing loyalty even at the expense of his
life. He reckoned that if he were to withdraw at that critical point,
people would be left with absolutely no one in whom they could
have confidence. His wholehearted loyalty and devotion to the
royal house and the nation allowed no alternative but dedication to
their cause and joining his fate to theirs. Having accepted the post,
he did not spend one day without tremendous anxiety or one moment without deep nervousness.

Toward the end of the third month, Prince Sado left incognito
for the northwest. The Governor of P'yŏngan Province at the time
was Chŏng Hwiryang, an uncle of Princess Hwawan's husband,
and the Prince rightly guessed that even if he were to make a trip
to P'yŏngyang, Chŏng Hwiryang would not dare report it to the
throne. Once the Prince-Regent arrived in P'yŏngyang, the Governor could not remain in his office undisturbed even though the
Prince was traveling under a false identity. I heard that Governor
Chŏng stood outside the Prince's lodging, waiting upon him. He
took care of meals for the Prince's party and supplied him with
necessary provisions. The Governor must have been in a state
of great agitation and nervousness. I heard that once, as he left
the Prince and passed through a wooded area, he coughed up
blood. He was a cautious man to begin with, but he was particularly afraid of the Prince. He was well aware that Princess Hwawan,
his nephew's widow, was greatly favored by His Majesty, and he
was greatly fearful that the Prince might turn against anyone connected with her. I can very well imagine how uncomfortable and
uneasy he must have felt.

My apprehension was beyond description. My father, too, was
quite literally at his wits' end. He was discreetly in touch with
Governor Chŏng and constantly informed of the Prince's where-
abouts. So restless was he that he stayed at the palace most nights.
Even on those rare days when he did go home, he did not retire to

---

* Lady Hyegyŏng maintains that her father's true desire was to retire into
private life. This seems to have been an accepted posture among the elite of this
period.

his bedroom but sat up in the reception room throughout the night. My father was in an impossible quandary. He deemed it out of the question that he report the Prince's doings to His Majesty, and yet it was equally out of the question that he admonish the Prince. Had there been the smallest possibility of admonition, what would have stopped him? As it was, not only was there not the slightest chance that the Prince would listen to him, just bringing up the topic might endanger my life and even my children's. It was not that my father did not wish to advise and correct the Prince, but after a long and careful deliberation, he came to the conclusion that the Prince was so hopelessly ill that nothing could be done about it. The only course was to protect the Grand Heir. This was, of course, a painful decision. Those who did not understand his motives accused him of neglecting his duty to guide the Prince. Neither he nor I wanted to defend him against this charge. There was no way my father could explain his situation or justify himself in the face of such criticism. We just lamented, in silence and in resignation, the adversity of our fate.

Prince Sado returned from his trip to P'yŏngyang around the twentieth of the fourth month, after some twenty days of absence.[19] Though I had spent the entire time in unrelieved anxiety, I could say nothing. While he was gone, we had to cover up his absence somehow. We pretended that the Prince was indisposed due to illness and maintained this impression with the cooperation of our eunuchs. The head eunuch, Yu Insik, lay in the inner room, speaking and giving orders in the manner of the Prince, while another, Pak Munhŭng, tended to him exactly as though he were the Prince. Perhaps it is best not to discuss the terror and shame this duplicity produced in each of us who participated.

Soon afterwards, Yun Chaegyŏm's memorial arrived.* Although Yun was right in insisting that all subjects had a solemn duty to admonish the Regent, the Prince was by now beyond the reach of official counsel. However, if His Majesty were to hear the smallest

---

* Yun Chaegyŏm's memorial, which arrived on the fifteenth of the fifth month, was not the first. On the eighth, Sŏ Myŏngŭng had sent a memorial to the Crown Prince, criticizing his secret trip to the northwestern region. He criticized the rough manners of those with whom the Prince was keeping company. Yun also criticized this trip and requested that those who allowed the Prince to make the trip be severely punished (*YS*, 97:20a–22a). Other officials also spoke of this matter in an audience. *YS*, 97:19a–b, 97:20b–21a.

word of the Prince's trip through official memorials, no one could predict the outcome.

Somehow the P'yŏngyang trip seemed to produce a calming effect on the Prince. He conducted his regular audiences with officials and held lecture sessions. How pitiable were the hoping hearts that anxiously searched for signs of improvement! Provoked by Kyehǔi, at an audience, the Prince was firm and chided him, alluding to the Han dynasty official Chiang Ch'ung.* My father came in one day excitedly relating this story to me, commenting on how well the Prince seemed.

Sometime after the tenth of the fifth month, the Prince went to Kyŏnghǔi Palace to pay his respect to His Majesty.[20] This was his first visit to his father since His Majesty's move to Kyŏnghǔi Palace. Fortunately, this visit was accomplished without mishap. Several days later, I took the Grand Heir to Kyŏnghǔi Palace to pay respect to His Majesty and to Lady Sŏnhǔi.[21] With so much on our minds, we could say very little to each other.

In the sixth month, Prince Sado came down with a disease and suffered terribly for several months. I felt that this illness probably occurred because he had not taken proper care of his noble self during his wanderings in disguise since the spring. It is against normal human affection to say this, but in retrospect, having seen him go through what he did—the saddest and most horrid fate, one unprecedented in human history—I regret that he did not die of this illness. Had he died then, we would have been left with only the grief of losing him, however profound. It would have spared him that deep affliction and his wife and children the unremitting bitterness that fell to them. It would have prevented the political volatility and the repercussions at court that reached such extremes. Many deaths would have been avoided. My family would not have suffered such vile slanders and the consequent misfortune. Unfathomable is the way of Heaven. The Prince recovered in the eighth month.

In the ninth month, His Majesty encountered in the course of reading the *Records of the Royal Secretariat* a memorial by Sŏ

---

* Chiang Ch'ung was an official in the court of Wu-ti of the Han dynasty who spoke ill of the Crown Prince to the emperor and thus brought harm to the prince. Hong Kyehǔi (1703–1771) was one of the supporters of Yŏngjo's position on military tax reform. He was regarded as belonging to a camp hostile to Prince Sado. Haboush, *Heritage*, 103–12.

Myŏngŭng referring to the Prince's trip to P'yŏngyang. Thus he discovered his son's secret trip.* It caused a terrible furor, but with the intervention of Chŏng Hwiryang,† it stopped short of a real disaster. For a brief moment, it seemed as if something drastic would happen. His Majesty announced a royal departure for Ch'angdŏk Palace and punished several eunuchs at the Prince's court.‡ This royal fury was entirely justified, but somehow His Majesty seemed unable to pursue the matter to its conclusion. This was, in a sense, his pattern of behavior. According to my observations over a long period, His Majesty was quite exacting and difficult on small matters because he was meticulous and attentive, but when he faced a matter of genuine gravity, he tended to be calmer and less harsh than he would have been with small transgressions. Thus, when he had heard that the Prince had killed many people because he was "hurt," he responded rather sympathetically and even consoled his son.

His Majesty's anger and consternation at his son's secret trip must have been profound, but it was a transgression too enormous and serious to confront, so he refrained from pursuing it to its conclusion.

When the announcement of the royal departure for Ch'angdŏk Palace came, the Prince seems to have felt that he might not be able to get through safely this time. He concealed the weapons and ornaments that he used in military games. The Prince had not spoken to me in a friendly or intimate manner for several years, but on that day he summoned me to Hwanch'wi Pavilion where he had been staying. He said to me, "I am afraid that I won't be safe this time. I wonder what I should do?"

Feeling heavy in the chest, I said, "It is a vexing situation, but even so, what can His Majesty possibly do?"

"Don't you see? He loves the Grand Heir. And as long as there

---

* On the twentieth of the ninth month, Yŏngjo ordered that the records from the fifth and sixth month be brought in and read to him. He discovered Sado's trip this way. *YS*, 98:18a–b.

† On the twenty-first, Yŏngjo stripped Hong Ponghan and Sado's tutors of their posts (*YS*, 98:18b–19a). In the interim, Chŏng Hwiryang had been appointed Minister of the Right. *YS*, 98:19a.

‡ On the twenty-second of the ninth month, Yŏngjo went to the gate of Ch'angdŏk Palace. There he ordered that several eunuchs be banished to distant islands and that a number of royal secretaries, who were on duty at Ch'angdŏk Palace, be stripped of their posts. *YS*, 98:19a.

is the Grand Heir, he would not care if he had to get rid of me," he said.

"The Grand Heir is Your Highness's son, and aren't father and son supposed to share the same fate?" I protested.

"You don't think of the obvious," he continued. "He hates me more and more. Really, it's getting unspeakably bad. He can, you see, obliterate me by first deposing me and then making the Grand Heir an adopted son of Prince Hyojang." The Prince said this in a doleful and measured tone, displaying no sign of illness.

Feeling a surge of grief, I said forcefully, "That can't be! That is impossible."

"You just wait and see," the Prince said. "He is fond of you, and so even though you and the children belong to me, all of you will be all right. But I won't be. I always had to bear it alone. No, he won't let me live. Don't you see what I am driven to? To this, this hopeless and wretched illness."

I listened to him weeping, overwhelmed by sadness. Later, after that cruel and baleful decree in the *kapsin* year (1764),* I remembered the Prince's words. I was struck by how strange it was that on that day he could so lucidly predict the future. This memory of his clairvoyance induced in me a violent sense of pain and bitterness.

The royal departure for Ch'angdŏk Palace was subsequently canceled. Thus the air of imminent danger was lifted. Nonetheless, whenever the Prince went through confrontation or conflict, his symptoms usually grew worse. In the tenth month, he was really badly off.

In that month a royal edict announced the selection of a wife for the Grand Heir. Some years before this, my father had been invited to the sixtieth birthday celebration of Madame Kim, the mother of Minister Kim Sŏngŭng, of the illustrious Ch'ŏngp'ung Kim family. There he saw Minister Kim Sŏngŭng's granddaughter and was quite struck by her grace. He mentioned an extraordinary young girl to us later. Now, Prince Sado noticed among the names of the candidates the daughter of Kim Simuk, the very girl his father-in-law had praised. He was strongly inclined toward choosing her as his daughter-in-law. He let his wishes be known by sending a message to his sister. He told her whom he wanted and intimated

---

* Yŏngjo's decree making the Grand Heir the posthumously adopted son of Crown Prince Hyojang.

that she had better see to it that the candidate of his choice was selected. But His Majesty, as well as the general opinion of the court, seemed inclined toward Yun Tŭngyang's daughter. Nonetheless, the Prince was in no state to be present at the selection and to argue for his preference. Without him, I could not go either. I felt it was against natural human feelings that I could not participate in the selection of a wife for my only son, the support of my future and the pivot of my affection. I spent the duration of the selection process in a dejected spirit. The Prince was also anguished lest his candidate not be chosen. To the immense joy and delight of the Prince, the news at last came reporting that Minister Kim's daughter was chosen.

After the second selection, the prospective bride contracted smallpox. The Grand Heir broke out with the same illness soon afterwards. Fortunately, they both recovered around the tenth of the twelfth month. Having been so anxious, His Majesty rejoiced over their recovery. Prince Sado was so elated that he was able to control his conduct. For several days he did not even seem ill. There is no need to go into detail over how ardently and ceaselessly I prayed to the gods and spirits in Heaven and on Earth for my son's recovery. Nor need I stress the care my father lavished upon the Grand Heir. He stayed at the Grand Heir's residence every night with no thought of retiring.* With the silent protection of ancestors, both the Grand Heir and his betrothed recovered in succession so that the final presentation was made in the twelfth month. The felicities of the occasion were great.

Custom demanded that the parents be present for the final presentation. His Majesty reluctantly invited the Prince and myself to the ceremony. I was elated over the prospect of finally meeting my future daughter-in-law, but at the same time I was apprehensive over how the Prince would fare. My foreboding proved right. The Prince had an exceedingly hard time dressing on that day, going through many suits of clothing. The cap presented equal difficulties. Unable to keep on pure jade headgear, he instead settled upon a cap decorated with jade of a type commonly worn by the officials of the third rank. Soon, father and son met at Sahyŏn

---

* The *Sillok* entry of the twenty-seventh of the twelfth month, 1761, records that Yŏngjo asked Hong Ponghan to stay with the Grand Heir during his illness. *YS*, 98:33b.

House. His Majesty simply could not have been kindly or sympathetically disposed toward the Prince. The headgear upon the Prince was large and ugly, almost like that worn by military officers, and let it be said also that it did nothing to enhance the dignity of the Prince-Regent. Nonetheless, His Majesty had invited the Prince, and the Prince was already there to witness one of the foremost events in his child's life. Besides, how could mere headgear be so important? Many things could have been worse. Yet before the prospective bride arrived, His Majesty became enraged by the Prince's cap and ordered the Prince to leave the room immediately. This was really too cruel. I simply could not imagine how His Majesty could have been so uncharitable to his son over such a minor matter. How aggrieved the Prince must have felt, turned away without a glimpse of his future daughter-in-law. I marveled at him for leaving so obediently without flying into a rage.

I really wanted to see my son's future wife, and so, inasmuch as I was there, I decided to stay, even if it meant that I might have to face a terrible scene later. When the ceremomy concluded, I felt even more strongly how heartless it had been that the Prince was turned away before the presentation. I was also apprehensive of how the Prince might react to this disappointment. I discussed the matter with the Queen, with Lady Sŏnhŭi, and Princess Hwawan. I suggested, "Since Ch'angdŏk Palace is on the way to the bride's pavilion, it would be possible to take her with me unnoticed. Of course, it is improper to do this on my own without receiving His Majesty's permission. But I would really like to have His Highness meet his daughter-in-law." They discussed it at length, but I simply ordered an attending eunuch, "When we pass the lower palace, please see to it that Her Ladyship's palanquin comes into the palace with mine." In this way, I brought her to Ch'angdŏk Palace.

Having gone to the upper palace in great anxiety and having been turned away before the ceremony, Prince Sado was lying still in Tŏksŏng House, dispirited and wounded. I announced, "Returning with the Grand Heir's Consort." Pleasantly surprised, the Prince welcomed his daughter-in-law and embraced her affectionately, his face beaming with delight. Not until late at night was he willing to send her back to the bride's pavilion where she was staying. I brought her to our residence to let the Prince see her because I felt that the circumstances warranted it. All the same I felt guilty, as though I had deliberately deceived His Majesty.

Feeling more aggrieved each day, the Prince grew worse daily. The disrespectful things he said of his father became unmanageable. It was ghastly. My mind was constantly in fright. I lived from one perilous moment to the next, not knowing when or how I would meet my end. I just wanted to see my son's wedding before anything happened.

The year ended and *imo* year (1762) began. The wedding was set for the second day of the second month, and I anxiously awaited the day, praying that the wedding would take place without mishap. Around the tenth of the first month, the Prince suddenly came down with what appeared to be seriously inflamed tonsils. I was very nervous. However, he recovered immediately after receiving acupuncture. I was greatly relieved. At last the day arrived when that most important of human affairs, the pledge of matrimony, was to be sworn. On that day, His Majesty sent for the Grand Heir, who left first. The Prince also started off early and, after resting a while in front of Sunghyŏn Gate, went to Kyŏnghyŏn Hall, in which the first ceremony took place. Thus the three generations gathered together in one place and grandfather and father saw the Grand Heir off to present a duck to the bride. The joyousness and the splendor of the occasion were not equaled by any that I have known. Afterwards, the grand ceremony took place at Kwangmyŏng Pavilion. That night the Prince stayed at Chŭphŭi Hall while the Grand Heir and the bride stayed at Kwangmyŏng Pavilion.*

On the following morning, the grandparents and parents were to receive the formal obeisances of the bride. For this we sat in one room. The Two Majesties† sat in chairs at the northern end of Kwangmyŏng Pavilion while the Crown Prince and the Crown Princess Consort were seated on the east and west of the room. The bride, young and new to the place, was not so quick of movement. While we waited, the tension grew palpable. The father and the son had not faced each other so closely for a long time. It was evident that His Majesty was quite displeased with his son's

---

* These buildings were within the Kyŏnghŭi Palace complex, which was demolished in 1910.

† King Yŏngjo and Queen Chŏngsun.

appearance and was restraining himself from saying something. I silently pleaded that His Majesty would not say anything to the Prince. I went out and hurried the bride in. I also instructed that a ritual meal, rice cooked with chestnut and jujube,* be served with no delay. The morning obeisance ended with no mishap. It was indeed fortunate.

Prince Sado carried himself with extreme caution. He wanted very much to spend all three days in the upper palace near the newlyweds. On such occasions he did not show symptoms of his illness. Treated properly, he would have done quite well. His Majesty, however, did not wish his son to stay the full three days. He had allowed the Prince to be present until the morning obeisance, as the protocols of the ceremony absolutely demanded it, but no more. He ordered the Prince to return to his own palace, allowing me to stay on for the three days. This presented many difficulties. I made excuses and slipped away soon afterwards.

After the three days at the upper palace, the Grand Heir and the Grand Heir Consort came down to Ch'angdŏk Palace. The Prince, who had been waiting for them, was happy to have them. He took the Grand Heir Consort to the Hwinyŏng Shrine and had her pay her respect. He was greatly moved on the occasion. He seemed to recover his true self. The Prince noticeably favored his daughter-in-law, and she responded to his affection. When he died, despite her extreme youth, she grieved deeply for him. As the years went by, she increasingly treasured his memory. She is still unable to speak of him without shedding tears. Perhaps this is because she received particular affection from him, but it is also because she has a truly filial heart.

The Prince had not seen his father-in-law privately for several years. My father† was about to leave for Hamgyŏng Province, where he had been assigned to perform a sacrifice at an ancient tomb. His Majesty instructed me to permit my father to see the Grand Heir Consort before departing, and so Father came to the lower palace. On that day, the Prince was a little better, and, evidently wanting to brag about his new daughter-in-law, he met my

* A dish that symbolized long life. The bride was to offer it to her in-laws as a pledge of her devotion to them.

† After being dismissed briefly on the twenty-first of the ninth month, 1761, Hong Ponghan was appointed Prime Minister within a week, on the twenty-seventh. *YS*, 98:20a.

father. While the Prince was growing up, he had no one he could speak to privately except for guidance officials or tutors. Thus he had no close contact with anyone outside the court until our marriage, when he met my father. He immediately took to his father-in-law; he respected him and felt close to him.

Though my father came to the palace for bimonthly greetings, he could see us only with royal permission, and even when he came to our quarters, he did not stay long. He would say, "The regulations of the court are very strict. An outsider should not stay too long," and he would leave shortly after. Still, whenever my father had an audience with the Prince, he would sincerely urge him on and help him in his studies. He made frequent references to relevant historical episodes and wrote out useful quotations from the classics and other texts for the Prince. The Prince used to send compositions to my father for comment, and Father unfailingly pointed out the merits and demerits of each sentence. In this way, the Prince learned a great deal from his father-in-law. As for devotion to the Prince and the sincere wish that he become a sage king of great peace, who among the officials could have honestly entertained one-thousandth of the feelings my father nurtured? Although his affection was limitless, he always guided the Prince to the right path. There were occasional instances in which royal affinal relatives catered to the whims and fancies of their royal in-laws by presenting them with playthings or curios. My father was completely disinclined to such practices. Whenever he saw the Prince, his words were invariably "Please exert yourself in filial devotion" or "Please diligently apply yourself to study." Perhaps because of this reticence, the Prince held my father in high esteem and behaved with great deference toward him. Even as the Prince came increasingly under the influence of his illness, he never once said anything disrespectful of his father-in-law.

On certain particularly trying occasions, I wrote to my father, telling him that things were becoming very difficult and that I trusted him to look after the situation. The Prince, however, never once wrote to my father asking for a favor. When the Prince's clothing phobia grew acute, so that having enough cloth became a desperate need or, literally, a matter of life and death, I turned to my father for assistance, but the Prince never asked him for it. The Prince took things from Lord Kŭmsŏng or from Madame Chŏng, but not one thing from my family. When he began his travels in disguise, one might have expected him to go to my family first. He went to Lord Kŭmsŏng's and changed into ordinary clothes there, but he never used my family's home as a stopover. The Prince continued to stand in awe of his father-in-law and remained deferential toward him. He was so ashamed of his bizarre behavior, including the outings in disguise, that if perchance he were to come into close contact with his father-in-law, he would hardly have been able to bring himself to look upon him squarely, and so he avoided him. Thus their encounters for several years, be they in audiences or in my father's attendance upon the Prince during his illness, had been exclusively public in nature, just ministerial attendance upon the Regent.

So on that day my father was pleasantly surprised to be greeted in that way by the Prince. He was pleased to see that the Prince, still young himself, had the good fortune of having already attained a daughter-in-law. He was happy to meet the young couple who came to greet him. My father extended heartfelt congratulations to the Prince. The Prince also responded in the affectionate manner of old, showing not the slightest symptom of his illness. It was really strange, but it was also heartbreaking.

In the third month the Prince again had great difficulties with His Majesty. His symptoms flared up uncontrollably. I can hardly bring myself to write of it. Gripped by rage, the Prince ordered eunuchs and ladies-in-waiting to say truly unspeakable things. Frightened as they were for their lives, in lèse-majesté, they would shout these blasphemies at the top of their lungs. These hellish scenes evoked in me such a terror of Heaven and such dread that I wished that I were dead, that I might be incognizant of what took place. Ever since pyŏngja (1756) when the Prince had been unjustly chastised by his father for drinking, the Prince had been deeply embittered at drink. Now, in the midst of a strict temperance campaign, he ordered that alcoholic beverages be brought to his residence in large quantity as if in fulfillment of his father's accusations. The Prince had little tolerance for alcohol, and though he could not drink very much, wine and liquor were scattered about everywhere. Everything that happened was cause for distress.

Since the kyŏngjin year (1760), many eunuchs and ladies-in-waiting had been killed. I cannot even remember all of them. Among the more conspicuous were Sŏ Kyŏngdal, in charge of supply and killed by the Prince for having brought something late;

many eunuchs on night duty at his residence; and one of the ladies-in-waiting belonging to Lady Sŏnhŭi's establishment. The situation was becoming insupportable. He had brought into the court several women he had met on his trips incognito, a nun he had picked up in his outings in *sinsa* (1761), and a *kisaeng** from his trip to P'yŏngan Province. When he held parties, there were, in addition to these, some lowly women servants at the court who had caught his fancy and many *kisaeng* from outside, all thrown together. These were truly bizarre events.

Toward the end of the second month, the Prince summoned Princess Hwawan and told her in a confidential manner that his illness was caused by a deep injury. Terror-stricken, the Princess responded sympathetically. She spoke of how sad it was and, to my horror, said some very disrespectful things about His Majesty. That was something I could not do. Even when my life hung in the balance, I could not utter anything disrespectful about His Majesty. Now the Prince, often attended by Princess Hwawan, held frequent parties at either T'ongmyŏng Pavilion or in the rear garden of Ch'angdŏk Palace. At night, he chose to stay at Hwanch'wi Pavilion.

The third month passed in horror and the fourth month arrived. By this time the Prince's residence no longer looked like that of a living person, but rather like a funeral chamber. He had red flags made exactly like funeral flags and had them set up in every room, including the one he used as his bedchamber. When parties ended, which was usually late at night, everyone, noble as well as base, would fall asleep here and there while the tables remained full of leftover food. The spectacle was not human; it belonged to the realm of ghosts and spectres. There was nothing I could do but resign myself to fate, thinking that all was dictated by Heaven.

The Prince often summoned blind fortunetellers. When they said something he did not like, he killed them. Many medical doctors, astronomers, and servants were also killed or injured. It reached the point where every day many dead bodies and victims of injury had to be carried out from the palace. Both in and out of the palace, people were terrified and angry, not knowing when they might meet their death or where they might find safe haven. Though the Prince had been endowed with a virtuous nature by

---

* A legally sanctioned courtesan. There were several categories of *kisaeng*.

Heaven, he had now lost it entirely and had gone completely astray. I cannot really talk about it.

Suddenly in the fifth month, the Prince excavated a space in which he built a house with three small rooms complete with sliding doors between them just like the inside of a grave. There was a passage to the outside through a small door in the ceiling. The door was nothing more than a wood panel that covered a small opening through which one could barely maneuver in and out. This door was covered by another panel of wood of the same size, which had earth and grass planted over it, so that there was no sign of anything underground. The Prince was satisfied with the result, and he spent many hours inside this subterranean chamber lit by a hanging lamp of jade. His intention was merely to have a place in which to hide all of his military weapons and equestrian equipment in the event that His Majesty were to come to the lower palace to ask for his things. He had no other motive than this, but this underground house added fuel to terrible suspicions. The Prince was doing these sinister things as if possessed by spirits; no human force could stop him.

In that month, for the first time since the Grand Heir's wedding, Lady Sŏnhŭi came to the lower palace to visit us, particularly the new Grand Heir Consort. The Prince was delighted and strangely moved by this visit. He lavished an extraordinary amount of attention on every detail of her stay. One might say in retrospect that his heart, not quite knowing it, was responding to a premonition that this was his farewell to his mother. Each meal was prepared in the manner of a feast with all sorts of delicacies. Cakes were piled high, and there were even cakes of ginseng. He composed a poem wishing her longevity, offered drinks wishing for the same, and took back her wine cup only after she drained it. In taking her to the rear garden, he insisted despite her resistance that she ride in a palanquin arranged in the manner of the king's sedan and accompanied by men carrying large military flags and a band consisting of trumpets and drums. This was obviously the Prince's idea of serving his mother with the utmost reverence and filial devotion.

Lady Sŏnhŭi, however, was shocked and dismayed at her son's deranged display of affection. She realized how hopeless his illness had become and was deeply disquieted at the uncertain prospect of where it might lead. Whenever she saw me, she would shed tears, murmuring fearfully, "What can happen?" After just a few days spent in this way, she left for the upper palace. Upon her departure, the mother wept and the son grieved deeply. They must have sensed that it could be their final parting. As for me, living in peril and chaos, I was not at all certain that I would ever see her again in this life. My heart felt as though pierced by a knife.

At about this time, Sin Man completed the mourning for his father and returned to the State Council as Prime Minister.[22] Seeing his old minister after three years, His Majesty felt as if he had met a new person and spoke to him frequently about the Prince-Regent. Now that Sin Man's return gave rise to much terrible talk about him, the Prince declared, "That minister is inauspicious. He is hateful." The Prince grew mistrustful and terrified of Sin Man, suspecting that he was slandering him to His Majesty. The Prince took such a deep aversion to Sin that just the thought of him would make him gnash his teeth in fury. His disease burst forth with even less restraint. I was simply at wits' end. Then, completely unexpectedly, the incident of Na Kyŏngŏn occurred.* At the time, my maternal cousin, Yi Haejung, was third minister in the Board of Punishment.

It was simply beyond me to reckon why, with what evil motives, that villainous Sangŏn brought this about.† Needless to say, it led to an alarming turn of events. His Majesty personally interrogated Kyŏngŏn and summoned the Prince, who hurried to the upper palace on foot.[23] As it was, the Prince had reached an irreversible point. Egged on by this villain, he plummeted into the abyss. At the same time, tension between father and son soared to a terrifying extreme. His Majesty had Kyŏngŏn executed. The Prince had Sangŏn, Kyŏngŏn's brother, brought in. In the courtyard before Sŏnji Pavilion in Simin Hall, he interrogated him under torture, demanding the name of the person behind the scheme, but Sangŏn did not tell. The Prince's hatred of Sin Man grew worse. He

---

* On the twenty-second of the fifth month, 1762, Na Kyŏngŏn sent a memorial to Yŏngjo, charging Prince Sado with ten heinous crimes. At this point Yŏngjo, furious at Sado and the incumbent ministers of the State Council, relieved Hong Ponghan and Yun Tongdo of the posts of Prime Minister and Minister of the Right, respectively. *YS*, 99:17b, 99:21a.

† Na Sangŏn was on the palace staff and was the brother of Na Kyŏngŏn. Lady Hyegyŏng is implying that Na Kyŏngŏn brought charges against Prince Sado at his brother's instigation.

threatened that he was going to seize Lord Yŏngsŏng, Sin Man's son,* and kill him in revenge. Calamity seemed imminent as the Prince daily thundered that he was going to get Lord Yŏngsŏng that day or the next. Probably because Lord Yŏngsŏng was not yet destined to die, the Prince did not actually carry out his threat.[†]

Seeing that the Prince's behavior grew each day wilder and more uncontrolled, Lady Sŏnhŭi seemed to give up hope. At about this time, the Prince wrote to Princess Hwawan complaining that she was not doing much for him. Several passages and the language he used were so terrible that one could not bear to look at them. Then he declared, "I am going to the upper palace through the water passage." He was also hell-bent on getting back at Lord Yŏngsŏng. Though he had not yet seized him and brought him in, he confiscated many things belonging to Yŏngsŏng—an official robe, a court robe, a military uniform, many items of everyday use such as jade headgear and buckles—and he burned them all. Lord Yŏngsŏng's life really hung by a thread. Lady Sŏnhŭi saw all this in horror. It was not so much that she was concerned for Lord Yŏngsŏng's life; rather, she was troubled by the Prince's wild and unbridled explosions of fury.

The Prince indeed attempted to go to the upper palace through the water passage, but he returned without success. He did this on the night of the eleventh and in the small hours of the twelfth of the intercalary fifth month. This led to a frightening rumor, which was exaggerated to terrifying proportions and spread rapidly throughout the court.[‡] True, the Prince did not do any of these things because he truly intended to. But when, propelled by rage, he lost his senses, he would say such things as how determined he was to do thus, or how much he wished to go with sword in hand to do so. If he had possessed an ounce of his normal senses, he certainly would not have behaved in that way. However, the Prince was born with a uniquely harrowing fate. It was his destiny not to live

* Lord Yŏngsŏng was the husband of Princess Hwahyŏp, who had died.
† The *Sillok* states that each day after Na Kyŏngŏn's report arrived, Prince Sado awaited punishment all day at a designated place (*YS*, 99:19a–22a). Apparently, though he was awaiting punishment, he was able to do other things.
‡ The *Sillok* describes Yŏngjo's decision thus: "Suddenly there was a rumor from the inner court. The king was truly astounded and went to Ch'angdŏk Palace" (*YS*, 99:22b). The allusive nature of these references suggests that Yŏngjo himself was thought to be Sado's target. For details, see Haboush, *Heritage*, 208.

out his natural span but to meet a hitherto unheard-of end. Thus Heaven contrived for him all sorts of evil situations to goad him on to his fate Oh! Heaven! Oh! Heaven! Did you have to press so cruelly?

Lady Sŏnhŭi realized that though her sick son could not be blamed, neither could he be trusted. The Prince was her only son, and she had entrusted her future to him. She certainly did not want to do what she felt she had to do. It was her lifelong pain that the Prince had turned out this way because he had received no affection in his youth, and that His Majesty simply could not grasp this point. But now that his illness had reached the irreversible point at which he could no longer recognize his parents, if she, out of private love, were to delay and do nothing, and if perchance the Prince, in a senseless state, were to be driven by his frenzy to commit an unthinkable act, then what would happen to the four-hundred-year-old dynasty? Duty called upon her to protect above all else His Majesty's royal person. The Prince was irretrievably ill, and perhaps it was best that his suffering come to an end. The bloodline of the Three August Royal Ancestors* now was solely carried by the person of the Grand Heir.

Reasoning thus, Lady Sŏnhŭi came to the conclusion that, though she loved her son, and loved him a thousand, ten thousand times as much as anyone else, there was no other way to preserve the dynasty than to do what duty required. She wrote to me on the thirteenth, saying, "The rumor about last night is even more frightening. Now that things have reached this state, I feel that, unless death were to cast me into oblivion, it is my duty to preserve the dynasty and to save the Grand Heir. I do not know whether I shall be able to meet the Crown Princess Consort in this life again." Reading that letter, I wept convulsively, but I still did not know that the great calamity would come on that very day.

That day, intending to hold an audience, His Majesty remained in the throne room at Kyŏnghyŏn Hall in Kwan'gwang Pavilion.[24] Lady Sŏnhŭi went to see him there. In tears, she said, "The horrible disease ever worsens; there is no hope. As a mother, this humble person can hardly bear to say this, but it is only right that

---

* *Samjong hyŏlmaek*, the bloodline of the three *chong*. The three *chong* here refer to Kings Hyojong, Hyŏnjong, and Sukchong, the direct line through which later Chosŏn kings descended.

Your Majesty secure the dynasty by protecting your sagacious person and the Grand Heir. Please make this decision." She continued, "With the affection of a father, Your Majesty might hesitate to do this. But it is all disease; he is no criminal. Though he cannot be saved, he cannot be blamed. Your Majesty must settle this; please extend your grace to the Grand Heir and his mother."[25]

As the wife [of the Prince], I dare not say that what she did was right. The situation, however, was irreparable. The right thing for me would have been to follow him in death. I would have been spared knowing what came afterwards. But I did not die. I could not; the thought of the Grand Heir prevented me. I can only grieve the pain of life, the misery of fate.

When His Majesty heard it, he did not hesitate or ponder, but at once ordered the departure for Ch'angdŏk Palace.*

Sundering her maternal love and crushing her parental attachment for the sake of great principle, Lady Sŏnhŭi had brought herself to inform His Majesty. Once this was done, she was seized by such pain that she could hardly breathe. She trod back to her residence at Yangdŏk Hall and took to bed, abjuring all food. Has there ever been such a painful predicament?

There were two routes for royal processions to Sŏnwŏn-jŏn. One was through Manan Gate, which carried no suggestion of misfortune. The other, through Kyŏnghwa Gate, signified misfortune. That day the procession was ordered to proceed through Kyŏnghwa Gate.

The Prince had hurt his back entering the water passage on the night of the eleventh. On the twelfth he was at T'ongmyŏng Pavilion. That day the main beam of the hall cracked loudly as if the wood was breaking. Frightened, the Prince groaned, "What can this mean? It must foretell my death."

A little before this, early in the fifth month, my father had elicited royal wrath. Dismissed, he had to stay in the eastern suburb for about a month.† The Prince must have felt the danger. He had directed Cho Yujin of the Crown Prince Protection Office to send

---

* A separate palace complex. It housed Prince Sado's residence.
† On the second of the intercalary fifth month, Hong Ponghan was dismissed from the post of Prime Minister, but five days later he was appointed Minister of the Left. *YS*, 99:21a–b.

word to Cho Chaeho, a former minister who was in Ch'unch'ŏn, to come to Seoul.* In matters of this sort, the Prince scarcely seemed inflicted by disease. Strange, the ways of Heaven!

The news of the royal departure on that day alarmed the Prince terribly. He quietly ordered that the military weapons and horses be hidden. And he set out for Tŏksŏng House through the back of Kyŏngch'un Pavilion. Before getting into the palanquin, he asked that I come to see him.

During the preceding days whenever he had caught sight of anyone, it had resulted in tragedy. Thus, when he rode in the palanquin, he had it enclosed on top and on all four sides with banners. To his tutors and to anyone outside, it was claimed that he was suffering from a disabling fever.

It was about noon when I received his summons to go to Tŏksŏng House. Suddenly, as I watched, a great flock of magpies surrounded Kyŏngch'un Pavilion and began to cry out in unison. I was seized by ominous foreboding. The Grand Heir was staying at Hwan'gyŏng Pavilion. I had been in a state of terrible agitation. Now, gripped by anxiety for my son, I ran to his residence and said to him, "No matter what happens, do not be alarmed. Bear everything in stride." I really did not know what to do.

The royal arrival was delayed somehow. News reached us that His Majesty might not reach Hwinyŏng Shrine until three in the afternoon.

The Prince again sent word that I should come to Tŏksŏng House. When I arrived, I found him drained, without his usual energy but with no sign of derangement in his face or in his voice. He was sitting with his back resting against a wall, his head lowered in a deep, meditative manner, his face devoid of color.

I was expecting that my appearance would lead to rage. This premonition that my life might end that day had caused me to plead with the Grand Heir and to warn him. Contrary to my anticipation, the Prince said calmly "It looks very bad, but they will

---

* Cho Chaeho (1702–1762), the son of Cho Munmyŏng and the brother of Queen Hyosun, was outspoken in his opinion that Crown Prince Sado should be protected. He was subsequently banished and executed. (*YS*, 99:30b.) In 1775, Cho was posthumously exonerated and restored to his former position. Yŏngjo's remark on this occasion was "I was angry at him at the time but he was not guilty." *YS*, 124:15a.

let you live. Oh, how I fear their intentions." In deep consternation, I sat there silently, just rubbing my hands together while
tears rolled down my face.

The royal procession had reached Hwinyŏng Shrine. A messenger came to summon the Prince. How strange! The Prince did
not say "Let's escape" or "Let's run away." Nor did he beat anyone. Without rage, he asked for the dragon robe of the Crown
Prince. Putting it on, he said, "I am going to say that I am suffering from a disabling fever. Bring the Grand Heir's winter cap."

As the Grand Heir's cap was small, I thought it would be better
for him to wear his own, so I asked a lady-in-waiting to fetch it.
This brought from the Prince a completely unexpected response:
"Your malevolence frightens me. You want to live long with the
Grand Heir at your side. Since I will die today, when I get out
there, you don't want me to wear his cap lest it bring misfortune
[to your son]. How very well I can fathom your cruel heart."

I did not know that he would meet that disaster on that day. I
could not see how it would all end. It was the sort of thing that
could end in death for all. What would become of my son, of me?
And so these words, coming as a thunderbolt, tormented me. I
fetched the Grand Heir's cap and gave it to him, saying, "What
Your Highness has said was indeed beyond my reckoning. Please
wear this." He refused. "No, why should I wear what you wish to
keep from me?" Could one have thought these the words of a
diseased person? Oh! Why did he go so obediently? It was, I guess,
all Heaven's will. Only pain and misery remain.

It grew late, and, with much urging, the Prince went out. His
Majesty, seated before Hwinyŏng Shrine, rapping his sword, enacted
that decision. It was too cruel; I cannot bear to record the scene.
Oh, grief!

When the Prince left, one could hear the fury of His Majesty's
voice. Hwinyŏng Shrine was not far from Tŏksŏng House; I had
someone go to the wall. He returned to say that the Prince had
already removed the dragon robe and was prostrate upon the
ground. I realized that it was the final decision; Heaven and Earth
seemed to sink around me; my heart and innards felt as though
they were being torn to pieces.

Too restless to stay at Tŏksŏng House, I went to the Grand
Heir's residence. We hugged each other desperately, not knowing
what to do.

At about four o'clock, I was informed that a eunuch had come requesting a rice chest from the kitchen. I could not understand what it meant, but I was too agitated to let him have it.

Realizing that a decision of an extreme nature had been taken, the Grand Heir went through the gate and begged, "Please spare my father." His Majesty ordered sternly, "You leave here." The Grand Heir left and went to the waiting room at the Prince's residence. My state at the time was simply beyond comparison to any ever known. After sending out the Grand Heir, the sky and the earth seemed to come together; the sun seemed to be losing light, and everything went dark. I had no desire to linger in this world for even one more second. I took a knife and was about to end my life, but someone took it and I could not achieve my wish. I desperately wanted to kill myself; I looked for something sharp, but found nothing.

I went out, passed Sungmun Hall, and reached Kŏnbok Gate that leads to Hwinyŏng Shrine. I could see nothing. I only heard the sound of a sword that His Majesty was rapping and the Prince's pleas: "Father, Father. I have done wrong. Herewith, I will do everything you say, I will study, I will obey you in everything, I promise. Please do not do this to me." My liver and gall were breaking into bits; everything was black around me. I just beat my breast. But what was to be done? What would be of use?

With your strength and with your energy, could you not have avoided getting into that rice chest even if it was a royal command? Why did you get in? Oh, why! At the beginning he tried to come out, but in the end, he was pressured into facing that dreadful fate.[26] How could Heaven be so cruel? There is only unparalleled grief. I wailed and wailed beneath the wall; there was no response.

Since the Prince had been stripped of his position, his wife and children ought not to have remained in the palace. Moreover, I was too fearful to let the Grand Heir stay out. I sat beneath the gate and wrote a letter to His Majesty: "Under Your Majesty's decision, it is most discomforting for the criminal's wife and son to remain at the palace. It is all the more fearful that the Grand Heir might stay out for long, and so this person humbly begs permission to leave for her [father's] home." I added, "By Your Majesty's heavenly grace, this humble person begs for the protection of the Grand Heir." I managed to find a eunuch and asked him to deliver it.

Not long afterwards, my older brother came in and said, "There was a royal decree commanding that, in accordance with the changed status of the crown prince, his family should leave for his wife's family home. We are bringing a palanquin for Her Ladyship and a sedan chair for the Grand Heir. So please come in them." Brother and sister embraced, crying bitterly.

I was carried on someone's back to the inner gate of Chŏsŭng Pavilion, passing through Ch'ŏnghwi Gate. A palanquin was waiting there. A lady-in-waiting named Yun rode with me, and eunuchs carried the palanquin. The ladies-in-waiting followed, wailing. Can there have been such a pitiful scene, ever?

When I got into the palanquin, I lost my senses. The lady-in-waiting Yun desperately massaged me, and I came back, but my misery was too much to bear.

When we reached my father's house, I was laid in a room in the inner quarter. The Grand Heir came, accompanied by my second uncle and my older brother.* The Grand Heir Consort was brought with Ch'ŏngyŏn in a palanquin sent by her family. What a pathetic sight.

I was just too miserable to live. I again attempted to kill myself. Again I failed. On further thought, I simply could not bear to inflict added grief upon the Grand Heir. Without me, who would see to his safety, his growing up? I restrained myself and preserved this cruel life of mine. I just cried out to Heaven. What a cruel fate!

At home, I met the Grand Heir. One could see his shock and grief. He had just witnessed, at his tender age, a scene of enormous terror and fright. Who can imagine the depth of his sorrow. Lest it make him ill, I hid my sorrow and said, "This is truly unbearable. But there is no way to deny that it is all Heaven's will. Only if you stay in good health and are good, only then will the country be at peace so that we can repay the sagacious grace. Although we are in deep sorrow, you should not harm yourself."

My father could not easily leave the court, and my older brother, because he held an official post, was also obliged to go in frequently. That left my younger brothers to attend the Grand Heir. The two older ones stayed with him, watching over him. My youngest brother had been the Grand Heir's playmate since child-

* Hong Inhan and Hong Nagin.

hood, and it was he who slept with him in the smaller room in the guest wing for eight or nine days. The Minister Kim Simuk* and his son, Kim Kidae, also wanted to be with the Grand Heir. But my father's house was quite small and all the ladies-in-waiting at the Grand Heir's establishment had come to stay with us, and so Minister Kim rented the house adjoining ours on the south that belonged to fifth special counselor Kim Kyŏngok. Minister Kim had his daughter-in-law stay to keep the Grand Heir Consort company. A passageway was cut through the walls separating the two houses.

My father had been recently dismissed from his post, and so he had stayed in the eastern suburbs for a while. Only after reaching that decision had His Majesty recalled my father and reappointed him to the State Council.[†] Learning of His Majesty's decision completely unawares, my father had rushed, stunned and dazed, into the palace and fainted at the gate.[‡] The Grand Heir was at the study hall. Upon hearing of his grandfather's condition, he sent some heart-clearing pills to him. My father regained his consciousness, but how could he have had any desire to live? Like me, his only thought and concern in this terrible time was to protect the Grand Heir. Thus he did not follow the Crown Prince in death. But Heaven and Earth, spirits and sentient beings stand witness to his loyalty, his wholehearted loyalty that sought only to ensure dynastic security by protecting the Grand Heir.[§]

This tenacious and odious life of mine remained unextinguished, but, as my thoughts stayed always on the Prince's plight—how could he possibly have endured it—I felt burned as though scorched by flames.

Two officials, O Yusŏn and Pak Sŏngwŏn, came and suggested that the Grand Heir be made to kneel on a straw mat in the open air to await punishment. This would have been proper. But who

* Chŏngjo's father-in-law.
[†] Hong Ponghan was reappointed to the State Council as the Minister of the Left on the seventh. Yŏngjo put Sado into the rice chest on the thirteenth of the intercalary fifth month.
[‡] According to Yi Kwanghyŏn, Hong Ponghan came into the court quite early along with two other ministers, but they were ordered to leave. He came back, but he was with other ministers. Haboush, *Heritage*, 211, 223–24.
[§] Once Sado was put into the chest, Hong Ponghan made a point of showing support for Yŏngjo's decision and a cool attitude toward Sado. *YS*, 99:23a, 99:25b.

had the heart to make the child do this? He was instead made to stay in the part of the house with the low eaves.*

It was not until the following day that my father received royal permission to leave the court. Upon seeing him, my son and I threw ourselves in his arms and cried unrestrainedly for a long time. My father then delivered a royal message to me: "Preserve yourself; secure the Grand Heir." Though we were under a most severe royal command, this sagacious instruction immensely moved and relieved me on behalf of the Grand Heir. In deep gratitude, I stroked the Grand Heir and said to him, "I, as your father's wife, and you, as your father's son, have met this misery. We can only grieve for our fate; we cannot blame or resent anyone. That we, mother and son, are saved today is entirely due to the sagacious grace of His Majesty to whom our lives are entrusted. In living up to his sagacious expectations, you should always do your very best to become a good man and always remain calm and correct. Only then will you be able to repay his sagacious grace and, at the same time, be a filial son to your father. There is no better course."

Then I turned to my father. First I thanked the royal grace, saying, "The days I have are exactly the days His Majesty bestows upon me. Please relay my message to His Majesty: this person humbly obeys his sagacious instructions." My words trailed into a sob. Indeed, not one word I said was untrue. What was sad was that the Prince had reached that condition in the first place; once he had reached that state, it could not be helped. I truly did not harbor any rancor in my heart and dared not feel resentful in any way. Embracing me and the Grand Heir, my father wept. He said, "Her Ladyship is right. Only by becoming a worthy and a sage can His Highness the Grand Heir repay the sagacious grace and also be a filial son to his father." Then he left for the court.

As the days passed, it was just too horrid to imagine the Prince's state. Unable to think of anything else, I spent days in near collapse. On the fifteenth, His Majesty had [the rice chest] bound very tightly [with rope], covered deeply [with grass], and moved to the upper palace. All hope was lost.

* A symbolic gesture signifying that the son shared in the state of disgrace with the father.

There was no way in which cloth could be brought out from the palace, and so my father provided the fabric for the suit that had to be readied for the body. For many years, through the Prince's clothing phobia, my father had supplied me with untold quantities of cloth. Now in preparing the burial suit, his last act of devotion to the Prince, he took care that not even the smallest detail was amiss.

On the twentieth, at about four o'clock in the afternoon, there was a torrential rain with much thunder. The thought of the Prince's terror of thunder made me so restless. I just could not bear to imagine it. All through this period, I thought constantly of death. I wished to die of starvation; I imagined jumping into deep water; I handled towels; and I frequently grabbed knives. Because of my weakness, I could not bring myself to complete the final act. But I could not eat at all; I could not drink water or eat wet gruel.

The Prince was reported to have responded until the storm, so it must be that he died during that rain. Oh, how did he bear up and meet that end? Every inch of my body ached with grief; it is but the cruelty of fate that life was restored to me.

In all urgency, Lady Sŏnhŭi had informed His Majesty. His Majesty, also, was compelled to carry out that act for the safety of the dynasty. We had still hoped that, since all had been caused by illness, His Majesty would take pity and extend his grace, stipulating that the Prince be mourned in accordance with his former position and that the mourners' costumes would reflect this. His Majesty's rage, however, showed no signs of abating even after the decision was carried out. He executed all of the Prince's cronies—a courtesan, the eunuch Pak P'ilsu, several palace servants, craftsmen, and even some shamans.* This was entirely reasonable and no one could dare complain. It was the fact that the Prince's illness was mistaken for unfiliality that was truly distressing.

Because of his clothing phobia, the Prince could barely manage, after innumerable tries, to put on a suit of unbleached cotton clothing. On that day, he was again wearing unbleached cotton. His Majesty had always seen him with the formal outer robe, the dragon robe, and so it was the first time that he saw him wearing

---

* The *Sillok* names the following: Pak P'ilsu, a Buddhist nun named Kasŏn, a courtesan from P'yŏngan Province, and two others. *YS*, 99:23a.

unbleached cotton clothes beneath. Not knowing of the Prince's illness, His Majesty was sharply provoked: "Even if you want to get rid of me, how can you wear mourning for me?"* Thus His Majesty was very thorough in going through the Prince's things. "Bring out everything that the Prince has used," he commanded. These included military flags and weapons; indeed, what was not there?† Even for the somberest royal funeral, descendants in mourning carried only one walking staff. The Prince, however, had many of these made. He had been particularly fond of swords and daggers, which he always kept near him. The mourning staffs he had made concealed swords within, and he would carry them with the swords inside as though they were walking staffs. He even showed them to me; I found them frightening, even horrifying. The Prince had not gotten rid of them, and they turned up among the things His Majesty unearthed. This further provoked and angered him,‡ and so he was not in a frame of mind to discuss mourning costumes for the Prince. It is just so grievous that, since His Majesty did not grasp his son's illness, he attributed all to unfiliality.

We had hoped that the mourning costumes of court officials would be those of subjects to the Prince-Regent. On such a terrible occasion as this, one ought to be thankful to his royal grace for saving the Grand Heir. Yet, until that moment of deposal, enacted as it was because of illness, His Highness had been Prince-Regent for fourteen years. His Majesty's virtue would have been better served if he had allowed the Prince to be mourned as the regent by those above and below. I found it extremely sad that this was not done.§

On the twentieth, when it was all over, the funeral arrangements had to proceed. But the Prince had first to be restored to his position as Crown Prince before this could commence. Though royal intent may not have been opposed to this, His Majesty seemed rather reluctant to restore his son and hesitated to allow him to be mourned in accordance with propriety. Only on the night of the

---

* Unbleached cotton was used for the mourning costume, and so Yŏngjo has interpreted Sado's clothes as a wish for his death.

† Yŏngjo had them all burned. *YS*, 99:23a–b.

‡ Yŏngjo's response to these objects was "With things like this, how can a nation not perish?" *YS*, 99:23b.

§ The Prince-Regent was treated as a ruler. The Crown Prince was not.

twenty-first did he relent, ordering the Prince's restoration.* Then, in consultation with the ministers, His Majesty decided on funeral arrangements. He suggested that the coffin be laid at Yongdong Palace.

At this point, my father had to exercise extreme caution. He was well aware that one wrong word or one wrong move might provoke His Majesty, whose rage was still searing as flame. That the Hong family might be exterminated was a matter of secondary importance; the preservation of the Grand Heir was at stake. Thus, seeking simultaneously not to oppose royal intentions, not to betray the deceased, and not to leave the Grand Heir with regrets, Father, in his devotion and loyalty, managed to have a posthumous title bestowed upon the Prince, the coffin laid at the Crown Prince Tutorial Office, and the three funeral committees formed and governed by precedent and law. He served as the president of the committees so that he could oversee everything personally until the burial, making certain that not the smallest detail would be amiss. Except for my father, who among those ministers would have dared to make any suggestion to His Majesty and who would have been able to turn his sagacious heart?

After the coffin was laid at the Crown Prince Tutorial Office, Father came home at dawn to see me and my son off to the palace. Holding my hand, Father wept as though he had taken leave of his senses. Still weeping, he said to me, "With the Grand Heir at your side, have a long life that you may enjoy comfort and peace in the late years of your life." The depth of my sorrow at the time cannot be equaled in history.

Upon our return to the palace, Prince Sado's funeral formally began at Simin Hall with calls for the soul of the departed. The Grand Heir let down his hair and wailed at Kŭndŏk House. The Grand Heir Consort wailed at my side with Ch'ŏngyŏn. We were a pitiful sight. A complete suit of burial clothes was brought in and put on the body. I heard that the body, despite the extreme heat, showed no sign of deterioration. The grief I felt at hearing this is unimaginable. After the body was clothed in burial garments, the time came for the washing of the body with wet towels

---

* The *Sillok* records that the Prince died on the twenty-first. Yŏngjo restored his son to the post of Crown Prince and granted him the posthumous title Crown Prince Sado, the title by which he is known to posterity. *YS*, 99:24b.

and the covering and tying of the nose, the mouth, the eyes, and the ears. As I advanced toward him, I became sharply aware of the utter uniqueness of my situation. His words came to me vividly, and I felt an unbearably sharp sense of shame at being alive. Now that we were divided by life and death, I would never again behold his majestic appearance. Deep and bitter was my regret at not having followed him.

Each detail, every step of the funeral, was heartbreaking. Since officials were not wearing mourning for a Prince-Regent, court attendants and eunuchs had to make do with pale blue. Then the offerings to the deceased posed problems. Fearful that our preparations might cause royal anger, we were exceedingly cautious. However, no royal order either to cancel or to lessen the offerings came. Thus the offerings on each morning and evening as well as the bimonthly offerings of the first and the fifteenth were duly performed. I just could not bear to permit my son, his wife, or my daughters to view their father before the body was enclosed in the coffin. It was only on the first day when we wore formal mourning costumes that I permitted them to wail with me. The Grand Heir's cry was so sorrowful, so truly heartrending, that no one remained unmoved. The funeral was scheduled for the seventh month. Before that, Lady Sŏnhŭi came to see me. Seeing the Prince's coffin, she hit her head against it and beat her breast, weeping violently. How bottomless her emotion must have been!

On the day of the funeral,[27] His Majesty went to the new grave and wrote the tablet himself.* How did it fare between them now, father and son separated by life and death? I could not imagine.

In the seventh month, the Crown Prince Tutorial Office was established, and the Grand Heir officially became the Crown Prince.[28] This, of course, was bestowed by his sagacious grace, but still, my father's devoted protection of the young heir shone brightly in this.

In the eighth month, His Majesty came to Ch'angdŏk Palace to attend the bimonthly sacrifice at the Ancestral Shrine. Though I was uncomfortable, not paying respect to him would have been too distressing, and so I went to see him at Sŭpch'wi Hall near

---

* Yŏngjo is reported to have said that although the affair of the thirteenth was a matter concerning the dynasty, on this day, he mourned his son as a father. *YS*, 100:4a–b.

the shrine. Though ten thousand grievous thoughts swirled inside me, I did not dare express even one. I merely said, "That mother and son are preserved is due entirely to Your Majesty's sagacious grace."

His Majesty took my hand and wept, "Not thinking that you would be like this, I was troubled by the thought of facing you. It is beautiful of you to put me at ease."

Upon hearing his words, my heart fell and I felt a great weight on my chest so oppressive that I could not breathe. The severity of my life grew suddenly vivid to me. Thereupon, I said to him, "This person humbly wishes that Your Majesty take the Grand Heir with you to Kyŏnghŭi Palace to instruct him."

He asked, "Do you think you could bear to part with him?"

I answered in tears, "It is a small matter that I would miss him, but it is a matter of great importance that he be properly instructed by being near Your Majesty."

It was thus decided that the Grand Heir would be sent to the upper palace. The parting of mother and son, situated as we were, was truly painful. The Grand Heir did not seem to be able to tear himself away from me. He finally left, soaked in tears. I felt as though my heart was being cut by a knife, but I had to endure it.

Boundless, indeed, was his sagacious grace. His love for the Grand Heir was most profound. Moreover, Lady Sŏnhŭi transferred her maternal love from her son to her grandson. With undivided attention, she looked after his daily needs and his meals, rendering the most devoted protection. Given her situation, how could she not be like that?

As the Grand Heir had been fond of books since he was four or five years old, I never worried that, even staying at a different palace, he might neglect his studies. But I missed him more intensely each day. His longing for his mother was also so great that each morning when he awoke he sent me a note of greeting. Only after receiving my reply before the morning study session could he put his mind at ease. He was like this for the entire three years that we lived apart. How strangely mature he was! During those three years, I was in poor health and almost continuously ill. From afar, my son consulted with physicians and had medicine prepared and sent to me, all in the manner of an adult. This was due to his Heaven-endowed filial nature. Still it was most unusual for a boy, just a little over ten years of age, to be like that.

On the Grand Heir's birthday* that year I felt poorly, but in compliance with royal orders, I went up to Kyŏnghŭi Palace. In an audience, His Majesty showed more sympathy and compassion than ever before. I was staying during the mourning period in a small house with a low ceiling to the south of Kyŏngch'un Pavilion. His Majesty conferred the name Kahyo Hall, the Hall of Praiseworthy Filiality, on that house. He wrote those characters on a piece of paper and ordered that this calligraphy be inscribed on a wooden plaque to be hung over the entrance. "Today I am writing this in repayment for your filial heart." I tearfully accepted his calligraphy, although I was uneasy because I felt undeserving of the encomium.

My father was profoundly moved when he heard of it. "His Majesty is having the two letters *ka hyo* inscribed on the plaque. This will be a treasure for our family for successive generations. I revere and admire both the parental affection of His Majesty and the filial devotion of Her Ladyship on whom this was so deservedly bestowed," he announced to the family. As a way of expressing proper gratitude to his sagacious grace, he then adopted the name of the hall as a family motto to be used in correspondence. Our gratitude was such that it was as though the characters were inscribed on our bones. Later when my son became king, he had a special house, Chagyŏng Pavilion, built for me. My situation did not warrant that I live in a tall and glittering house, but I was persuaded by his sagacious filial piety and decided to spend the remaining years of my life there. So I had the plaque with Kahyo Hall inscribed upon it moved and hung over the southern gate of Chagyŏng Pavilion. This was in remembrance of my indebtedness to His Majesty King Yŏngjo and to pay tribute to his boundless affection.

In the twelfth month of that year, the Manchu envoy came.† Accompanied by the Grand Heir, His Majesty went to Prince Sado's mourning chamber to receive the imperial condolences. He was about to return to his palace with the Grand Heir, but he saw that his grandson was crying, sad to part again from his mother. He

---

* Chŏngjo's tenth birthday.
† The envoy came to pay condolences to Yŏngjo for the death of Prince Sado. *YS*, 100:26a–b.

said, "The Grand Heir cannot bring himself to part from you. How about leaving him here?"

Lest His Majesty feel wounded that his wholehearted affection for his grandson was not reciprocated or that this child thought only of his mother, I said, "He says that when he is down here, he longs for Your Majesty, and when he goes up to the upper palace, he longs for his mother. He would cry like this if Your Majesty were to go back without him, so please take him with you."

His Majesty immediately broke into a happy smile. "As you say." He took the Grand Heir with him.

Hurt that his mother was sending him away with no regard for human sentiment, my son went away crying endlessly. I do not have to say how I felt. His staying with me, however, was the way of private affection; the right way lay in his going up to attend His Majesty, learning and being trained in governance, and taking up the duties of a descendant, those same duties that his father had left unfulfilled. So I sent him away, sundering the attachment that causes us to cling in parting and to miss one another in separation.

Remembering the past as a warning, I was deeply concerned that the Grand Heir be wholeheartedly filial to His Majesty and that he not in the slightest degree betray His Majesty's affection. It was not purely for the private love of my son that I was worried. The safety and danger of the monarchy hung upon the person of the Grand Heir, and Heaven can vouch for the depth of anxiety that this caused me. This was not because I was naturally public-spirited, but rather because my father had guided me, instructing me with great principle to ignore the feminine tendency toward softhearted partiality. No one knows how thoroughly and tirelessly my father worked, with devotion and loyalty, for the Grand Heir and for the state.

When, after an interval, the Grand Heir would come down to the mourning chamber, he would wail with such true sorrow that no one who heard it was unmoved. As soon as the Grand Heir came to wail, Prince Sado's wooden tablet, which had seemed solitary and unattended, seemed to welcome his son, and the lonely mourning chamber appeared to be shrouded in light. Amidst that deep sorrow, this was quite comforting. I often wondered what would have happened to the monarchy and the nation if I had not given birth to the Grand Heir. It must be that the monarchy, thrown prostrate, was meant to be preserved by this felicitous birth in *imsin* (1752) that followed the birth in the *kyŏngo* year (1750).

The calamity of the *imo* year (1762) was unprecedented in history; my husband was terribly unfortunate to meet such a fate. But as he had a son who inherited his father's place and as there was no gap between His Majesty's love and the Grand Heir's filial devotion, who would have dreamed that further misfortune would be inflicted upon him? Thus the royal decree that came in the second month of *kapsin* (1764) was beyond my most overwrought imaginings.* Though subordinates should not say anything about what superiors do, the dismay and wretchedness this act caused in me was simply incomparable. Bitter regret that I lived rather than doing away with this odious life of mine at the time of the tragedy again swelled within me. Was this what I had lived for? How keenly did I feel the temptation to end my life right then and there! However, lest my death appear to be a protest against the royal decision, I resolutely took hold of myself and restrained the urge. My inconsolable misery was not less than what I had felt during that tragic year. Lady Sŏnhŭi also was so shocked and grieved that she was unable to take food for days. How can I record how it felt?

The Grand Heir in his tender years had borne pain unmatched by anyone past or present. The terrifying event of that year was something unwonted in the royal house, and he grieved deeply. When he took off the heavy mourning garb at the conclusion of the mourning for his father, he wailed so pitifully that his cries seemed to penetrate Heaven and Earth; indeed, they sounded even more sorrowful than did the Heaven-and-Earth-stopping cries that began his mourning.

By the *kapsin* year (1764), the Grand Heir was two years older; what he had to bear seemed to be even more trying and bitter. When I saw him, my liver and spleen felt as though metal was being melted or a stone was being ground inside of me, and I was again seized with the desire to instantaneously end my life. However, I could not bear the thought of the deep sorrow this would inflict upon the Grand Heir. Without me, he would be even lonelier and more isolated. As the situation became more precarious, it

---

* The decree that made Chŏngjo a posthumously adopted son of Prince Hyojang.

grew ever more vitally important that I protect him. Having resolved not to kill myself, I consoled the Grand Heir. I told him
again and again that the sadder he felt, the more careful he should
be in taking care of his precious person, and though things did
seem terribly regrettable, he should be good so that he might one
day repay his father. With repeated pleas and exhortations, I managed to calm him. He had taken no food at all that day, crying the
whole time. He looked so pitiable that I let him lie down next to
me. I hugged him and whispered soothing words to make him fall
asleep. It took a long time before he did. What a miserable sight!

That fateful day was the eleventh day of the second month.[29] I
simply could not fathom why His Majesty made that decision.* He
suddenly and unexpectedly arrived at Ch'angdŏk Palace, paid a
long ritual visit to the Sŏnwŏn-jŏn,† and came to see me afterward.
I dared not say anything. I just said, "That mother and son are
alive today is due to your sagacious grace. Though Your Majesty
made that decision, what can this humble person say." "It is right
that you be that way," he answered. Living as I was with that
painful memory, would that I had been spared this grievous bitterness! Life seemed to hold still greater trials for me. The desire to
thrash myself was indeed strong. Ah! How beyond compare was
my situation!

In the seventh month, Lady Sŏnhŭi came to attend a post-
mourning sacrifice for Prince Sado. On that occasion, Her Ladyship promised me firmly that in the autumn she and I would get
together to talk things over. Suddenly it was found that she had a
stomach tumor; on the twenty-sixth of the seventh month, she
passed away.‡ My grief cannot be compared to the usual grief of
daughter-in-law for mother-in-law. For the sake of the country,

* The most probable rationale was to remove any connotation of criminality
from Chŏngjo by dissociating him as far as possible from Prince Sado. See
Introduction, 18.

† To ritually announce his decision to make Chŏngjo an adopted son of his
older son, Prince Hyojang.

‡ After reporting Lady Sŏnhŭi's death, the *Sillok* contains a passage saying that,
to her great merit, she had protected the state and the king in a time of misfortune
and crisis (*YS*, 104:6a). Yŏngjo composed a eulogy in which he pays tribute to her
"loyalty transcending private love, which saved the dynasty from the brink of
ruin." He then conferred a title on her, *Ŭiyŏl* (Shining righteousness). See Yŏngjo,
Ŏje py'oŭirok, manuscript, 1764, Changsŏgak. Yŏngjo also wrote a necrology that
is inscribed on porcelain tablets. He attributes the preservation of the dynasty to
her. See figure 9.

she was forced to do what a loving mother cannot, and though this was for her lord the King, what terrible pain she must have suffered. She used to say, "I did that unbearable thing; not even grass will grow on my grave."

She also said, "My true concern was for the monarchy and the safety of the sagacious person; still it was cruel and heartless. You know my intention, but what will the Grand Heir and his sisters think?" At night she would not go to bed. She would sit in the wooden corridor to the east of her chamber. Gazing toward the east, she would ponder sadly: "Could the monarchy have survived without my resorting to that act? Did I err? Was I wrong?" But then she would correct herself: "Oh, no. It is but the weakness of women that I think thus. Never! I could not have been wrong!" When Her Ladyship came to the Prince's temporary shrine,* she called to her son and wept inconsolably. Her grief seemed to turn into that tumor that ended her. Ah! Sadness.

Who among those now living knows the event of that year as I do, and whose grief is as deep as mine or my son's? Whose devotion to Prince Sado has been as constant as mine? That is why I used to say to my son, the late King, "True, Your Highness is his son, but you were young at that time, and so you would not know about it in such detail as do I. When it comes to that year, Your Highness should ask me.† Do not believe what others have to say. To gain Your Highness's favor, they may gather rumors from all over the country and repeat them to you, but all are unscrupulous fabrications." The late King used to answer, "Please do not think that I don't know it. Those rascals are always accusing me of being wanting in filial devotion [to my father], and I wish to avoid their criticism. Neither can I bring myself, as a son, to contradict anyone if someone is held up as having been good to Prince Sado. So I offer posthumous offices and titles to anyone they name. When it comes to things that concern that matter, I cannot avoid being confused, one who, knowing the truth, still does as he is urged." I could not bear to think of his inner pain.

There are two versions of the incident of that year. Both are equally narrow, one-sided, and untrue. One is that His Majesty's decision was noble and just, one to be upheld as estimable to

---

* A temporary shrine was set up during the mourning period.
† Chŏngjo is said to have expressed admiration for his mother's memory. *Sunjo sillok*, in *Chosŏn wangjo sillok*, 19:5a–b.

Heaven and Earth. This view holds that for that great deed, His Majesty should be praised for sagacious virtue. It expresses no regret for Prince Sado's death. In short, Prince Sado is turned into an unfilial person and a criminal, while His Majesty's act is placed in the same category as casting out an enemy nation or pacifying a rebellion. In this case, what would become of Prince Sado and where would this leave the late King, his son? This certainly is too disparaging of them.

The other version is that, though Prince Sado had no illness, His Majesty listened to slanders and committed that terribly excessive act. Those who subscribe to this view promote revenge and the restoration of honor. They might sound as though they wish to clear Prince Sado of wrongdoing, but from this viewpoint, His Late Majesty inflicted that cruel fate on the guiltless Crown Prince on account of some slander. Of what malfeasance does this accuse His Late Majesty? Both versions are defamatory to the three generations, and neither is factually correct in any way.

I agree with the way my late father often described the event: The illness [of Prince Sado] reached such a point that the safety of His Late Majesty's person and the dynasty hung in the balance. Though immensely grieved and pained, His Majesty had no choice but to resort to that act. As for Prince Sado, when he was his true self, he was deeply concerned lest he commit misconduct. Frustratingly, illness deprived him of Heaven's endowment; he did not know what he was doing. It was lamentable that he fell victim to that illness, but there is a saying that even a sage cannot escape illness. Under the circumstances, he cannot be charged with misconduct in the slightest degree. I speak the truth and describe the situation as it was. I say this because I believe that only when the truth is known will His Late Majesty's act be perceived as unavoidable, one to which he turned, in agony and grief, as a very last resort. Only then will Prince Sado be seen as having met that misfortune because of that terrible illness. When it comes to the late King [Chŏngjo], one should speak of his grief separately from his duty, in order not to distort the truth. Only then will his human emotion, as well as his duty, receive their just due.

As for these two versions, one attributes misdeeds to His Late Majesty. The other blames the misconduct on Prince Sado and invites embarrassment to the late King. They are both clearly blasphemous to the three generations. Those who uphold His Late Majesty's decision as noble wish to find fault with my late father, saying that it was he who brought in 'that thing.'* I have noted elsewhere that it could not possibly have been my father, and so I will not discuss it here. But when one speaks thus, is he being loyal to His Late Majesty, faithful to Prince Sado? Since the late King accepted everything concerning the event of that year, regardless of the truthfulness or origin of the claim, and since he could not bring himself to deny a charge if it concerned events of that day, the unscrupulous knowingly took advantage of this weakness. They distorted truth and fabricated what suited them. Hurting people in this way, they proclaimed themselves to be loyal officials. Where else in all of history does one see such things?

The event of that year has caused confusion between loyalty and disloyalty and between truth and falsity for these last forty years. Things have not been dealt with straightforwardly. Once Prince Sado's illness reached its height, nothing could be done; His Late Majesty's decision could not have been avoided. As for 'that fateful thing,' it was His Late Majesty himself who thought of it. Both myself and the late King had our deep private pain, but we also knew our duty. Despite our grief, we were thankful to his sagacious grace, who perpetuated the dynastic mission by letting us live. It is very unfortunate that what ministers and officals said or might have said during that trying time has been willfully misinterpreted and imagined by those who came afterwards and that many unlikely stories are circulating about. There simply is no room to allow even one loose word about the event of that year, be it from the ruler or his officials, be it from above or below.

I really did not have the heart to record the way the event of that year came about. Upon reconsideration, I felt that it was not right that the present King, a direct descendant, did not know how things stood at the time. I was also concerned that he might not be able to discern right from wrong. Compelled by these consid-erations, I forced myself to write. Many things were hard to speak of; some were just too painful for me to write about—and these amounted to quite a few in number—and I have left them out. Still, I have managed to write this in my white-haired old age. The hatefulness and hard-heartedness of humans are simply without limit. Calling upon Heaven and weeping in pain, I lament my fate.

* The rice chest.

Appendixes

Appendix 1: Genealogical Table of the Yi Royal House

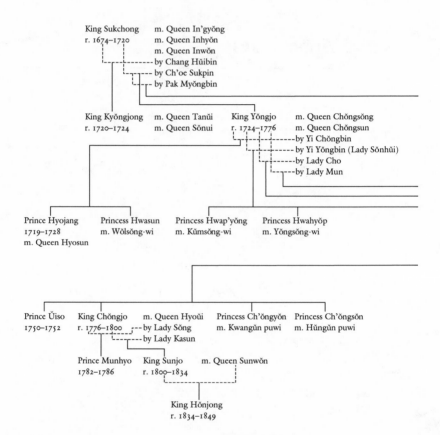

King Sukchong   m. Queen In'gyŏng
r. 1674–1720   m. Queen Inhyŏn
                 m. Queen Inwŏn
                 by Chang Hŭibin
                 by Ch'oe Sukpin
                 by Pak Myŏngbin

King Kyŏngjong   m. Queen Tanŭi   King Yŏngjo   m. Queen Chŏngsŏng
r. 1720–1724   m. Queen Sŏnui   r. 1724–1776   m. Queen Chŏngsun
                                                    by Yi Chŏngbin
                                                    by Yi Yŏngbin (Lady Sŏnhŭi)
                                                    by Lady Cho
                                                    by Lady Mun

Prince Hyojang   Princess Hwasun   Princess Hwap'yŏng   Princess Hwahyŏp
1719–1728   m. Wŏlsŏng-wi   m. Kŭmsŏng-wi   m. Yŏngsŏng-wi
m. Queen Hyosun

Prince Ŭiso   King Chŏngjo   m. Queen Hyoŭi   Princess Ch'ŏngyŏn   Princess Ch'ŏngsŏn
1750–1752   r. 1776–1800   by Lady Sŏng   m. Kwangŭn puwi   m. Hŭngŭn puwi
                               by Lady Kasun

Prince Munhyo   King Sunjo   m. Queen Sunwŏn
1782–1786   r. 1800–1834

King Hŏnjong
r. 1834–1849

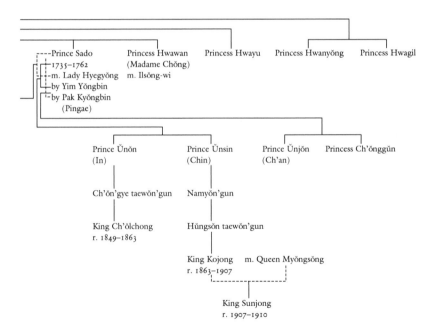

Prince Yŏllyŏng
1699–1719

----Prince Sado
  ┌1735–1762
  ┼-m. Lady Hyegyŏng
  └by Yim Yŏngbin
  ┴-by Pak Kyŏngbin
    (Pingae)

Princess Hwawan   Princess Hwayu   Princess Hwanyŏng   Princess Hwagil
(Madame Chŏng)
m. Ilsŏng-wi

Prince Ŭnŏn   Prince Ŭnsin   Prince Ŭnjŏn   Princess Ch'ŏnggŭn
(In)   (Chin)   (Ch'an)

Ch'ŏn'gye taewŏn'gun   Namyŏn'gun

King Ch'ŏlchong   Hŭngsŏn taewŏn'gun
r. 1849–1863

King Kojong   m. Queen Myŏngsŏng
r. 1863–1907

King Sunjong
r. 1907–1910

Appendix 2: Genealogical Table of the Hong Family

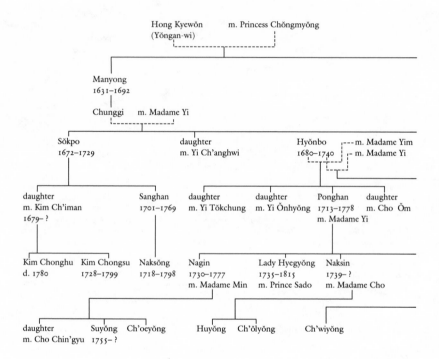

Hong Kyewŏn   m. Princess Chŏngmyŏng
(Yŏngan-wi)

Manyong
1631–1692

Chunggi   m. Madame Yi

Sŏkpo   daughter   Hyŏnbo   ---m. Madame Yim
1672–1729   m. Yi Ch'anghwi   1680–1740 ---m. Madame Yi

daughter   Sanghan   daughter   daughter   Ponghan   daughter
m. Kim Ch'iman   1701–1769   m. Yi Tŏkchung   m. Yi Ŏnhyŏng   1713–1778   m. Cho Ŏm
1679–?   m. Madame Yi

Kim Chonghu   Kim Chongsu   Naksŏng   Nagin   Lady Hyegyŏng   Naksin
d. 1780   1728–1799   1718–1798   1730–1777   1735–1815   1739–?
                                         m. Madame Min m. Prince Sado m. Madame Cho

daughter   Suyŏng   Ch'oeyŏng   Huyŏng   Ch'ŏlyŏng   Ch'wiyŏng
m. Cho Chin'gyu   1755–?

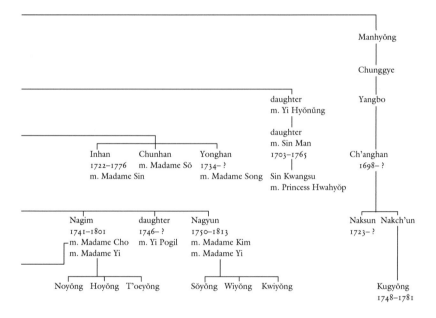

Manhyŏng

Chunggye

			daughter m. Yi Hyŏnŭng	Yangbo
			daughter m. Sin Man	
Inhan	Chunhan	Yonghan	1703–1765	Ch'anghan
1722–1776	m. Madame Sŏ	1734–?		1698–?
m. Madame Sin		m. Madame Song	Sin Kwangsu	
			m. Princess Hwahyŏp	

Nagim	daughter	Nagyun		Naksun Nakch'un
1741–1801	1746–?	1750–1813		1723–?
m. Madame Cho	m. Yi Pogil	m. Madame Kim		
m. Madame Yi		m. Madame Yi		

Noyŏng Hoyŏng T'oeyŏng   Sŏyŏng Wiyŏng Kwiyŏng   Kugyŏng
                                                                        1748–1781

Appendix 3: Genealogical Table of the Kyŏngju Kim Family

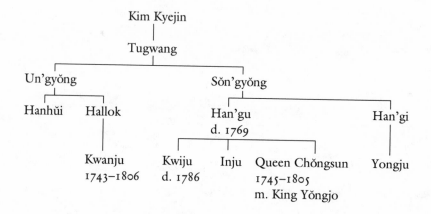

Notes

Introduction

1. In Chosŏn Korea, the personal name of a woman was not recorded. In most records, a woman was referred to by her familial position as a daughter, wife, or mother of someone. Within the royal family, women were known by their titles. Lady Hyegyŏng was one of her titles, and the one by which she is most widely known.

2. If there were no children and no dependent parents, a widow's following her husband to death was viewed as the ultimate in conjugal loyalty. The Chosŏn government even recognized widows who chose this alternative by posthumously granting them a red gate before their houses in commemoration. For details, see Pak Chu, *Chosŏn ŭi chŏngp'yo chŏngch'aek* (Seoul: Ilchogak, 1990).

3. Prince Sado's "crimes," which may have included an attempted regicide, would have belonged to a category that required the punishment of his family. For a discussion of this, see JaHyun Kim Haboush, *A Heritage of Kings: One Man's Monarchy in the Confucian World* (New York: Columbia University Press, 1988), 230–31.

4. I am referring to Chŏngjo, Prince Sado's son by Lady Hyegyŏng, who was then the Grand Heir. Apparently, Chŏngjo was regarded as the only heir at the time of Sado's death. Nonetheless, Sado had three secondary sons born of secondary consorts. Strictly speaking, they were potential heirs, and when Chŏngjo's line came to an end in the nineteenth century, the Yi royal house was continued by the descendants of Sado's secondary sons.

5. Estelle C. Jelinek, *The Tradition of Women's Autobiography: From Antiquity to the Present* (Boston: Twayne Publishers, 1986). For a discussion of women autobiographers' difficulty in self-assertion, see Patricia Meyer Spacks, "Selves in Hiding," in *Women's Autobiography*, ed. Estelle C. Jelinek (Bloomington: Indiana University Press, 1980), 93–111.

6. Major works include *The Gossamer Years*, trans. Edward Seiden-sticker (Tokyo and Rutland, Vt.: Tuttle, 1964); *Murasaki Shikibu: Her Diary and Poetic Memoirs*, trans. Richard Bowring (Princeton: Princeton University Press, 1982); *The Izumi Shikibu Diary*, trans. Edwin A. Cranston (Cambridge, Mass.: Harvard University Press, 1969). For a discussion of the introspective nature of these diaries, see Richard Bowring, "The Female Hand in Heian Japan: A First Reading," in *The Female Autograph*, ed. Domna C. Stanton (Chicago: University of Chicago Press, 1984), 49–56.

7. This is Laden's phrase. See Marie-Paule Laden, *Self-Imitation in the Eighteenth Century Novel* (Princeton: Princeton University Press, 1987), 12.

8. Ibid., 13.

9. On the relationship between narratives and society, see William Ray, *Story and History* (Oxford: Basil Blackwell, 1990), 1–29.

10. Beginning with the *Wang Och'ŏnch'ukkuk chŏn* (Travel diary to the five Indias), a travel journal written by a monk in the eighth century, there are numerous travel diaries, mostly to China and Japan. See *The Hye Ch'o Diary: Memoir of the Pilgrimage to the Five Regions of India* trans. Han-sung Yang et al. (Berkeley: Asian Humanities Press); *Yŏnhaengnok sŏnjip*, 2 vols. (Seoul: Taedong munhwa yŏn'guwŏn, Sŏnggyun'gwan University, 1960–1962); *Kugyŏk haehaeng ch'ongjae*, 11 vols. (Seoul: Minjok munhwa ch'ujinhoe, 1978–1988). For a discussion of miscellaneous writings, see Peter H. Lee, *A Korean Storyteller's Miscellany* (Princeton: Princeton University Press, 1989), 1–56.

11. *Tanam mallok* by Min Chinwŏn (1664–1736), the famous states-man and leader of the Noron faction, is an exception to the norm. It reports King Sukchong's cruel chastisement of his son, Kyŏngjong, and the latter's mental inertia. Min Chinwŏn, *Tanam mallok*, 2 *ch'aek*, manuscript, n.d., Kyujanggak, 1:47b–48a.

12. A memorial is a formal composition sent to the ruler. During the Chosŏn dynasty, those who were allowed to send memorials included offi-cials and educated men who could write the memorial in literary Chinese. Memorials offered a channel of participation in public discourse. Most memorials concerned public policy.

13. Hong Ponghan, *Igikchae mallok*, 2 *ch'aek*, manuscript, n.d., Kyujanggak.

14. Pei-yi Wu, *The Confucian's Progress* (Princeton: Princeton Univer-sity Press, 1990), 4–10.

15. As for these subgenres, ibid., 4–5, 20, 24, 32, 35, 53, 156.

16. Because Hong Nagin predeceased his father by one year, this life chronology was completed by someone else. Hong Nagin, *Sŏnbugun yŏnboryak*, manuscript, n.d., Kyujanggak. See *The Memoir of 1802*.

17. His younger sons are Hong Naksin (1739–?), Hong Nagim (1741–1801), and Hong Nagyun (1750–1813).

18. Hong Naksin, *Sŏnbugun yusa*, manuscript, n.d., Kyujanggak.

19. Kim Ilgŭn, *Ŏn'gan ŭi yŏn'gu* (Seoul: Kŏn'guk taehakkyo ch'ul-p'anbu, 1986), 187–250.

20. For a discussion of the effectiveness of the epistolary form, see Ian Watt, *The Rise of the Novel* (Berkeley: University of California Press, 1957), 187–211. For examples in Korea, see Kim Ilgŭn, *Ŏn'gan*, 186–87, 238–39.

21. Examples of romans à clef include *Kyech'uk ilgi* (The Notebook of 1613) and *Inhyŏn wanghu chŏn* (The story of Queen Inhyŏn). For a translation of the latter, see *The True History of Queen Inhyŏn*, in *Virtuous Women: Three Classic Korean Novels* (Seoul: Royal Asiatic Society, Korea Branch, 1974), 181–233. For a discussion of these works as court novels, see So Chaeyŏng, "Kungjŏng sosŏl non" in *Ko sosŏl t'ongnon* (Seoul: Iu ch'ulp'ansa, 1983), 211–43. For a discussion classifying them as documentary literature, see Chŏng Ŭnim, *Kungjŏng munhak yŏn'gu* (Seoul: Sŏlt'ŏ, 1993).

22. For example, *Sangdŏk ch'ongnok*, a necrology of Ch'ae Chegong (1720–1799), the famous statesman, by his daughter-in-law. Chŏng Ssi puin, *Sangdŏk ch'ongnok*, *Munhak sasang* (Oct., 1977): 384–94; (Nov., 1977): 382–88; (Jan., 1978): 328–34.

23. Prose fiction, for example, was written in Chinese and vernacular Korean and works written in one language were frequently translated into the other. For a discussion of the relationship between the two traditions, see JaHyun Kim Haboush, "Dual Nature of Culture Discourse in Chosŏn Korea," in *Contact between Cultures, East Asia: History and Social Science*, ed. Bernard Hung-Kay Luk (Lampeter, Dyfed, U.K.: Ellen Mellen Press, 1992), 4:194–96.

24. Patricia Meyer Spacks, *Imagining a Self* (Cambridge: Harvard University Press, 1976), 209.

25. Georges Gusdorf, "Conditions and Limits of Autobiography," in *Autobiography: Essays Theoretical and Critical*, ed. James Olney (Princeton: Princeton University Press, 1980), 29–30.

26. There are numerous articles and books on this topic. Notable ones include Nancy Chodorow, *The Reproduction of Mothering: Psychoanalysis and the Sociology of Gender* (Berkeley: University of California Press, 1978); Elaine Showalter, ed., *Speaking of Gender* (London: Routledge, 1989).

27. Mary G. Mason, "The Other Voice: Autobiographies of Women Writers," in *Autobiography*, ed. Olney, 210–12.

28. See her reasons for writing her autobiography as quoted in ibid., 208.

29. Ibid., 212–13.

30. See the discussion on the texts. For details, see JaHyun Kim Haboush, "The Texts of the *Memoirs of Lady Hyegyŏng*: The Problem of Authenticity," *Gest Library Journal* 5, no. 2 (Winter 1992): 29–48.

31. So, "Kungjŏng sosŏl non," 211–43.

32. For various opinions concerning the genre of this work, see Kim Yongsuk, *Hanjungnok yŏn'gu* (Seoul: Han'guk yŏn'guwŏn, 1983), 288–91. More recently, So Chaeyŏng termed *Hanjungnok* a "family novel [*kajŏng/kamun sosŏl*]." So Chaeyŏng, "*Hanjungnok*," in *Han'guk kojŏn*

sosŏl chakp'umnon, ed. Kim Chinse (Seoul: Chipmundang, 1990), 725–38.

33. For a discussion of the relationship between narration and power, see Ray, *Story and History*, 133–85.

34. For examples, see Philippe Lejeune, *On Autobiography*, trans. Katherine Leary (Minneapolis: University of Minnesota Press, 1989), 177–84.

35. For numerous examples of family injunctions, see Kim Chonggwŏn, *Myŏngga ŭi kahun* (Seoul: Myŏngmundang, 1988).

36. Lejeune, *On Autobiography*, 3–30.

37. Northrop Frye, *Anatomy of Criticism* (Princeton: Princeton University Press, 1957), 307–8.

38. On the persecution of Catholics, see James Huntly Grayson, *Early Buddhism and Christianity in Korea* (Leiden: Brill, 1985), 70–100. On Catholic martyrs, see Kim Chang-seok Thaddeus, *Lives of 103 Martyr Saints of Korea* (Seoul: Catholic Publishing House, 1984).

39. Charles Dallet, *Histoire de l'Eglise de Corée* (Paris: n.p., 1874), 1:145.

40. The memorial was sent by Yi Simdo, the censor general, in the ninth month of 1808. It discusses the ill-effects of royal affinal relatives, concentrating especially on the Hong family. *Sunjo sillok* (hereafter *SS*), in *Chosŏn wangjo sillok*, 48 vols. plus index (Seoul: Kuksa p'yŏnch'an wiwŏnhoe, 1955–1963), 11:27a–28a.

41. *SS*, 12:3a–9a.

42. For a discussion of a similar phenomenon in China, see Wu, *Confucian's Progress*, 8–9.

43. Lady Hyegyŏng's memory is reputed to have been remarkable. Chŏngjo is said to have expressed his admiration for her memory, erudition, and intelligence. *SS*, 19:5a–b.

44. For a discussion of this conflict as it is represented in Korean popular literature, see JaHyun Kim Haboush, "Filial Emotions and Filial Values: Changing Patterns in the Discourse of Filiality in Late Chosŏn Korea." *Harvard Journal of Asiatic Studies* 55, no. 1 (June 1995): 168–75.

45. In Chosŏn Korea, an unmarried daughter observed three years of mourning for her parents. A married woman, however, observed one year of mourning for her natal parents but three years of mourning for her parents-in-law. See Martina Deuchler, *Confucian Transformation of Korea* (Cambridge: Harvard University Press, 1993), 267. Since Lady Hyegyŏng became the Crown Princess Consort, her mourning for her mother was further shortened.

46. Valerie Sanders, *The Private Lives of Victorian Women: Autobiography in Nineteenth-Century England* (Brighton: Harvester Wheatsheaf, 1989), 53, 67, 71.

47. This was done right after Sado's funeral. *Yŏngjo sillok* (hereafter *YS*), in *Chosŏn wangjo sillok*, 99:24b, 100:4b.

48. Kyŏngjong's mental malfunction is mentioned in several accounts by his tutors and officials. Yi Chae, *Samgwan'gi*, 2:22b in *P'aerim* 10 vols. (Seoul: T'amgudang, 1970); Min, *Tanam mallok*, 2:8b–9a.

49. Kyŏngjong was responsible for every administrative decision except appointments and dismissals of officials, criminal cases, and military affairs. *Sŭngjŏngwŏn ilgi*, 115 vols. (Seoul: Kuksa p'yŏnch'an wiwŏnhoe, 1961–1970), 27:194.

50. Kyŏngjong was said to have been impotent. Min, *Tanam mallok*, 2:8b–9a.

51. Procedurally, Sado's regency followed that of Kyŏngjong (*YS*, 69:5b–6b). For details of Sado's regency, see *The Memoir of 1805*. Also, Haboush, *Heritage*, 166–230.

52. For the *Sillok* view, see *YS*, 125:18a–b. The compilation of *Yŏngjo sillok* began in 1776, soon after Hong Inhan's execution. It was completed in 1780.

53. *YS*, 125:19b–21b.

54. See p. 100. The *Sillok* says that Hong Inhan, in alliance with Hugyŏm, repeatedly persecuted Chŏngjo and tried to harm him. *YS*, 125:23b.

55. *SS*, 10:2b–3b.

56. *Ch'ŏlchong sillok*, in *Chosŏn wangjo sillok*, 7:5b. Kim Yongsuk, *Hanjungnok yŏn'gu*, 360–64.

57. *Chŏngjo sillok* (hereafter *CS*), in *Chosŏn wangjo sillok*, 1:2b.

58. It was not until 1899 that Prince Sado and Lady Hyegyŏng were offered full honors and given the titles King Changjo and Queen Kyŏngŭi. *Kojong sillok*, 4 vols. (Seoul: T'amgudang, 1970–1979), 39:84b–85b.

59. In fact, there was mounting pressure to do this. *CS*, 34:58a–60b, 35:8b–10b.

60. *CS*, 35:14a–19b.

61. One of these paintings was auctioned at Christie's in New York for about $600,000 in the fall of 1991. See JaHyun Kim Haboush, "Private and Public in the Court Art of Late Chosŏn Korea," *Korean Culture* 14, no. 2 (Summer 1993). Figures 4 and 5 are two panels from an eight-panel screen-painting depicting Chŏngjo's 1795 visit to Prince Sado's tomb.

62. Haboush, *Heritage*, 224.

63. Ibid., 7–28.

64. For memorials requesting the reversal of this policy, see *CS*, 34:58a–60b, 35:8b–10b, 35:12b–14b.

65. Michel Foucault, *Mental Illness and Psychology* (Berkeley: University of California Press, 1987), 64–75.

66. In 1776, Chŏngjo, then the heir apparent, requested and received permission from Yŏngjo to destroy these records. *YS*, 127:13b–15a.

67. On this, see Haboush, *Heritage*, 117–65.

68. In narrating these memoirs, she seems to embody a spirit reminiscent of that which Burton Watson attributes to the great Chinese historian Ssu-ma Ch'ien (145–90 B.C.), a conviction that "the love and understanding of the historian, in an act resembling religious salvation, rights all the injustices, assuages all the sorrow, and sets down in imperishable words the true form of the individual's life where it may await the understanding of all sympathetic men of the future." Burton Watson, *Ssu-ma*

Ch'ien: Grand Historian of China (New York: Columbia University Press, 1958), 128.

69. See *Hanjungnok* in *Munjang* 1, no. 1 (February 1939): 102–14; 1, no. 2 (March 1939): 177–86; 1, no. 3 (April 1939): 180–6; 1, no. 4 (May 1939): 182–7; 1, no. 5 (June 1939): 189–98; 1, no. 6 (July 1939): 197–201; 1, no. 7 (August 1939): 189–95; 1, no. 8 (September 1939): 195–202; 1, no. 9 (October 1939): 266–77; 1, no. 10 (November 1939): 203–13; 1, no. 11 (December 1939): 179–88; 2, no. 1 (January 1940): 208–19.

70. For a more detailed discussion of texts, see Haboush, "The Texts of the *Memoirs of Lady Hyegyŏng*," 31–46.

71. Kim Yongsuk, *Hanjungnok yŏn'gu*, 22–41.

72. Chaoying Fang, *The Asami Library: A Descriptive Catalogue* (Berkeley: University of California Press, 1969), 193–95.

73. Kim Yongsuk, *Hanjungnok yŏn'gu*, 96–130.

The Memoir of 1795

1. Hong Suyŏng was the oldest son of Hong Nagin, Lady Hyegyŏng's older brother. Since Hong Nagin was the oldest son of Hong Ponghan, Hong Suyŏng was the heir to that branch of the Hong family.

2. Hong Inhan's wife, the daughter of the Deputy Minister of Personnel, Sin Pang.

3. In the Asami Memoir 1-A manuscript that I am following for this memoir, this sentence comes about ten pages later. In putting this sentence here, I am following the arrangement in the Asami complete manuscript version. I am making this exception because it reads much better this way.

4. Hong Hyŏnbo was the great-grandson of Hong Chuwŏn (1606–1672) and Princess Chŏngmyŏng, King Sŏnjo's daughter. He had a respectable official career that included an appointment as Minister of Rites.

5. Hong Ponghan's first sister was the wife of Yi Tŏkchung, who served as first counselor in the Office of the Special Counselors. His second sister married Yi Ŏnhyŏng, whose posts included a governorship. He was the son of Prince Ch'ŏngnŭng, a member of the royal clan. The youngest sister was married to Cho Ŏm (1719–1777), who had an illustrious but troubled career. He was well known for his financial and agricultural management. He died in his place of banishment.

6. Lord Chirye was Lady Hyegyŏng's mother's brother, Yi Pyŏnggŏn.

7. Lady Hyegyŏng's mother's oldest sister married Kim Tarhaeng, the great-grandson of Kim Suhang (1629–1689), a renowned minister of the Noron faction.

8. Lady Hyegyŏng's cousin's father was Song Chaehŭi, who married her mother's sister.

9. The uncle from the main house was Hong Sanghan (1701–1769), who had an illustrious official career that included appointments as Minister of Rites, of Punishment, and of Military Affairs.

10. For details of the wedding, see *Changjo Hŏn'gyŏnghu karye togam ŭigwe*, manuscript, 1744, Kyujanggak.

11. Lord Kwangsŏng was Kim Man'gi (1633–1687), the father of King Sukchong's (r. 1674–1720) first queen, Queen In'gyŏng (1661–1680). He passed the palace examination in 1653 and had a good official career. Lord Yŏyang was Min Yujung (1630–1687), the father of King Sukchong's second queen, Queen Inhyŏn (1667–1701). He passed the palace examination in 1650 and had an illustrious official career. A disciple of the famous Song Siyŏl, he was a renowned scholar.

12. Lord P'ungnŭng was Cho Munmyŏng (1680–1732). Cho was the father of Queen Hyosun, the wife of Prince Hyojang. He passed the preliminary examination in 1705 and the regular *munkwa* in 1713. He had an illustrious career, serving at one point as Minister of the Left. He was Soron but an enthusiastic supporter of Yŏngjo's *t'angp'yŏng* policy, which emphasized balance between factions. See JaHyun Kim Haboush, *A Heritage of Kings: One Man's Monarchy in the Confucian World* (New York: Columbia University Press, 1988), 129–35.

13. Hong Ponghan was appointed Governor of P'yŏngan Province on the third of the tenth month, 1756, and had his farewell audience with Yŏngjo on the following day. *YS*, 88:17b–18a.

14. Queen Chŏngsŏng died on the fifteenth of the second month, 1757 (*YS*, 89:5a). Her funeral cortege left the palace on the third day of the sixth month, 1757, and she was interred at Hongnŭng on the fourth. The *Sillok* notes Sado's grief. *YS*, 89:27a.

15. The *Sillok* does not record Hong Ponghan's dismissal, but the entry of the third of the twelfth month, 1757, says that Hong Ponghan, the former General of the Palace Guard, was reinstated. *YS*, 90:32b.

16. Queen Dowager Inwŏn died on the twenty-sixth of the third month, 1757. *YS*, 89:11a.

17. The uncle of Chŏng Ch'idal, Princess Hwawan's husband, Chŏng Hwiryang was renowned for his scholarship and had an illustrious official career, which included a term as Minister of the Left. Chŏng Ch'idal was Soron, whereas Hong Ponghan was Noron.

18. Chŏng Hugyŏm passed the palace examination in 1766.

19. Hong Ponghan's reappointment as Prime Minister was in the eleventh month of 1768. *YS*, 111:28b.

20. Hong Ponghan was sent into confinement on the ninth of the second month. Ch'ŏngju was in Ch'ungch'ŏng Province. *YS*, 116:9a.

21. Hong Ponghan was appointed Prime Minister in the eleventh month of 1768. He served about fourteen months.

22. Hong Ponghan's confinement was lifted on the eleventh of the second month, two days after it began. *YS*, 116:10a.

23. Princess Ch'ŏngyŏn married Kim Kisŏng in 1764, and Princess Ch'ŏngsŏn married Chŏng Chaehwa in 1766.

24. Chŏngjo posthumously cleared Hong Ponghan of the three charges. *CS*, 18:17b–18b. Also see Chŏngjo, *Hongjae chŏnsŏ*, 5 vols. (Seoul: T'aehaksa, 1986), 32:15b–18b.

25. The splendor of this celebration is described in CS, 42:33b-36a. Also see *Chagung im Hwasŏng haenggung chinsŏn akchang*, manuscript, 1795, Kyujanggak.

26. Lord Kyŏngŭn was Kim Chusin, the father of Queen Inwŏn, and Lord P'ungnŭng was Cho Munmyŏng, the father of Queen Hyosun. See note 12.

27. This novel circulated widely in various manuscript versions. It has a complicated plot centering around Yu Usŏng and his descendants for three generations. Kim Kidong, *Yijo sidae sosŏl ŭi yŏn'gu* (Seoul: Song-mun'gak, 1974), 183-90.

28. Yi Pogil. Very little is known about him.

The Memoir of 1801

NOTE: Approximately two pages at the beginning of *The Memoir of 1801* are missing from the Asami comp-A and Ilsa manuscripts. The Asami text begins with "chinnyŏk haya chusŏn haya naego" (using every means available, [she] succeeded in obtaining royal permission). The Ilsa manuscript begins one and a half lines after the Asami text: "Manil kŭ puma ka yomulch'i anihago" (Had Lord Ilsŏng not died so early). I have followed the Karam manuscript for the missing portion.

1. From this point on, I am following the Asami comp-A manuscript.

2. Hugyŏm passed the final civil examinations in 1766.

3. For a detailed discussion of Yŏngjo's policy to contain the factional politics of the Chosŏn court, see Haboush, *Heritage*, 117-65.

4. The furor erupted early in the third month, and Kim Ch'iin and Kim Chongsu were banished later in the month. Several others were punished along with them. *YS*, 118:21b-26a.

5. After passing the civil service examination in 1753, Hong Inhan served in important positions for most of his career. He was Minister of the Right in 1774 and Minister of the Left in 1775.

6. Hong Kugyŏng (1748-1781) passed the *munkwa* in 1771, served in the Crown Prince Tutorial Office, and became a trusted confidant of the Heir Apparent, Chŏngjo. After Chŏngjo's accession in 1776, to which he was supposed to have contributed by protecting the King during a volatile time of political intrigues, Kugyŏng wielded power.

7. Hong Naksun (1723-?) passed the *munkwa* in 1757 and served in various positions. After his nephew Kugyŏng became powerful, he was appointed to higher office, reaching Minister of the Left in 1779. With Kugyŏng's loss of power in 1780, he was dismissed from the post.

8. Hong Nakch'un, the younger brother of Hong Naksun.

9. For details, see CS, 1:17b-18a.

10. Kim Chin'gwi (1651-1704), the older brother of Queen In'gyŏng, had a relatively illustrious official career punctuated by banishment, as was the norm during this period of intense factional conflict.

11. The regency was enacted on the tenth of the twelfth month, 1775. *YS*, 126:10a-b.

12. After this sentence, about eight lines starting with "kŭ sase rŭl sangsanghakŏndae" and concluding with "NoSoron irŭn tŏok kŭmgi kattaya" are omitted for reasons of repetitiveness. Lady Hyegyŏng is repeatedly saying that Hong Inhan only said, "Why is it necessary for His Highness to know about the Noron and the Soron." She emphatically denies that he said that it was not necessary for Chŏngjo to know about personnel matters or state affairs.

13. This is a paraphrase of what Chŏngjo said. *Sŭngjŏngwŏn ilgi*, 90:506c.

14. *Mujŏng pogam* was first compiled in 1468, but it went through several revisions. *Munhŏn pigo*, 3 vols. (Seoul: Tongguk munhwasa, 1964), vol. 3, 245:17a–b.

15. Sŏnjo restored Yun in 1577, the tenth year of his reign. Queen Dowager Kongŭi (1514–1577) is better known as Queen Insŏng, the wife of King Injong.

16. Kim Chonghu (d. 1780) had a reputation for scholarship. In his political activities, he joined forces with his brother, Chongsu.

17. Kim Chongsu (1728–1799) passed the preliminary examination in 1750 and the final civil examination in 1768.

18. She was chosen in the sixth month of 1778. *CS*, 5:60a.

19. Wŏnbin died in the fifth month of 1779. *CS*, 7:43b–44a.

20. Kugyŏng's persecution of the Queen, though not specified, is described in the *Sillok* as having been quite extreme. *CS*, 8:26b.

21. For details, see *CS*, 8:26a–b. The title Wanp'ung was removed from Tam in 1780. *CS*, 10:19a.

22. In the second month of 1780, in response to mounting official clamor, Chŏngjo agreed to Kugyŏng's confinement. Kugyŏng died in the fourth month of 1781. *CS*, 9:17a–b, 11:58b–59a.

23. About eight lines after this, from "Chongsu ga Kugyŏng ŭl tarigo" to "Kugyŏng kwa tongsimhanjul i ŏtchi soyŏnch'i aniriyo," have been omitted due to repetition.

24. Hong Nagim's own account of why he befriended Chŏng Hugyŏm is more or less similar. *CS*, 5:22a–b.

25. This request is recorded in the *Sillok*. *CS*, 5:22b.

26. See Hong Sanggil's confession in *CS*, 4:25a.

27. This book was published in 1778 under royal auspices. It describes the events from the seventh month of 1777 to the second month of 1778. *Sok Myŏngŭirok*, ed. Kim Ch'iin, 1778, Kyujanggak.

28. The funeral cortege left the palace on the fourth, and the burial took place on the sixth of the eleventh month, 1800. *SS*, 1:32a–33a.

29. Hong Manyong (1631–1692), who served in various offices including Minister of Personnel.

The Memoir of 1802

1. There are a number of official biographies of Chŏngjo at the end of *Chŏngjo sillok*. See *Chŏngjo sillok purok*, in *Chosŏn wangjo sillok*, 1a–59a.

2. Yŏngjo made this point very clearly to his grandson. *Yŏngjo sillok* (hereafter *YS*), in *Chosŏn wangjo sillok*, 104:15a.

3. Chŏngjo's compositions are also found in Chŏngjo's collected works. They come to sixty-eight pieces. Chŏngjo, *Hongjae chŏnsŏ*, 5 vols. (Seoul: T'aehaksa, 1986), 11:1a–13:41a.

4. Hong Ponghan served as the Director of the Relief Agency and later as the civilian head of the Palace Guard.

5. See Chŏngjo's preface. Chŏngjo, ed., *Ŏjŏng Hong Ikchŏnggong chugo*, 18 *ch'aek*, 1815, Kyujanggak, 1:1a–5b.

6. The pressure to exonerate Han Yu mounted in the later years of Chŏngjo's reign, and Chŏngjo acquiesced to it in 1798. *CS*, 50:1a.

7. For details, see *Sado seja yejang togam toch'ŏng ŭigwe*, 2 *ch'aek*, manuscript, 1762, Kyujanggak.

8. Lady Hyegyŏng here says *munjip* (collected works), but as far as can be ascertained, Hong Ponghan's collected works were not published. In addition to *Ŏjŏng Hong Ikchŏnggong chugo* in 18 volumes, which was published in 1815, there is *Igikchae mallok* (Leisurely writings of Igikchae) by Hong Ponghan, 2 *ch'aek*, date unknown. Hong Ponghan was the editor of a number of important court-sponsored works on law and the economy.

9. Kwiju's uncle, Kim Hallok, was a well-known scholar, but the Kim family does not seem to have produced many important officials.

10. Kim Kwanju was the son of Kim Hallok and cousin of Kim Kwiju. He was exiled to Kapsan in 1772. From 1793 he was appointed to minor positions in the provinces including such positions as Magistrate of Tongnae. In 1800 when Sunjo ascended the throne, his group gained power. He served as the Minister of the Right in 1802.

11. The full title of Yŏngjo's book was *Ŏmjebang Yugollok*. The book charged that the so-called scholars of the mountains and forests (*sallim*) were forming themselves into a dangerous faction. *YS*, 104:33a.

12. The *Sillok* records that it was the Censorate that requested Ch'oe Ingnam's trial. *YS*, 115:17a–b.

13. For details, see *YS*, 115:18a–20a.

14. This exchange is also recorded in the *Sillok*. *YS*, 117:7b.

15. Chŏngjo, quoting Yŏngjo, confirms this view. Chŏngjo, *Hongjae chŏnsŏ*, 42:1a.

16. Hong Ponghan was made a commoner on the twelfth of the eighth month, 1771. *YS*, 117:11a–b.

17. For details, see *YS*, 119:6a–12b.

18. For more details on these memorials, mentioned earlier in this memoir, see *CS*, 1:9b–10a, 1:16b–17a.

The Memoir of 1805

1. Lord Kŭmsŏng was Pak Myŏngwŏn (1725–1790). Later, he headed ambassadorial missions to China on several occasions.

2. For a discussion of the daily life of heirs-apparent in the Chosŏn dynasty, see JaHyun Kim Haboush, "The Education of the Yi Crown Prince: A Study in Confucian Pedagogy," in *The Rise of Neo-Confucianism in Korea*, ed. Wm. Theodore de Bary and JaHyun Kim Haboush (New York: Columbia University Press, 1985), 204–7.

3. Princess Hwasun's mother was Lady Yi Chŏngbin.

4. Princess Hwahyŏp was born of Lady Sŏnhŭi.

5. Neither the *Sillok* nor the *Records of the Royal Secretariat* records this memorial.

6. For this episode, see Haboush, *Heritage*, 181–85.

7. Sado sent in a number of memorials begging for rescission of the abdication edict. *Yŏngjo sillok* (hereafter *YS*), in *Chosŏn wangjo sillok*, 78: 10b–20a.

8. *Yangje*, the term for a Crown Prince's secondary consorts of the junior second rank. The person in question was Lady Yim, who was later awarded the title Yŏngbin.

9. Ŭnsŏn and Ŭnŏn were born of the same mother, Lady Yim.

10. For the trial, see *Ch'uan kŭp kugan*, 331 *ch'aek*, manuscript, 1601–1892, Kyujanggak, *ch'aek*, 191–92.

11. The celebration lasted two days, the seventh and eighth of the seventh month. Prince Sado led the congratulatory proceedings on the occasion. *YS*, 88:4a–b.

12. Princess Hwayu was born of Lady Cho.

13. Lord Wŏlsŏng was Kim Hanjin, the son of Prime Minister Kim Hŭnggyŏng (1677–1750).

14. Princess Hwasun died on the seventeenth, thirteen days after her husband, who had died on the fourth. *YS*, 91:2a–b, 91:6a–b.

15. Yŏngjo announced this decision on the twelfth of the second month, and his tutorial staff was appointed on that day. *YS*, 93:6b.

16. The selection was done on the ninth of the sixth month. Kim Han'gu's daughter was chosen to be the new queen, Queen Chŏngsun. *YS*, 93:22b. The royal wedding took three days, from the twentieth to the twenty-second. *YS*, 93:24a. For details, see *Yŏngjo Chŏngsunhu karye togam toch'ŏng ŭigwe*, 2 *ch'aek*, manuscript, 1759, Kyujanggak.

17. The *Sillok* gives similar accounts. *YS*, 96:5a.

18. Chŏngjo performed the ceremony of entrance on the tenth of the third month, 1761. *YS*, 97:10a.

19. The *Sillok* records Prince Sado's meeting with officials on the twenty-second of the fourth month. *YS*, 97:17b.

20. Sado went to Kyŏnghŭi Palace on the seventeenth of the fifth month. *YS*, 97:22b.

21. Lady Hyegyŏng went to the palace on the nineteenth of the fifth month. *YS*, 97:23a.

22. Sin Man (1703–1765) was appointed Prime Minister on the second of the intercalary fifth month, 1762 (*YS*, 99:21a). His father, Sin Sach'ŏl (1671–1759), had a long official career that included directorship at the Board of Rites.

23. For Yŏngjo's reaction and his confrontation with Sado on this day, see Haboush, *Heritage*, 204–5.

24. There are other accounts of this day: a terse *Sillok* account (*YS*, 99:22b–23a) and a minute by minute eyewitness account by a royal historian, Yi Kwanghyŏn (*Yi Kwanghyŏn ilgi*, manuscript, date unknown, Changsŏgak). For a complete translation of these accounts, see Haboush, *Heritage*, 210–12, 219–30.

25. Other sources also confirm that Lady Sŏnhŭi was the one who informed Yŏngjo. Haboush, *Heritage*, 212, 231. Also see the caption to figure 9.

26. That Prince Sado entered the rice chest on his own is very significant. This was an attempt to avoid the appearance of a criminal execution. Yi royal family custom forbade the killing of a member by a method which would disfigure or dismember the body. This left the possibility of a cup of poison, which was often used for members of the upper class. This method, however, connoted a criminal execution, and Prince Sado's wife and children would have suffered. The alternative was for Prince Sado to kill himself by self-strangulation. He tried this several times, but on each occasion the knot was loosened by his tutors, whose duty was to save the Prince. Hence the rice chest. Prince Sado entered it, it was sealed under royal order, and the Prince died in it after eight days. Haboush, *Heritage*, 230–31.

27. The funeral was held on the twenty-third of the seventh month. For details of Prince Sado's funeral, see *Sado seja sangjang tŭngnok*, manuscript, 1762, Changsŏgak.

28. Chŏngjo became Crown Prince on the twenty-fourth of the seventh month, the day after Sado's burial. *YS*, 100:4b.

29. According to the *Sillok*, it was the twentieth of the second month, 1764. *YS*, 103:7b–9a.

Glossary

An'guk-dong	安國洞	Ch'in Kuei	秦檜
Anwa yugo	安窩遺稿	Chinjong	眞宗
Ch'ae Chegong	蔡濟恭	Chiphyŏn-mun	集賢門
Chagyŏng-jŏn	慈慶殿	Chippok-hŏn	集福軒
Ch'an	襸	Cho Chaeho	趙載浩
Chang Hŭibin	張禧嬪	Cho Chin'gyu	趙鎭奎
Chang Kung-i	張公藝	Cho Kwanbin	趙觀彬
Ch'angdŏk-gung	昌德宮	Cho Mun-myŏng	趙文命
Changgyŏng wanghu	章敬王后	Cho Ŏm	趙曮
Changjo	莊祖	Cho T'aeŏk	趙泰億
Ch'angŭi-gung	彰義宮	Cho Ugyu	趙羽逵
Changyun yungbŏm kimyŏng ch'anghyu	章倫隆範基命 昌休	Cho Yŏngsun	趙榮順
		Cho Yŏngŭi	趙榮毅
		Cho Yujin	趙維進
Ch'ao	趙	Ch'oe Ingnam	崔益男
Chao-lieh	昭烈	Ch'oe Myŏng-gil	崔鳴吉
chapki	雜記	Ch'oe Sang-gung	崔尙宮
chapnok	雜錄		
Ch'ech'ŏn kŏn'gŭk sŏnggong sinhwa	體天建極聖功 神化	Ch'oe Sŏkhang	崔錫恒
		Ch'oe Suwŏn	崔守元
		Ch'ŏlchong	哲宗
Cheju-do	濟州島	Ch'ŏmjŏng-gong	僉正公
Ch'ewŏn-hap	體元閤	chŏn/chuan	傳
Chiang Ch'ung	江充	Chŏn Sŏnghae	전 성 해
Chin	禛	Chŏng Chaehwa	鄭在和

355

Chŏng Ch'idal	鄭致達	chubu	主簿
Chŏng Ch'ŏ	鄭妻	chukch'aeng-mun	竹册文
Chŏng Chon'gyŏm	鄭存謙	Ch'unch'ŏn	春川
Chŏng Hong-sun	鄭弘淳	ch'ung	忠
Chŏng Hugyŏm	鄭厚謙	Ch'ungch'ŏng-do	忠清道
Chŏng Hwi-ryang	鄭翬良	Ch'unghŏn-gong	忠獻公
Chŏng Ihwan	鄭履煥	Chungjong	中宗
Chŏng Kwang-han	鄭光漢	Chungjŏng-mun	중정문
Chŏnggan-gong	貞簡公	ch'ungsin	忠臣
Ch'ŏnggŭn hyŏnju	清瑾縣主	Chŭphŭi-dang	緝熙堂
		Ch'wisŏn-dang	就善堂
Chŏnghŏn-gong	貞獻公	Fen-yang wang	汾陽王
		Feng-lai	蓬萊
Ch'ŏnghwi-mun	清輝門	Fu Hsi	伏羲
		Haeju	海州
Chŏngjo	正祖	Han Ch'i	韓琦
Ch'ŏngju	清州	Han Fu-p'i	韓富弼
Chŏngmyŏng kongju	貞明公主	Han Ingmo	韓翼謩
		Han Sanggung	韓尚宮
Chongno-gu	鍾路區	Han Wŏnjin	韓元震
Ch'ŏngnŭng-gun	青陵君	Han Yonggwi	韓用龜
		Han Yu	韓鍮
Ch'ŏngp'ung Kim	清風金	han'gŭl	한글
		Hanjung mallok	한중 만록
Ch'ŏngsŏn kunju	清璿郡主	Hanjungnok	한중록
		Hoesang-jŏn	會祥殿
Chŏngsŏng wanghu	貞聖王后	Hong Ch'ang-han	洪昌漢
Chŏngsun wanghu	貞純王后	Hong Ch'oeyŏng	洪最榮
Ch'ŏngwŏn puwŏn'gun	清原府院君	Hong Ch'ŏlyŏng	洪徹榮
		Hong Chunggi	洪重基
Chŏn'gye taewŏn'gun	全溪大院君	Hong Chung-gye	洪重楷
Ch'ŏngyŏn kunju	清衍郡主	Hong Chunhae	洪準海
		Hong Chunhan	洪駿漢
chonho	尊號	Hong Chuwŏn	洪柱元
Chosŏn	朝鮮	Hong Ch'wiyŏng	洪就榮
Chŏsŭng-jŏn	儲承殿	Hong Hoyŏng	洪好榮
Chou Wen-mu	周文謨	Hong Huyŏng	洪後榮
Chu-ko Liang	諸葛亮	Hong Hyŏnbo	洪鉉輔

Hong Ikchu	洪翊周	Hwagil ongju	和吉翁主
Hong Inhan	洪麟漢	Hwahyŏp ongju	和協翁主
Hong Kambo	洪鑑輔	Hwanch'wi-	環翠堂
Hong Kugyŏng	洪國榮	dang	
Hong Kwiyŏng	洪貴榮	hwangch'ŏn	黃泉
Hong Kyehŭi	洪啓禧	Hwanghae-do	黃海道
Hong Man-	洪萬衡	Hwangsŏng-	橫城縣
hyŏng		hyŏn	
Hong Manyong	洪萬容	Hwan'gyŏng-	歡慶殿
Hong Nagim	洪樂任	jŏn	
Hong Nagin	洪樂仁	Hwanyŏng	和寧翁主
Hong Nagyun	洪樂倫	ongju	
Hong Nakchin	洪樂進	Hwap'yŏng	和平翁主
Hong Nakch'un	洪樂春	ongju	
Hong Nakp'a	洪樂波	Hwasŏng	華城
Hong Naksin	洪樂信	Hwasun ongju	和順翁主
Hong Naksul	洪樂述	Hwawan ongju	和緩翁主
Hong Naksun	洪樂純	Hwayu ongju	和柔翁主
Hong Noyŏng	洪魯榮	Hwinyŏng-jŏn	徽寧殿
Hong Ponghan	洪鳳漢	Hye Ch'o	惠超
Hong Sangbŏm	洪相範	Hyegyŏng-	惠慶宮
Hong Sanggil	洪相吉	gung	
Hong Sanghan	洪象漢	hyo	孝
Hong Seju	洪世周	*Hyogyŏng*/	孝經
Hong Seyŏng	洪世榮	*Hsiao-ching*	
Hong Sŏkpo	洪錫輔	Hyojang seja	孝章世子
Hong Sŏnho	洪善浩	Hyojong	孝宗
Hong Sŏyŏng	洪緖榮	Hyŏllyung-wŏn	顯隆園
Hong Surhae	洪述海	Hyŏnjong	顯宗
Hong Suyŏng	洪守榮	Hyŏnju	縣主
Hong	洪退榮	Hyoso-jŏn	孝昭殿
T'oeyŏng		Hyosun	孝純王后
Hong Ŭiyŏng	洪義榮	wanghu	
Hong Wiyŏng	洪緯榮	Hyoŭi wanghu	孝懿王后
Hong Yangbo	洪良輔	*Igikchae mallok*	翼翼齊漫錄
Hong Yonghan	洪龍漢	Ikchŏng-gong	翼靖公
Hongju	洪州	Illyŏng-hŏn	逸寧軒
Hongnŭng	弘陵	Ilsa	일사
Hŏnjong	憲宗	Ilsŏng-wi	日城尉
Horak	湖洛	imo	壬午
Hŭijŏng	희정	In	祠
Hŭijŏng-dang	熙政堂	In'gyŏng	仁敬王后
Hŭksan-do	黑山島	wanghu	
Hŭngjŏng-	興政堂	Inhyŏn wanghu	仁顯王后
dang		*Inhyŏn wanghu*	인현왕후전
Hŭngsŏn	興宣大院君	*chŏn*	
taewŏn'gun		Inmok wanghu	仁穆王后
Hŭngŭn puwi	興恩副尉	Insŏng wanghu	仁聖王后

Insu wanghu	仁粹王后	Kim Simuk	金時默
Inwŏn wanghu	仁元王后	Kim Sŏngŭng	金聖應
Ka hyo	嘉孝	Kim Sŏn'gyŏng	金選慶
Kaesŏng	開城	Kim Suwan	金수완
Kahyo-dang	嘉孝堂	Kim Tarhaeng	金達行
kajŏng/kamun sosŏl	家庭家門小說	Kim Tonguk	金東旭
		Kim Tugwang	金斗光
Kang	堈	Kim Un'gyŏng	金運慶
Kanghwa-do	江華島	Kim Yakhaeng	金若行
Kangnŭng	江陵	Kim Yongju	金龍柱
Kansin	姦臣	Kim Yongsuk	金用淑
Kapsan	甲山	kisa	己巳
Karam	가람	Kisaeng	妓生
Kasŏn	假仙	Kojong	高宗
Kasun-gung	嘉順宮	Kŏnbok-mun	建福門
Kim Chaero	金在魯	Kongju	公州
Kim Ch'angjip	金昌集	Kongmuk-hap	恭默閣
Kim Ch'iin	金致仁	Kongŭi taebi	恭懿大妃
Kim Ch'iman	金致萬	Kŏnyang-mun	建陽門
Kim Chimuk	金持默	Kŏp'yŏng-dong	居平洞
Kim Chin'gwi	金鎭龜	Kosŏ-hŏn	古書軒
Kim Chonghu	金鍾厚	Koyang	高陽
Kim Chongsu	金鍾秀	Kuang-wu	光武
Kim Chusin	金柱臣	Kŭmsŏng-wi	錦城尉
Kim Hallok	金漢祿	kungjŏng silgi munhak	宮庭實記文學
Kim Hanch'ae	金한채		
Kim Han'gi	金漢耆	kungjŏng sosŏl	宮庭小說
Kim Han'gu	金漢耉	Kuo Tzu-i	郭子儀
Kim Hanhŭi	金漢禧	*Kuun mong*	九雲夢
Kim Hansin	金漢藎	Kwalli-hap	觀理閣
Kim Hŭng-gyŏng	金興慶	Kwangju	廣州
		Kwangmyŏng-jŏn	光明殿
Kim Hyodŏk	金孝德		
Kim Igi	金履基	Kwangsŏng puwŏn'gun	光城府院君
Kim Inju	金麟柱		
Kim Isŏng	金履成	Kwangŭn puwi	光恩副尉
Kim Kidae	金基大	Kwanhŭi-hap	觀熙閣
Kim Kisŏng	金箕性	kwi	歸
Kim Kwanju	金觀柱	*Kyech'uk ilgi*	계축일기
Kim Kwiju	金龜柱	Kyŏngbok-jŏn	景福殿
Kim Kyejin	金季珍	Kyŏngchun-jŏn	景春殿
Kim Kyŏngok	金敬玉	Kyŏnghŭi-gung	慶熙宮
Kim Man'gi	金萬基	Kyŏnghun-gak	景薰閣
Kim Myŏnggi	金明基	Kyŏnghwa-mun	景華門
Kim Sangmuk	金尙默	Kyŏnghyŏn-dang	景賢堂
Kim Sangno	金尙魯		
Kim Sanjung	金山重	Kyŏngjong	景宗
Kim Sich'an	金時粲	Kyŏngju Kim	慶州金

Kyŏngmo-gung	景慕宮	nwe	雷
Kyŏngŭi	敬懿王后	O Sisu	吳始壽
wanghu		O Sŏkch'ung	吳錫忠
Kyŏngŭn	慶恩府院君	Ŏ taebi	魚大妃
puwŏn'gun		O Yusŏn	오유선
Kyujanggak	奎章閣	Ohŭng	鰲興府院君
Li-chi	禮記	puwŏn'gun	
Lien P'o	廉頗	*Ŏjŏng Hong*	御定洪翼靖公
Lin Hsiang-ju	藺相如	*Ikchŏnggong*	奏藁
Liu Pei	柳備	*chugo*	
Ma-ku	麻姑	*Okch'ugyŏng*	玉樞經
mallok	漫錄	Okhwa-dang	玉華堂
Manan-mun	萬安門	*Ŏmjebang*	嚴隄防裕昆錄
Min Chinwŏn	閔鎭遠	*Yugollok*	
Min Paeksang	閔百祥	Onyang	溫陽
Min Yujung	閔維重	Ŏŭi-dong	於義洞
Ming-ti	明帝	Padukp'an	바둑판
Minjung	民衆書館	Pak Chunwŏn	朴準源
sŏgwan		Pak Kyŏngbin	朴景嬪
Mirohan-jŏng	未老閒亭	Pak Munhŭng	朴文興
mo-shu-yu	莫須有	Pak Myŏngwŏn	朴明源
Mujŏng pogam	武定寶鑑	Pak P'ilsu	朴弼秀
Mun Sŏngguk	文性國	Pak Sech'e	朴世采
Mun Taebok	文大福	Pak Segŭn	박세근
Munhyo	文孝	Pak Sŏngwŏn	朴性源
Munjang	文章	Pang	方鍾鉉
munjip	文集	Chonghyŏn	
Munjŏng	文定王后	Pansong-bang	盤松坊
wanghu		Pingae	빙애
munkwa	文科	Pohwa-mun	普化門
musin	戊申	Pŏlli	磻里
Myŏngjong	明宗	pongjoha	奉朝賀
Myŏngjŏng-jŏn	明政殿	Pongnyŏ	福女
Myŏngnŭng	明陵	pongsa	奉事
Myŏngŭirok	明義錄	Pongsŏng-gun	鳳城君
Na Kyŏngŏn	羅景彦	Pongsu-dang	奉壽堂
Na Sangŏn	羅尙彦	P'ungsan Hong	豊山洪
Naegak	內閣	pyŏk	霹
Naehun	內訓	pyŏkp'a	僻派
Naju	羅州	P'yŏngan-do	平安道
Naksŏn-dang	樂善堂	P'yŏngdong	平洞
Nam Yuyong	南有容	P'yŏngsan	平山
Namdang	南塘	P'yŏngyang	平壤
Namin	南人	ri	里
Namyŏn'gun	南延君	sa	死
Nangnam-hŏn	洛南軒	Sado seja	思悼世子
Nonae-dang	老來堂	Sahyŏn-hap	思賢閤
Noron	老論	sallim	山林

sambulp'ilchi	三不必知	Song Hwanŏk	宋煥億
samgant'aek	三揀擇	Song Myŏng-	宋明欽
samjŏn	三殿	hŭm	
samjong	三宗血脈	Song Tŏksang	宋德相
hyŏlmaek		Sŏnggyun'gwan	成均館
Samsu	三水	*Songsa*	宋史
Sangdŏk ch'ong-	상덕총록	Sŏnhŭi-gung	宣禧宮
nok		Sŏnhwa-mun	宣化門
sanggung	尙宮	Sonji-gak	遜志閣
se	才	Sŏnjo	宣祖
sejabin	世子嬪	Sŏnŭi wanghu	宣懿王后
Sejong	世宗	Sŏnwŏn-jŏn	璿源殿
seson	世孫	Soron	小論
Shu-ching	書經	Ssu-ma Ch'ien	司馬遷
Shun	舜	Sukch'ang	淑昌
Sillok	實錄	Sukchong	肅宗
Sim Hwanji	沈煥之	*Sukhyang chŏn*	淑香傳
Sim Nŭngp'il	沈能弼	Sunghyŏn-mun	崇賢門
Sim Sangun	沈翔雲	Sungjŏng-mun	崇政門
Sim Ŭiji	沈儀之	*Sŭngjŏngwŏn*	承政院日記
Simin-dang	時敏堂	*ilgi*	
simyukcha	十六字兇言	Sungmun-dang	崇文堂
hyungŏn		Sunjo	純祖
Sin Kwangsu	申光綏	Sunjong	純宗
Sin Kyŏng	申暻	Sunwŏn	純元王后
Sin Man	申晩	wanghu	
Sin Pang	申昉	Suwŏn	水原
Sin Sach'ŏl	申思喆	T'aejo	太祖
sinim sahwa	申壬士禍	T'aejong	太宗
Sinp'ung-lu	新豊樓	taewang	大王
sip'a	時派	T'ai-chia	太甲
So Chaeyŏng	蘇在英	Talsŏng	達城府院君
Sŏ Chongje	徐宗悌	puwŏn'gun	
Sŏ Kyŏngdal	徐京達	Tam	湛
Sŏ Myŏngsŏn	徐命善	tamje	禫祭
Sŏ Myŏngŭng	徐命膺	*Tanam mallok*	丹巖漫錄
Sŏ Yongbo	徐龍輔	T'anghwa rŭl	탕화를 피치아
Sŏ Yunyŏng	徐有寧	p'ich'i anih-	니하게 만다니
Sohak/Hsiao-	小學	age mandani	
hsüeh		t'angp'yŏng	蕩平
Sohŏn wanghu	昭憲王后	Tŏkchong	德宗
Sohye wanghu	昭惠王后	Tŏksŏng-hap	德成閣
Sok Myŏngŭirok	續明義錄	Tonggung	東宮
Sok Yugollok	續裕昆錄	T'ongmyŏng-	通明殿
Sŏnbugun	先府君年譜略	jŏn	
yŏnboryak		Tongnae	東萊
Sŏnbugun yusa	先府君遺事	T'ongŭi-dong	通義洞
Song Chaehŭi	宋載禧	*Tso-chuan*	左傳

Ŭinŭng	懿陵
Ŭiso	懿昭
Ŭiyŏl	義烈
ŭlsa sahwa	乙巳士禍
Ŭn	垠
Ŭnjŏn-gun	恩全君
Ŭnŏn-gun	恩彦君
Ŭnsin-gun	恩信君
wagul	窩窟
Wang Och'ŏn-ch'ukkuk chŏn	往五天竺國傳
Wanp'ung-gun	完豊君
Wŏlsŏng-wi	月城尉
Wŏn Inson	元仁孫
Wŏnbin	元嬪
Wu-ti	武帝
yangban	兩班
Yangdŏk-dang	養德堂
Yangje	良娣
Yangjŏng-hap	養正閣
Yangju	楊州
Yi Anmuk	李安默
Yi Ch'anghwi	李昌輝
Yi Chip	李潗
Yi Ch'ŏnbo	李天輔
Yi Chŏngbin	李靖嬪
Yi Haejung	李海重
Yi Hu	李㷞
Yi Hyŏnŭng	李顯應
Yi Ik	李瀷
Yi In'gang	李仁剛
Yi Isang	李頤祥
Yi Kahwan	李家煥
Yi Kan	李柬
Yi Kwanghyŏn	李光鉉
Yi Kyehŭng	李啓興
Yi Ŏnhyŏng	李彦衡
Yi Pogil	李復一
Yi Pyŏnggi	李秉岐
Yi Pyŏnggŏn	李秉健
Yi Sanggung	李尙宮
Yi Sanjung	李山重
Yi Sebak	李世璞
Yi Simdo	李審度
Yi Sisu	李時秀
Yi Sŭnghun	李承薰
Yi Tŏkchung	李德重

Yi Toyŏng	李道永
Yi Yin	伊尹
Yim Yŏngbin	林英嬪
Yin huang-hou	陰皇后
Yŏbŏm	女範
yŏgŏl	逆孽
Yŏhŭng Min	驪興閔
yŏk	逆
Yŏllyŏng-gun	延齡君
yŏnbo/nien-p'u	年譜
Yŏngan-wi	永安尉
Yŏngch'un-hŏn	迎春軒
Yongdong-gung	龍洞宮
Yŏngjo	英祖
Yŏngjo sillok	英祖實錄
Yŏngmi-jŏng	永美亭
Yŏngmo-dang	永慕堂
Yŏngsŏn-dang	迎善堂
Yŏngsŏng-wi	永城尉
Yŏngu-wŏn	永祐園
Yŏn'gyŏng-dang	延慶堂
Yŏsan	礪山
Yosŏ-mun	燿西門
yŏŭiju	如意珠
Yŏyang puwŏn'gun	驪陽府院君
Yu Insik	柳仁植
Yu Kang	柳焵
Yu Ssi samdae rok	劉氏三代錄
Yu Usŏng	劉祐星
Yueh Fei	岳飛
Yugollok	裕昆錄
Yun Chaegyŏm	尹在謙
Yun Hongnyŏl	尹弘烈
Yun Im	尹任
Yun Oŭm	尹梧陰
Yun Sanghu	尹象厚
Yun Sidong	尹著東
Yun Tongdo	尹東度
Yun Tŭngyang	尹得養
Yun Tusu	尹斗壽
Yun Wŏnhyŏng	尹元衡
Yun Yanghu	尹養厚
Yunggyŏng-hŏn	隆慶軒

Index

Designer: Ina Clausen
Compositor: Asco Trade Typesetting, Ltd.
Text: 10/13 Galliard
Display: Galliard
Printer: Sheridan
Binder: Sheridan